THE VOICE
THAT IS GREAT
WITHIN US

"This anthology is original, sensitive, and beautifully balanced. It will certainly be a touchstone for future anthologies of this kind."

—Karl Shapiro

"When an intelligent man undertakes an anthology of the poetry of his time, it is as though a steamy window has been wiped clean. The landscape that appears is one man's country perhaps, but it has been resolved out of its mists and streaks and smears, and become coherent. Hayden Carruth is an intelligent man, and he has done us an indispensable service. His anthology will be essential, in school and at home, for a long time."

—Wendell Berry

"The work of a man who is both a poet and a distinguished critic, who has been observing and participating for years in the development of American poetry, and who is attached to no region or clique but only to what is good.

"In teaching poetry-writing workshops at Swarthmore and Columbia, and more recently in teaching at City College, I have been longing for such a collection. The scope and variousness are unmatched by any anthology of modern poetry I have ever seen. The individual choices are revealing of the richness and fertility of American verse in this epoch, but also of the editorial care and devotion which has refused to plagiarize other anthologies, and which has given serious attention to the range of each poet's work in making selections."

—Adrienne Rich

"THE VOICE THAT IS GREAT . . . sets forth main strands of the past now coming clear, and then displays our whole squirming immediate scene, not curried and exclusive, but unclear, a rush of talents yoked—as they have to be—by violence together. All regions and colors and tones among American poets of this century get their say in this collection. It has God's—and as some will no doubt opine, the Devil's—plenty."

—William Stafford

THE VOICE THAT IS GREAT WITHIN US

AMERICAN POETRY OF THE TWENTIETH CENTURY

EDITED BY HAYDEN CARRUTH

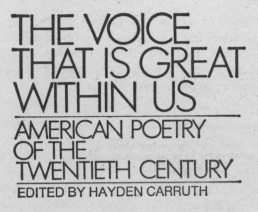

"Where the voice that is in us makes a true response,
Where the voice that is great within us rises up . . ."
—Wallace Stevens

BANTAM BOOKS
NEW YORK · TORONTO · LONDON · SYDNEY · AUCKLAND

THE VOICE THAT IS GREAT WITHIN US
AMERICAN POETRY OF THE TWENTIETH CENTURY
A Bantam Book / November 1970

Published simultaneously in the United States and Canada

Bantam Books are published by Bantam Books, a division of Bantam Doubleday Dell Publishing Group, Inc. Its trademark, consisting of the words "Bantam Books" and the portrayal of a rooster, is Registered in U.S. Patent and Trademark Office and in other countries. Marca Registrada. Bantam Books, 1540 Broadway, New York, New York 10036.

PRINTED IN THE UNITED STATES OF AMERICA

KR   23 22 21

ACKNOWLEDGMENTS

For permission to reprint all works in this volume by each of the following poets, grateful acknowledgment is made to the holders of copyright, publishers or representatives named below and on the following pages (pages vi–xvi), which constitute an extension of the copyright page.

"In Neglect," "Mowing," "Mending Wall," "The Black Cottage," "The Wood-Pile," "An Old Man's Winter Night," "The Hill Wife," "'Out, Out,'" "A Fountain, a Bottle, a Donkey's Ears and Some Books," "Nothing Gold Can Stay," "The Runaway," "Gathering Leaves," "Once by the Pacific," "Acquainted with the Night," "In Divés' Dive," "Never Again Would Birds' Song Be the Same," by Robert Frost. From *Complete Poems of Robert Frost*. Copyright 1916, 1923, 1928, 1930, 1934, 1939 by Holt, Rinehart & Winston, Inc. Copyright 1936, 1942, 1944, 1951, © 1956, 1958, 1962 by Robert Frost. Copyright © 1964, 1967 by Leslie Frost Ballantine. Reprinted by permission of Holt, Rinehart & Winston, Inc.

"Chicago," by Carl Sandburg. From his *Chicago Poems*. Copyright 1916 by Holt, Rinehart & Winston, Inc. Copyright 1944 by Carl Sandburg. Reprinted by permission of Holt, Rinehart & Winston, Inc.

"River Roads," by Carl Sandburg. From his *Cornhuskers*. Copyright 1918 by Holt, Rinehart & Winston, Inc. Copyright 1946 by Carl Sandburg. Reprinted by permission of Holt, Rinehart & Winston, Inc.

"Crapshooters," "Prayer After World War," "The Sins of Kalamazoo," by Carl Sandburg. From his *Smoke and Steel*. Copyright 1920 by Harcourt, Brace & World, Inc. Copyright 1948 by Carl Sandburg. Reprinted by permission of Harcourt, Brace & World, Inc.

"Love in Labrador," by Carl Sandburg. From his *Good Morning, America* by Carl Sandburg. Copyright 1928, © 1956 by Carl Sandburg. Reprinted by permission of Harcourt, Brace & World, Inc.

"Abraham Lincoln Walks at Midnight," "The Spider and the Ghost," "At Mass," by Vachel Lindsay. From his *Collected Poems*. Copyright 1914 by The Macmillan Company, renewed 1942 by Elizabeth C. Lindsay. Reprinted by permission of The Macmillan Co., Inc.

"The Flower-fed Buffaloes," by Vachel Lindsay. Copyright 1926 by D. Appleton & Co. Copyright © renewed 1954 by Elizabeth C. Lindsay. Reprinted by permission of Appleton Century, Inc. affiliate of Meredith Press.

"In the Carolinas," "Sea Surface Full of Clouds," by Wallace Stevens. From *The Collected Poems of Wallace Stevens*. Copyright 1923, renewed 1951 by Wallace Stevens. Reprinted by permission of Alfred A. Knopf, Inc.

"Evening Without Angels," by Wallace Stevens. From *The Collected Poems of Wallace Stevens*. Copyright 1936 by Wallace Stevens. Reprinted by permission of Alfred A. Knopf, Inc.

"Metamorphosis," by Wallace Stevens. From *The Collected Poems of Wallace Stevens*. Copyright 1942 by Wallace Stevens. Reprinted by permission of Alfred A. Knopf, Inc.

"Men Made out of Words," by Wallace Stevens. From *The Collected Poems of Wallace Stevens*. Copyright 1947 by Wallace Stevens. Reprinted by permission of Alfred A. Knopf, Inc.

"The House Was Quiet and the World Was Calm," by Wallace Stevens. From *The Collected Poems of Wallace Stevens*. Copyright 1942, 1947 by Wallace Stevens. Reprinted by permission of Alfred A. Knopf, Inc.

"Martial Cadenza," by Wallace Stevens. From *The Collected Poems of Wallace Stevens*. Copyright 1942 by Wallace Stevens. Reprinted by permission of Alfred A. Knopf, Inc.

"No Possum, No Sop, No Taters," "The Beginning," "Less and Less Human, O Savage Spirit," by Wallace Stevens. From *The Collected Poems of Wallace Stevens*. Copyright 1947 by Wallace Stevens. Reprinted by permission of Alfred A. Knopf, Inc.

"The Irish Cliffs of Moher," by Wallace Stevens. From *The Collected Poems of Wallace Stevens*. Copyright 1952 by Wallace Stevens. Reprinted by permission of Alfred A. Knopf, Inc.

"The River of Rivers in Connecticut," by Wallace Stevens. From *The Collected Poems of Wallace Stevens*. Copyright © 1954 by Wallace Stevens. Reprinted by permission of Alfred A. Knopf, Inc.

"Lunar Baedeker," "Love Songs," by Mina Loy. From her *Lunar Baedeker and Time Tables*. Copyright © 1958 by Mina Loy. Reprinted by permission of Jargon Books.

"First Praise," "The House," "Death," "Tract," "To a Solitary Disciple," "To a Friend Concerning Several Ladies," "Between Walls," "The Predicter of Famine," by William Carlos Williams. From his *Collected Earlier Poems*. Copyright 1938 by William Carlos Williams. Reprinted by permission of New Directions Publishing Corporation.

x

To E.P.
from us all.

FOREWORD

When I was a young poet in the 1940's I felt chronologically deprived, and so did my friends. We had been born too late, that was our trouble. The great epoch of "modern poetry" was in the past; its works, which we desperately admired, *The Waste Land, Lustra, Harmonium, Spring and All* and so many others, had been written long ago and had exhausted the poetic impetus. Nothing was left for us to do. Avidly we sought old magazines in which to experience vicariously the fervor of once-ringing manifestoes and the exciting first appearances of tradition-shattering poems. We sought, too, the old-timers who could regale us with the gossip that never dies. What was it really like in Paris during the 1920's, or in London a decade earlier? These were the issues that seemed to us most interesting.

Now, of course, I have come to understand that my own life has been equally blest, my own time equally interesting. Not only were members of my generation already beginning, in 1945, to produce works that would rival the past, but the old-timers themselves, at least many of them, were still looking forward to their best poems; and the quarter-century since then has been rich in poetic experience. I remember a day when my mail unexpectedly brought me a little pamphlet of poems so beautifully articulated within their own intentions that I spent the afternoon reading them over and over: my first acquaintance with the work of Denise Levertov. I remember another day and another pamphlet, this one containing "To the Holy Spirit," by Yvor Winters, a poem that has never ceased to astonish, frighten and console me. I remember the time when I was editing a magazine and received one morning a shiny manila envelope which enclosed a crisp sheaf of bond paper, professionally typed and fastened with a copper clip—a new batch of poems from Wallace Stevens—or another day when a twice-used envelope brought manuscripts equally well typed, but nonprofessionally and on an old machine—poems from E. E. Cummings—and what could be better than that? Nor have my pleasures diminished; in making this book I have found many superb poems hitherto unknown to me, while a few poets who had been scarcely more than names in my mind are now authors of works I shall prize until the end.

These sixty years of American poetry have been a high moment of the creative spirit. We say this without chauvinism because we know that other moments, higher than ours, have from time to time flourished and disappeared, leaving only shards of clay or scraps of papyrus behind them; and we live in the constant knowledge that our own moment may be eclipsed instantaneously, blasted into rubble. Moreover, we are aware that America's poetic emergence from the provincialism that warped our culture for three centuries before 1900 has been accompanied in other spheres by actions much less agreeable. Yet we cannot fail to see what our poets have done. If, in surveying our poetic accomplishment, we are too wise to be proud, I hope we are wise enough to be pleased, for surely these sixty years have been glorious—and they are not ended. Sometimes in the daily grind of literary and editorial labor we become too impressed by the imitativeness and stylization we find inevitably in the working of the cultural mechanism; but when we stand back and take a longer view we see that the opposite is the case. Not imitation but originality; not stylization but great diversity and spontaneity. Few periods of cultural evolution, however splendid their effects, can equal ours in its vitality: the remarkable diversity of forms, the ability to find strength within itself for successive waves of renewal and change. Naturally, and with justice, we are pleased.

This book is supposed to be a collection of poems to represent these remarkable years. To say, as some anthologists in the past have said of theirs, that this is the best, or that it is a "treasury" or even in the literal sense an anthology (meaning a garland), would strike me as arrogant. It is what one moderately experienced and immoderately diligent reader has selected during two and a half years of reading. Yet I hope it is not simply a personal selection. Actually, a few poets included here have produced work which, taken as a whole, is repugnant to my taste, though they are poets of such prominence that I felt my book would be incomplete without them. In short, I have tried to make a book which will give pleasure and enlightenment to readers, and which at the same time will suggest by its shape and structure a generalized historical verity, the "canon" of modern American poetry as viewed from the present. To put it another way, I have tried to combine my own judgment with what I understand of the needs of others.

Of course, I have failed. That goes without saying, and not only because of personal fallibility. An anthology at best is a system of compromises, because its field of interest is inevitably too big to be encompassed by its physical limits. How can a book of "American" poetry omit the work of those Americans to our north and south who write in French and Spanish as well as English? The limits are arbitrary; and though at first I had hoped to use at least some of the Canadian poems which to my mind definitely belong here, in the end I had to exclude them. Or how can a book of "modern" poetry omit Whitman, Stephen Crane, Robinson? Again it is a question of limits. One must draw the line somewhere between "forerunners" and "true moderns," and if I have a feeling that it is right to begin with Robert Frost, certainly this is a feeling, not an arguable proposition. Some readers will ask, I am sure, why such a book omits famous early poets like Edgar Lee Masters, Amy Lowell, Alfred Kreymborg and Stephen Vincent Benét; to which I can answer only that in rereading their books I found their importance to be less poetic than historical, a matter of example and influence. Since this book is for readers whose first interest is presumed to be the poem rather than history, I have omitted them.

Yet whatever else an anthologist may be, he is a worker in time, a kind of historian. His aim is the present, but his material is the past; and the farther back he looks the deeper he sees. Hence as his anthology moves from early to late his criteria of selection progressively change from narrow to broad, from deep to shallow. Young poets are more widely, though more tenuously, represented than their elders. This is regrettable; worse, it is fundamentally inhumane; but I see no way to avoid it.

A further question: Who, within the determined geographical limits, is an American by right of nationality? Should one poet born in England but later transplanted to the United States (e.g., W. H. Auden) be left out, when another (Mina Loy or Denise Levertov) is included? At best the answer is an intuition. The one poet seems to me, in his work as in his broader affinities, to have remained essentially British, while the others have become American. One case is unique, however. The American and British elements in the work of T. S. Eliot are equally strong, making him truly international, to be claimed by either country.

Beyond this my principles of selection, which are general rather than absolute, have been few:

1. To admit no poem merely because it is famous, but rather to reexamine the entire work of each poet and to choose the poems that seem now, in current taste and feeling, his strongest.

2. To exclude all translations, excerpts from long poems, and poems with extensive notes, epigraphs or other appendages.

3. To give primacy among all criteria to my own feeling, and to select no particular poem that does not seem to me genuine within its given modality, whatever that may be.

Finally a word about the supplementary apparatus. In recent years a custom has grown up of equipping anthologies with more and more impedimenta: notes, bibliographies, statements by poets, editorials, chronologies, pedagogical aids, etc. At first some such scheme was contemplated for this anthology too, but then I changed my mind; partly because I found, as the competition for space intensified, that I wished to save as much space as possible for the poems themselves, and partly because I came to feel that it would be presumptuous to anticipate the needs of students, teachers or other readers in the variety of their situations. Consequently I decided to keep my notes to the merest biographical detail; only to find, when I set out to write them, that biography and criticism are bound together, especially where older poets are concerned. I hope the elements of criticism I have introduced are impersonal, historical and generally agreed upon. As for the bibliographies, they are nonscholarly, intended simply to help readers look up the most important books by poets who appeal to them. Wherever possible I have listed the latest books in print, I have given selected and collected editions in place of single volumes and I have omitted all but a few works of prose. In some cases the latest books listed in the bibliographies appeared too late to be consulted in compiling the anthology itself.

Many people have helped me in this work. Three old friends have been especially generous, giving me valuable advice and access to their personal collections of books and manuscripts: Adrienne Rich, Denise Levertov and James Laughlin. I am extremely grateful to them, as I am also to those on the publisher's staff who have made the work possible at all by taking on themselves a large part of the immense clerical burden; I mean particularly Betsy Nordstrom, Jody Burnett and Gregory Armstrong. Equally valuable to me have been the resourcefulness and friendliness of many librarians, and acknowledgments are due especially to those at the Dewey Memorial Library of Johnson State College in Vermont, at the Baker Memorial Library of Dartmouth College and at the Harris Collection of Contemporary American Poetry and Drama of Brown University. Finally to my daughter, Martha Herbert, her only recompense for a summer's good company and help with research: thanks and love.

H.C.

Note: In my original manuscript, I had included several poems by Laura Riding. Unfortunately, arrangements for reprinting Miss Riding's poems could not be made—the one case in which my choice has been so thwarted—and hence I simply record my belief that her work belongs in such a book as this.

CONTENTS

xli

THE VOICE
THAT IS GREAT
WITHIN US

AMERICAN POETRY OF THE TWENTIETH CENTURY

ROBERT FROST (1875–1963)

Born in San Francisco, Frost moved to New England ten years later upon the death of his father, and in effect remained there the rest of his life, becoming the New Englander par excellence of his age. Yet his early life was not notably successful. Twice interrupted in attempts to secure a college degree, he farmed for a while in New Hampshire, worked as a mill hand, a schoolteacher, a newspaperman. His first poem was published in 1894; but during the next twenty years his work was consistently rejected by American editors. Finally, discouraged but still determined, Frost went to England in 1912, and there won the support of influential poets and critics, including Ezra Pound. His first two books, *A Boy's Will* (1913) and *North of Boston* (1914), were published in London. In 1915 he returned to America. Thereafter his success was unquestioned: he won many honors, including four Pulitzer Prizes for poetry, and became not only the most popular serious poet in the country but one of the most generally respected among fellow writers. Frost's poetic practice was based on what he called "sentence sounds," the natural tones and rhythms of speech cast loosely against standard poetic forms. Conventional as it may seem today, it was a new departure in its time, making Frost a distinctly modern poet. Similarly his combination of Emersonian spiritual aspiration with back-country Yankee pragmatism placed him squarely among his contemporaries, to whom his metaphysically probing lyrics and narratives, sometimes cynical or playful but often genuinely anguished, spoke with force. These factors, together with his superb poetic gift, make him dominant in the American tradition, a figure with whom younger poets, even the most rebellious, must come to terms.

Complete Poems of Robert Frost. Holt, Rinehart & Winston, 1949 ff.

IN NEGLECT

They leave us so to the way we took,
    As two in whom they were proved mistaken,
That we sit sometimes in the wayside nook,
With mischievous, vagrant, seraphic look,
    And *try* if we cannot feel forsaken.

MOWING

There was never a sound beside the wood but one,
And that was my long scythe whispering to the ground.
What was it it whispered? I knew not well myself;
Perhaps it was something about the heat of the sun,
Something, perhaps, about the lack of sound—
And that was why it whispered and did not speak.
It was no dream of the gift of idle hours,
Or easy gold at the hand of fay or elf:
Anything more than the truth would have seemed too
    weak
To the earnest love that laid the swale in rows,
Not without feeble-pointed spikes of flowers
(Pale orchises), and scared a bright green snake.
The fact is the sweetest dream that labor knows.
My long scythe whispered and left the hay to make.

MENDING WALL

Something there is that doesn't love a wall,
That sends the frozen-ground-swell under it,
And spills the upper boulders in the sun;
And makes gaps even two can pass abreast.
The work of hunters is another thing:
I have come after them and made repair
Where they have left not one stone on a stone,
But they would have the rabbit out of hiding,
To please the yelping dogs. The gaps I mean,
No one has seen them made or heard them made,
But at spring mending-time we find them there.
I let my neighbor know beyond the hill;
And on a day we meet to walk the line
And set the wall between us once again.
We keep the wall between us as we go.
To each the boulders that have fallen to each.
And some are loaves and some so nearly balls
We have to use a spell to make them balance:
'Stay where you are until our backs are turned!'
We wear our fingers rough with handling them.
Oh, just another kind of outdoor game,
One on a side. It comes to little more:

There where it is we do not need the wall:
He is all pine and I am apple orchard.
My apple trees will never get across
And eat the cones under his pines, I tell him.
He only says, 'Good fences make good neighbors.'
Spring is the mischief in me, and I wonder
If I could put a notion in his head:
'*Why* do they make good neighbors? Isn't it
Where there are cows? But here there are no cows.
Before I built a wall I'd ask to know
What I was walling in or walling out,
And to whom I was like to give offense.
Something there is that doesn't love a wall,
That wants it down.' I could say 'Elves' to him,
But it's not elves exactly, and I'd rather
He said it for himself. I see him there
Bringing a stone grasped firmly by the top
In each hand, like an old-stone savage armed.
He moves in darkness as it seems to me,
Not of woods only and the shade of trees.
He will not go behind his father's saying,
And he likes having thought of it so well
He says again, 'Good fences make good neighbors.'

THE BLACK COTTAGE

We chanced in passing by that afternoon
To catch it in a sort of special picture
Among tar-banded ancient cherry trees,
Set well back from the road in rank lodged grass,
The little cottage we were speaking of,
A front with just a door between two windows,
Fresh painted by the shower a velvet black.
We paused, the minister and I, to look.
He made as if to hold it at arm's length
Or put the leaves aside that framed it in.
'Pretty,' he said. 'Come in. No one will care.'
The path was a vague parting in the grass
That led us to a weathered window-sill.
We pressed our faces to the pane. 'You see,' he said,
'Everything's as she left it when she died.

Her sons won't sell the house or the things in it.
They say they mean to come and summer here
Where they were boys. They haven't come this year.
They live so far away—one is out west—
It will be hard for them to keep their word.
Anyway they won't have the place disturbed.'
A buttoned hair-cloth lounge spread scrolling arms
Under a crayon portrait on the wall,
Done sadly from an old daguerreotype.
'That was the father as he went to war.
She always, when she talked about the war,
Sooner or later came and leaned, half knelt
Against the lounge beside it, though I doubt
If such unlifelike lines kept power to stir
Anything in her after all the years.
He fell at Gettysburg or Fredericksburg,
I ought to know—it makes a difference which:
Fredericksburg wasn't Gettysburg, of course.
But what I'm getting to is how forsaken
A little cottage this has always seemed;
Since she went more than ever, but before—
I don't mean altogether by the lives
That had gone out of it, the father first,
Then the two sons, till she was left alone.
(Nothing could draw her after those two sons.
She valued the considerate neglect
She had at some cost taught them after years.)
I mean by the world's having passed it by—
As we almost got by this afternoon.
It always seems to me a sort of mark
To measure how far fifty years have brought us.
Why not sit down if you are in no haste?
These doorsteps seldom have a visitor.
The warping boards pull out their own old nails
With none to tread and put them in their place.
She had her own idea of things, the old lady.
And she liked talk. She had seen Garrison
And Whittier, and had her story of them.
One wasn't long in learning that she thought
Whatever else the Civil War was for,
It wasn't just to keep the States together,
Nor just to free the slaves, though it did both.
She wouldn't have believed those ends enough
To have given outright for them all she gave.

6

Her giving somehow touched the principle
That all men are created free and equal.
And to hear her quaint phrases—so removed
From the world's view today of all those things.
That's a hard mystery of Jefferson's.
What did he mean? Of course the easy way
Is to decide it simply isn't true.
It may not be. I heard a fellow say so.
But never mind, the Welshman got it planted
Where it will trouble us a thousand years.
Each age will have to reconsider it.
You couldn't tell her what the West was saying,
And what the South to her serene belief.
She had some art of hearing and yet not
Hearing the latter wisdom of the world.
White was the only race she ever knew.
Black she had scarcely seen, and yellow never.
But how could they be made so very unlike
By the same hand working in the same stuff?
She had supposed the war decided that.
What are you going to do with such a person?
Strange how such innocence gets its own way.
I shouldn't be surprised if in this world
It were the force that would at last prevail.
Do you know but for her there was a time
When to please younger members of the church,
Or rather say non-members in the church,
Whom we all have to think of nowadays,
I would have changed the Creed a very little?
Not that she ever had to ask me not to;
It never got so far as that; but the bare thought
Of her old tremulous bonnet in the pew,
And of her half asleep was too much for me.
Why, I might wake her up and startle her.
It was the words "descended into Hades"
That seemed too pagan to our liberal youth.
You know they suffered from a general onslaught.
And well, if they weren't true why keep right on
Saying them like the heathen? We could drop them.
Only—there was the bonnet in the pew.
Such a phrase couldn't have meant much to her.
But suppose she had missed it from the Creed
As a child misses the unsaid Good-night,
And falls asleep with heartache—how should *I* feel?

7

I'm just as glad she made me keep hands off,
For, dear me, why abandon a belief
Merely because it ceases to be true.
Cling to it long enough, and not a doubt
It will turn true again, for so it goes.
Most of the change we think we see in life
Is due to truths being in and out of favor.
As I sit here, and oftentimes, I wish
I could be monarch of a desert land
I could devote and dedicate forever
To the truths we keep coming back and back to.
So desert it would have to be, so walled
By mountain ranges half in summer snow,
No one would covet it or think it worth
The pains of conquering to force change on.
Scattered oases where men dwelt, but mostly
Sand dunes held loosely in tamarisk
Blown over and over themselves in idleness.
Sand grains should sugar in the natal dew
The babe born to the desert, the sand storm
Retard mid-waste my cowering caravans—
There are bees in this wall.' He struck the clapboards,
Fierce heads looked out; small bodies pivoted.
We rose to go. Sunset blazed on the windows.

THE WOOD-PILE

Out walking in the frozen swamp one gray day,
I paused and said, 'I will turn back from here.
No, I will go on farther—and we shall see.'
The hard snow held me, save where now and then
One foot went through. The view was all in lines
Straight up and down of tall slim trees
Too much alike to mark or name a place by
So as to say for certain I was here
Or somewhere else: I was just far from home.
A small bird flew before me. He was careful
To put a tree between us when he lighted,
And say no word to tell me who he was
Who was so foolish as to think what *he* thought.
He thought that I was after him for a feather—

8

The white one in his tail; like one who takes
Everything said as personal to himself.
One flight out sideways would have undeceived him.
And then there was a pile of wood for which
I forgot him and let his little fear
Carry him off the way I might have gone,
Without so much as wishing him good-night.
He went behind it to make his last stand.
It was a cord of maple, cut and split
And piled—and measured, four by four by eight.
And not another like it could I see.
No runner tracks in this year's snow looped near it.
And it was older sure than this year's cutting,
Or even last year's or the year's before.
The wood was gray and the bark warping off it
And the pile somewhat sunken. Clematis
Had wound strings round and round it like a bundle.
What held it though on one side was a tree
Still growing, and on one a stake and prop,
These latter about to fall. I thought that only
Someone who lived in turning to fresh tasks
Could so forget his handiwork on which
He spent himself, the labor of his ax,
And leave it there far from a useful fireplace
To warm the frozen swamp as best it could
With the slow smokeless burning of decay.

AN OLD MAN'S WINTER NIGHT

All out-of-doors looked darkly in at him
Through the thin frost, almost in separate stars,
That gathers on the pane in empty rooms.
What kept his eyes from giving back the gaze
Was the lamp tilted near them in his hand.
What kept him from remembering what it was
That brought him to that creaking room was age.
He stood with barrels round him—at a loss.
And having scared the cellar under him
In clomping here, he scared it once again
In clomping off;—and scared the outer night,
Which has its sounds, familiar, like the roar

Of trees and crack of branches, common things,
But nothing so like beating on a box.
A light he was to no one but himself
Where now he sat, concerned with he knew what,
A quiet light, and then not even that.
He consigned to the moon, such as she was,
So late-arising, to the broken moon
As better than the sun in any case
For such a charge, his snow upon the roof,
His icicles along the wall to keep;
And slept. The log that shifted with a jolt
Once in the stove, disturbed him and he shifted,
And eased his heavy breathing, but still slept.
One aged man—one man—can't keep a house,
A farm, a countryside, or if he can,
It's thus he does it of a winter night.

THE HILL WIFE

Loneliness

Her Word

One ought not to have to care
    So much as you and I
Care when the birds come round the house
    To seem to say good-by;

Or care so much when they come back
    With whatever it is they sing;
The truth being we are as much
    Too glad for the one thing

As we are too sad for the other here—
    With birds that fill their breasts
But with each other and themselves
    And their built or driven nests.

House Fear

Always—I tell you this they learned—
Always at night when they returned
To the lonely house from far away
To lamps unlighted and fire gone gray,

They learned to rattle the lock and key
To give whatever might chance to be
Warning and time to be off in flight:
And preferring the out- to the in-door night,
They learned to leave the house-door wide
Until they had lit the lamp inside.

'OUT, OUT—'

The buzz saw snarled and rattled in the yard
And made dust and dropped stove-length sticks of wood,
Sweet-scented stuff when the breeze drew across it.
And from there those that lifted eyes could count
Five mountain ranges one behind the other
Under the sunset far into Vermont.
And the saw snarled and rattled, snarled and rattled,
As it ran light, or had to bear a load.
And nothing happened: day was all but done.
Call it a day, I wish they might have said
To please the boy by giving him the half hour
That a boy counts so much when saved from work.
His sister stood beside them in her apron
To tell them 'Supper.' At the word, the saw,
As if to prove saws knew what supper meant,
Leaped out at the boy's hand, or seemed to leap—
He must have given the hand. However it was,
Neither refused the meeting. But the hand!
The boy's first outcry was a rueful laugh,
As he swung toward them holding up the hand
Half in appeal, but half as if to keep
The life from spilling. Then the boy saw all—
Since he was old enough to know, big boy
Doing a man's work, though a child at heart—
He saw all spoiled. 'Don't let him cut my hand off—
The doctor, when he comes. Don't let him, sister!'
So. But the hand was gone already.
The doctor put him in the dark of ether.
He lay and puffed his lips out with his breath.
And then—the watcher at his pulse took fright.
No one believed. They listened at his heart.
Little—less—nothing!—and that ended it.
No more to build on there. And they, since they
Were not the one dead, turned to their affairs.

A FOUNTAIN, A BOTTLE,
A DONKEY'S EARS AND SOME BOOKS

Old Davis owned a solid mica mountain
In Dalton that would some day make his fortune.
There'd been some Boston people out to see it:
And experts said that deep down in the mountain
The mica sheets were big as plate glass windows.
He'd like to take me there and show it to me.

'I'll tell you what you show me. You remember
You said you knew the place where once, on Kinsman,
The early Mormons made a settlement
And built a stone baptismal font outdoors—
But Smith, or someone, called them off the mountain
To go West to a worse fight with the desert.
You said you'd seen the stone baptismal font.
Well, take me there.'

     'Some day I will.'

        'Today.'

'Huh, that old bathtub, what is that to see?
Let's talk about it.'

      'Let's go see the place.'

'To shut you up I'll tell you what I'll do:
I'll find that fountain if it takes all summer,
And both of our united strengths, to do it.'

'You've lost it, then?'

      'Not so but I can find it.
No doubt it's grown up some to woods around it.
The mountain may have shifted since I saw it
In eighty-five.'

    'As long ago as that?'

'If I remember rightly, it had sprung
A leak and emptied then. And forty years

Can do a good deal to bad masonry.
You won't see any Mormon swimming in it.
But you have said it, and we're off to find it.
Old as I am, I'm going to let myself
Be dragged by you all over everywhere—'

'I thought you were a guide.'

                              'I am a guide,
And that's why I can't decently refuse you.'

We made a day of it out of the world,
Ascending to descend to reascend.
The old man seriously took his bearings,
And spoke his doubts in every open place.

We came out on a look-off where we faced
A cliff, and on the cliff a bottle painted,
Or stained by vegetation from above,
A likeness to surprise the thrilly tourist.

'Well, if I haven't brought you to the fountain,
At least I've brought you to the famous Bottle.'

'I won't accept the substitute. It's empty.'

'So's everything.'

                              'I want my fountain.'

'I guess you'd find the fountain just as empty.
And anyway this tells me where I am.'

'Hadn't you long suspected where you were?'

'You mean miles from that Mormon settlement?
Look here, you treat your guide with due respect
If you don't want to spend the night outdoors.
I vow we must be near the place from where
The two converging slides, the avalanches,
On Marshall, look like donkey's ears.
We may as well see that and save the day.'

'Don't donkey's ears suggest we shake our own?'

'For God's sake, aren't you fond of viewing nature?
You don't like nature. All you like is books.
What signify a donkey's ears and bottle,
However natural? Give you your books!
Well then, right here is where I show you books.
Come straight down off this mountain just as fast
As we can fall and keep a-bouncing on our feet.
It's hell for knees unless done hell-for-leather.'

'Be ready,' I thought, 'for almost anything.'

We struck a road I didn't recognize,
But welcomed for the chance to lave my shoes
In dust once more. We followed this a mile,
Perhaps, to where it ended at a house
I didn't know was there. It was the kind
To bring me to for broad-board paneling.
I never saw so good a house deserted.

'Excuse me if I ask you in a window
That happens to be broken,' Davis said.
'The outside doors as yet have held against us.
I want to introduce you to the people
Who used to live here. They were Robinsons.
You must have heard of Clara Robinson,
The poetess who wrote the book of verses
And had it published. It was all about
The posies on her inner window sill,
And the birds on her outer window sill,
And how she tended both, or had them tended:
She never tended anything herself.
She was "shut in" for life. She lived her whole
Life long in bed, and wrote her things in bed.
I'll show you how she had her sills extended
To entertain the birds and hold the flowers.
Our business first's up attic with her books.'

We trod uncomfortably on crunching glass
Through a house stripped of everything
Except, it seemed, the poetess's poems.
Books, I should say!—if books are what is needed.
A whole edition in a packing-case,
That, overflowing like a horn of plenty,

14

Or like the poetess's heart of love,
Had spilled them near the window toward the light
Where driven rain had wet and swollen them.
Enough to stock a village library—
Unfortunately all of one kind, though.
They had been brought home from some publisher
And taken thus into the family.
Boys and bad hunters had known what to do
With stone and lead to unprotected glass:
Shatter it inward on the unswept floors.
How had the tender verse escaped their outrage?
By being invisible for what it was,
Or else by some remoteness that defied them
To find out what to do to hurt a poem.
Yet oh! the tempting flatness of a book,
To send it sailing out the attic window
Till it caught wind, and, opening out its covers,
Tried to improve on sailing like a tile
By flying like a bird (silent in flight,
But all the burden of its body song),
Only to tumble like a stricken bird,
And lie in stones and bushes unretrieved.
Books were not thrown irreverently about.
They simply lay where someone now and then,
Having tried one, had dropped it at his feet
And left it lying where it fell rejected.
Here were all those the poetess's life
Had been too short to sell or give away.

'Take one,' Old Davis bade me graciously.

'Why not take two or three?'

                    'Take all you want.
Good-looking books like that.' He picked one fresh
In virgin wrapper from deep in the box,
And stroked it with a horny-handed kindness.
He read in one and I read in another,
Both either looking for or finding something.

The attic wasps went missing by like bullets.

I was soon satisfied for the time being.

All the way home I kept remembering
The small book in my pocket. It was there.
The poetess had sighed, I knew, in heaven
At having eased her heart of one more copy—
Legitimately. My demand upon her,
Though slight, was a demand. She felt the tug.
In time she would be rid of all her books.

NOTHING GOLD CAN STAY

Nature's first green is gold,
Her hardest hue to hold.
Her early leaf's a flower;
But only so an hour.
Then leaf subsides to leaf.
So Eden sank to grief,
So dawn goes down to day.
Nothing gold can stay.

THE RUNAWAY

Once when the snow of the year was beginning to fall,
We stopped by a mountain pasture to say, 'Whose colt?'
A little Morgan had one forefoot on the wall,
The other curled at his breast. He dipped his head
And snorted at us. And then he had to bolt.
We heard the miniature thunder where he fled,
And we saw him, or thought we saw him, dim and gray,
Like a shadow against the curtain of falling flakes.
'I think the little fellow's afraid of the snow.
He isn't winter-broken. It isn't play
With the little fellow at all. He's running away.
I doubt if even his mother could tell him, "Sakes,
It's only weather." He'd think she didn't know!
Where is his mother? He can't be out alone.'
And now he comes again with clatter of stone,
And mounts the wall again with whited eyes
And all his tail that isn't hair up straight.
He shudders his coat as if to throw off flies.
'Whoever it is that leaves him out so late,
When other creatures have gone to stall and bin,
Ought to be told to come and take him in.'

GATHERING LEAVES

Spades take up leaves
No better than spoons,
And bags full of leaves
Are light as balloons.

I make a great noise
Of rustling all day
Like rabbit and deer
Running away.

But the mountains I raise
Elude my embrace,
Flowing over my arms
And into my face.

I may load and unload
Again and again
Till I fill the whole shed,
And what have I then?

Next to nothing for weight,
And since they grew duller
From contact with earth,
Next to nothing for color.

Next to nothing for use.
But a crop is a crop,
And who's to say where
The harvest shall stop?

ONCE BY THE PACIFIC

The shattered water made a misty din.
Great waves looked over others coming in,
And thought of doing something to the shore
That water never did to land before.
The clouds were low and hairy in the skies,
Like locks blown forward in the gleam of eyes.
You could not tell, and yet it looked as if
The shore was lucky in being backed by cliff,
The cliff in being backed by continent;

It looked as if a night of dark intent
Was coming, and not only a night, an age.
Someone had better be prepared for rage.
There would be more than ocean-water broken
Before God's last *Put out the Light* was spoken.

ACQUAINTED WITH THE NIGHT

I have been one acquainted with the night.
I have walked out in rain—and back in rain.
I have outwalked the furthest city light.

I have looked down the saddest city lane.
I have passed by the watchman on his beat
And dropped my eyes, unwilling to explain.

I have stood still and stopped the sound of feet
When far away an interrupted cry
Came over houses from another street,

But not to call me back or say good-by;
And further still at an unearthly height,
One luminary clock against the sky

Proclaimed the time was neither wrong nor right.
I have been one acquainted with the night.

IN DIVÉS' DIVE

It is late at night and still I am losing,
But still I am steady and unaccusing.

As long as the Declaration guards
My right to be equal in number of cards,

It is nothing to me who runs the Dive.
Let's have a look at another five.

NEVER AGAIN WOULD BIRDS' SONG BE THE SAME

He would declare and could himself believe
That the birds there in all the garden round
From having heard the daylong voice of Eve
Had added to their own an oversound,
Her tone of meaning but without the words.
Admittedly an eloquence so soft
Could only have had an influence on birds
When call or laughter carried it aloft.
Be that as may be, she was in their song.
Moreover her voice upon their voices crossed
Had now persisted in the woods so long
That probably it never would be lost.
Never again would birds' song be the same.
And to do that to birds was why she came.

CARL SANDBURG (1878–1967)

The son of Swedish immigrants, Sandburg grew up in Galesburg, Ill., a railroad town, where he attended school until he was thirteen, then dropped out and wandered for years through the West and Midwest, working at varied jobs. He served in the Spanish-American War and for a while attended college. Finally he settled in Milwaukee, where he married, became a Socialist and a newspaperman, and began devoting himself seriously to poetry. In 1913 he moved to Chicago. Harriet Monroe, founder of *Poetry*, gave his work a prominent place in her magazine, where it attracted attention for its robust and Whitmanesque freedom. Two books, *Chicago Poems* (1916) and *Cornhuskers* (1918), assured his reputation. During the twenties and thirties Sandburg toured widely, lecturing, reading his poems, singing and collecting folk songs, playing his guitar. His two collections, *The American Songbag* (1927) and *The New American Songbag* (1950), are important contributions to folklore. At the same time he became deeply interested in the life and achievement of Abraham Lincoln, and spent many years in producing a multi-volume biography. In addition his works include several first-rate books for children (the Rootabaga series), novels, autobiographies, screen plays, and much journalism. Sandburg's poetry was scorned during his middle and later life by the European-oriented critics of the time, and in part rightly so; he wrote too much and too facilely. But some of his early poems have a fresh vision and incantatory vigor that remain firm. In style, attitude, and temperament, he was closer to the young poets of today than most of them recognize.

Complete Poems. Harcourt, Brace, 1950.

CHICAGO

Hog Butcher for the World,
Tool Maker, Stacker of Wheat,
Player with Railroads and the Nation's Freight Handler;
Stormy, husky, brawling,
City of the Big Shoulders:

They tell me you are wicked and I believe them, for I have seen your painted women under the gas lamps luring the farm boys.

And they tell me you are crooked and I answer: Yes, it is true I have seen the gunman kill and go free to kill again.

And they tell me you are brutal and my reply is: On the faces of women and children I have seen the marks of wanton hunger.

And having answered so I turn once more to those who sneer at this my city, and I give them back the sneer and say to them:

Come and show me another city with lifted head singing so proud to be alive and coarse and strong and cunning.

Flinging magnetic curses amid the toil of piling job on job, here is a tall bold slugger set vivid against the little soft cities;

Fierce as a dog with tongue lapping for action, cunning as a savage pitted against the wilderness,

    Bareheaded,

    Shoveling,

    Wrecking,

    Planning,

    Building, breaking, rebuilding,

Under the smoke, dust all over his mouth, laughing with white teeth,

Under the terrible burden of destiny laughing as a young man laughs,

Laughing even as an ignorant fighter laughs who has never lost a battle,

Bragging and laughing that under his wrist is the pulse, and under his ribs the heart of the people,

    Laughing!

Laughing the stormy, husky, brawling laughter of Youth, half-naked, sweating, proud to be Hog Butcher, Tool Maker, Stacker of Wheat, Player with Railroads and Freight Handler to the Nation.

RIVER ROADS

Let the crows go by hawking their caw and caw.
They have been swimming in midnights of coal mines
  somewhere.
Let 'em hawk their caw and caw.

Let the woodpecker drum and drum on a hickory stump.
He has been swimming in red and blue pools somewhere
  hundreds of years
And the blue has gone to his wings and the red has gone
  to his head.
Let his red head drum and drum.

Let the dark pools hold the birds in a looking-glass.
And if the pool wishes, let it shiver to the blur of many
  wings, old swimmers from old places.

Let the redwing streak a line of vermilion on the green
  wood lines.
And the mist along the river fix its purple in lines of a
  woman's shawl on lazy shoulders.

CRAPSHOOTERS

Somebody loses whenever somebody wins.
This was known to the Chaldeans long ago.
And more: somebody wins whenever somebody loses.
This too was in the savvy of the Chaldeans.

They take it heaven's hereafter is an eternity of crap
  games where they try their wrists years and years and
  no police come with a wagon; the game goes on for-
  ever.
The spots on the dice are the music signs of the songs of
  heaven here.
God is Luck: Luck is God: we are all bones the High
  Thrower rolled: some are two spots, some double sixes.

The myths are Phoebe, Little Joe, Big Dick.
Hope runs high with a: Huh, seven—huh, come seven.
This too was in the savvy of the Chaldeans.

THE SINS OF KALAMAZOO

The sins of Kalamazoo are neither scarlet nor crimson.
The sins of Kalamazoo are a convict gray, a dishwater
drab.
And the people who sin the sins of Kalamazoo are neither
scarlet nor crimson.
They run to drabs and grays—and some of them sing
they shall be washed whiter than snow—and some: We
should worry.

Yes, Kalamazoo is a spot on the map
And the passenger trains stop there
And the factory smokestacks smoke
And the grocery stores are open Saturday nights
And the streets are free for citizens who vote
And inhabitants counted in the census.
Saturday night is the big night.
   Listen with your ears on a Saturday night in Kalamazoo
   And say to yourself: I hear America, I hear, *what* do I
   hear?

Main street there runs through the middle of the town
And there is a dirty post office
And a dirty city hall
And a dirty railroad station
And the United States flag cries, cries the Stars and
Stripes to the four winds on Lincoln's birthday and the
Fourth of July.

Kalamazoo kisses a hand to something far off.
Kalamazoo calls to a long horizon, to a shivering silver
angel, to a creeping mystic what-is-it.
"We're here because we're here," is the song of Kalamazoo.
"We don't know where we're going but we're on our way,"
are the words.
There are hound dogs of bronze on the public square,
hound dogs looking far beyond the public square.

Sweethearts there in Kalamazoo
Go to the general delivery window of the post office
And speak their names and ask for letters
And ask again, "Are you sure there is nothing for me?
I wish you'd look again—there must be a letter for me."

And sweethearts go to the city hall
And tell their names and say, "We want a license."
And they go to an installment house and buy a bed on
time and a clock
And the children grow up asking each other, "What can
we do to kill time?"
They grow up and go to the railroad station and buy tickets
for Texas, Pennsylvania, Alaska.
"Kalamazoo is all right," they say. "But I want to see the
world."
And when they have looked the world over they come
back saying it is all like Kalamazoo.

The trains come in from the east and hoot for the crossings,
And buzz away to the peach country and Chicago to the
west
Or they come from the west and shoot on to the Battle
Creek breakfast bazaars
And the speedbug heavens of Detroit.

"I hear America, I hear, *what* do I hear?"
Said a loafer lagging along on the sidewalks of Kalamazoo,
Lagging along and asking questions, reading signs.

Oh yes, there is a town named Kalamazoo,
A spot on the map where the trains hesitate.
I saw the sign of a five and ten cent store there
And the Standard Oil Company and the International
Harvester
And a graveyard and a ball grounds
And a short order counter where a man can get a stack
of wheats
And a pool hall where a rounder leered confidential like
and said:
"Lookin' for a quiet game?"

The loafer lagged along and asked,
"Do you make guitars here?
Do you make boxes the singing wood winds ask to sleep
in?
Do you rig up strings the singing wood winds sift over
and sing low?"
The answer: "We manufacture musical instruments here."

Here I saw churches with steeples like hatpins,
Undertaking rooms with sample coffins in the show window
And signs everywhere satisfaction is guaranteed,
Shooting galleries where men kill imitation pigeons,
And there were doctors for the sick,
And lawyers for people waiting in jail,
And a dog catcher and a superintendent of streets,
And telephones, water-works, trolley cars,
And newspapers with a splatter of telegrams from sister cities of Kalamazoo the round world over.

And the loafer lagging along said:
Kalamazoo, you ain't in a class by yourself;
I seen you before in a lot of places.
If you are nuts America is nuts.

And lagging along he said bitterly:
Before I came to Kalamazoo I was silent.
Now I am gabby, God help me, I am gabby.

Kalamazoo, both of us will do a fadeaway.
I will be carried out feet first
And time and the rain will chew you to dust
And the winds blow you away.
And an old, old mother will lay a green moss cover on my bones
And a green moss cover on the stones of your post office and city hall.

Best of all
I have loved your kiddies playing run-sheep-run
And cutting their initials on the ball ground fence.
They knew every time I fooled them who was fooled and how.

Best of all
I have loved the red gold smoke of your sunsets;
I have loved a moon with a ring around it
Floating over your public square;
I have loved the white dawn frost of early winter silver
And purple over your railroad tracks and lumber yards.

The wishing heart of you I loved, Kalamazoo.
I sang bye-lo, bye-lo to your dreams.
I sang bye-lo to your hopes and songs.
I wished to God there were hound dogs of bronze on
your public square,
Hound dogs with bronze paws looking to a long horizon
with a shivering silver angel,
a creeping mystic what-is-it.

PRAYER AFTER WORLD WAR

Wandering oversea dreamer,
Hunting and hoarse, Oh daughter and mother,
Oh daughter of ashes and mother of blood,
Child of the hair let down, and tears,
Child of the cross in the south
And the star in the north,
Keeper of Egypt and Russia and France,
Keeper of England and Poland and Spain,
Make us a song for tomorrow.
Make us one new dream, us who forget,
Out of the storm let us have one star.

Struggle, Oh anvils, and help her.
Weave with your wool, Oh winds and skies.
Let your iron and copper help,
Oh dirt of the old dark earth.

Wandering oversea singer,
Singing of ashes and blood,
Child of the scars of fire,
Make us one new dream, us who forget.
Out of the storm let us have one star.

LOVE IN LABRADOR

One arch of the sky
Took on a spray of jewels.

The crystals gleamed on the windows
Weaving their wintrish alphabets
Of spears and ovals fixed in frost
Fastened to a glass design
With a word: This must be.

There are shooters of the moon far north.
There are dying eyes holding diadems.
There are deaths sweet as laughing waters.
There are gold heelprints on the fading
    staircases of the stars.

VACHEL LINDSAY (1879–1931)

Born in Springfield, Ill., Lindsay as a young man desired to become a missionary; later his thought turned toward mystical, Swedenborgian, and radical concepts, and he did not lose his crusading zeal. Once he walked from Illinois to New Mexico, preaching the "gospel of beauty" wherever he could and exchanging poems for his keep. But although he admired Whitman and tried to imitate him, his poetry was closer in spirit to Poe, Sidney Lanier, and Swinburne, and his most famous poems, "General William Booth Enters into Heaven" and "The Congo" —heavily cadenced set pieces in whose tumultuous performance Lindsay often asked his audience to take part—now betray a flaccid structure and lack of depth which Lindsay himself came to recognize. Discouraged, he fell victim to the morbid element in his half-mystical, half-puritanical nature, and ended by committing suicide.

Collected Poems. Macmillan, 1934.

ABRAHAM LINCOLN WALKS AT MIDNIGHT

(In Springfield, Illinois)

It is portentous, and a thing of state
That here at midnight, in our little town
A mourning figure walks, and will not rest,
Near the old court-house pacing up and down,

Or by his homestead, or in shadowed yards
He lingers where his children used to play,
Or through the market, on the well-worn stones
He stalks until the dawn-stars burn away.

A bronzed, lank man! His suit of ancient black,
A famous high top-hat and plain worn shawl
Make him the quaint great figure that men love,
The prairie-lawyer, master of us all.

He cannot sleep upon his hillside now.
He is among us:—as in times before!
And we who toss and lie awake for long
Breathe deep, and start, to see him pass the door.

His head is bowed. He thinks on men and kings.
Yea, when the sick world cries, how can he sleep?
Too many peasants fight, they know not why,
Too many homesteads in black terror weep.

The sins of all the war-lords burn his heart.
He sees the dreadnaughts scouring every main.
He carries on his shawl-wrapped shoulders now
The bitterness, the folly and the pain.

He cannot rest until a spirit-dawn
Shall come;—the shining hope of Europe free:
The league of sober folk, the Workers' Earth,
Bringing long peace to Cornland, Alp and Sea.

It breaks his heart that kings must murder still,
That all his hours of travail here for men
Seem yet in vain. And who will bring white peace
That he may sleep upon his hill again?

THE SPIDER AND THE GHOST OF THE FLY

Once I loved a spider
When I was born a fly,
A velvet-footed spider
With a gown of rainbow-dye.
She ate my wings and gloated.
She bound me with a hair.
She drove me to her parlor
Above her winding stair.
To educate young spiders
She took me all apart.
My ghost came back to haunt her.
I saw her eat my heart.

AT MASS

No doubt to-morrow I will hide
My face from you, my King.
Let me rejoice this Sunday noon,
And kneel while gray priests sing.

It is not wisdom to forget.
But since it is my fate
Fill thou my soul with hidden wine
To make this white hour great.

My God, my God, this marvelous hour
I am your son, I know.
Once in a thousand days your voice
Has laid temptation low.

THE FLOWER-FED BUFFALOES

The flower-fed buffaloes of the spring
In the days of long ago,
Ranged where the locomotives sing
And the prairie flowers lie low;
The tossing, blooming, perfumed grass
Is swept away by wheat,
Wheels and wheels and wheels spin by
In the spring that still is sweet.
But the flower-fed buffaloes of the spring
Left us long ago.
They gore no more, they bellow no more,
They trundle around the hills no more:—
With the Blackfeet lying low,
With the Pawnees lying low.

WALLACE STEVENS (1879–1955)

Stevens determined, early in life, to create a life-style that would accommodate his first vocation, poetry. The course he chose would have seemed paradoxical to many, but not to him. He studied law, entered the insurance business at Hartford, Conn., and spent a number of years working upward to an executive position and a life of affluence. Consequently his first book, *Harmonium* (1923), did not appear until he was forty-three years old; but then it made an immediate hit. Many of its poems became favorites: "Hibiscus on the Sleeping Shores," "Sunday Morning," "The Emperor of Ice-Cream," "Tea at the Palaz of Hoon," "Sea Surface Full of Clouds," etc. They were as exotic as their titles; full of tropical imagery and unusual diction, armored in brilliant stylized rhetoric; but despite their ornamentation they dealt with disturbing themes, particularly man's attempt to find, or create, meaning in a universe from which the spiritual rationale had apparently departed. For Stevens, the way lay through aesthetic experience; yet he was never merely willing to substitute art for reality. The real world, he insisted, was the "necessary angel" who announced to imaginative man the plenitude of life. As his books succeeded one another, perceptive readers saw that although the famous stylization of the early poems had moderated, the new work was more exact, better integrated, and more profoundly felt. Indeed some of Stevens's most moving poems, written in his last years, were not published until after his death, in a volume which also contains his "Adagia," brilliant prose aphorisms and philosophical aperçus. No other poetry of the twentieth century has been more consistently, flawlessly individual; none has been more attractive; none has been harder to imitate. Hence the influence of Stevens on younger poets, though pervasive, has been indirect.

The Collected Poems of Wallace Stevens. Knopf, 1954.
Opus Posthumous. Ed. Samuel French Morse. Knopf, 1957.
The Necessary Angel. (Essays.) Knopf, 1951.
Selected Letters of Wallace Stevens. Ed. Holly Stevens. Knopf, 1966.

IN THE CAROLINAS

The lilacs wither in the Carolinas.
Already the butterflies flutter above the cabins.
Already the new-born children interpret love
In the voices of mothers.

Timeless mother,
How is it that your aspic nipples
For once vent honey?

The pine-tree sweetens my body
The white iris beautifies me.

SEA SURFACE FULL OF CLOUDS

I

In that November off Tehuantepec,
The slopping of the sea grew still one night
And in the morning summer hued the deck

And made one think of rosy chocolate
And gilt umbrellas. Paradisal green
Gave suavity to the perplexed machine

Of ocean, which like limpid water lay.
Who, then, in that ambrosial latitude
Out of the light evolved the moving blooms,

Who, then, evolved the sea-blooms from the clouds
Diffusing balm in that Pacific calm?
C'était mon enfant, mon bijou, mon âme.

The sea-clouds whitened far below the calm
And moved, as blooms move, in the swimming green
And in its watery radiance, while the hue

Of heaven in an antique reflection rolled
Round those flotillas. And sometimes the sea
Poured brilliant iris on the glistening blue.

II

In that November off Tehuantepec
The slopping of the sea grew still one night.
At breakfast jelly yellow streaked the deck

And made one think of chop-house chocolate
And sham umbrellas. And a sham-like green
Capped summer-seeming on the tense machine

Of ocean, which in sinister flatness lay.
Who, then, beheld the rising of the clouds
That strode submerged in that malevolent sheen,

Who saw the mortal massives of the blooms
Of water moving on the water-floor?
C'était mon frère du ciel, ma vie, mon or.

The gongs rang loudly as the windy booms
Hoo-hooed it in the darkened ocean-blooms.
The gongs grew still. And then blue heaven spread

Its crystalline pendentives on the sea
And the macabre of the water-glooms
In an enormous undulation fled.

In that November off Tehuantepec,
The slopping of the sea grew still one night
And a pale silver patterned on the deck

And made one think of porcelain chocolate
And pied umbrellas. An uncertain green,
Piano-polished, held the tranced machine

Of ocean, as a prelude holds and holds.
Who, seeing silver petals of white blooms
Unfolding in the water, feeling sure

Of the milk within the saltiest spurge, heard, then,
The sea unfolding in the sunken clouds?
Oh! C'était mon extase et mon amour.

So deeply sunken were they that the shrouds,
The shrouding shadows, made the petals black
Until the rolling heaven made them blue,

A blue beyond the rainy hyacinth,
And smiting the crevasses of the leaves
Deluged the ocean with a sapphire blue.

IV

In that November off Tehuantepec
The night-long slopping of the sea grew still.
A mallow morning dozed upon the deck

And made one think of musky chocolate
And frail umbrellas. A too-fluent green
Suggested malice in the dry machine

Of ocean, pondering dank stratagem.
Who then beheld the figures of the clouds
Like blooms secluded in the thick marine?

Like blooms? Like damasks that were shaken off
From the loosed girdles in the spangling must.
C'était ma foi, la nonchalance divine.

The nakedness would rise and suddenly turn
Salt masks of beard and mouths of bellowing,
Would—But more suddenly the heaven rolled

Its bluest sea-clouds in the thinking green,
And the nakedness became the broadest blooms,
Mile-mallows that a mallow sun cajoled.

V

In that November off Tehuantepec
Night stilled the slopping of the sea. The day
Came, bowing and voluble, upon the deck,

Good clown. . . . One thought of Chinese chocolate
And large umbrellas. And a motley green
Followed the drift of the obese machine

34

Of ocean, perfected in indolence.
What pistache one, ingenious and droll,
Beheld the sovereign clouds as jugglery

And the sea as turquoise-turbaned Sambo, neat
At tossing saucers—cloudy-conjuring sea?
C'était mon esprit bâtard, l'ignominie.

The sovereign clouds came clustering. The conch
Of loyal conjuration trumped. The wind
Of green blooms turning crisped the motley hue

To clearing opalescence. Then the sea
And heaven rolled as one and from the two
Came fresh transfigurings of freshest blue.

EVENING WITHOUT ANGELS

the great interests of man: air and light,
the joy of having a body,
the voluptuousness of looking.

—Mario Rossi

Why seraphim like lutanists arranged
Above the trees? And why the poet as
Eternal *chef d'orchestre?*

              Air is air,
Its vacancy glitters round us everywhere.
Its sounds are not angelic syllables
But our unfashioned spirits realized
More sharply in more furious selves.

              And light
That fosters seraphim and is to them
Coiffeur of haloes, fecund jeweller—
Was the sun concoct for angels or for men?
Sad men made angels of the sun, and of
The moon they made their own attendant ghosts,
Which led them back to angels, after death.

Let this be clear that we are men of sun
And men of day and never of pointed night,
Men that repeat antiquest sounds of air
In an accord of repetitions. Yet,
If we repeat, it is because the wind
Encircling us, speaks always with our speech.

Light, too, encrusts us making visible
The motions of the mind and giving form
To moodiest nothings, as, desire for day
Accomplished in the immensely flashing East,
Desire for rest, in that descending sea
Of dark, which in its very darkening
Is rest and silence spreading into sleep.

. . . Evening, when the measure skips a beat
And then another, one by one, and all
To a seething minor swiftly modulate.
Bare night is best. Bare earth is best. Bare, bare,
Except for our own houses, huddled low
Beneath the arches and their spangled air,
Beneath the rhapsodies of fire and fire,
Where the voice that is in us makes a true response,
Where the voice that is great within us rises up,
As we stand gazing at the rounded moon.

MARTIAL CADENZA

I

Only this evening I saw again low in the sky
The evening star, at the beginning of winter, the star
That in spring will crown every western horizon,
Again . . . as if it came back, as if life came back,
Not in a later son, a different daughter, another place,
But as if evening found us young, still young,
Still walking in a present of our own.

II

It was like sudden time in a world without time,
This world, this place, the street in which I was,

Without time: as that which is not has no time,
Is not, or is of what there was, is full
Of the silence before the armies, armies without
Either trumpets or drums, the commanders mute, the arms
On the ground, fixed fast in a profound defeat.

III

What had this star to do with the world it lit,
With the blank skies over England, over France
And above the German camps? It looked apart.
Yet it is this that shall maintain—Itself
Is time, apart from any past, apart
From any future, the ever-living and being,
The ever-breathing and moving, the constant fire,

IV

The present close, the present realized,
Not the symbol but that for which the symbol stands,
The vivid thing in the air that never changes,
Though the air change. Only this evening I saw it again,
At the beginning of winter, and I walked and talked
Again, and lived and was again, and breathed again
And moved again and flashed again, time flashed again.

METAMORPHOSIS

Yillow, yillow, yillow,
Old worm, my pretty quirk,
How the wind spells out
Sep - tem - ber. . . .

Summer is in bones.
Cock-robin's at Caracas.
Make o, make o, make o,
Oto - otu - bre.

And the rude leaves fall.
The rain falls. The sky
Falls and lies with the worms.
The street lamps

37

Are those that have been hanged,
Dangling in an illogical
To and to and fro
Fro Niz - nil - imbo.

NO POSSUM, NO SOP, NO TATERS

He is not here, the old sun,
As absent as if we were asleep.

The field is frozen. The leaves are dry.
Bad is final in this light.

In this bleak air the broken stalks
Have arms without hands. They have trunks

Without legs or, for that, without heads.
They have heads in which a captive cry

Is merely the moving of a tongue.
Snow sparkles like eyesight falling to earth,

Like seeing fallen brightly away.
The leaves hop, scraping on the ground.

It is deep January. The sky is hard.
The stalks are firmly rooted in ice.

It is in this solitude, a syllable,
Out of these gawky flitterings,

Intones its single emptiness,
The savagest hollow of winter-sound.

It is here, in this bad, that we reach
The last purity of the knowledge of good.

The crow looks rusty as he rises up.
Bright is the malice in his eye . . .

One joins him there for company,
But at a distance, in another tree.

LESS AND LESS HUMAN, O SAVAGE SPIRIT

If there must be a god in the house, must be,
Saying things in the rooms and on the stair,

Let him move as the sunlight moves on the floor,
Or moonlight, silently, as Plato's ghost

Or Aristotle's skeleton. Let him hang out
His stars on the wall. He must dwell quietly.

He must be incapable of speaking, closed,
As those are: as light, for all its motion, is;

As color, even the closest to us, is;
As shapes, though they portend us, are.

It is the human that is the alien,
The human that has no cousin in the moon.

It is the human that demands his speech
From beasts or from the incommunicable mass.

If there must be a god in the house, let him be one
That will not hear us when we speak: a coolness,

A vermilioned nothingness, any stick of the mass
Of which we are too distantly a part.

MEN MADE OUT OF WORDS

What should we be without the sexual myth,
The human revery or poem of death?

Castratos of moon-mash—Life consists
Of propositions about life. The human

Revery is a solitude in which
We compose these propositions, torn by dreams,

By the terrible incantations of defeats
And by the fear that defeats and dreams are one.

The whole race is a poet that writes down
The eccentric propositions of its fate.

THE HOUSE WAS QUIET AND
THE WORLD WAS CALM

The house was quiet and the world was calm.
The reader became the book; and summer night

Was like the conscious being of the book.
The house was quiet and the world was calm.

The words were spoken as if there was no book,
Except that the reader leaned above the page,

Wanted to lean, wanted much most to be
The scholar to whom his book is true, to whom

The summer night is like a perfection of thought.
The house was quiet because it had to be.

The quiet was part of the meaning, part of the mind:
The access of perfection to the page.

And the world was calm. The truth in a calm world,
In which there is no other meaning, itself

Is calm, itself is summer and night, itself
Is the reader leaning late and reading there.

THE BEGINNING

So summer comes in the end to these few stains
And the rust and rot of the door through which she went.

The house is empty. But here is where she sat
To comb her dewy hair, a touchless light,

Perplexed by its darker iridescences.
This was the glass in which she used to look

At the moment's being, without history,
The self of summer perfectly perceived,

And feel its country gayety and smile
And be surprised and tremble, hand and lip.

This is the chair from which she gathered up
Her dress, the carefulest, commodious weave

Inwoven by a weaver to twelve bells . . .
The dress is lying, cast-off, on the floor.

Now, the first tutoyers of tragedy
Speak softly, to begin with, in the eaves.

THE IRISH CLIFFS OF MOHER

Who is my father in this world, in this house,
At the spirit's base?

My father's father, his father's father, his—
Shadows like winds

Go back to a parent before thought, before speech,
At the head of the past.

They go to the cliffs of Moher rising out of the mist,
Above the real,

Rising out of present time and place, above
The wet, green grass.

This is not landscape, full of the somnambulations
Of poetry

And the sea. This is my father or, maybe,
It is as he was,

A likeness, one of the race of fathers: earth
And sea and air.

THE RIVER OF RIVERS IN CONNECTICUT

There is a great river this side of Stygia,
Before one comes to the first black cataracts
And trees that lack the intelligence of trees.

In that river, far this side of Stygia,
The mere flowing of the water is a gayety,
Flashing and flashing in the sun. On its banks,

No shadow walks. The river is fateful,
Like the last one. But there is no ferryman.
He could not bend against its propelling force.

It is not to be seen beneath the appearances
That tell of it. The steeple at Farmington
Stands glistening and Haddam shines and sways.

It is the third commonness with light and air,
A curriculum, a vigor, a local abstraction . . .
Call it, once more, a river, an unnamed flowing,

Space-filled, reflecting the seasons, the folk-lore
Of each of the senses; call it, again and again,
The river that flows nowhere, like a sea.

MINA LOY (1882–1966)

Born in London of English parents, Miss Loy nevertheless was
associated closely with American poets in the imagist movement,
especially with Ezra Pound, who respected her writing and
publicized it in the U.S. Her output remained small, but dis-
tinguished by extreme toughness and originality. After some
years in France and Spain, she eventually made her home in
America, where she died at Aspen, Colo., at age eighty-four,
having lived to see her work reprinted and rediscovered by the
younger generation of American poets.

Lunar Baedeker and Time-Tables. Highlands, N.C.:
Jonathan Williams, 1958.

LUNAR BAEDEKER

A silver Lucifer
serves
cocaine in cornucopia

To some somnambulists
of adolescent thighs
draped
in satirical draperies

Peris in livery
prepare
Lethe
for posthumous parvenues

Delirious Avenues
lit
with the chandelier souls
of infusoria
from Pharaoh's tombstones

lead
to mercurial doomsdays

Odious oasis
in furrowed phosphorous

the eye-white sky-light
white-light district
of lunar lusts

Stellectric signs
"Wing shows on Starway"
"Zodiac carrousel"

Cyclones
of ecstatic dust
and ashes whirl
crusaders
from hallucinatory citadels
of shattered glass
into evacuate craters

A flock of dreams
browse on Necropolis

From the shores
of oval oceans
in the oxidized Orient

Onyx-eyed Odalisques
and ornithologists
observe
the flight
of Eros obsolete

And "Immortality"
mildews . . .
in the museums of the moon

"Nocturnal cyclops"
"Crystal concubine"

Pocked with personification
the fossil virgin of the skies
waxes and wanes

LOVE SONGS

1

Spawn of fantasies
Sifting the appraisable
Pig Cupid   his rosy snout
Rooting erotic garbage
"Once upon a time"
Pulls a weed   white star-topped
Among wild oats sown in mucous membrane
I would   an eye in a Bengal light
Eternity in a sky-rocket
Constellations in an ocean
Whose rivers run no fresher
Than a trickle of saliva

These are suspect places

I must live in my lantern
Trimming subliminal flicker
Virginal   to the bellows
Of experience
                    Colored glass.

2

At your mercy
Our Universe
Is only
A colorless onion
You derobe
Sheath by sheath
          Remaining
A disheartening odour
About your nervy hands

3

          Night
Heavy with shut-flowers' nightmares

          Noon
Curled to the solitaire
Core of the
Sun

4

Evolution fall foul of
Sexual equality
Prettily miscalculate
Similitude

Unnatural selection
Breed such sons and daughters
As shall jibber at each other
Uninterpretable cryptonyms
Under the moon

Give them some way of braying brassily
For caressive calling
Or to homophonous hiccoughs
Transpose the laugh
Let them suppose that tears
Are snowdrops or molasses
Or anything
Than human insufficiencies
Begging dorsal vertebrae

Let meeting be the turning
To the antipodean
And Form   a blurr
Anything
Than seduce them
To the one
As simple satisfaction
For the other

5

Shuttle-cock and battle-dore
A little pink-love
And feathers are strewn

6

Let Joy go solace-winged
To flutter whom she may concern

7

Once in a messanino
The starry ceiling
Vaulted an unimaginable family
Bird-like abortions
With human throats
And Wisdom's eyes
Who wore lamp-shade red dresses
And woolen hair

One bore a baby
In a padded porte-enfant
Tied with a sarsenet ribbon
To her goose's wings

But for the abominable shadows
I would have lived
Among their fearful furniture
To teach them to tell me their secrets
Before I guessed
—Sweeping the brood clean out

8

Midnight empties the street
      To the left a boy .
  One wing has been washed in the rain
  The other will never be clean any more—
Pulling door-bells to remind
Those that are snug
      To the right a haloed ascetic
      Threading houses
Probes wounds for souls
—The poor can't wash in hot water—
And I don't know which turning to take—

9

We might have coupled
In the bed-ridden monopoly of a moment
Or broken flesh with one another
At the profane communion table
Where wine is spill't on promiscuous lips

We might have given birth to a butterfly
With the daily-news
Printed in blood on its wings

10

In some
Prenatal plagiarism
Foetal buffoons
Caught tricks

From archetypal pantomime
Stringing emotions
Looped aloft

For the blind eyes
That Nature knows us with
And the most of Nature   is green

11

Green things grow
Salads
For the cerebral
Forager's revival . . .
And flowered flummery
Upon bossed bellies
Of mountains
Rolling in the sun

12

Shedding our petty pruderies
From slit eyes

We sidle up
to Nature
                that irate pornographist

13

The wind stuffs the scum of the white street
Into my lungs and my nostrils
Exhilarated birds
Prolonging flight into the night
Never reaching

WILLIAM CARLOS WILLIAMS (1883–1963)

Williams lived all his life in the town where he was born, Rutherford, N.J. A physician specializing in pediatrics, he wrote in his spare time, tapping out many of his short poems on a portable typewriter kept beside his office desk; yet he was far from a haphazard or occasional writer. In addition to short poems, published in a score of volumes, he wrote a multivolume poem entitled *Paterson*, four novels, several plays, short stories, a book of superb historical essays, an autobiography, and hundreds of reviews, literary essays, introductions, manifestoes, and other pieces. His output, considering his busy professional life, is astonishing. Although influenced by his lifelong friendship with Ezra Pound, Williams was too much an individualist to belong to any "school." He distrusted Pound's European associations, particularly the symbolist affinities of Pound's early colleague T. S. Eliot; and during the period of Eliot's dominance in Anglo-American literature, Williams felt estranged from the mainstream. But he never lacked admirers; and toward the end of his life, when his work was taken as model by the Black Mountain poets and their followers, he was quickly elevated to dominance himself, willy-nilly the founder of a school. Williams worked all his life, though more by practice than precept, to establish and define a native poetry, using American idiom and cadence to create a flexible but controlled language that could be truly expressive of our civilization. To the extent that a faultless ear, an unclouded eye, and an instinct for poetic drama, together with unshakable artistic integrity, could do the job, he undoubtedly succeeded, although his statements of theory were sometimes not very helpful. Today he is probably the most widely read, and certainly the most widely imitated, of all American poets.

The Collected Earlier Poems. New Directions, 1951.
The Collected Later Poems. New Directions, 1950.
Paterson, Books I–V. New Directions, 1963.
Pictures from Breughel and Other Poems. New Directions, 1962.
Selected Essays. Random House, 1954.
Selected Letters. Ed. John C. Thirlwall. McDowell, Obolensky, 1957.
Autobiography. Random House, 1951.
Many Loves and Other Plays. New Directions, 1961.
In the American Grain. New Directions, 1939.
I Wanted to Write a Poem. Ed. Edith Head. Beacon, 1958.

FIRST PRAISE

Lady of dusk-wood fastnesses,
    Thou art my Lady.
I have known the crisp, splintering leaf-tread with thee
    on before,
White, slender through green saplings;
I have lain by thee on the brown forest floor
    Beside thee, my Lady.

Lady of rivers strewn with stones,
    Only thou art my Lady.
Where thousand the freshets are crowded like peasants to
    a fair;
Clear-skinned, wild from seclusion
They jostle white-armed down the tent-bordered
    thoroughfare
    Praising my Lady.

THE HOUSE

The house is yours
to wander in as you please—
Your breakfasts will be kept
ready for you until

you choose to arise!
This is the front room
where we stood penniless
by the hogshead of crockery.

This is the kitchen—
We have a new
hotwater heater and a new
gas-stove to please you

And the front stairs
have been freshly painted—
white risers
and the treads mahogany.

50

Come upstairs
to the bedroom—
Your bed awaits you—
the chiffonier waits—

the whole house
is waiting—for you
to walk in it at your pleasure—
It is yours.

DEATH

He's dead
the dog won't have to
sleep on his potatoes
any more to keep them
from freezing

he's dead
the old bastard—
He's a bastard because

there's nothing
legitimate in him any
more
      he's dead
He's sick-dead

                 he's
a godforsaken curio
without
any breath in it

He's nothing at all
      he's dead
shrunken up to skin

     Put his head on
one chair and his
feet on another and
he'll lie there
like an acrobat—

Love's beaten. He
beat it. That's why
he's insufferable—

because
he's here needing a
shave and making love
an inside howl
of anguish and defeat—

He's come out of the man
and he's let
the man go—
the liar

Dead
his eyes
rolled up out of
the light—a mockery

which
love cannot touch—

just bury it
and hide its face
for shame.

TRACT

I will teach you my townspeople
how to perform a funeral
for you have it over a troop
of artists—
unless one should scour the world—
you have the ground sense necessary.

See! the hearse leads.
I begin with a design for a hearse.
For Christ's sake not black—
nor white either—and not polished!
Let it be weathered—like a farm wagon—
with gilt wheels (this could be

52

applied fresh at small expense)
or no wheels at all:
a rough dray to drag over the ground.

Knock the glass out!
My God—glass, my townspeople!
For what purpose? Is it for the dead
to look out or for us to see
how well he is housed or to see
the flowers or the lack of them—
or what?
To keep the rain and snow from him?
He will have a heavier rain soon:
pebbles and dirt and what not.
Let there be no glass—
and no upholstery, phew!
and no little brass rollers
and small easy wheels on the bottom—
my townspeople what are you thinking of?

A rough plain hearse then
with gilt wheels and no top at all.
On this the coffin lies
by its own weight.

           No wreaths please—
especially no hot house flowers.
Some common memento is better,
something he prized and is known by:
his old clothes—a few books perhaps—
God knows what! You realize
how we are about these things
my townspeople—
something will be found—anything
even flowers if he had come to that.
So much for the hearse.

For heaven's sake though see to the driver!
Take off the silk hat! In fact
that's no place at all for him—
up there unceremoniously
dragging our friend out to his own dignity!
Bring him down—bring him down!

Low and inconspicuous! I'd not have him ride
on the wagon at all—damn him—
the undertaker's understrapper!
Let him hold the reins
and walk at the side
and inconspicuously too!

Then briefly as to yourselves:
Walk behind—as they do in France,
seventh class, or if you ride
Hell take curtains! Go with some show
of inconvenience; sit openly—
to the weather as to grief.
Or do you think you can shut grief in?
What—from us? We who have perhaps
nothing to lose? Share with us
share with us—it will be money
in your pockets.
                    Go now
I think you are ready.

TO A SOLITARY DISCIPLE

Rather notice, mon cher,
that the moon is
tilted above
the point of the steeple
than that its color
is shell-pink.

Rather observe
that it is early morning
than that the sky
is smooth
as a turquoise.

Rather grasp
how the dark
converging lines
of the steeple
meet at the pinnacle—

54

perceive how
its little ornament
tries to stop them—

See how it fails!
See how the converging lines
of the hexagonal spire
escape upward—
receding, dividing!
—sepals
that guard and contain
the flower!

Observe
how motionless
the eaten moon
lies in the protecting lines.
It is true:
in the light colors
of morning

brown-stone and slate
shine orange and dark blue.

But observe
the oppressive weight
of the squat edifice!
Observe
the jasmine lightness
of the moon.

TO A FRIEND CONCERNING SEVERAL LADIES

You know there is not much
that I desire, a few chrysanthemums
half lying on the grass, yellow
and brown and white, the
talk of a few people, the trees,
an expanse of dried leaves perhaps
with ditches among them.

But there comes
between me and these things
a letter
or even a look—well placed,
you understand,
so that I am confused, twisted
four ways and—left flat,
unable to lift the food to
my own mouth:
Here is what they say: Come!
and come! and come! And if
I do not go I remain stale to
myself and if I go—
                    I have watched
the city from a distance at night
and wondered why I wrote no poem.
Come! yes,
the city is ablaze for you
and you stand and look at it.

And they are right. There is
no good in the world except out of
a woman and certain women alone
for certain things. But what if
I arrive like a turtle,
with my house on my back or
a fish ogling from under water?
It will not do. I must be
steaming with love, colored
like a flamingo. For what?
To have legs and a silly head
and to smell, pah! like a flamingo
that soils its own feathers behind?
Must I go home filled
with a bad poem?
And they say:
Who can answer these things
till he has tried? Your eyes
are half closed, you are a child,
oh, a sweet one, ready to play
but I will make a man of you and
with love on his shoulder—!

And in the marshes
the crickets run
on the sunny dike's top and
make burrows there, the water
reflects the reeds and the reeds
move on their stalks and rattle drily.

BETWEEN WALLS

the back wings
of the

hospital where
nothing

will grow lie
cinders

in which shine
the broken

pieces of a green
bottle

THE PREDICTER OF FAMINE

White day, black river
corrugated and swift—

as the stone of the sky
on the prongy ring
of the tarnished city
is smooth and without motion:

A gull flies low
upstream, his beak tilted
sharply, his eye
alert to the providing water.

LAMENT

What face, in the water,
distinct
yet washed by an obscurity?

The willow supplants its own
struggling rafters
(of winter branches)

by a green radiance. Is it
old or young?
But what this face

reflected beyond the bare structures
of a face
shining from the creaseless

water? A face
overlaid with evil, brown water;
the good insecure, the evil

sure beyond the buried sun. Lift
it. Turn away.
There was beside you

but now another face,
with long nose and clear blue eyes,
secure . . .

A HISTORY OF LOVE

1

And would you gather turds
for your grandmother's garden?
Out with you then, dustpan and broom;
she has seen the horse passing!

Out you go, bold again
as you promise always to be.
Stick your tongue out at the neighbors
that her flowers may grow.

Let me stress your
            loveliness
and its gravity

its counter-hell: Reading
finds you on the page

where sight enlarges
to confound the mind
            and only

a child is frightened
by its father's headgear

while a bird jigs and ol' Bunk
Johnson blows his horn.

RUSSIA

The Williams Avenue Zionist Church
                        (colored)
a thing to hold in the palm of the hand,
your big hand—
the dwarf campanile piled up, improvised
of blue cinder-blocks, badly aligned
(except for the incentive)

                        unvarnished,
the cross at the top slapped together
(in this lumber shortage) of sticks from
an old barrel top, I think

                        —painted white

Russia, idiot of the world, blind idiot
—do you understand me?

                        This also
I place in your hands . . .

I dream! and my dream is folly. While
armies rush to the encounter
I, alone, dream before the impending
onslaught. And the power in me,
to be crushed out: this paper, forgotten
—not even known ever to have existed,
proclaims the power of my dream . . .

Folly! I call upon folly to save us—
and scandal and disapproval, the restless
angels of the mind—

                              (I omit
the silly word exile. For from what and
to what land shall I be exiled and talk of
the cardinal bird and the starling
as though they were strange?)

                              I am
at home in my dream, Russia; and only there,
before the obliterating blow
                              that shall flatten everything
and its crazy masonry,
                              am I at home.

Inspired by my dream I do not call upon
a party to save me, nor a government
of whatever sort.

                    Rather I descend into
my dream as into a quiet lake
and there, already there, I find
my kinships. Thence I rise by my own
propulsions into a world beyond the moon.

O Russia, Russia! must we begin to call
you idiot of the world? When
you were a dream the world lived in you
inviolate—

O Russia! Russians! come with me into
my dream and let us be lovers,
connoisseurs, idlers—Come with me

60

in the spirit of Walt Whitman's earliest
poem, let us loaf at our ease—a moment
at the edge of destruction

                              Look.
Look through my eyes a moment. I am
a poet, uninfluential, with no skill
in polemics—my friends tell me I lack
the intellect. Look,
I once met Mayakovsky. Remember
Mayakovsky? I have a little paper-bound
volume of his in my attic, inscribed by him
in his scrawling hand to our mutual
friendship. He put one foot up
on the table that night at 14th St. when
he read to us—and his voice came
like the outpourings of the Odyssey.

                              Russians!
let Mayakovsky be my sponsor—he
and his Willie, the Havana street-cleaner—
Mayakovsky was a good guy and killed
himself, I suppose, not to embarrass you.

And so I go about.

And now I want to call your attention—
that you may know what keen eyes
I have in my dream—
to Leonardo's Last Supper! a small print
I saw today in a poor kitchen.

                              Russia!
for the first time in my life, I noticed
this famous picture not because
of the subject matter but because
of the severity and simplicity
of the background! Oh there was
the passion of the scene, of course,
generally. But particularly,
ignoring the subject, I fell upon
the perpendiculars of the paneled
woodwork standing there, submissive,
in exaggerated perspective.

There you have it. It's that background
from which my dreams have sprung. These
I dedicate now to you, now when I am
about to die. I hold back nothing. I lay
my spirit at your feet and say to you:
Here I am, a dreamer. I do not
resist you. Among many others, undistinguished,
of no moment—I am the background
upon which you will build your empire.

THE ACT

There were the roses, in the rain.
Don't cut them, I pleaded.
     They won't last, she said
But they're so beautiful
     where they are.
Agh, we were all beautiful once, she
     said,
and cut them and gave them to me
     in my hand.

THE CLOUDS

I

Filling the mind
upon the rim of the overarching sky, the
     horses of
the dawn charge from south to north,
     gigantic beasts
rearing flame-edged above the pit,
a rank confusion of the imagination still
     uncured
a rule, piebald under the streetlamps,
     reluctant
to be torn from its hold.

               Their flanks still
caught among low, blocking forms their
     fore-parts

rise lucid beyond this smell of a swamp, a mud
livid with decay and life! turtles
that burrowing among the white roots lift
    their green
red-striped faces startled before the dawn.

A black flag, writhing and whipping at the
    staff-head
mounts the sepulcher of the empty bank,
    fights
to be free . . .
        South to north! the direction
unmistakable, they move, distinct beyond
    the unclear
edge of the world, clouds! like statues
before which we are drawn—in darkness,
    thinking of
our dead, unable, knowing no place
where else rightly to lodge them.

                Tragic outlines
and the bodies of horses, mindfilling—but
visible! against the invisible; actual against
the imagined and the concocted; unspoiled
    by hands
and unshaped also by them but caressed by
    sight only,
moving among them, not that that propels
the eyes from under, while it blinds:

—upon whose backs the dead ride, high!
undirtied by the putridity we fasten upon
    them—
South to north, for this moment distinct
    and undeformed,
into the no-knowledge of their nameless
    destiny.

II

Where are the good minds of past days, the unshorn?
Villon, to be sure, with his
saw-toothed will and testament? Erasmus
who praised folly and

63

Shakespeare who wrote so that
no school man or churchman could sanction him without
revealing his own imbecility? Aristotle,
shrewd and alone, a onetime herb peddler?

They all, like Aristophanes, knew the clouds and
said next to nothing of the soul's flight
but kept their heads and died—
like Socrates, Plato's better self, unmoved.

Where? They live today in their old state because
of the pace they kept that keeps
them now fresh in our thoughts, their
relics, ourselves: Toulouse-Lautrec, the

deformed who lived in a brothel and painted
the beauty of whores. These were
the truth-tellers of whom we are the sole heirs
beneath the clouds that bring

shadow and darkness full of thought deepened
by rain against the clatter
of an empty sky. But anything to escape humanity!
Now it's spiritualism—again,

as if the certainty of a future life
were any solution to our dilemma: how to get
published not what we write but what we would write
    were
it not for the laws against libelous truth.

The poor brain unwilling to own the obtrusive body
would crawl from it like a crab and
because it succeeds, at times, in doffing that,
by its wiles of drugs or other "ecstasies," thinks

at last that it is quite free—exulted, scurrying to
some slightly larger shell some snail
has lost (where it will live). And so, thinking,
pretends a mystery! an unbodied

thing that would still be a brain—but no body,
something that does not eat but flies by the propulsions
of pure—what? into the sun itself, illimitedly
and exists so forever, blest, washed, purged

and at ease in non-representational bursts
of shapeless flame, sentient (naturally!)—and keeps
touch with the earth (by former works) at least.
The intellect leads, leads still! Beyond the clouds.

III

(Scherzo)

I came upon a priest once at St. Andrew's
in Amalfi in crimson and gold brocade riding
the clouds of his belief.

It happened that we tourists had intervened
at some mid-moment of the ritual—
tipped the sacristan or whatever it was.

No one else was there—porphyry and alabaster,
the light flooding in scented
with sandalwood—but this holy man

jiggling upon his buttocks to the litany
chanted, in response, by two kneeling altar boys!
I was amazed and stared in such manner

that he, caught half off the earth
in his ecstasy—though without losing a beat—
turned and grinned at me from his cloud.

IV

With each, dies a piece of the old life, which he carries,
a precious burden, beyond! Thus each
is valued by what he carries and that is his soul—
diminishing the bins by that much
unless replenished.

It is that which is the brotherhood:
the old life, treasured. But if they live?
What then?

The clouds remain
—the disordered heavens, ragged, ripped by winds
or dormant, a caligraphy of scaly dragons and bright
moths,

of straining thought, bulbous or smooth,
ornate, the flesh itself (in which
the poet foretells his own death); convoluted, lunging
   upon
a pismire, a conflagration, a . . . .

THE HORSE SHOW

Constantly near you, I never in my entire
sixty-four years knew you so well as yesterday
or half so well. We talked. You were never
so lucid, so disengaged from all exigencies
of place and time. We talked of ourselves,
intimately, a thing never heard of between us.
How long have we waited? almost a hundred years.

You said, Unless there is some spark, some
spirit we keep within ourselves, life, a
continuing life's impossible—and it is all
we have. There is no other life, only the one.
The world of the spirits that comes afterward
is the same as our own, just like you sitting
there they come and talk to me, just the same.

They come to bother us. Why? I said. I don't
know. Perhaps to find out what we are doing.
Jealous, do you think? I don't know. I
don't know why they should want to come back.
I was reading about some men who had been
buried under a mountain, I said to her, and
one of them came back after two months,

digging himself out. It was in Switzerland,
you remember? Of course I remember. The
villagers tho't it was a ghost coming down
to complain. They were frightened. They
do come, she said, what you call
my "visions." I talk to them just as I
am talking to you. I see them plainly.

Oh if I could only read! You don't know
what adjustments I have made. All
I can do is to try to live over again

what I knew when your brother and you
were children—but I can't always succeed.
Tell me about the horse show. I have
been waiting all week to hear about it.

Mother darling, I wasn't able to get away.
Oh that's too bad. It was just a show;
they make the horses walk up and down
to judge them by their form. Oh is that
all? I tho't it was something else. Oh
they jump and run too. I wish you had been
there, I was so interested to hear about it.

TO BE RECITED TO FLOSSIE ON HER BIRTHDAY

Let him who may
among the continuing lines
seek out

that tortured constancy
affirms
where I persist

let me say
across cross purposes
that the flower bloomed

struggling to assert itself
simply under
the conflicting lights

you will believe me
a rose
to the end of time

POEM

on getting a card
long delayed
from a poet whom I love
but

with whom I differ
touching
the modern poetic
technique

I was much moved
to hear
from him if
as yet he does not

concede the point
nor is he
indeed conscious of it
no matter

his style
has other outstanding
virtues
which delight me

FOR ELEANOR AND BILL MONAHAN

Mother of God! Our Lady!
        the heart
                is an unruly Master:
Forgive us our sins
        as we
                forgive
those who have sinned against
        us.
                We submit ourselves
to Your rule
        as the flowers in May
                submit themselves to
                Your Holy rule—against
that impossible springtime
        when men
                shall be the flowers
spread at your feet.

As far as spring is
        from winter
            so are we
from you now. We have not come
        easily
            to your environs
but painfully
        across sands
            that have scored our
feet. That which we have suffered
        was for us
            to suffer. Now,
in the winter of the year,
        the birds who know how
            to escape suffering
by flight
        are gone. Man alone
            is that creature who
cannot escape suffering
        by flight   .

I do not come to you
        save that I confess
            to being
                half man and half
woman. I have seen the ivy
        cling
            to a piece of crumbled
wall so that
        you cannot tell
            by which either
stands: this is to say
        if she to whom I cling
            is loosened both
of us go down.

Mother of God
        I have seen you stoop
            to a merest flower
and raise it
        and press it to your cheek.
            I could have called out

69

joyfully
    but you were too far off.
        You are a woman and
it was
    a woman's gesture.

You have no lovers now
    in the bare skies
        to bring you flowers,
to whisper to you
    under a hedge
        howbeit
you are young
    and fit to be loved.
        I declare it boldly
with my heart
    in my teeth
        and my knees knocking
together. Yet I declare
    it, and by God's word
        it is no lie. Make us
humble and obedient to His rule.

There are men
    who as they live
        fling caution to the
wind and women praise them
    and love them for it.
        Cruel as the claws of
a cat   .   .

The moon which
    they have vulgarized recently
        is still
your planet
    as it was Dian's before
        you. What
do they think they will attain
    by their ships
        that death has not
already given
    them? Their ships
        should be directed

inward upon   .   But I
    am an old man. I
        have had enough.
The female principle of the world
    is my appeal
        in the extremity
to which I have come.
    O clemens! O pia! O dolcis!
    Maria!

THE SPARROW

(To My Father)

This sparrow
    who comes to sit at my window
        is a poetic truth
more than a natural one.
    His voice,
        his movements,
his habits—
    how he loves to
        flutter his wings
in the dust—
    all attest it;
        granted, he does it
to rid himself of lice
    but the relief he feels
        makes him
cry out lustily—
    which is a trait
        more related to music
than otherwise.
    Wherever he finds himself
        in early spring,
on back streets
    or beside palaces,
        he carries on
unaffectedly
    his amours.
        It begins in the egg,

his sex genders it:
        What is more pretentiously
                useless
or about which
        we more pride ourselves?
                It leads as often as not
to our undoing.
        The cockerel, the crow
                with their challenging voices
cannot surpass
        the insistence
                of his cheep!
Once
        at El Paso
                toward evening,
I saw—and heard!—
        ten thousand sparrows
                who had come in from
the desert
        to roost. They filled the trees
                of a small park. Men fled
(with ears ringing!)
        from their droppings,
                leaving the premises
to the alligators
        who inhabit
                the fountain. His image
is familiar
        as that of the aristocratic
                unicorn, a pity
there are not more oats eaten
        nowadays
                to make living easier
for him.
        At that,
                his small size,
keen eyes,
        serviceable beak
                and general truculence
assure his survival—
        to say nothing
                of his innumerable

brood.
      Even the Japanese
         know him
and have painted him
      sympathetically,
         with profound insight
into his minor
      characteristics.
         Nothing even remotely
subtle
      about his lovemaking.
         He crouches
before the female,
      drags his wings,
         waltzing,
throws back his head
      and simply—
         yells! The din
is terrific.
      The way he swipes his bill
         across a plank
to clean it,
      is decisive.
         So with everything
he does. His coppery
      eyebrows
         give him the air
of being always
      a winner—and yet
         I saw once,
the female of his species
      clinging determinedly
         to the edge of
a water pipe,
      catch him
         by his crown-feathers
to hold him
      silent,
         subdued,
hanging above the city streets
      until
         she was through with him.

What was the use
        of that?
                She hung there
herself,
        puzzled at her success.
                I laughed heartily.
Practical to the end,
        it is the poem
                of his existence
that triumphed
        finally;
                a wisp of feathers
flattened to the pavement,
        wings spread symmetrically
                as if in flight,
the head gone,
        the black escutcheon of the breast
                undecipherable,
an effigy of a sparrow,
        a dried wafer only,
                left to say
and it says it
        without offense,
                beautifully;
This was I,
        a sparrow.
                I did my best;
farewell.

SARA TEASDALE (1884–1933)

Neurotically intense, Miss Teasdale moved in the company of poets, it is said, like a "recessive flame." After one particularly tempestuous affair, with Vachel Lindsay, she married a businessman; but later divorced him, retired to seclusion, and in the end died from an overdose of sleeping pills. Her poems, though popular in her lifetime, seem fragile and dated today; but a few retain, within slight conventional forms, the force of genuine originality.

Collected Poems. Macmillan, 1937.

"I AM NOT YOURS"

I am not yours, not lost in you,
    Not lost, although I long to be
Lost as a candle lit at noon,
    Lost as a snowflake in the sea.

You love me, and I find you still
    A spirit beautiful and bright,
Yet I am I, who long to be
    Lost as a light is lost in light.

Oh plunge me deep in love—put out
    My senses, leave me deaf and blind,
Swept by the tempest of your love,
    A taper in a rushing wind.

"WHAT DO I CARE"

What do I care, in the dreams and the languor of spring,
    That my songs do not show me at all?
For they are a fragrance, and I am a flint and a fire,
    I am an answer, they are only a call.

But what do I care, for love will be over so soon,
  Let my heart have its say and my mind stand idly by,
For my mind is proud and strong enough to be silent,
  It is my heart that makes my songs, not I.

MOONLIGHT

It will not hurt me when I am old,
  A running tide where moonlight burned
    Will not sting me like silver snakes;
The years will make me sad and cold,
  It is the happy heart that breaks.

The heart asks more than life can give,
  When that is learned, then all is learned;
    The waves break fold on jewelled fold,
But beauty itself is fugitive,
  It will not hurt me when I am old.

EZRA POUND (1885-   )

To suggest in a note the breadth of Pound's activities is impossible. As poet, translator, critic, editor, counselor, correspondent, impresario, manifesto writer, inventor of movements—in these capacities and more he has been untiring, and has left his mark on every aspect of modern Anglo-American poetry. Many of his contemporaries have acknowledged not only his influence but his direct help, notably Eliot, Joyce, Hemingway, Frost, and Yeats. The son of an assayer, Pound was born in Hailey, Ida., a mining town; then later lived in Philadelphia and attended the University of Pennsylvania. Before completing his doctoral studies, however, he left the U.S., going first to Italy, where his first book, *A Lume Spento*, was published at Venice in 1908, and then to England, where he helped to found the imagist movement. Though he soon became disaffected and took up other, more advanced positions, his statements of theory during this period left a deep impress on all contemporary writing, especially his advocacy of a functional rather than a forced metric in poetry, and his insistence on utter clarity and hardness of detail in all writing, with an avoidance of the least trace of conventional sentimentalism. Meanwhile his own writing progressed rapidly. In 1915 he published the first of his many translations from Chinese poetry. In 1917 his first cantos appeared, inaugurating the sequence which has occupied him since then. In 1924 he settled at Rapallo, in Italy, which became his permanent home. At the same time he took up Social Credit, an economic philosophy developed by C. H. Douglas, and turned his attention more and more to political and social questions. During World War II he conducted a series of broadcasts from Italy which were thought to contain statements inimical to American interests. After the war he was brought to the U.S. and indicted for treason; but his trial was never held. Instead he was lodged in federal custody at St. Elizabeth's Hospital, Washington, D.C., where he remained for thirteen years, until his release was brought about through the intercession of fellow poets, particularly E. E. Cummings and Robert Frost. Today he lives in retirement in Italy. Irascible, hypersensitive, dauntless, always controversial, Pound has cheerfully given offense to many people; yet no one has been more generous to fellow artists, more helpful or more influential. In freeing poetry from the formal and attitudinal conventions that had grown progressively more restrictive during the nineteenth century, i.e., in originating modern poetry, Pound's role was not only central and crucial but veritably unique. Today few working poets could be found who do not regard him with veneration and affection.

Personae. Rev. ed. New Directions, 1949.
The Cantos. (Numbers 1–95.) New Directions, 1963.
Thrones. (Cantos 96–109.) New Directions, 1959.
The Literary Essays of Ezra Pound. Ed. T. S. Eliot. New Directions, 1954.
The Translations of Ezra Pound. Rev. ed. New Directions, 1963.
Guide to Kulchur. New Directions, 1952.
The ABC of Reading. New Directions, 1960.
The Spirit of Romance. New Directions, 1952.
The Confucian Odes. (Translation of the *Shih-ching*.) New Directions, 1959.

CINO

Italian Campagna 1309, the open road

Bah! I have sung women in three cities,
But it is all the same;
And I will sing of the sun.

Lips, words, and you snare them,
Dreams, words, and they are as jewels,
Strange spells of old deity,
Ravens, nights, allurement:
And they are not;
Having become the souls of song.

Eyes, dreams, lips, and the night goes.
Being upon the road once more,
They are not.
Forgetful in their towers of our tuneing
Once for Wind-runeing
They dream us-toward and
Sighing, say, "Would Cino,
Passionate Cino, of the wrinkling eyes,
Gay Cino, of quick laughter,
Cino, of the dare, the jibe,
Frail Cino, strongest of his tribe
That tramp old ways beneath the sun-light,
Would Cino of the Luth were here!"

Once, twice, a year—
Vaguely thus word they:

"Cino?" "Oh, eh, Cino Polnesi
The singer is't you mean?"
"Ah yes, passed once our way,
A saucy fellow, but . . .
(Oh they are all one these vagabonds),
Peste! 'tis his own songs?
Or some other's that he sings?
But *you*, My Lord, how with your city?"

But you "My Lord," God's pity!
And all I knew were out, My Lord, you
Were Lack-land Cino, e'en as I am,
O Sinistro.

I have sung women in three cities.
But it is all one.
I will sing of the sun.
. . . eh? . . . they mostly had grey eyes,
But it is all one, I will sing of the sun.

" 'Pollo Phoibee, old tin pan, you
Glory to Zeus' aegis-day,
Shield o' steel-blue, th' heaven o'er us
Hath for boss thy lustre gay!

'Pollo Phoibee, to our way-fare
Make thy laugh our wander-lied;
Bid thy 'fulgence bear away care.
Cloud and rain-tears pass they fleet!

Seeking e'er the new-laid rast-way
To the gardens of the sun . . .
. . . .
I have sung women in three cities
But it is all one.

I will sing of the white birds
In the blue waters of heaven,
The clouds that are spray to its sea.

DE AEGYPTO

I, even I, am he who knoweth the roads
Through the sky, and the wind thereof is my body.

I have beheld the Lady of Life,
I, even I, who fly with the swallows.

Green and gray is her raiment,
Trailing along the wind.

I, even I, am he who knoweth the roads
Through the sky, and the wind thereof is my body.

Manus animam pinxit,
My pen is in my hand

To write the acceptable word. . . .
My mouth to chant the pure singing!

Who hath the mouth to receive it,
The song of the Lotus of Kumi?

I, even I, am he who knoweth the roads
Through the sky, and the wind thereof is my body.

I am flame that riseth in the sun,
I, even I, who fly with the swallows.

The moon is upon my forehead,
The winds are under my lips.

The moon is a great pearl in the waters of sapphire,
Cool to my fingers the flowing waters.

I, even I, am he who knoweth the roads
Through the sky, and the wind thereof is my body.

AND THUS IN NINEVEH

"Aye! I am a poet and upon my tomb
Shall maidens scatter rose leaves
And men myrtles, ere the night
Slays day with her dark sword.

"Lo! this thing is not mine
Nor thine to hinder,
For the custom is full old,
And here in Nineveh have I beheld
Many a singer pass and take his place
In those dim halls where no man troubleth
His sleep or song.
And many a one hath sung his songs
More craftily, more subtle-souled than I;
And many a one now doth surpass
My wave-worn beauty with his wind of flowers,
Yet am I poet, and upon my tomb
Shall all men scatter rose leaves
Ere the night slay light
With her blue sword.

"It is not, Raana, that my song rings highest
Or more sweet in tone than any, but that I
Am here a Poet, that doth drink of life
As lesser men drink wine."

BALLATETTA

The light became her grace and dwelt among
Blind eyes and shadows that are formed as men;
Lo, how the light doth melt us into song:

The broken sunlight for a healm she beareth
Who hath my heart in jurisdiction.
In wild-wood never fawn nor fallow fareth
So silent light; no gossamer is spun
So delicate as she is, when the sun
Drives the clear emeralds from the bended grasses
Lest they should parch too swiftly, where she passes.

THE RETURN

See, they return; ah, see the tentative
      Movements, and the slow feet,
      The trouble in the pace and the uncertain
      Wavering!

See, they return, one, and by one,
With fear, as half-awakened;
As if the snow should hesitate
And murmur in the wind,
       and half turn back;
These were the "Wing'd-with-Awe,"
      Inviolable.

Gods of the wingèd shoe!
With them the silver hounds,
      sniffing the trace of air!

Haie! Haie!
   These were the swift to harry;
These the keen-scented;
These were the souls of blood.

Slow on the leash,
      pallid the leash-men!

SALUTATION

O generation of the thoroughly smug
   and thoroughly uncomfortable,
I have seen fishermen picnicking in the sun,
I have seen them with untidy families,
I have seen their smiles full of teeth
   and heard ungainly laughter.
And I am happier than you are,
And they were happier than I am;
And the fish swim in the lake
   and do not even own clothing.

LIU CH'E

The rustling of the silk is discontinued,
Dust drifts over the court-yard,
There is no sound of foot-fall, and the leaves
Scurry into heaps and lie still,
And she the rejoicer of the heart is beneath them:

A wet leaf that clings to the threshold.

IN A STATION OF THE METRO

The apparition of these faces in the crowd;
Petals on a wet, black bough.

LAMENT OF THE FRONTIER GUARD

By the North Gate, the wind blows full of sand,
Lonely from the beginning of time until now!
Trees fall, the grass goes yellow with autumn.
I climb the towers and towers
      to watch out the barbarous land:
Desolate castle, the sky, the wide desert.
There is no wall left to this village.
Bones white with a thousand frosts,
High heaps, covered with trees and grass;
Who brought this to pass?
Who has brought the flaming imperial anger?
Who has brought the army with drums and with kettle-
    drums?
Barbarous kings.
A gracious spring, turned to blood-ravenous autumn,
A turmoil of wars-men, spread over the middle kingdom,
Three hundred and sixty thousand,
And sorrow, sorrow like rain.
Sorrow to go, and sorrow, sorrow returning.
Desolate, desolate fields,
And no children of warfare upon them,
    No longer the men for offence and defence.
Ah, how shall you know the dreary sorrow at the North
   Gate,
With Rihoku's name forgotten,
And we guardsmen fed to the tigers.

By Rihaku

ALBA

When the nightingale to his mate
Sings day-long and night late
My love and I keep state

In bower,
In flower,
'Till the watchman on the tower
Cry:
  "Up! Thou rascal, Rise,
  I see the white
    Light
     And the night
      Flies."

FROM *HUGH SELWYN MAUBERLEY*

I

E.P. Ode Pour l'Election de Son Sépulchre

For three years, out of key with his time,
He strove to resuscitate the dead art
Of poetry; to maintain "the sublime"
In the old sense. Wrong from the start—

No, hardly, but seeing he had been born
In a half savage country, out of date;
Bent resolutely on wringing lilies from the acorn;
Capaneus; trout for factitious bait;

ἴδμεν γάρ τοι πάνθ', δο' ἐνὶ Τροίῃ
Caught in the unstopped ear;
Giving the rocks small lee-way
The chopped seas held him, therefore, that year.

His true Penelope was Flaubert,
He fished by obstinate isles;
Observed the elegance of Circe's hair
Rather than the mottoes on sun-dials.

Unaffected by "the march of events,"
He passed from men's memory in *l'an trentiesme*
De son eage; the case presents
No adjunct to the Muses' diadem.

84

The age demanded an image
Of its accelerated grimace,
Something for the modern stage,
Not, at any rate, an Attic grace;

Not, not certainly, the obscure reveries
Of the inward gaze;
Better mendacities
Than the classics in paraphrase!

The "age demanded" chiefly a mould in plaster,
Made with no loss of time,
A prose kinema, not, not assuredly, alabaster
Or the "sculpture" of rhyme.

These fought in any case,
and some believing,
          pro domo, in any case . . .

Some quick to arm,
some for adventure,
some from fear of weakness,
some from fear of censure,
some for love of slaughter, in imagination,
learning later . . .
some in fear, learning love of slaughter;

Died some, pro patria,
          non "dulce" non "et decor" . . .
walked eye-deep in hell
believing in old men's lies, then unbelieving
came home, home to a lie,
home to many deceits,
home to old lies and new infamy;
usury age-old and age-thick
and liars in public places.

Daring as never before, wastage as never before.
Young blood and high blood,
fair cheeks, and fine bodies;

fortitude as never before

frankness as never before,
disillusions as never told in the old days,
hysterias, trench confessions,
laughter out of dead bellies.

ENVOI (1919)

Go, dumb-born book,
Tell her that sang me once that song of Lawes:
Hadst thou but song
As thou hast subjects known,
Then were there cause in thee that should condone
Even my faults that heavy upon me lie,
And build her glories their longevity.

Tell her that sheds
Such treasure in the air,
Recking naught else but that her graces give
Life to the moment,
I would bid them live
As roses might, in magic amber laid,
Red overwrought with orange and all made
One substance and one colour
Braving time.

Tell her that goes
With song upon her lips
But sings not out the song, nor knows
The maker of it, some other mouth,
May be as fair as hers,
Might, in new ages, gain her worshippers,
When our two dusts with Waller's shall be laid,
Siftings on siftings in oblivion,
Till change hath broken down
All things save Beauty alone.

V

1

Now if ever it is time to cleanse Helicon;
                   to lead Emathian horses afield,
And to name over the census of my chiefs in the Roman
    camp.
If I have not the faculty, "The bare attempt would be
    praise-worthy."
"In things of similar magnitude
                   the mere will to act is sufficient."

The primitive ages sang Venus,
                   the last sings of a tumult,
And I also will sing war when this matter of a girl is
    exhausted.
I with my beak hauled ashore would proceed in a more
    stately manner,
My Muse is eager to instruct me in a new gamut, or
    gambetto,
Up, up my soul, from your lowly cantilation,
                   put on a timely vigour.

Oh august Pierides! Now for a large-mouthed product.
Thus:
"The Euphrates denies its protection to the Parthian and
    apologizes for Crassus,"
And "It is, I think, India which now gives necks to your
    triumph,"
And so forth, Augustus. "Virgin Arabia shakes in her in-
    most dwelling."
If any land shrink into a distant seacoast,
              it is a mere postponement of your domination.
And I shall follow the camp, I shall be duly celebrated for
    singing the affairs of your cavalry.
May the fates watch over my day.

Yet you ask on what account I write so many love-lyrics
And whence this soft book comes into my mouth.
Neither Calliope nor Apollo sung these things into my ear,
                        My genius is no more than a girl.

If she with ivory fingers drive a tune through the lyre,
                        We look at the process.
How easy the moving fingers; if hair is mussed on her
     forehead,
If she goes in a gleam of Cos, in a slither of dyed stuff,
There is a volume in the matter; if her eyelids sink into
     sleep,
There are new jobs for the author;
And if she plays with me with her shirt off,
                        We shall construct many Iliads.
And whatever she does or says
                        We shall spin long yarns out of nothing.

Thus much the fates have allotted me, and if, Maecenas,
I were able to lead heroes into armour, I would not,
Neither would I warble of Titans, nor of Ossa spiked onto
     Olympus,
Nor of causeways over Pelion,
Nor of Thebes in its ancient respectability,
                        nor of Homer's reputation in Pergamus,
Nor of Xerxes' two-barreled kingdom, nor of Remus and
     his royal family,
Nor of dignified Carthaginian characters,
Nor of Welsh mines and the profit Marus had out of them.

I should remember Caesar's affairs . . .
                        for a background,
Although Callimachus did without them,
                        and without Theseus,
Without an inferno, without Achilles attended of gods,
Without Ixion, and without the sons of Menoetius and the
     Argo and without Jove's grave and the Titans.

And my ventricles do not palpitate to Caesarial *ore ro-
tundos*,
Nor to the tune of the Phrygian fathers.
Sailor, of winds; a plowman, concerning his oxen;

Soldier, the enumeration of wounds; the sheep-feeder, of
ewes;
We, in our narrow bed, turning aside from battles:
Each man where he can, wearing out the day in his man-
ner.

3

It is noble to die of love, and honourable to remain un-
cuckolded for a season.
And she speaks ill of light women,
                              and will not praise Homer
Because Helen's conduct is "unsuitable."

VII

Me happy, night, night full of brightness;
Oh couch made happy by my long delectations;
How many words talked out with abundant candles;
Struggles when the lights were taken away;
Now with bared breasts she wrestled against me,
          Tunic spread in delay;
And she then opening my eyelids fallen in sleep,
Her lips upon them; and it was her mouth saying:
     Sluggard!

In how many varied embraces, our changing arms,
Her kisses, how many, lingering on my lips.
"Turn not Venus into a blinded motion,
     Eyes are the guides of love,
Paris took Helen naked coming from the bed of Menelaus,
Endymion's naked body, bright bait for Diana,"
     —such at least is the story.

While our fates twine together, sate we our eyes with love;
For long night comes upon you
                         and a day when no day returns.
Let the gods lay chains upon us
                    so that no day shall unbind them.

Fool who would set a term to love's madness,
For the sun shall drive with black horses,
     earth shall bring wheat from barley,

The flood shall move toward the fountain
  Ere love know moderations,
  The fish shall swim in dry streams.
No, now while it may be, let not the fruit of life cease.

  Dry wreaths drop their petals,
       their stalks are woven in baskets,
  To-day we take the great breath of lovers,
       to-morrow fate shuts us in.

Though you give all your kisses
      you give but few.

Nor can I shift my pains to other,
  Hers will I be dead,
If she confer such nights upon me,
      long is my life, long in years,
If she give me many,
  God am I for the time.

CANTO I

And then went down to the ship,
Set keel to breakers, forth on the godly sea, and
We set up mast and sail on that swart ship,
Bore sheep aboard her, and our bodies also
Heavy with weeping, and winds from sternward
Bore us out onward with bellying canvas,
Circe's this craft, the trim-coifed goddess.
Then sat we amidships, wind jamming the tiller,
Thus with stretched sail, we went over sea till day's end.
Sun to his slumber, shadows o'er all the ocean,
Came we then to the bounds of deepest water,
To the Kimmerian lands, and peopled cities
Covered with close-webbed mist, unpierced ever
With glitter of sun-rays
Nor with stars stretched, nor looking back from heaven
Swartest night stretched over wretched men there.
The ocean flowing backward, came we then to the place
Aforesaid by Circe.
Here did they rites, Perimedes and Eurylochus,

And drawing sword from my hip
I dug the ell-square pitkin;
Poured we libations unto each the dead,
First mead and then sweet wine, water mixed with white
    flour.
Then prayed I many a prayer to the sickly death's-heads;
As set in Ithaca, sterile bulls of the best
For sacrifice, heaping the pyre with goods,
A sheep to Tiresias only, black and a bell-sheep.
Dark blood flowed in the fosse,
Souls out of Erebus, cadaverous dead, of brides
Of youths and of the old who had borne much;
Souls stained with recent tears, girls tender,
Men many, mauled with bronze lance heads,
Battle spoil, bearing yet dreory arms,
These many crowded about me; with shouting,
Pallor upon me, cried to my men for more beasts;
Slaughtered the herds, sheep slain of bronze;
Poured ointment, cried to the gods,
To Pluto the strong, and praised Proserpine;
Unsheathed the narrow sword,
I sat to keep off the impetuous impotent dead,
Till I should hear Tiresias.
But first Elpenor came, our friend Elpenor,
Unburied, cast on the wide earth,
Limbs that we left in the house of Circe,
Unwept, unwrapped in sepulchre, since toils urged
    other.
Pitiful spirit. And I cried in hurried speech:
"Elpenor, how art thou come to this dark coast?
"Cam'st thou afoot, outstripping seamen?"
        And he in heavy speech:
"Ill fate and abundant wine. I slept in Circe's ingle.
"Going down the long ladder unguarded,
"I fell against the buttress,
"Shattered the nape-nerve, the soul sought Avernus.
"But thou, O King, I bid remember me, unwept, unburied,
"Heap up mine arms, be tomb by sea-bord, and inscribed:
"*A man of no fortune, and with a name to come.*
"And set my oar up, that I swung mid fellows."

And Anticlea came, whom I beat off, and then Tiresias
    Theban,

Holding his golden wand, knew me, and spoke first:
"A second time? why? man of ill star,
"Facing the sunless dead and this joyless region?
"Stand from the fosse, leave me my bloody bever
"For soothsay."
        And I stepped back,
And he strong with the blood, said then: "Odysseus
"Shalt return through spiteful Neptune, over dark seas,
"Lose all companions." And then Anticlea came.
Lie quiet Divus. I mean, that is Andreas Divus,
In officina Wecheli, 1538, out of Homer.
And he sailed, by Sirens and thence outward and away
And unto Circe.
        Venerandam,
In the Cretan's phrase, with the golden crown, Aphrodite,
Cypri munimenta sortita est, mirthful, oricalchi, with
        golden
Girdles and breast bands, thou with dark eyelids
Bearing the golden bough of Argicida. So that:

CANTO XLVII

Who even dead, yet hath his mind entire!
This sound came in the dark
First must thou go the road
                        to hell
And to the bower of Ceres' daughter Proserpine,
Through overhanging dark, to see Tiresias,
Eyeless that was, a shade, that is in hell
So full of knowing that the beefy men know less than he,
Ere thou come to thy road's end.
        Knowledge the shade of a shade,
Yet must thou sail after knowledge
Knowing less than drugged beasts. *phtheggometha
thasson*
φθεγγώμεθα θᾶσσον
        The small lamps drift in the bay
And the sea's claw gathers them.
Neptunus drinks after neap-tide.
Tamuz! Tamuz!!
The red flame going seaward.
        By this gate art thou measured.

From the long boats they have set lights in the water,
The sea's claw gathers them outward.
Scilla's dogs snarl at the cliff's base,
The white teeth gnaw in under the crag,
But in the pale night the small lamps float seaward

Τυ Δ ὥνα
TU DIONA

Καὶ Μοῖραιτ' "Αδονιν
Kai MOIRAI' ADONIN
The sea is streaked red with Adonis,
The lights flicker red in small jars.
Wheat shoots rise new by the altar,
    flower from the swift seed.
Two span, two span to a woman,
Beyond that she believes not. Nothing is of any impor-
    tance.
To that is she bent, her intention
To that art thou called ever turning intention,
Whether by night the owl-call, whether by sap in shoot,
Never idle, by no means by no wiles intermittent
Moth is called over mountain
The bull runs blind on the sword, *naturans*
To the cave art thou called, Odysseus,
By Molü hast thou respite for a little,
By Molü art thou freed from the one bed
    that thou may'st return to another
The stars are not in her counting,
    To her they are but wandering holes.
Begin thy plowing
When the Pleiades go down to their rest,
Begin thy plowing
40 days are they under seabord,
Thus do in fields by seabord
And in valleys winding down toward the sea.
When the cranes fly high
    think of plowing.
By this gate art thou measured
Thy day is between a door and a door
Two oxen are yoked for plowing
Or six in the hill field
White bulk under olives, a score for drawing down stone,
Here the mules are gabled with slate on the hill road.
Thus was it in time.

And the small stars now fall from the olive branch,
Forked shadow falls dark on the terrace
More black than the floating martin
    that has no care for your presence,
His wing-print is black on the roof tiles
And the print is gone with his cry.
So light is thy weight on Tellus
Thy notch no deeper indented
Thy weight less than the shadow
Yet hast thou gnawed through the mountain,
    Scylla's white teeth less sharp.
Hast thou found a nest softer than cunnus
Or hast thou found better rest
Hast'ou a deeper planting, doth thy death year
Bring swifter shoot?
Hast thou entered more deeply the mountain?

The light has entered the cave. Io! Io!
The light has gone down into the cave,
Splendour on splendour!
By prong have I entered these hills:
That the grass grow from my body,
That I hear the roots speaking together,
The air is new on my leaf,
The forked boughs shake with the wind.
Is Zephyrus more light on the bough, Apeliota
more light on the almond branch?
By this door have I entered the hill.
Falleth,
Adonis falleth.
Fruit cometh after. The small lights drift out with the tide,
sea's claw has gathered them outward,
Four banners to every flower
The sea's claw draws the lamps outward.
Think thus of thy plowing
When the seven stars go down to their rest
Forty days for their rest, by seabord
And in valleys that wind down toward the sea
     Καὶ Μοῖραι᾽ "Αδονιν
     KAI MOIRAI' ADONIN
When the almond bough puts forth its flame,
When the new shoots are brought to the altar,
     Τυ Διώνα, Καὶ Μοῖραι
     TU DIONA, KAI MOIRAI

94

Καὶ Μοῖραι' Ἄδονιν
KAI MOIRAI' ADONIN
　　　that hath the gift of healing,
that hath the power over wild beasts.

CANTO LXXXI

Zeus lies in Ceres' bosom
Taishan is attended of loves
　　　under Cythera, before sunrise
and he said: Hay aquí mucho catolicismo—(sounded
　　　　　　　　　　　　　　　　　catoli*th*ismo)
　　　y muy poco reliHion"
and he said: Yo creo que los reyes desparecen"
That was Padre José Elizondo
　　　in 1906 and in 1917
or about 1917
　　　and Dolores said: Come pan, niño," eat bread, me lad
Sargent had painted her
　　　　　　before he descended
(i.e. if he descended
　　　but in those days he did thumb sketches,
impressions of the Velasquez in the Museo del Prado
and books cost a peseta,
　　　brass candlesticks in proportion,
hot wind came from the marshes
　　　and death-chill from the mountains.
And later Bowers wrote: "but such hatred,
　　I had never conceived such"
and the London reds wouldn't show up his friends.
　　　(i.e. friends of Franco
working in London) and in Alcazar
forty years gone, they said: go back to the station to eat
you can sleep here for a peseta"
　　　goat bells tinkled all night
　　　and the hostess grinned: Eso es luto, *haw!*
mi marido es muerto
　　　(it is mourning, my husband is dead)
when she gave me paper to write on
with a black border half an inch or more deep,
　　　say ⅝ths, of the locanda
"We call *all* foreigners frenchies"

and the egg broke in Cabranez' pocket,
        thus making history. Basil says
they beat drums for three days
till all the drumheads were busted
        (simple village fiesta)
and as for his life in the Canaries...
Possum observed that the local   folk dance
was danced by the same dancers in divers localities
        in political welcome...
the technique of demonstration
        Cole studied that (not G.D.H., Horace)
"You will find" said old André Spire,
that every man on that board (Crédit Agricole)
has a brother-in-law
        "You the one, I the few"
        said John Adams
speaking of fears in the abstract
    to his volatile friend Mr Jefferson
(to break the pentameter, that was the first heave)
or as Jo Bard says: they never speak to each other,
if it is baker and concierge visibly
        it is La Rochefoucauld and de Maintenon audibly.
"Te cavero le budelle"
            "La corata a te"
In less than a geological epoch
            said Henry Mencken
"Some cook, some do not cook
    some things cannot be altered"
Ἴυγξ. . . . . ἐμὸν ποτὶ δῶμα τὸν ἄνδρα
What counts is the cultural level,
    thank Benin for this table ex packing box
    "doan yu tell no one I made it"
        from a mask fine as any in Frankfurt
"It'll get you offn th' groun"
        Light as the branch of Kuanon
And at first disappointed with shoddy
the bare ram-shackle quais, but then saw the
high buggy wheels
        and was reconciled,
George Santayana arriving in the port of Boston
and kept to the end of his life that faint *thethear*
of the Spaniard
        as a grace quasi imperceptible

96

as did Muss the *v* for *u* of Romagna
and said the grief was a full act
    repeated for each new condoleress
working up to a climax.
and George Horace said he wd/"get Beveridge" (Senator)
Beveridge wouldn't talk and he wouldn't write for the
    papers
but George got him by campin' in his hotel
and assailin' him at lunch breakfast an' dinner
      three articles
and my ole man went on hoein' corn
   while George was a-tellin' him,
come across a vacant lot
    where you'd occasionally see a wild rabbit
or mebbe only a loose one
    AOI!
    a leaf in the current
             at my grates no Althea

libretto

    Yet
    Ere the season died a-cold
    Borne upon a zephyr's shoulder
    I rose through the aureate sky
           Lawes and Jenkyns guard thy rest
           Dolmetsch ever be thy guest,
    Has he tempered the viol's wood
    To enforce   both the grave   and the acute?
    Has he curved us the bowl of the lute?
           Lawes and Jenkyns guard thy rest
           Dolmetsch ever be thy guest
    Hast 'ou fashioned so airy a mood
    To draw up leaf from the root?
    Hast 'ou found   a cloud   so light
    As seemed neither mist nor shade?

           Then resolve me, tell me aright
           If Waller sang or Dowland played.

           Your eyen two wol sleye me sodenly
           I may the beauté of hem nat susteyne

And for 180 years almost nothing.

Ed ascoltando al leggier mormorio
    there came new subtlety of eyes into my tent,
whether of spirit or hypostasis,
    but what the blindfold hides
or at carneval
                nor any pair showed anger
Saw but the eyes and stance between the eyes,
colour, diastasis,
    careless or unaware it had not the
    whole tent's room
nor was place for the full Εἰδὼς
interpass, penetrate
    casting but shade beyond the other lights
        sky's clear
        night's sea
        green of the mountain pool
        shone from the unmasked eyes in half-mask's space.
What thou lovest well remains,
                the rest is dross
What thou lov'st well shall not be reft from thee
What thou lov'st well is thy true heritage
Whose world, or mine or theirs
                or is it of none?
First came the seen, then thus the palpable
    Elysium, though it were in the halls of hell,
What thou lovest well is thy true heritage

The ant's a centaur in his dragon world.
Pull down thy vanity, it is not man
Made courage, or made order, or made grace,
    Pull down thy vanity, I say pull down.
Learn of the green world what can be thy place
In scaled invention or true artistry,
Pull down thy vanity,
                Paquin pull down!
The green casque has outdone your elegance.

"Master thyself, then others shall thee beare"
    Pull down thy vanity
Thou art a beaten dog beneath the hail,
A swollen magpie in a fitful sun,
Half black half white
Nor knowst'ou wing from tail

Pull down thy vanity
        How mean thy hates
Fostered in falsity,
        Pull down thy vanity,
Rathe to destroy, niggard in charity,
Pull down thy vanity,
        I say pull down.

But to have done instead of not doing
        this is not vanity
To have, with decency, knocked
That a Blunt should open
        To have gathered from the air a live tradition
or from a fine old eye the unconquered flame
This is not vanity.
    Here error is all in the not done,
all in the diffidence that faltered,

CANTO 90

> *Animus humanus amor non est,*
> *sed ab ipso amor procedit, et*
> *ideo seipso non diligit, sed amore*
> *qui seipso procedit.*

"From the colour the nature
        & by the nature the sign!"
Beatific spirits welding together
        as in one ash-tree in Ygdrasail.
        Baucis, Philemon.
Castalia is the name of that fount in the hill's fold,
        the sea below,
                        narrow beach.
Templum aedificans, not yet marble,
        "Amphion!"

And from the San Ku   三

        孤

to the room in Poitiers where one can stand
        casting no shadow,

That is Sagetrieb,
                    that is tradition.
Builders had kept the proportion,
        did Jacques de Molay
            know these proportions?
and was Erigena ours?
        Moon's barge over milk-blue water
Kuthera δεινά
Kuthera sempiterna
                    Ubi amor, ibi oculus.
Vae qui cogitatis inutile.
    quam in nobis similitudine divinae
                                    reperetur imago.
"Mother Earth in thy lap"
                    said Randolph
                    ἠγάπησεν πολύ
liberavit masnatos.
Castalia like the moonlight
        and the waves rise and fall,
Evita, beer-halls, semina motuum,
        to parched grass, now is rain
not arrogant from habit,
    but furious from perception,
                                Sibylla,
from under the rubble heap
                        m'elevasti
from the dulled edge beyond pain,
                        m'elevasti
out of Erebus, the deep-lying
    from the wind under the earth,
                        m'elevasti
from the dulled air and the dust,
                        m'elevasti
by the great flight,
                m'elevasti,
                            Isis Kuanon
    from the cusp of the moon,
                        m'elevasti
the viper stirs in the dust,
                the blue serpent
glides from the rock pool
    And they take lights now down to the water
the lamps float from the rowers
    the sea's claw drawing them outward.

"De fondo" said Juan Ramon,
    like a mermaid, upward,
but the light perpendicular, upward
and to Castalia,
                water jets from the rock
and in the flat pool as Arethusa's
                    a hush in papyri.
Grove hath its altar
    under elms, in that temple, in silence
a lone nymph by the pool.
    Wei and Han rushing together
two rivers together
    bright fish and flotsam
torn bough in the flood
        and the waters clear with the flowing
Out of heaviness where no mind moves at all
    "birds for the mind" said Richardus,
"beasts as to body, for know-how"
Gaio! Gaio!
            To Zeus with the six seraphs before him
The architect from the painter,
            the stone under elm
Taking form now,
            the rilievi,
    the curled stone at the marge
Faunus, sirenes,
    the stone taking form in the air
    ac ferae,
                cervi,
                the great cats approaching.
Pardus, leopardi, Bagheera
    drawn hither from woodland,
woodland ἐπὶ χθονί
    the trees rise
    and there is a wide sward between them
οἱ χθόνιοι myrrh and olibanum on the altar stone
giving perfume,
                and where was nothing
now is furry assemblage
        and in the boughs now are voices
grey wing, black wing, black wing shot with crimson
and the umbrella pines
                    as in Palatine,
as in pineta. χελιδών, χελιδών

For the procession of Corpus
                  come now banners
comes flute tone
               οἱ χθόνιοι
to new forest,
     thick smoke, purple, rising
bright flame now on the altar
            the crystal funnel of air
out of Erebus, the delivered,
        Tyro, Alcmene, free now, ascending
e i cavalieri,
              ascending,
no shades more,
                lights among them, enkindled,
and the dark shade of courage
                  'Ηλέκτρα
     bowed still with the wrongs of Aegisthus.
Trees die & the dream remains
       Not love but that love flows from it
       ex animo
       & cannot ergo delight in itself
       but only in the love flowing from it.
       UBI AMOR IBI OCULUS EST.

ELINOR WYLIE (1885–1928)

In both her life and her writing Elinor Wylie furnished an example to the Flaming Twenties. Married to millionaire Philip Hichborn, she eloped to Europe with Horace Wylie, whom she married when Hichborn committed suicide; then, divorcing Wylie, she married the poet William Rose Benét. A few years later, after a "wasting illness," she died. Beautiful, impulsive, gifted, she wrote poems in a shrewd but graceful manner, influenced by the English metaphysicals and Shelley, as well as several historical fantasies in prose. Both were extremely popular during her lifetime.

Collected Poems of Elinor Wylie. Knopf, 1932.
Last Poems of Elinor Wylie. Knopf, 1943.
The Collected Prose of Elinor Wylie. Knopf, 1933.

FULL MOON

My bands of silk and miniver
Momently grew heavier;
The black gauze was beggarly thin;
The ermine muffled mouth and chin;
I could not suck the moonlight in.

Harlequin in lozenges
Of love and hate, I walked in these
Striped and ragged rigmaroles;
Among the pavement my footsoles
Trod warily on living coals.

Shoulding the thoughts I loathed,
In their corrupt disguises clothed,
Mortality I could not tear
From my ribs, to leave them bare
Ivory in silver air.

There I walked, and there I raged;
The spiritual savage caged

103

Within my skeleton, raged afresh
To feel, behind a carnal mesh,
The clean bones crying in the flesh.

PROPHECY

I shall lie hidden in a hut
    In the middle of an alder wood,
With the back door blind and bolted shut,
    And the front door locked for good.

I shall lie folded like a saint,
    Lapped in a scented linen sheet,
On a bedstead striped with bright-blue paint,
    Narrow and cold and neat.

The midnight will be glassy black
    Behind the panes, with wind about
To set his mouth against a crack
    And blow the candle out.

LET NO CHARITABLE HOPE

Now let no charitable hope
Confuse my mind with images
Of eagle and of antelope:
I am in nature none of these.

I was, being human, born alone;
I am, being woman, hard beset;
I live by squeezing from a stone
The little nourishment I get.

In masks outrageous and austere
The years go by in single file;
But none has merited my fear,
And none has quite escaped my smile.

H.D. (1886–1961)

Hilda Doolittle, who was born in Bethlehem, Pa., signed her published work simply with her initials; and so she became known—"H.D."—to her readers and even her friends. After education in the U.S., she went to England in 1911 and never returned. She joined Ezra Pound in the early phases of the imagist movement, but soon, like him, abandoned its programmatic aspects; yet in her later work she hewed closer than Pound to the basic principles: clarity, brevity, precision, flexibility. Her work is delicate and musical, but never fragile or easy; in tone it is classical. She was, in fact, a classicist, who made translations from Greek poetry and drama, and used classical themes often in her own poems and novels. Never a polemicist or controversialist, preferring instead to write in obscurity, she saw her work, though always admired, fail of the attention its evident virtues merited. Recently, however, owing in part to an extended critical appreciation by the poet Robert Duncan, readers are turning more and more to her books.

Collected Poems. Liveright, 1940.
The Walls Do Not Fall. Oxford University Press, 1944.
Tribute to Angels. Oxford University Press, 1945.
The Flowering of the Rod. Oxford University Press, 1946.
Selected Poems. Grove Press, 1957.
Helen in Egypt. Grove Press, 1961.
By Avon River. (Essays.) Macmillan, 1949.

EVENING

The light passes
from ridge to ridge,
from flower to flower—
the hypaticas, wide-spread
under the light
grow faint—
the petals reach inward,
the blue tips bend
toward the bluer heart
and the flowers are lost.

The cornel-buds are still white,
but shadows dart
from the cornel-roots—
black creeps from root to root,
each leaf
cuts another leaf on the grass,
shadow seeks shadow,
then both leaf
and leaf-shadow are lost.

ACON

I

Bear me to Dictaeus,
and to the steep slopes;
to the river Erymanthus.

I choose spray of dittany,
cyperum, frail of flower,
buds of myrrh,
all-healing herbs,
close pressed in calathes.

For she lies panting,
drawing sharp breath,
broken with harsh sobs,
she, Hyella,
whom no god pities.

II

Dryads
haunting the groves,
nereids
who dwell in wet caves,
for all the white leaves of olive-branch,
and early roses,
and ivy wreaths, woven gold berries,
which she once brought to your altars,
bear now ripe fruits from Arcadia,
and Assyrian wine
to shatter her fever.

The light of her face falls from its flower,
as a hyacinth,
hidden in a far valley,
perishes upon burnt grass.

Pales,
bring gifts,
bring your Phoenician stuffs,
and do you, fleet-footed nymphs,
bring offerings,
Illyrian iris,
and a branch of shrub,
and frail-headed poppies.

EURYDICE

I

So you have swept me back,
I who could have walked with the live souls
above the earth,
I who could have slept among the live flowers
at last;

so for your arrogance
and your ruthlessness
I am swept back
where dead lichens drip
dead cinders upon moss of ash;

so for your arrogance
I am broken at last,
I who had lived unconscious,
who was almost forgot;

if you had let me wait
I had grown from listlessness
into peace,
if you had let me rest with the dead,
I had forgot you
and the past.

II

Here only flame upon flame
and black among the red sparks,
streaks of black and light
grown colourless;

why did you turn back,
that hell should be reinhabited
of myself thus
swept into nothingness?

why did you turn?
why did you glance back?
why did you hesitate for that moment?
why did you bend your face
caught with the flame of the upper earth,
above my face?

what was it that crossed my face
with the light from yours
and your glance?
what was it you saw in my face?
the light of your own face,
the fire of your own presence?

What had my face to offer
but reflex of the earth,
hyacinth colour
caught from the raw fissure in the rock
where the light struck,
and the colour of azure crocuses
and the bright surface of gold crocuses
and of the wind-flower,
swift in its veins as lightning
and as white.

III

Saffron from the fringe of the earth,
wild saffron that has bent
over the sharp edge of earth,
all the flowers that cut through the earth,
all, all the flowers are lost;

everything is lost,
everything is crossed with black,
black upon black
and worse than black,
this colourless light.

IV

Fringe upon fringe
of blue crocuses,
crocuses, walled against blue of themselves,
blue of that upper earth,
blue of the depth upon depth of flowers,
lost;

flowers,
if I could have taken once my breath of them,
enough of them,
more than earth,
even than of the upper earth,
had passed with me
beneath the earth;

if I could have caught up from the earth,
the whole of the flowers of the earth,
if once I could have breathed into myself
the very golden crocuses
and the red,
and the very golden hearts of the first saffron,
the whole of the golden mass,
the whole of the great fragrance,
I could have dared the loss.

V

So for your arrogance
and your ruthlessness
I have lost the earth
and the flowers of the earth,
and the live souls above the earth,
and you who passed across the light
and reached
ruthless;

you who have your own light,
who are to yourself a presence,
who need no presence;

yet for all your arrogance
and your glance,
I tell you this:

such loss is no loss,
such terror, such coils and strands and pitfalls
of blackness,
such terror
is no loss;

hell is no worse than your earth
above the earth,
hell is no worse,
no, nor your flowers
nor your veins of light
nor your presence,
a loss;

my hell is no worse than yours
though you pass among the flowers and speak
with the spirits above earth.

VI

Against the black
I have more fervour
than you in all the splendour of that place,
against the blackness
and the stark grey
I have more light;

and the flowers,
if I should tell you,
you would turn from your own fit paths
toward hell,
turn again and glance back

and I would sink into a place
even more terrible than this.

VII

At least I have the flowers of myself,
and my thoughts, no god
can take that;
I have the fervour of myself for a presence
and my own spirit for light;

and my spirit with its loss
knows this;
though small against the black,
small against the formless rocks,
hell must break before I am lost;

before I am lost,
hell must open like a red rose
for the dead to pass.

CENTAUR SONG

Now that the day is done,
now that the night creeps soft
and dims the chestnut clusters'
radiant spike of flower,
O sweet, till dawn
break through the branches
of our orchard-garden,
rest in this shelter
of the osier-wood and thorn.

They fall,
the apple-flowers;
nor softer grace has Aphrodite
in the heaven afar,
nor at so fair a pace
open the flower-petals
as your face bends down,
while, breath on breath,
your mouth wanders
from my mouth o'er my face.

What have I left
to bring you in this place,
already sweet with violets?
(those you brought
with swathes of earliest grass,
forest and meadow balm,
flung from your giant arms
for us to rest upon.)

Fair are these petals
broken by your feet;
your horse's hooves
tread softer than a deer's;
your eyes, startled,
are like the deer eyes
while your heart
trembles more than the deer.

O earth, O god,
O forest, stream or river,
what shall I bring
that all the day hold back,
that Dawn remember Love
and rest upon her bed,
and Zeus, forgetful not of Danaë or Maia,
bid the stars shine forever.

AT ITHACA

Over and back,
the long waves crawl
and track the sand with foam;
night darkens and the sea
takes on that desperate tone
of dark that wives put on
when all their love is done.

Over and back,
the tangled thread falls slack,
over and up and on;
over and all is sewn;

now while I bind the end,
I wish some fiery friend
would sweep impetuously
these fingers from the loom.

My weary thoughts
play traitor to my soul,
just as the toil is over;
swift while the woof is whole,
turn now my spirit, swift,
and tear the pattern there,
the flowers so deftly wrought,
the border of sea-blue,
the sea-blue coast of home.

The web was over-fair,
that web of pictures there,
enchantments that I thought
he had, that I had lost;
weaving his happiness
within the stitching frame,
weaving his fire and fame,
I thought my work was done,
I prayed that only one
of those that I had spurned,
might stoop and conquer this
long waiting with a kiss.

But each time that I see
my work so beautifully
inwoven and would keep
the picture and the whole,
Athene steels my soul,
slanting across my brain,
I see as shafts of rain
his chariot and his shafts,
I see the arrows fall,
I see my lord who moves
like Hector, lord of love,
I see him matched with fair
bright rivals and I see
those lesser rivals flee.

FRAGMENT THIRTY-SIX

I know not what to do:
my mind is divided.
—Sappho

I know not what to do,
my mind is reft:
is song's gift best?
is love's gift loveliest?
I know not what to do,
now sleep has pressed
weight on your eyelids.

Shall I break your rest,
devouring, eager?
is love's gift best?
nay, song's the loveliest:
yet were you lost,
what rapture
could I take from song?
what song were left?

I know not what to do:
to turn and slake
the rage that burns,
with my breath burn
and trouble your cool breath?
so shall I turn and take

snow in my arms?
(is love's gift best?)
yet flake on flake
of snow were comfortless,
did you lie wondering,
wakened yet unawake.

Shall I turn and take
comfortless snow within my arms?
press lips to lips
that answer not,
press lips to flesh
that shudders not nor breaks?

Is love's gift best?
shall I turn and slake
all the wild longing?
O I am eager for you!
as the Pleiads shake
white light in whiter water
so shall I take you?

My mind is quite divided,
my minds hesitate,
so perfect matched,
I know not what to do:
each strives with each
as two white wrestlers

standing for a match,
ready to turn and clutch
yet never shake muscle nor nerve
        nor tendon;
so my mind waits
to grapple with my mind,
yet I lie quiet,
I would seem at rest.

I know not what to do:
strain upon strain,
sound surging upon sound
makes my brain blind;
as a wave-line may wait to fall
yet (waiting for its falling)
still the wind may take
from off its crest,
white flake on flake of foam,
that rises,
seeming to dart and pulse
and rend the light,
so my mind hesitates
above the passion
quivering yet to break,
so my mind hesitates
above my mind,
listening to song's delight.

I know not what to do:
will the sound break,
rending the night
with rift on rift of rose
and scattered light?
will the sound break at last
as the wave hesitant,
or will the whole night pass
and I lie listening awake?

LETHE

Nor skin nor hide nor fleece
    Shall cover you,
Nor curtain of crimson nor fine
Shelter of cedar-wood be over you,
    Nor the fir-tree
    Nor the pine.

Nor sight of whin nor gorse
    Nor river-yew,
Nor fragrance of flowering bush,
Nor wailing of reed-bird to waken you,
    Nor of linnet,
    Nor of thrush.

Nor word nor touch nor sight
    Of lover, you
Shall long through the night but for this:
The roll of the full tide to cover you
    Without question,
    Without kiss.

THE MYSTERIES REMAIN

The mysteries remain,
I keep the same
cycle of seed-time
and of sun and rain;

116

Demeter in the grass,
I multiply,
renew and bless
Iacchus in the vine;
I hold the law,
I keep the mysteries true,
the first of these
to name the living, dead;
I am red wine and bread.

> *I keep the law,*
> *I hold the mysteries true,*
> *I am the vine,*
> *the branches, you*
> *and you.*

"WE HAVE SEEN HER"

We have seen her
the world over,

Our Lady of the Goldfinch,
Our Lady of the Candelabra,

Our Lady of the Pomegranate,
Our Lady of the Chair;

we have seen her, an empress,
magnificent in pomp and grace,

and we have seen her
with a single flower

or a cluster of garden-pinks
in a glass beside her;

we have seen her snood
drawn over her hair,

or her face set in profile
with the blue hood and stars;

we have seen her head bowed down
with the weight of a domed crown,

or we have seen her, a wisp of a girl
trapped in a golden halo;

we have seen her with arrow, with doves
and a heart like a valentine;

we have seen her in fine silks imported
from all over the Levant,

and hung with pearls brought
from the city of Constantine;

we have seen her sleeve
of every imaginable shade

of damask and figured brocade;
it is true,

the painters did very well by her;
it is true, they missed never a line

of the suave turn of the head
or subtle shade of lowered eye-lid

or eye-lids half-raised; you find
her everywhere (or did find),

in cathedral, museum, cloister,
at the turn of the palace stair.

"TIME HAS AN END, THEY SAY"

Time has an end, they say,
sea-walls are worn away
by wind and the sea-spray,
not the herb,
      rosemary.

Queens have died, I am told,
faded the cloth-of-gold,
no Caesar half so bold,
as the herb,
    rosemary.

Rooted within the grave,
spreading to heaven, save
us by the grace He gave
to the herb,
    rosemary.

SIGIL

Now let the cycle sweep us here and there,
we will not struggle;
somewhere,
under a forest-ledge,
a wild white-pear
will blossom;

somewhere,
under an edge of rock,
a sea will open;
slice of the tide-shelf
will show in coral, yourself,
in conch-shell,
myself;

somewhere,
over a field-hedge,
a wild bird
will lift up wild, wild throat,
and that song, heard,
will stifle out this note.

ROBINSON JEFFERS (1887–1962)

Long before Carmel became a popular hangout on the Pacific Coast, Jeffers settled there. He built his house above the rocky shore, and in isolation from what he considered the vulgarity and self-destructiveness of commercial civilization, he practiced the art of epic verse more diligently than any other modern poet in America, basing his powerfully rhetorical stories on classical and biblical themes. Because his characteristic poems are long and unexcerptible, he is a difficult poet to anthologize; but his work has been extremely popular, especially such narratives as "Tamar," "Roan Stallion," "The Women at Point Sur," "The Tower Beyond Tragedy," "Cawdor," and "Dear Judas." His greatest success was his free adaptation of the Euripidean *Medea*, produced on the stage in 1947 with Judith Anderson in the leading role. In his later work, however, Jeffers reached such a pitch of bitter antihumanism, calling out for war and the atomic holocaust as the only means by which the universe could be rid of human greed and complacency, that he repelled many readers who had been attracted to his earlier poems.

> *Selected Poetry.* Random House, 1938.
> *Medea.* Random House, 1946.
> *Be Angry at the Sun.* Random House, 1941.
> *The Double Axe.* Random House, 1948.
> *Hungerfield and Other Poems.* Random House, 1954.

BIRDS

The fierce musical cries of a couple of sparrowhawks
  hunting on the headland,
Hovering and darting, their heads northwestward,
Prick like silver arrows shot through a curtain the noise of
  the ocean
Trampling its granite; their red backs gleam
Under my window around the stone corners; nothing
  gracefuller, nothing
Nimbler in the wind. Westward the wave-gleaners,
The old gray sea-going gulls are gathered together, the
  north-west wind wakening

Their wings to the wild spirals of the wind-dance.
Fresh as the air, salt as the foam, play birds in the bright
    wind, fly falcons
Forgetting the oak and the pinewood, come gulls
From the Carmel sands and the sands at the river-mouth,
    from Lobos and out of the limitless
Power of the mass of the sea, for a poem
Needs multitude, multitudes of thoughts, all fierce, all
    flesh-eaters, musically clamorous
Bright hawks that hover and dart headlong, and ungainly
Gray hungers fledged with desire of transgression, salt
    slimed beaks, from the sharp
Rock-shores of the world and the secret waters.

SHINE, PERISHING REPUBLIC

While this America settles in the mould of its vulgarity,
    heavily thickening to empire,
And protest, only a bubble in the molten mass, pops and
    sighs out, and the mass hardens,

I sadly smiling remember that the flower fades to make
    fruit, the fruit rots to make earth.
Out of the mother; and through the spring exultances,
    ripeness and decadence; and home to the mother.

You making haste haste on decay: not blameworthy; life
    is good, be it stubbornly long or suddenly
A mortal splendor: meteors are not needed less than
    mountains: shine, perishing republic.

But for my children, I would have them keep their dis-
    tance from the thickening center; corruption
Never has been compulsory, when the cities lie at the
    monster's feet there are left the mountains.

And boys, be in nothing so moderate as in love of man, a
    clever servant, insufferable master.
There is the trap that catches noblest spirits, that caught
    —they say—God, when he walked on earth.

AN ARTIST

That sculptor we knew, the passionate-eyed son of a
    quarryman,
Who astonished Rome and Paris in his meteor youth, and
    then was gone, at his high tide of triumphs,
Without reason or good-bye; I have seen him again lately,
    after twenty years, but not in Europe.

In desert hills I rode a horse slack-kneed with thirst.
    Down a steep slope a dancing swarm
Of yellow butterflies over a shining rock made me hope
    water. We slid down to the place,
The spring was bitter but the horse drank. I imagined
    wearings of an old path from that wet rock
Ran down the canyon; I followed, soon they were lost, I
    came to a stone valley in which it seemed
No man nor his mount had ever ventured, you wondered
    whether even a vulture'd ever spread sail there.
There were stones of strange form under a cleft in the far
    hill; I tethered the horse to a rock
And scrambled over. A heap like a stone torrent, a
    moraine,
But monstrously formed limbs of broken carving ap-
    peared in the rock-fall, enormous breasts, defaced heads
Of giants, the eyes calm through the brute veils of
    fracture. It was natural then to climb higher and go in
Up the cleft gate. The canyon was a sheer-walled crack
    winding at the entrance, but around its bend
The walls grew dreadful with stone giants, presences
    growing out of the rigid precipice, that strove
In dream between stone and life, intense to cast their
    chaos . . . or to enter and return . . . stone-fleshed,
    nerve-stretched
Great bodies ever more beautiful and more heavy with
    pain, they seemed leading to some unbearable
Consummation of the ecstasy . . . but there, troll among
    Titans, the bearded master of the place accosted me
In a cold anger, a mallet in his hand, filthy and ragged.
    There was no kindness in that man's mind,
But after he had driven me down to the entrance he
    spoke a little.

The merciless sun had found the slot now
To hide in, and lit for the wick of that stone lamp-bowl
  a sky almost, I thought, abominably beautiful;
While our lost artist we used to admire: for now I knew
  him: spoke of his passion.

                    He said, "Marble?
White marble is fit to model a snow-mountain: let man
  be modest. Nor bronze: I am bound to have my tool
In my material, no irrelevances. I found this pit of dark-
  gray freestone, fine-grained, and tough enough
To make sketches that under any weathering will last
  my lifetime. . . .

The town is eight miles off, I can fetch food and no one
  follows me home. I have water and a cave
Here; and no possible lack of material. I need, therefore,
  nothing. As to companions, I make them.
And models? They are seldom wanted; I know a Basque
  shepherd I sometimes use; and a woman of the town.
What more? Sympathy? Praise? I have never desired
  them and also I have never deserved them. I will not
  show you
More than the spalls you saw by accident.

                              What I see is the
enormous beauty of things, but what I attempt
Is nothing to that. I am helpless toward that.
It is only to form in stone the mould of some ideal
  humanity that might be worthy to *be*
Under that lightning. Animalcules that God (if he were
  given to laughter) might omit to laugh at.
Those children of my hands are tortured, because they
  feel," he said, "the storm of the outer magnificence.
They are giants in agony. They have seen from my eyes
The man-destroying beauty of the dawns over their
  notch yonder, and all the obliterating stars.
But in their eyes they have peace. I have lived a little
  and I think
Peace marrying pain alone can breed that excellence in
  the luckless race, might make it decent
To exist at all on the star-lit stone breast.

I hope," he said,
that when I grow old and the chisel drops,
I may crawl out on a ledge of the rock and die like a wolf."

These fragments are all I can remember,
These in the flare of the desert evening. Having been driven so brutally forth I never returned;
Yet I respect him enough to keep his name and the place secret. I hope that some other traveller
May stumble on that ravine of Titans after their maker has died. While he lives, let him alone.

ANTRIM

No spot of earth where men have so fiercely for ages of time
Fought and survived and cancelled each other,
Pict and Gael and Dane, McQuillan, Clandonnel, O'Neill,
Savages, the Scot, the Norman, the English,
Here in the narrow passage and the pitiless north, perpetual
Betrayals, relentless resultless fighting.
A random fury of dirks in the dark: a struggle for survival
Of hungry blind cells of life in the womb.
But now the womb has grown old, her strength has gone forth; a few red carts in a fog creak flax to the dubs,
And sheep in the high heather cry hungrily that life is hard; a plaintive peace; shepherds and peasants.

We have felt the blades meet in the flesh in a hundred ambushes
And the groaning blood bubble in the throat;
In a hundred battles the heavy axes bite the deep bone,
The mountain suddenly stagger and be darkened.
Generation on generation we have seen the blood of boys
And heard the moaning of women massacred,
The passionate flesh and nerves have flamed like pitchpine and fallen

And lain in the earth softly dissolving.
I have lain and been humbled in all these graves, and
mixed new flesh with the old and filled the hollow of
my mouth
With maggots and rotten dust and ages of repose. I lie
here and plot the agony of resurrection.

MARIANNE MOORE (1887–   )

A leader, with Pound and Eliot, of the poetic revolution, Miss Moore extended the imagist demand for clarity and precision into a method that has been called "poetic literalism." Usually her poems derive from the curiosa of nature or art, analyzed in prosaic detail. Her work is frankly pedantic, with elaborate notes and quotations, and is further depoeticized by her dryly syllabic meters and unobtrusive rhymes. Yet from this literalness arises, often by way of irony, a concentration of ethical concern that is, in her best poems, forceful in its scrupulosity. Her poems are at once elegant and honest, characteristic of the intellectual period in which most of them were written; if her manner today seems finical, and her sensibility remote, nevertheless neither her poetic integrity, nor its exemplary importance in the evolution of modern poetry, can be questioned.

> *Collected Poems.* Macmillan, 1951.
> *Like a Bulwark.* Viking, 1956.
> *O to Be a Dragon.* Viking, 1959.
> *The Fables of La Fontaine.* (Translations.) Viking, 1954.

TO A STEAM ROLLER

The illustration
is nothing to you without the application.
    You lack half wit. You crush all the particles down
        into close conformity, and then walk back and forth
        on them.

Sparkling chips of rock
are crushed down to the level of the parent block.
    Were not 'impersonal judgment in aesthetic
        matters a metaphysical impossibility,' you

might fairly achieve
it. As for butterflies, I can hardly conceive
    of one's attending upon you, but to question
        the congruence of the complement is vain, if it exists.

THE PAPER NAUTILUS

For authorities whose hopes
are shaped by mercenaries?
    Writers entrapped by
    teatime fame and by
commuters' comforts? Not for these
    the paper nautilus
    constructs her thin glass shell.

Giving her perishable
souvenir of hope, a dull
    white outside and smooth-
    edge inner surface
glossy as the sea, the watchful
    maker of it guards it
    day and night; she scarcely

eats until the eggs are hatched.
Buried eight-fold in her eight
    arms, for she is in
    a sense a devil-
fish, her glass ramshorn-cradled freight
    is hid but is not crushed.
    As Hercules, bitten

by a crab loyal to the hydra,
was hindered to succeed,
    the intensively
    watched eggs coming from
the shell free it when they are freed,—
    leaving its wasp-nest flaws
    of white on white, and close-

laid Ionic chiton-folds
like the lines in the mane of
    a Parthenon horse,
    round which the arms had
wound themselves as if they knew love
    is the only fortress
    strong enough to trust to.

T. S. ELIOT (1888–1965)

In outline, Eliot's biography is well known: his boyhood in St. Louis, his education at Harvard and abroad, his decision to settle permanently in England, his lifelong friendship with Ezra Pound, his influential editing (*The Egoist, The Criterion,* and with the publishing house of Faber & Faber), his many honors, including the Nobel Prize in 1948, his early attachment to the neohumanism of Irving Babbitt, his conversion to Anglo-Catholicism, his deepening commitment to a conservative socioreligious view of history and civilization. Few poets anywhere have enjoyed more prestige and authority. Eliot's poems, especially "The Waste Land" (1923), and his essays, established the tone of moral concern, intellectual rigor, and emotional integrity that shaped Anglo-American literature for three decades. Now that the younger generation of American poets has swung toward the objectivism of Pound and Williams, rejecting Eliot's influence and the European symbolist tradition, Eliot's bearing on American poetry seems less crucial than formerly. But in other respects his work and teaching will always remain significant: his experimentalism, which made each major poem a technical departure; his search for means to expand the metrical and verbal resources of poetry; his hospitality to young writers. And in the end the debate between objectivism and symbolism may come to seem, at least to readers more interested in poetry than in theory, no more than hairsplitting.

> *Collected Poems, 1909–1962.* Harcourt, Brace & World, 1963.
> *Collected Plays.* London: Faber & Faber, 1962.
> *Essays, Ancient and Modern.* Harcourt, Brace, 1936.
> *Essays in Elizabethan Drama.* Harcourt, Brace, 1956.
> *The Idea of a Christian Society.* Harcourt, Brace, 1940.
> *Of Poetry and Poets.* Farrar, Straus & Cudahy, 1957.

PRELUDES

I

The winter evening settles down
With smell of steaks in passageways.
Six o'clock.

The burnt-out ends of smoky days.
And now a gusty shower wraps
The grimy scraps
Of withered leaves about your feet
And newspapers from vacant lots;
The showers beat
On broken blinds and chimney-pots,
And at the corner of the street
A lonely cab-horse steams and stamps.

And then the lighting of the lamps.

II

The morning comes to consciousness
Of faint stale smells of beer
From the sawdust-trampled street
With all its muddy feet that press
To early coffee-stands.

With the other masquerades
That time resumes,
One thinks of all the hands
That are raising dingy shades
In a thousand furnished rooms.

III

You tossed a blanket from the bed,
You lay upon your back, and waited;
You dozed, and watched the night revealing
The thousand sordid images
Of which your soul was constituted;
They flickered against the ceiling.
And when all the world came back
And the light crept up between the shutters
And you heard the sparrows in the gutters,
You had such a vision of the street
As the street hardly understands;
Sitting along the bed's edge, where
You curled the papers from your hair,
Or clasped the yellow soles of feet
In the palms of both soiled hands.

His soul stretched tight across the skies
That fade behind a city block,
Or trampled by insistent feet
At four and five and six o'clock;
And short square fingers stuffing pipes,
And evening newspapers, and eyes
Assured of certain certainties,
The conscience of a blackened street
Impatient to assume the world.

I am moved by fancies that are curled
Around these images, and cling:
The notion of some infinitely gentle
Infinitely suffering thing.

Wipe your hand across your mouth, and laugh;
The worlds revolve like ancient women
Gathering fuel in vacant lots.

LA FIGLIA CHE PIANGE

O quam te memorem virgo . . .

Stand on the highest pavement of the stair—
Lean on a garden urn—
Weave, weave the sunlight in your hair—
Clasp your flowers to you with a pained surprise—
Fling them to the ground and turn
With a fugitive resentment in your eyes:
But weave, weave the sunlight in your hair.

So I would have had him leave,
So I would have had her stand and grieve,
So he would have left
As the soul leaves the body torn and bruised,
As the mind deserts the body it has used.
I should find
Some way incomparably light and deft,
Some way we both should understand,
Simple and faithless as a smile and shake of the hand.

She turned away, but with the autumn weather
Compelled my imagination many days,
Many days and many hours:
Her hair over her arms and her arms full of flowers.
And I wonder how they should have been together!
I should have lost a gesture and a pose.
Sometimes these cogitations still amaze
The troubled midnight and the noon's repose.

SWEENEY ERECT

> *And the trees about me,*
> *Let them be dry and leafless; let the rocks*
> *Groan with continual surges; and behind me*
> *Make all a desolation. Look, look, wenches!*

Paint me a cavernous waste shore
    Cast in the unstilled Cyclades,
Paint me the bold anfractuous rocks
    Faced by the snarled and yelping seas.

Display me Aeolus above
    Reviewing the insurgent gales
Which tangle Ariadne's hair
    And swell with haste the perjured sails.

Morning stirs the feet and hands
    (Nausicaa and Polypheme).
Gesture of orang-outang
    Rises from the sheets in steam.

This withered root of knots of hair
    Slitted below and gashed with eyes,
This oval O cropped out with teeth:
    The sickle motion from the thighs

Jackknifes upward at the knees
    Then straightens out from heel to hip
Pushing the framework of the bed
    And clawing at the pillow slip.

Sweeney addressed full length to shave
Broadbottomed, pink from nape to base,
Knows the female temperament
And wipes the suds around his face.

(The lengthened shadow of a man
Is history, said Emerson
Who had not seen the silhouette
Of Sweeney straddled in the sun.)

Tests the razor on his leg
Waiting until the shriek subsides.
The epileptic on the bed
Curves backward, clutching at her sides.

The ladies of the corridor
Find themselves involved, disgraced,
Call witness to their principles
And deprecate the lack of taste

Observing that hysteria
Might easily be misunderstood;
Mrs. Turner intimates
It does the house no sort of **good.**

But Doris, towelled from the bath,
Enters padding on broad feet,
Bringing sal volatile
And a glass of brandy neat.

THE HIPPOPOTAMUS

Similiter et omnes revereantur Diaconos, ut mandatum Jesu Christi; et Episcopum, ut Jesum Christum, existentem filium Patris; Presbyteros autem, ut concilium Dei et conjunctionem Apostolorum. Sine his Ecclesia non vocatur; de quibus suadeo vos sic habeo.

S. Ignatii ad Trallianos

And when this epistle is read among you, cause that it be read also in the church of the Laodiceans.

The broad-backed hippopotamus
Rests on his belly in the mud;
Although he seems so firm to us
He is merely flesh and blood.

Flesh and blood is weak and frail,
Susceptible to nervous shock;
While the True Church can never fail
For it is based upon a rock.

The hippo's feeble steps may err
In compassing material ends,
While the True Church need never stir
To gather in its dividends.

The 'potamus can never reach
The mango on the mango-tree;
But fruits of pomegranate and peach
Refresh the Church from over sea.

At mating time the hippo's voice
Betrays inflexions hoarse and odd,
But every week we hear rejoice
The Church, at being one with God.

The hippopotamus's day
Is passed in sleep; at night he hunts;
God works in a mysterious way—
The Church can sleep and feed at once.

I saw the 'potamus take wing
Ascending from the damp savannas,
And quiring angels round him sing
The praise of God, in loud hosannas.

Blood of the Lamb shall wash him clean
And him shall heavenly arms enfold,
Among the saints he shall be seen
Performing on a harp of gold.

He shall be washed as white as snow,
By all the martyr'd virgins kist,
While the True Church remains below
Wrapt in the old miasmal mist.

ASH-WEDNESDAY

I

Because I do not hope to turn again
Because I do not hope
Because I do not hope to turn
Desiring this man's gift and that man's scope
I no longer strive to strive towards such things
(Why should the agèd eagle stretch its wings?)
Why should I mourn
The vanished power of the usual reign?

Because I do not hope to know again
The infirm glory of the positive hour
Because I do not think
Because I know I shall not know
The one veritable transitory power
Because I cannot drink
There, where trees flower, and springs flow, for there is
 nothing again

Because I know that time is always time
And place is always and only place
And what is actual is actual only for one time
And only for one place
I rejoice that things are as they are and
I renounce the blessèd face
And renounce the voice

Because I cannot hope to turn again
Consequently I rejoice, having to construct something
Upon which to rejoice

And pray to God to have mercy upon us
And I pray that I may forget
These matters that with myself I too much discuss
Too much explain
Because I do not hope to turn again
Let these words answer
For what is done, not to be done again
May the judgement not be too heavy upon us

Because these wings are no longer wings to fly
But merely vans to beat the air
The air which is now thoroughly small and dry
Smaller and dryer than the will
Teach us to care and not to care
Teach us to sit still.

Pray for us sinners now and at the hour of our death
Pray for us now and at the hour of our death.

II

Lady, three white leopards sat under a juniper-tree
In the cool of the day, having fed to satiety
On my legs my heart my liver and that which had been
    contained
In the hollow round of my skull. And God said
Shall these bones live? shall these
Bones live? And that which had been contained
In the bones (which were already dry) said chirping:
Because of the goodness of this Lady
And because of her loveliness, and because
She honours the Virgin in meditation,
We shine with brightness. And I who am here dissembled
Proffer my deeds to oblivion, and my love
To the posterity of the desert and the fruit of the gourd.
It is this which recovers
My guts the strings of my eyes and the indigestible por-
    tions
Which the leopards reject. The Lady is withdrawn
In a white gown, to contemplation, in a white gown.
Let the whiteness of bones atone to forgetfulness.
There is no life in them. As I am forgotten
And would be forgotten, so I would forget
Thus devoted, concentrated in purpose. And God said
Prophesy to the wind, to the wind only for only
The wind will listen. And the bones sang chirping
With the burden of the grasshopper, saying

Lady of silences
Calm and distressed
Torn and most whole
Rose of memory
Rose of forgetfulness

Exhausted and life-giving
Worried reposeful
The single Rose
Is now the Garden
Where all loves end
Terminate torment
Of love unsatisfied
The greater torment
Of love satisfied
End of the endless
Journey to no end
Conclusion of all that
Is inconclusible
Speech without word and
Word of no speech
Grace to the Mother
For the Garden
Where all love ends.

Under a juniper-tree the bones sang, scattered and shining
We are glad to be scattered, we did little good to each
    other,
Under a tree in the cool of the day, with the blessing of
    sand,
Forgetting themselves and each other, united
In the quiet of the desert. This is the land which ye
Shall divide by lot. And neither division nor unity
Matters. This is the land. We have our inheritance.

III

At the first turning of the second stair
I turned and saw below
The same shape twisted on the banister
Under the vapour in the fetid air
Struggling with the devil of the stairs who wears
The deceitful face of hope and of despair.

At the second turning of the second stair
I left them twisting, turning below;
There were no more faces and the stair was dark,
Damp, jaggèd, like an old man's mouth drivelling, beyond
    repair,
Or the toothed gullet of an agèd shark.

At the first turning of the third stair
Was a slotted window bellied like the fig's fruit
And beyond the hawthorn blossom and a pasture scene
The broadbacked figure drest in blue and green
Enchanted the maytime with an antique flute.
Blown hair is sweet, brown hair over the mouth blown,
Lilac and brown hair;
Distraction, music of the flute, stops and steps of the
    mind over the third stair,
Fading, fading; strength beyond hope and despair
Climbing the third stair.

Lord, I am not worthy
Lord, I am not worthy

      but speak the word only.

IV

Who walked between the violet and the violet
Who walked between
The various ranks of varied green
Going in white and blue, in Mary's colour,
Talking of trivial things
In ignorance and in knowledge of eternal dolour
Who moved among the others as they walked,
Who then made strong the fountains and made fresh the
    springs

Made cool the dry rock and made firm the sand
In blue of larkspur, blue of Mary's colour,
Sovegna vos

Here are the years that walk between, bearing
Away the fiddles and the flutes, restoring
One who moves in the time between sleep and waking,
    wearing

White light folded, sheathed about her, folded.
The new years walk, restoring
Through a bright cloud of tears, the years, restoring
With a new verse the ancient rhyme. Redeem
The time. Redeem
The unread vision in the higher dream
While jewelled unicorns draw by the gilded hearse.

The silent sister veiled in white and blue
Between the yews, behind the garden god,
Whose flute is breathless, bent her head and sighed but
    spoke no word

But the fountain sprang up and the bird sang down
Redeem the time, redeem the dream
The token of the word unheard, unspoken

Till the wind shake a thousand whispers from the yew

And after this our exile

V

If the lost word is lost, if the spent word is spent
If the unheard, unspoken
Word is unspoken, unheard;
Still is the unspoken word, the Word unheard,
The Word without a word, the Word within
The world and for the world;
And the light shone in darkness and
Against the Word the unstilled world still whirled
About the centre of the silent Word.

    O my people, what have I done unto thee.

Where shall the word be found, where will the word
Resound? Not here, there is not enough silence
Not on the sea or on the islands, not
On the mainland, in the desert or the rain land,
For those who walk in darkness
Both in the day time and in the night time
The right time and the right place are not here
No place of grace for those who avoid the face
No time to rejoice for those who walk among noise and
    deny the voice

Will the veiled sister pray for
Those who walk in darkness, who chose thee and oppose
    thee,
Those who are torn on the horn between season and sea-
    son, time and time, between

Hour and hour, word and word, power and power, those
    who wait
In darkness? Will the veiled sister pray
For children at the gate
Who will not go away and cannot pray:
Pray for those who chose and oppose

O my people, what have I done unto thee.

Will the veiled sister between the slender
Yew trees pray for those who offend her
And are terrified and cannot surrender
And affirm before the world and deny between the rocks
In the last desert between the last blue rocks
The desert in the garden the garden in the desert
Of drouth, spitting from the mouth the withered apple-
seed.

O my people.

VI

Although I do not hope to turn again
Although I do not hope
Although I do not hope to turn

Wavering between the profit and the loss
In this brief transit where the dreams cross
The dreamcrossed twilight between birth and dying
(Bless me father) though I do not wish to wish these
    things
From the wide window towards the granite shore
The white sails still fly seaward, seaward flying
Unbroken wings

And the lost heart stiffens and rejoices
In the lost lilac and the lost sea voices
And the weak spirit quickens to rebel
For the bent golden-rod and the lost sea smell
Quickens to recover
The cry of quail and the whirling plover
And the blind eye creates
The empty forms between the ivory gates
And smell renews the salt savour of the sandy earth

This is the time of tension between dying and birth
The place of solitude where three dreams cross
Between blue rocks
But when the voices shaken from the yew-tree drift away
Let the other yew be shaken and reply.

Blessèd sister, holy mother, spirit of the fountain, spirit of
    the garden,
Suffer us not to mock ourselves with falsehood
Teach us to care and not to care
Teach us to sit still
Even among these rocks,
Our peace in His will
And even among these rocks
Sister, mother
And spirit of the river, spirit of the sea,
Suffer me not to be separated

And let my cry come unto Thee.

EAST COKER

I

In my beginning is my end. In succession
Houses rise and fall, crumble, are extended,
Are removed, destroyed, restored, or in their place
Is an open field, or a factory, or a by-pass.
Old stone to new building, old timber to new fires,
Old fires to ashes, and ashes to the earth
Which is already flesh, fur and faeces,
Bone of man and beast, cornstalk and leaf.
Houses live and die: there is a time for building
And a time for living and for generation
And a time for the wind to break the loosened pane
And to shake the wainscot where the field-mouse trots
And to shake the tattered arras woven with a silent motto.

In my beginning is my end. Now the light falls
Across the open field, leaving the deep lane
Shuttered with branches, dark in the afternoon,
Where you lean against a bank while a van passes,

And the deep lane insists on the direction
Into the village, in the electric heat
Hypnotised. In a warm haze the sultry light
Is absorbed, not refracted, by grey stone.
The dahlias sleep in the empty silence.
Wait for the early owl.

                    In that open field
If you do not come too close, if you do not come too
    close,
On a summer midnight, you can hear the music
Of the weak pipe and the little drum
And see them dancing around the bonfire
The association of man and woman
In daunsinge, signifying matrimonie—
A dignified and commodious sacrament.
Two and two, necessarye coniunction,
Holding eche other by the hand or the arm
Whiche betokeneth concorde. Round and round the fire
Leaping through the flames, or joined in circles,
Rustically solemn or in rustic laughter
Lifting heavy feet in clumsy shoes,
Earth feet, loam feet, lifted in country mirth
Mirth of those long since under earth
Nourishing the corn. Keeping time,
Keeping the rhythm in their dancing
As in their living in the living seasons
The time of the seasons and the constellations
The time of milking and the time of harvest
The time of the coupling of man and woman
And that of beasts. Feet rising and falling.
Eating and drinking. Dung and death.

Dawn points, and another day
Prepares for heat and silence. Out at sea the dawn wind
Wrinkles and slides. I am here
Or there, or elsewhere. In my beginning.

II

What is the late November doing
With the disturbance of the spring
And creatures of the summer heat,
And snowdrops writhing under feet

And hollyhocks that aim too high
Red into grey and tumble down
Late roses filled with early snow?
Thunder rolled by the rolling stars
Simulates triumphal cars
Deployed in constellated wars
Scorpion fights against the Sun
Until the Sun and Moon go down
Comets weep and Leonids fly
Hunt the heavens and the plains
Whirled in a vortex that shall bring
The world to that destructive fire
Which burns before the ice-cap reigns.

That was a way of putting it—not very satisfactory:
A periphrastic study in a worn-out poetical fashion,
Leaving one still with the intolerable wrestle
With words and meanings. The poetry does not matter
It was not (to start again) what one had expected.
What was to be the value of the long looked forward to,
Long hoped for calm, the autumnal serenity
And the wisdom of age? Had they deceived us,
Or deceived themselves, the quiet-voiced elders,
Bequeathing us merely a receipt for deceit?
The serenity only a deliberate hebetude,
The wisdom only the knowledge of dead secrets
Useless in the darkness into which they peered
Or from which they turned their eyes. There is, it seems
    to us,
At best, only a limited value
In the knowledge derived from experience.
The knowledge imposes a pattern, and falsifies,
For the pattern is new in every moment
And every moment is a new and shocking
Valuation of all we have been. We are only undeceived
Of that which, deceiving, could no longer harm.
In the middle, not only in the middle of the way
But all the way, in a dark wood, in a bramble,
On the edge of a grimpen, where is no secure foothold,
And menaced by monsters, fancy lights,
Risking enchantment. Do not let me hear
Of the wisdom of old men, but rather of their folly,
Their fear of fear and frenzy, their fear of possession,
Of belonging to another, or to others, or to God.

The only wisdom we can hope to acquire
Is the wisdom of humility: humility is endless.

The houses are all gone under the sea.

The dancers are all gone under the hill.

III

O dark dark dark. They all go into the dark,
The vacant interstellar spaces, the vacant into the vacant,
The captains, merchant bankers, eminent men of letters,
The generous patrons of art, the statesmen and the rulers,
Distinguished civil servants, chairmen of many commit-
    tees,
Industrial lords and petty contractors, all go into the dark,
And dark the Sun and Moon, and the Almanach de Gotha
And the Stock Exchange Gazette, the Directory of
    Directors,
And cold the sense and lost the motive of action.
And we all go with them, into the silent funeral,
Nobody's funeral, for there is no one to bury.
I said to my soul, be still, and let the dark come upon
    you
Which shall be the darkness of God. As, in a theatre,
The lights are extinguished, for the scene to be changed
With a hollow rumble of wings, with a movement of
    darkness on darkness,
And we know that the hills and the trees, the distant
    panorama
And the bold imposing façade are all being rolled away—
Or as, when an underground train, in the tube, stops too
    long between stations
And the conversation rises and slowly fades into silence
And you see behind every face the mental emptiness
    deepen
Leaving only the growing terror of nothing to think
    about;
Or when, under ether, the mind is conscious but conscious
    of nothing—
I said to my soul, be still, and wait without hope
For hope would be hope for the wrong thing; wait
    without love
For love would be love of the wrong thing; there is yet
    faith

But the faith and love and the hope are all in the waiting.
Wait without thought, for you are not ready for thought:
So the darkness shall be the light, and the stillness the
    dancing.
Whisper of running streams, and winter lightning.
The wild thyme unseen and the wild strawberry,
The laughter in the garden, echoed ecstasy
Not lost, but requiring, pointing to the agony
Of death and birth.

              You say I am repeating
Something I have said before. I shall say it again.
Shall I say it again? In order to arrive there,
To arrive where you are, to get from where you are not,
    You must go by a way wherein there is no ecstasy.
In order to arrive at what you do not know
    You must go by a way which is the way of ignorance.
In order to possess what you do not possess
    You must go by the way of dispossession.
In order to arrive at what you are not
    You must go through the way in which you are not.
And what you do not know is the only thing you know
And what you own is what you do not own
And where you are is where you are not.

IV

The wounded surgeon plies the steel
That questions the distempered part;
Beneath the bleeding hands we feel
The sharp compassion of the healer's art
Resolving the enigma of the fever chart.

Our only health is the disease
If we obey the dying nurse
Whose constant care is not to please
But to remind of our, and Adam's curse,
And that, to be restored, our sickness must grow worse.

The whole earth is our hospital
Endowed by the ruined millionaire,
Wherein, if we do well, we shall
Die of the absolute paternal care
That will not leave us, but prevents us everywhere.

The chill ascends from feet to knees,
The fever sings in mental wires.
If to be warmed, then I must freeze
And quake in frigid purgatorial fires
Of which the flame is roses, and the smoke is briars.

The dripping blood our only drink,
The bloody flesh our only food:
In spite of which we like to think
That we are sound, substantial flesh and blood—
Again, in spite of that, we call this Friday good.

V

So here I am, in the middle way, having had twenty
    years—
Twenty years largely wasted, the years of *l'entre deux
    guerres*—
Trying to learn to use words, and every attempt
Is a wholly new start, and a different kind of failure
Because one has only learnt to get the better of words
For the thing one no longer has to say, or the way in
    which
One is no longer disposed to say it. And so each venture
Is a new beginning, a raid on the inarticulate
With shabby equipment always deteriorating
In the general mess of imprecision of feeling,
Undisciplined squads of emotion. And what there is to
    conquer
By strength and submission, has already been discovered
Once or twice, or several times, by men whom one cannot
    hope
To emulate—but there is no competition—
There is only the fight to recover what has been lost
And found and lost again and again: and now, under
    conditions
That seem unpropitious. But perhaps neither gain nor loss.
For us, there is only the trying. The rest is not our busi-
    ness.

Home is where one starts from. As we grow older
The world becomes stranger, the pattern more compli-
    cated

Of dead and living. Not the intense moment
Isolated, with no before and after,
But a lifetime burning in every moment
And not the lifetime of one man only
But of old stones that cannot be deciphered.
There is a time for the evening under starlight,
A time for the evening under lamplight
(The evening with the photograph album).
Love is most nearly itself
When here and now cease to matter.
Old men ought to be explorers
Here and there does not matter
We must be still and still moving
Into another intensity
For a further union, a deeper communion
Through the dark cold and the empty desolation,
The wave cry, the wind cry, the vast waters
Of the petrel and the porpoise. In my end is my begin-
    ning.

JOHN CROWE RANSOM (1888–   )

Though his output is small, some of Ransom's poems, with their deeply tragic view masked in gentle irony, are among the most famous of this century in America. Born in Tennessee, Ransom attended Vanderbilt and Oxford, then returned to Vanderbilt as a teacher. There he became a member of the Fugitives, a group, including Allen Tate and Robert Penn Warren, which advocated in general a return to the values of the Old South; but it was as poets and literary critics that the Fugitives made their mark. Ransom, who originated the term "New Criticism," was its most acute exponent, bringing a warmly philosophical attitude to his work. In 1937 he became professor of poetry at Kenyon College, where he founded the *Kenyon Review*, a quarterly which was, under his editorship, one of the country's most distinguished. He retired in 1958.

Selected Poems. Rev. ed. Knopf, 1963.
The New Criticism. (Essays.) New Directions, 1941.
Poems and Essays. Vintage, 1955.

WINTER REMEMBERED

Two evils, monstrous either one apart,
Possessed me, and were long and loath at going:
A cry of Absence, Absence, in the heart,
And in the wood the furious winter blowing.

Think not, when fire was bright upon my bricks,
And past the tight boards hardly a wind could enter,
I glowed like them, the simple burning sticks,
Far from my cause, my proper heat and center.

Better to walk forth in the murderous air
And wash my wound in the snows; that would be healing;
Because my heart would throb less painful there,
Being caked with cold, and past the smart of feeling.

And where I went, the hugest winter blast
Would have this body bowed, these eyeballs streaming,

And though I think this heart's blood froze not fast
It ran too small to spare one drop for dreaming.

Dear love, these fingers that had known your touch,
And tied our separate forces first together,
Were ten poor idiot fingers not worth much,
Ten frozen parsnips hanging in the weather.

BELLS FOR JOHN WHITESIDE'S DAUGHTER

There was such speed in her little body,
And such lightness in her footfall,
It is no wonder her brown study
Astonishes us all.

Her wars were bruited in our high window.
We looked among orchard trees and beyond,
Where she took arms against her shadow,
Or harried unto the pond

The lazy geese, like a snow cloud
Dripping their snow on the green grass,
Tricking and stopping, sleepy and proud,
Who cried in goose, Alas,

For the tireless heart within the little
Lady with rod that made them rise
From their noon apple-dreams and scuttle
Goose-fashion under the skies!

But now go the bells, and we are ready,
In one house we are sternly stopped
To say we are vexed at her brown study,
Lying so primly propped.

VAUNTING OAK

He is a tower unleaning. But how will he not break,
If Heaven assault him with full wind and sleet,
And what uproar tall trees concumbent make!

More than a hundred years, more than a hundred feet
Naked he rears against the cold skies eruptive;
Only his temporal twigs are unsure of seat,

And the frail leaves of a season, which are susceptive
Of the mad humor of wind, and turn and flee
In panic round the stem on which they are captive.

Now a certain heart, too young and mortally
Linked with an unbeliever of bitter blood,
Observed, as an eminent witness of life, the tree,

And exulted, wrapped in a phantasy of good:
"Be the great oak for its long winterings
Our love's symbol, better than the summer's brood."

Then the venerable oak, delivered of his pangs,
Put forth profuse his green banners of peace
And testified to her with innumerable tongues.

And what but she fetch me up to the steep place
Where the oak vaunted? A flat where birdsong flew
Had to be traversed; and a quick populace

Of daisies, and yellow kinds; and here she knew,
Who had been instructed of much mortality,
Better than brag in this distraught purlieu.

Above the little and their dusty tombs was he
Standing, sheer on his hill, not much soiled over
By the knobs and broken boughs of an old tree,

And she murmured, "Established, you see him there!
forever."
But, that her pitiful error be undone,
I knocked on his house loudly, a sorrowing lover,

And drew forth like a funeral a hollow tone.
"The old gentleman," I grieved, "holds gallantly,
But before our joy shall have lapsed, even, will be gone."

I knocked more sternly, and his dolorous cry
Boomed till its loud reverberance outsounded
The singing of bees; or the coward birds that fly

Otherwhere with their songs when summer is sped,
And if they stayed would perish miserably;
Or the tears of a girl remembering her dread.

HERE LIES A LADY

Here lies a lady of beauty and high degree.
Of chills and fever she died, of fever and chills,
The delight of her husband, her aunt, an infant of three,
And of medicos marveling sweetly on her ills.

For either she burned, and her confident eyes would
    blaze,
And her fingers fly in a manner to puzzle their heads—
What was she making? Why, nothing; she sat in a maze
Of old scraps of laces, snipped into curious shreds—

Or this would pass, and the light of her fire decline
Till she lay discouraged and cold, like a stalk white and
    blown,
And would not open her eyes, to kisses, to wine;
The sixth of these states was her last; the cold settled
    down.

Sweet ladies, long may ye bloom, and toughly I hope ye
    may thole,
But was she not lucky? In flowers and lace and mourning,
In love and great honor we bade God rest her soul
After six little spaces of chill, and six of burning.

BLUE GIRLS

Twirling your blue skirts, travelling the sward
Under the towers of your seminary,
Go listen to your teachers old and contrary
Without believing a word.

Tie the white fillets then about your hair
And think no more of what will come to pass
Than bluebirds that go walking on the grass
And chattering on the air.

Practise your beauty, blue girls, before it fail;
And I will cry with my loud lips and publish
Beauty which all our power shall never establish,
It is so frail.

For I could tell you a story which is true;
I know a lady with a terrible tongue,
Blear eyes fallen from blue,
All her perfections tarnished—yet it is not long
Since she was lovelier than any of you.

SURVEY OF LITERATURE

In all the good Greek of Plato
I lack my roastbeef and potato.

A better man was Aristotle,
Pulling steady on the bottle.

I dip my hat to Chaucer,
Swilling soup from his saucer,

And to Master Shakespeare
Who wrote big on small beer.

The abstemious Wordsworth
Subsisted on a curd's-worth,

But a slick one was Tennyson,
Putting gravy on his venison.

What these men had to eat and drink
Is what we say and what we think.

The influence of Milton
Came wry out of Stilton.

Sing a song for Percy Shelley,
Drowned in pale lemon jelly,

And for precious John Keats,
Dripping blood of pickled beets.

Then there was poor Willie Blake,
He foundered on sweet cake.

God have mercy on the sinner
Who must write with no dinner,

No gravy and no grub,
No pewter and no pub,

No belly and no bowels,
Only consonants and vowels.

CONRAD AIKEN (1889–   )

Grandson of W. J. Potter, the Unitarian minister of New Bedford who, under the influence of Darwin and Humboldt, took his congregation out of the church and founded the Free Religious Association, Aiken has said that his work as a writer has been a continuation of his grandfather's search for evolving forms of consciousness under the impact of modern science, especially psychoanalysis. His first book was published in 1914. Although he was a lifelong friend of T. S. Eliot, his work has been thematically freer than Eliot's, and in form more lyrical. As editor, anthologist, and critic, Aiken played a conspicuous role in winning an audience for modern poetry during the twenties and thirties.

Collected Poems. Oxford University Press, 1953.
Selected Poems. Oxford University Press, 1961.
A Letter from Li Po. Oxford University Press, 1955.
The Morning Song of Lord Zero. Oxford University Press, 1963.
A Seizure of Limericks. Holt, Rinehart & Winston, 1964.
Thee. Braziller, 1967.
Ushant. (Autobiography.) Duell, Sloan & Pearce, 1952.
Collected Short Stories. World, 1960.
Collected Novels. Holt, Rinehart & Winston, 1964.
Collected Criticism. Oxford University Press, 1968.

FROM *TIME IN THE ROCK, OR PRELUDES TO DEFINITION*

XI

Mysticism, but let us have no words,
angels, but let us have no fantasies,
churches, but let us have no creeds,
no dead gods hung on crosses in a shop,
nor beads nor prayers nor faith nor sin nor penance:
and yet, let us believe, let us believe.

Let it be the flower
seen by the child for the first time, plucked without
    thought
broken for love and as soon forgotten:

and the angels, let them be our friends,
used for our needs with selfish simplicity,
broken for love and as soon forgotten;

and let the churches be our houses
defiled daily, loud with discord,—
where the dead gods that were our selves may hang,
our outgrown gods on every wall;
Christ on the mantelpiece, with downcast eyes;
Buddha above the stove;
the Holy Ghost by the hatrack, and God himself
staring like Narcissus from the mirror,
clad in a raincoat, and with hat and gloves.

Mysticism, but let it be a flower,
let it be the hand that reaches for the flower,
let it be the flower that imagined the first hand,
let it be the space that removed itself to give place
for the hand that reaches, the flower to be reached—
let it be self displacing self
as quietly as a child lifts a pebble,
as softly as a flower decides to fall,—
self replacing self
as seed follows flower to earth.

XXXVII

Where we were walking in the day's light, seeing
the flight of bones to the stars, the voyage of dead men,
those who go forth like dead leaves on the air
in the long journey, those who are swept
on the last current, the cold and shoreless ones,
who do not speak, do not answer, have no names,
nor are assembled again by any thought, but voyage
in the wide circle, the great circle

where we were talking, in the day's light, watching
even as I took your hand, even as I kissed you,

ah the unspeakable voyage of the dead men
those who go up from the grass without laughter
who take leave of the wheat and water without speech
who pass us without memory and without murmur
as they begin the endless voyage

                           where we stood
in the little round of colour, perilously poised
in the bright instant between two instant deaths,
whispering yes, whispering no, greeting and permitting,
touching and recalling, and with our eyes
looking into the past to see if there the future
might grow like a leaf, might grow like a bough with
    flowers,
might grow like a tree with beneficent shade

but what delight that was, O wave who broke
out of the long dark nothing against my breast,
you who lifted me violently so that we rose together,
what delight that was, in that clear instant,
even as we shone thus, the first, the last,
to see the flight of bones, the everlasting,
the noiseless unhurrying flight
of the cold and shoreless ones, the ones who no more
answer to any names, whose voyage in space
does not remember the earth or stars
nor is recalled by any spider, or any flower,
the joyless and deathless dancers—

                       speak once, speak twice,
before we join them, lady, and speak no more.

LXII

The bird flying past my head said previous previous
the clock too said previous
I was warned, I was too soon, but I went on
taking with me a buzzing headful of omens
as this, and that, and the other, all to no good
turn back, go to the right, no no go forward,
under that tree, under that cliff, through that man's
    house
his wife will tell you, ask her the way

I went and asked, it was all as I had foreseen,
one thing and then another all as if planned
the bird saying previous previous and the clock croaking
the cliff and the tree and the house and the wife
the husband looking askance at me over his work
why it is all a dream I said and hurried
with leaden or golden steps in dream's bravado
past bird clock cliff tree wife and husband

into the beyond—but what was the beyond but nothing
nothing nothing—a shore a shape a silence
an edge a falling off—a loaf of fog
sliced by a knife. It was then that I turned back,
and found the past was changed and strange as future—
cliff tree wife and husband changed and strange;
and the same or a different bird flew past my head
saying previous previous, as if I were again too soon.

LXXXIV

What face she put on it, we will not discuss:
she went hence an hour since. Where she went,
is another matter. To the north, to the south,
as the man whistled, or the whim bade, she went,
or even—who can say—following a star.
Her heart is like an hourglass, from which the sand runs—
no sooner run than tilted to run again;
her mind, a mirror, which reflects the last moment;
her face, you would know it anywhere, it gives you back
your own light, like the moon. Tell her a lie,
threefold she reflects it; tell her the truth,
and its returned brilliance will strike you dead.
She is of quicksilver. You might as well
pillow your head on a cloud, as on that breast,
or strive to sleep with a meteor: when you wake,
she is gone, your own hand is under your cheek.

Yet she is of the material that earth is made of:
will breed as quick as a fly; bloom like the cherry,
fearless of frost: and has a nimble fancy
as tropic in pattern as a fernleaf. She walks
as naturally as a young tree might walk:
with no pretence: picks up her roots and goes

out of your world, and into the secret darkness,
as a lady with lifted train will leave a ballroom,
and who knows why.

               Wherefor do you love her, gentlemen?
Because, like the spring earth, she is fruitfulness?
and you are seed? you need no other reason?
and she no other than her perpetual season.

XCII

But no, the familiar symbol, as that the
curtain lifts on a current of air, the rain
drips at the window, the green leaves seen in the
lamplight are bright against the darkness, these
will no longer serve your appetite, you must have
something fresh, something sharp—

The coarse grassblade, such as will cut
a careless finger, the silver pencil
lying straight along the crack in the table
in its pure rondure a multitude of reflections
or else your own thumbnail suddenly seen
and as if for the first time

Strongly ridged, warm-coloured as flesh but cool,
the pale moon at the base, and the fleck of scar
which grows slowly towards the tip—you think of a river
down which a single dead leaf perhaps is carried
or you think of a glacier in which
an acorn has been frozen—

But these too are familiar, it is not these
which will say your thought, you lift desperately
your eyes to the wall—the smooth surface
awaits them as precisely and coldly
as the paper awaits the gleaming pencil, giving
nothing, not even a resistance—

Where will you turn now if not to the rain,
to the curtain in the wind, the leaf tapping the window,
these are the wilderness, these are beyond
your pencil with its reflections
your thumbnail with its suggestion of rivers and glaciers
now you must go abroad

To the wild night which everywhere awaits you
and the deep darkness full of sounds
to the deep terror in which shines for a moment
a single light, far-off, which is suddenly quenched
this is the meaning for which you seek a phrase
this is your phrase.

FROM *A LETTER FROM LI PO*

IX

The winds of doctrine blow both ways at once.
The wetted finger feels the wind each way,
presaging plums from north, and snow from south.
The dust-wind whistles from the eastern sea
to dry the nectarine and parch the mouth.
The west wind from the desert wreathes the rain
too late to fill our wells, but soon enough,
the four-day rain that bears the leaves away.
Song with the wind will change, but is still song
and pierces to the rightness in the wrong
or makes the wrong a rightness, a delight.
Where are the eager guests that yesterday
thronged at the gate? Like leaves, they could not stay,
the winds of doctrine blew their minds away,
and we shall have no loving-cup tonight.
No loving-cup: for not ourselves are here
to entertain us in that outer year,
where, so they say, we see the Greater Earth.
The winds of doctrine blow our minds away,
and we are absent till another birth.

JOHN PEALE BISHOP (1892–1944)

Born a southerner, Bishop attended Princeton, lived in Paris among other literary expatriates during the twenties, then settled in Connecticut; his poems, fiction, and essays often reflect the conflict between his southern background and the larger world in which he lived.

Collected Poems. Ed. Allen Tate. Scribner's, 1948.

ALWAYS, FROM MY FIRST BOYHOOD

Always, from my first boyhood,
I have known how, lying awake in a straightened
Nakedness—curtains of rain drawn at the window—
To summon from dimness beautiful bodies,
While, over my iron pallet, the painful
Windiness of lilacs spread an
Impalpable coverlet.

Bodies of young men centaured on horses:
Pliant and tawny as leopards, they ride
Over a ground made spongy by April and rains,
Against the drawn lines of a forest
Misty as rain, clouded with torn green;
Their thighs are pressed like bronze to the gleaming
White flanks of the horses; stirrupless, their feet
Toe in abandon; for their eyes are upraised
Where, blue and afar, the jutted mountains
Renew their ancient march in sunrise.

Scarcely has the brittle bickering of twigs
Subsided from their hoofbeats, when I have, with words,
Disenchanted from the grey web of the wood's edge
The tenuous, rose-frosted beauty of women.
Their mouths are claret-wet from some mystery,
Virginal, awful, performed in the forest;
Or else they have seen, by the yellow flame of crocuses,

The flushed and long-sought touching of lovers.
For now, with burnt savage hair outshaken,
Tremulous, exulted, they front the east wind,
Complaining toward the curveting fading horsemen.

Always it is the same: the fixed, blue-radiant
Mountains; the horsemen on horses, the young men
Staring afar off, and the women crying, crying—
The retreating lure and the sinuous beautiful bodies.

So, beginning at midnight, I am as one
Steeped in intolerable wine, and lie
Throbbing; exhausted only when the arid dawn
Cracks its light on the fissile planes of the mirror.

IN THE DORDOGNE

We stood up before day
and shaved by metal mirrors
in the faint flame of a faulty candle.

And we hurried down the wide stone stairs
with a clirr of spur chains
on stone. And we thought
when the cocks crew
that the ghosts of a dead dawn
would rise and be off. But they stayed
under the window, crouched on the staircase,
the window now the color of morning.

The colonel asleep in the bed of Sully
slept on: but we descended
and saw in a niche in the white wall
a Virgin and child, serene
who were stones: we saw sycamores:
three aged mages
scattering gifts of gold.
But when the wind blew, there were autumn odors
and the shadowed trees
had the dapplings of young fawns.

And each day one died or another
died: each week we sent out thousands
that returned by hundreds
wounded or gassed. And those that died
we buried close to the old wall
within a stone's throw of Perigord
under the tower of the troubadours.

And because we had courage;
because there was courage and youth
ready to be wasted; because we endured
and were prepared for all endurance;
we thought something must come of it:
that the Virgin would raise her child and smile;
the trees gather up their gold and go;
that courage would avail something
and something we had never lost
be regained through wastage, by dying,
by burying the others under the English tower.

The colonel slept on in the bed of Sully
under the ravelling curtains: the leaves fell
and were blown away: the young men rotted
under the shadow of the tower
in a land of small clear silent streams
where the coming on of evening is
the letting down of blue and azure veils
over the clear and silent streams
delicately bordered by poplars.

O PIONEERS!

The white sagebrush desert. Noon.
All day heat. But the nights cool. And
Again yellowing dawn. Aspens on
Mountains and yellow sagebrush on sand.

Blind light bewilders. Blown or trampled out,
You cannot follow in the apparent wind
Your father's footsteps. It is to this end
They must have led you. Turn and turn about,

The way is lost to fortune. Forward, back,
Delirium will never find a stream
Running gold sands. Rather the earth will crack
Dry on skeletons, skulls in some daft scheme,

Sockets of eyes that perished crazily,
Ignorant of sun, the sagebrush, mad
Even to the dew. A continent they had
To ravage, and raving romped from sea to sea.

ARCHIBALD MACLEISH (1892–   )

An expatriate in France during the twenties, MacLeish was influenced by Pound and Eliot, his early poems reflecting a metaphysical and symbolist preoccupation. Later, when he had returned to the U.S., his poems veered toward patriotic and socially oriented themes, and he began writing verse dramas for radio. His long poem *Conquistador*, based on the conquests of Cortez, won the Pulitzer Prize in 1932. In 1939 he was appointed Librarian of Congress, and during World War II he served in several governmental posts, becoming Assistant Secretary of State in 1944. In 1949 he assumed the Boylston Professorship at Harvard. His work of the past fifteen years has concentrated on drama, and several of his verse plays have been staged with remarkable success on Broadway. Altogether MacLeish has published more than forty volumes of poetry, drama, and criticism.

Collected Poems, 1917–1952. Houghton Mifflin, 1963.
J. B. (Drama.) Houghton Mifflin, 1958.
Poetry and Experience. (Criticism.) Houghton Mifflin, 1961.

UNFINISHED HISTORY

We have loved each other in this time twenty years
And with such love as few men have in them even for
One or for the marriage month or the hearing of

Three nights' carts in the street but it will leave them:
We have been lovers the twentieth year now:
Our bed has been made in many houses and evenings:

The apple-tree moves at the window in this house:
There were palms rattled the night through in one:
In one there were red tiles and the sea's hours:

We have made our bed in the changes of many months—
and the
Light of the day is still overlong in the windows
Till night shall bring us the lamp and one another:

Those that have seen her have no thought what she is:
Her face is in the sun as a palmful of water:
Only by night and in love are the dark winds on it . . .

I wrote this poem that day when I thought
Since we have loved we two so long together
Shall we have done together—all love gone?

Or how then will it change with us when the breath
Is no more able for such joy and the blood is
Thin in the throat and the time not come for death?

THE END OF THE WORLD

Quite unexpectedly as Vasserot
The armless ambidextrian was lighting
A match between his great and second toe
And Ralph the lion was engaged in biting
The neck of Madame Sossman while the drum
Pointed, and Teeny was about to cough
In waltz-time swinging Jocko by the thumb—
Quite unexpectedly the top blew off:

And there, there overhead, there, there, hung over
Those thousands of white faces, those dazed eyes,
There in the starless dark the poise, the hover,
There with vast wings across the canceled skies,
There in the sudden blackness, the black pall
Of nothing, nothing, nothing—nothing at all.

SIGNATURE FOR TEMPO

I

Think that this world against the wind of time
Perpetually falls the way a hawk
Falls at the wind's edge but is motionless—

Think that this silver snail the moon will climb
All night upon time's curving stalk
That as she climbs bends, bends beneath her—

                                        Yes

And think that we remember the past time.

II

These live people,
These more
Than three dimensional
By time protracted edgewise into heretofore
People,
How shall we bury all
These queer-shaped people,
In graves that have no more
Than three dimensions?
Can we dig
With such sidlings and declensions
As to coffin bodies big
With memory?
And how
Can the earth's contracted Now
Enclosed these knuckles and this crooked knee
Sprawled over hours of a sun long set?

Or do these bones forget?

III

Borne
Landward on relinquishing seas,
Worn
By the sliding of water

Whom time goes over wave by wave, do I lie
Drowned in a crumble of surf at the sea's edge?—

And wonder now what ancient bones are these
That flake on sifting flake
Out of deep time have shelved this shallow ledge
Where the waves break—

VOYAGE WEST

There was a time for discoveries—
For the headlands looming above in the
First light and the surf and the
Crying of gulls: for the curve of the
Coast north into secrecy.

That time is past.
The last lands have been peopled.
The oceans are known now.

Señora: once the maps have all been made
A man were better dead than find new continents.

A man would better never have been born
Than find upon the open ocean flowers
Drifted from islands where there are no islands

Or midnight, out of sight of any land,
Smell on the altering air the odor of rosemary.

No fortune passes that misfortune—

To lift along the evening of the sky,
Certain as sun and sea, a new-found land
Steep from an ocean where no landfall can be.

EDNA ST. VINCENT MILLAY (1892–1950)

Miss Millay won attention for her poems while she was a student at Vassar. Later, having moved to Greenwich Village, where she acted with the Provincetown Players and took up a life of "emancipation," she began writing poems that were impudent, sardonic, yet sentimental: keepsakes of the twenties. They became widely popular. Of all the young women in those years whose poetry celebrated a life "this side of paradise," Miss Millay was both the most typical and the most talented. Today, however, the work of her more mature period, written while she was living on a farm in rural New York, isolated and often ill and despondent, seems stronger than her youthful poems. Her best are her frankly, not to say recklessly, traditional sonnets, called *Fatal Interview* (1931).

Collected Poems. Harper, 1956.

FROM *FATAL INTERVIEW*

II

This beast that rends me in the sight of all,
This love, this longing, this oblivious thing,
That has me under as the last leaves fall,
Will glut, will sicken, will be gone by spring.
The wound will heal, the fever will abate,
The knotted hurt will slacken in the breast;
I shall forget before the flickers mate
Your look that is today my east and west.
Unscathed, however, from a claw so deep
Though I should love again I shall not go:
Along my body, waking while I sleep,
Sharp to the kiss, cold to the hand as snow,
The scar of this encounter like a sword
Will lie between me and my troubled lord.

XI

Not in a silver casket cool with pearls
Or rich with red corundum or with blue,
Locked, and the key withheld, as other girls

Have given their loves, I give my love to you;
Not in a lovers'-knot, not in a ring
Worked in such fashion, and the legend plain—
Semper fidelis, where a secret spring
Kennels a drop of mischief for the brain:
Love in the open hand, no thing but that,
Ungemmed, unhidden, wishing not to hurt,
As one should bring you cowslips in a hat
Swung from the hand, or apples in her skirt,
I bring you, calling out as children do:
"Look what I have!—And these are all for you."

XIV

Since of no creature living the last breath
Is twice required, or twice the ultimate pain,
Seeing how to quit your arms is very death,
'Tis likely that I shall not die again;
And likely 'tis that Time whose gross decree
Sends now the dawn to clamour at our door,
Thus having done his evil worst to me,
Will thrust me by, will harry me no more.
When you are corn and roses and at rest
I shall endure, a dense and sanguine ghost,
To haunt the scene where I was happiest,
To bend above the thing I loved the most;
And rise, and wring my hands, and steal away
As I do now, before the advancing day.

XIX

My most distinguished guest and learnèd friend,
The pallid hare that runs before the day
Having brought your earnest counsels to an end
Now have I somewhat of my own to say:
That it is folly to be sunk in love,
And madness plain to make the matter known,
These are no mysteries you are verger of;
Everyman's wisdoms these are, and my own.
If I have flung my heart unto a hound
I have done ill, it is a certain thing;
Yet breathe I freer, walk I the more sound
On my sick bones for this brave reasoning?
Soon must I say, " 'Tis prowling Death I hear!"
Yet come no better off, for my quick ear.

XX

Think not, nor for a moment let your mind,
Wearied with thinking, doze upon the thought
That the work's done and the long day behind,
And beauty, since 'tis paid for, can be bought.
If in the moonlight from the silent bough
Suddenly with precision speak your name
The nightingale, be not assured that now
His wing is limed and his wild virtue tame.
Beauty beyond all feathers that have flown
Is free; you shall not hood her to your wrist,
Nor sting her eyes, nor have her for your own
In any fashion; beauty billed and kissed
Is not your turtle; treat her like a dove—
She loves you not; she never heard of love.

XXVIII

When we are old and these rejoicing veins
Are frosty channels to a muted stream,
And out of all our burning there remains
No feeblest spark to fire us, even in dream,
This be our solace: that it was not said
When we were young and warm and in our prime,
Upon our couch we lay as lie the dead,
Sleeping away the unreturning time.
O sweet, O heavy-lidded, O my love,
When morning strikes her spear upon the land,
And we must rise and arm us and reprove
The insolent daylight with a steady hand,
Be not discountenanced if the knowing know
We rose from rapture but an hour ago.

XXXVI

Hearing your words, and not a word among them
Tuned to my liking, on a salty day
When inland woods were pushed by winds that flung them
Hissing to leeward like a ton of spray,
I thought how off Matinicus the tide
Came pounding in, came running through the Gut,
While from the Rock the warning whistle cried,
And children whimpered, and the doors blew shut;
There in the autumn when the men go forth,

With slapping skirts the island women stand
In gardens stripped and scattered, peering north,
With dahlia tubers dripping from the hand:
The wind of their endurance, driving south,
Flattened your words against your speaking mouth.

XL

You loved me not at all, but let it go;
I loved you more than life, but let it be.
As the more injured party, this being so,
The hour's amenities are all to me—
The choice of weapons; and I gravely choose
To let the weapons tarnish where they lie,
And spend the night in eloquent abuse
Of senators and popes and such small fry
And meet the morning standing, and at odds
With heaven and earth and hell and any fool
That calls his soul his own, and all the gods,
And all the children getting dressed for school . . .
And you will leave me, and I shall entomb
What's cold by then in an adjoining room.

XLVI

Even in the moment of our earliest kiss,
When sighed the straitened bud into the flower,
Sat the dry seed of most unwelcome this;
And that I knew, though not the day and hour.
Too season-wise am I, being country-bred,
To tilt at autumn or defy the frost:
Snuffing the chill even as my fathers did,
I say with them, "What's out tonight is lost."
I only hoped, with the mild hope of all
Who watch the leaf take shape upon the tree,
A fairer summer and a later fall
Than in these parts a man is apt to see,
And sunny clusters ripened for the wine:
I tell you this across the blackened vine.

E. E. CUMMINGS (1894–1962)

Cummings' first published work, *The Enormous Room* (1922), was a novel based on his experience as a prisoner in France during World War I; it remains among the best works of fiction written in that period. Later, although he continued to write fiction and drama, and worked also as a painter, Cummings devoted his greatest effort to lyric poetry. His early poems were conventional and Shelleyan; but his mature writing was persistently experimental, using distorted typography and syntax, as well as a diction which was scandalous at the time, to create new effects. A few of these experiments were clearly intended to shock, but most were attempts to reinforce the poem's inner structure and rhythm, and to sharpen its focus. Throughout his writing, Cummings' lyric gift seldom faltered, his humane concern rarely left him. For years he lived at Patchin Place in New York's Greenwich Village, an address which became in effect the center of the American avant-garde during the thirties, forties, and fifties.

Poems 1923–1954. Harcourt, Brace, 1954.
95 Poems. Harcourt, Brace, 1958.
73 Poems. (Posthumous.) Harcourt, Brace & World, 1963.
The Enormous Room. Modern Library, 1948.
Him. (Drama.) Boni & Liveright, 1927.
Eimi. (Travel diary.) Covici, Friede, 1933.
Santa Claus, a Morality. Holt, 1946.
I, Six Nonlectures. Harvard University Press, 1953.

"MY LOVE"

my love
thy hair is one kingdom
  the king whereof is darkness
thy forehead is a flight of flowers

thy head is a quick forest
  filled with sleeping birds
thy breasts are swarms of white bees
  upon the bough of thy body
thy body to me is April
in whose armpits is the approach of spring

thy thighs are white horses yoked to a chariot
    of kings
they are the striking of a good minstrel
between them is always a pleasant song

my love
thy head is a casket
    of the cool jewel of thy mind
the hair of thy head is one warrior
    innocent of defeat
thy hair upon thy shoulders is an army
    with victory and with trumpets

thy legs are the trees of dreaming
whose fruit is the very eatage of forgetfulness

thy lips are satraps in scarlet
    in whose kiss is the combining of kings
thy wrists
are holy
    which are the keepers of the keys of thy blood
thy feet upon thy ankles are flowers in vases
    of silver

in thy beauty is the dilemma of flutes

    thy eyes are the betrayal
of bells comprehended through incense

"BUFFALO BILL 'S"

Buffalo Bill 's
defunct
            who used to
            ride a watersmooth-silver
                                    stallion
and break onetwothreefourfive pigeonsjustlikethat
                                                    Jesus

he was a handsome man
                            and what i want to know is
how do you like your blueeyed boy
Mister Death

"NOTICE THE CONVULSED ORANGE INCH OF MOON"

notice the convulsed orange inch of moon
perching on this silver minute of evening.

We'll choose the way to the forest—no offense
to you, white town whose spires softly dare.
Will take the houseless wisping rune
of road lazily carved on sharpening air.

Fields lying miraculous in violent silence

fill with microscopic whithering
. . .(that's the Black People, chérie,
who live under stones.) Don't be afraid

and we will pass the simple ugliness
of exact tombs, where a large road crosses
and all the people are minutely dead.

Then you will slowly kiss me

"RAISE THE SHADE"

raise the shade
will youse dearie?
rain
wouldn't that

get yer goat but
we don't care do
we dearie we should
worry about the rain

huh
dearie?
yknow
i'm

sorry for awl the
poor girls that
gets up god
knows when every

day of their
lives
aint you,
              oo-oo.   dearie

not so
hard dear

you're killing me

"I WILL BE"

                                    i will be

   M o ving in the Street of her

   bodyfee l inga ro undMe the traffic of
   lovely; muscles-sinke x p i r i n g S
         uddenl
   Y   totouch
                     the curvedship of
                                         Her-
   ....kIss   her:hands
                            will play on,mE as
   dea d tunes OR s-cra p-y leaVes flut te rin g
   from Hideous trees or

         Maybe Mandolins
                      l oo k-
      pigeons fly ingand

   whee(:are,SpRiN,kLiNg an in-stant with sunLight
   t h e n)l-
      ing all go BlacK wh-eel-ing
      oh
         ver
            mYveRylitTle

                        174

```
     street
     where
     you will come,

                    at twi li ght
     s(oon & there's
     a              m oo
)n.
```

"SPRING IS LIKE A PERHAPS HAND"

Spring is like a perhaps hand
(which comes carefully
out of Nowhere)arranging
a window,into which people look(while
people stare
arranging and changing placing
carefully there a strange
thing and a known thing here)and

changing everything carefully

spring is like a perhaps
Hand in a window
(carefully to
and fro moving New and
Old things,while
people stare carefully
moving a perhaps
fraction of flower here placing
an inch of air there)and

without breaking anything.

"IF I SHOULD SLEEP WITH A LADY CALLED DEATH"

if i should sleep with a lady called death
get another man with firmer lips
to take your new mouth in his teeth
(hips pumping pleasure into hips).

Seeing how the limp huddling string
of your smile over his body squirms
kissingly, i will bring you every spring
handfuls of little normal worms.

Dress deftly your flesh in stupid stuffs,
phrase the immense weapon of your hair.
Understanding why his eye laughs,
i will bring you every year

something which is worth the whole,
an inch of nothing for your soul.

"I LIKE MY BODY WHEN IT IS WITH YOUR"

i like my body when it is with your
body.   It is so quite new a thing.
Muscles better and nerves more.
i like your body.   i like what it does,
i like its hows.   i like to feel the spine
of your body and its bones, and the trembling
-firm-smooth ness and which i will
again and again and again
kiss,   i like kissing this and that of you,
i like, slowly stroking the, shocking fuzz
of your electric fur, and what-is-it comes
over parting flesh .... And eyes big love-crumbs,

and possibly i like the thrill

of under me you so quite new

"WHY DID YOU GO"

why did you go
little fourpaws?
you forgot to shut
your big eyes.

where did you go?
like little kittens
are all the leaves
which open in the rain.

little kittens who
are called spring,
is what we stroke
maybe asleep?

do you know? or maybe did
something go away
ever so quietly
when we weren't looking.

"WHO'S MOST AFRAID OF DEATH?"

who's most afraid of death? thou
                              art of him
utterly afraid, i love of thee
(beloved) this

                    and truly i would be
near when his scythe takes crisply the whim
of thy smoothness.   and mark the fainting
murdered petals.   with the caving stem.

But of all most would i be one of them

round the hurt heart which do so frailly cling. . . .)
i who am but imperfect in my fear

Or with thy mind against my mind, to hear
nearing our hearts' irrevocable play—
through the mysterious high futile day

an enormous stride
                    (and drawing thy mouth toward

my mouth, steer our lost bodies carefully downward)

"THAN(BY YON SUNSET'S WINTRY GLOW"

than(by yon sunset's wintry glow
revealed)this tall strong stalwart youth,
what sight shall human optics know
more quite ennobling forsooth?

One wondrous fine sonofabitch
(to all purposes and intents)
in which distinct and rich
portrait should be included,gents

these(by the fire's ruddy glow
united)not less than sixteen
children and of course you know
their mother,of his heart the queen

—incalculable bliss!
Picture it gents:our hero,Dan
who as you've guessed already is
the poorbuthonest workingman

(by that bright flame whose myriad tints
enrich a visage simple,terse,
seated like any king or prince
upon his uncorrupted arse

with all his hearty soul aglow)
his nightly supper sups
it isn't snowing snow you know
it's snowing buttercups

"'NEXT TO OF COURSE GOD AMERICA I'"

"next to of course god america i
love you land of the pilgrims' and so forth oh
say can you see by the dawn's early my
country 'tis of centuries come and go
and are no more what of it we should worry
in every language even deafanddumb
thy sons acclaim your glorious name by gorry
by jingo by gee by gosh by gum

why talk of beauty what could be more beaut-
iful than these heroic happy dead
who rushed like lions to the roaring slaughter
they did not stop to think they died instead
then shall the voice of liberty be mute?"

He spoke. And drank rapidly a glass of water

"I SING OF OLAF GLAD AND BIG"

i sing of Olaf glad and big
whose warmest heart recoiled at war:
a conscientious object-or

his wellbelovéd colonel(trig
westpointer most succinctly bred)
took erring Olaf soon in hand;
but—though an host of overjoyed
noncoms(first knocking on the head
him)do through icy waters roll
that helplessness which others stroke
with brushes recently employed
anent this muddy toiletbowl,
while kindred intellects evoke
allegiance per blunt instruments—
Olaf(being to all intents
a corpse and wanting any rag
upon what God unto him gave)
responds,without getting annoyed
"I will not kiss your f.ing flag"

straightway the silver bird looked grave
(departing hurriedly to shave)

but—though all kinds of officers
(a yearning nation's blueeyed pride)
their passive prey did kick and curse
until for wear their clarion
voices and boots were much the worse,
and egged the firstclassprivates on
his rectum wickedly to tease

by means of skilfully applied
bayonets roasted hot with heat—
Olaf (upon what were once knees)
does almost ceaselessly repeat
"there is some s. I will not eat"

our president,being of which
assertions duly notified
threw the yellowsonofabitch
into a dungeon,where he died

Christ(of His mercy infinite)
i pray to see;and Olaf,too

preponderatingly because
unless statistics lie he was
more brave than me:more blond than you.

"SOMEWHERE I HAVE NEVER TRAVELLED,
GLADLY BEYOND"

somewhere i have never travelled,gladly beyond
any experience,your eyes have their silence:
in your most frail gesture are things which enclose me,
or which i cannot touch because they are too near

your slightest look easily will unclose me
though i have closed myself as fingers,
you open always petal by petal myself as Spring opens
(touching skilfully,mysteriously)her first rose

or if your wish to be close me,i and
my life will shut very beautifully,suddenly,
as when the heart of this flower imagines
the snow carefully everywhere descending;

nothing which we are to perceive in this world equals
the power of your intense fragility:whose texture
compels me with the colour of its countries,
rendering death and forever with each breathing

(i do not know what it is about you that closes
and opens;only something in me understands
the voice of your eyes is deeper than all roses)
nobody,not even the rain,has such small hands

"WHAT A PROUD DREAMHORSE"

what a proud dreamhorse pulling(smoothloomingly)
    through
(stepp)this(ing)crazily seething of this
raving city screamingly street wonderful

flowers And o the Light thrown by Them opens

sharp holes in dark places paints eyes touches hands with
    new-
ness and these startled whats are a(piercing clothes
    thoughts kiss
-ing wishes bodies)squirm-of-frightened shy are whichs
    small
its hungry for Is for Love Spring thirsty for happens
only and beautiful
                    there is a ragged beside the who limps
man crying silence upward
                    —to have tasted Beautiful to have known
Only to have smelled Happens—skip dance kids hop point
    at
red blue yellow violet white orange green-
ness

    o what a proud dreamhorse moving(whose feet
almost walk air). now who stops. Smiles.he
                                        stamps

"AS FREEDOM IS A BREAKFASTFOOD"

as freedom is a breakfastfood
or truth can live with right and wrong
or molehills are from mountains made

181

—long enough and just so long
will being pay the rent of seem
and genius please the talentgang
and water most encourage flame

as hatracks into peachtrees grow
or hopes dance best on bald men's hair
and every finger is a toe
and any courage is a fear
—long enough and just so long
will the impure think all things pure
and hornets wail by children stung

or as the seeing are the blind
and robins never welcome spring
nor flatfolk prove their world is round
nor dingsters die at break of dong
and common's rare and millstones float
—long enough and just so long
tomorrow will not be too late

worms are the words but joy's the voice
down shall go which and up come who
breasts will be breasts thighs will be thighs
deeds cannot dream what dreams can do
—time is a tree(this life one leaf)
but love is the sky and i am for you
just so long and long enough

"ANYONE LIVED IN A PRETTY HOW TOWN"

anyone lived in a pretty how town
(with up so floating many bells down)
spring summer autumn winter
he sang his didn't he danced his did.

Women and men(both little and small)
cared for anyone not at all
they sowed their isn't they reaped their same
sun moon stars rain

children guessed (but only a few
and down they forgot as up they grew
autumn winter spring summer)
that noone loved him more by more

when by now and tree by leaf
she laughed his joy she cried his grief
bird by snow and stir by still
anyone's any was all to her

someones married their everyones
laughed their cryings and did their dance
(sleep wake hope and then) they
said their nevers they slept their dream

stars rain sun moon
(and only the snow can begin to explain
how children are apt to forget to remember
with up so floating many bells down)

one day anyone died i guess
(and noone stooped to kiss his face)
busy folk buried them side by side
little by little and was by was

all by all and deep by deep
and more by more they dream their sleep
noone and anyone earth by april
wish by spirit and if by yes.

Women and men (both dong and ding)
summer autumn winter spring
reaped their sowing and went their came
sun moon stars rain

"IT'S OVER A (SEE JUST"

it's over a (see just
over this) wall
the apples are (yes
they're gravensteins) all
as red as to lose
and as round as to find.

Each why of a leaf says
(floating each how)
you're which as to die
(each green of a new)
you're who as to grow
but you're he as to do

what must(whispers)be must
be(the wise fool)
if living's to give
so breathing's to steal—
five wishes are five
and one hand is a mind

then over our thief goes
(you go and i)
has pulled(for he's we)
such fruit from what bough
that someone called they
made him pay with his now.

But over a(see just
over this)wall
the red and the round
(they're gravensteins)fall
with kind of a blind
big sound on the ground

"MR U WILL NOT BE MISSED"

mr u will not be missed
who as an anthologist
sold the many on the few
not excluding mr u

"NO MAN,IF MEN ARE GODS"

no man,if men are gods;but if gods must
be men,the sometimes only man is this
(most common,for each anguish is his grief;
and,for his joy is more than joy,most rare)

a fiend,if fiends speak truth;if angels burn

by their own generous completely light,
an angel;or(as various worlds he'll spurn
rather than fail immeasurable fate)
coward,clown,traitor,idiot,dreamer,beast—

such was a poet and shall be and is

—who'll solve the depths of horror to defend
a sunbeam's architecture with his life:
and carve immortal jungles of despair
to hold a mountain's heartbeat in his hand

"THE FIRST OF ALL MY DREAMS WAS OF"

the first of all my dreams was of
a lover and his only love,
strolling slowly(mind in mind)
through some green mysterious land

until my second dream begins—
the sky is wild with leaves;which dance
and dancing swoop(and swooping whirl
over a frightened boy and girl)

but that mere fury soon became
silence:in huger always whom
two tiny selves sleep(doll by doll)
motionless under magical

foreverfully falling snow.
And then this dreamer wept:and so
she quickly dreamed a dream of spring
—how you and i are blossoming

"ALL WHICH ISN'T SINGING IS MERE TALKING"

all which isn't singing is mere talking
and all talking's talking to oneself
(whether that oneself be sought or seeking
master or disciple sheep or wolf)

185

gush to it as deity or devil
—toss in sobs and reasons threats and smiles
name it cruel fair or blessed evil—
it is you (né i) nobody else

drive dumb mankind dizzy with haranguing
—you are deafened every mother's son—
all is merely talk which isn't singing
and all talking's to oneself alone

but the very song of (as mountains
feel and lovers) singing is silence

CHARLES REZNIKOFF (1894–   )

A lawyer and legal editor, Reznikoff was associated in the thirties with the objectivist poets of New York, a group, including also Louis Zukofsky, which was organized loosely under the mentorship of William Carlos Williams. Some of his early work was published by The Objectivist Press, other books were privately published; but not until a selected edition of his poetry was brought out in 1962 did Reznikoff earn the attention his work deserves. Clear, mystical, sometimes bitter or disconsolate, his poems evoking the Hebrew tradition and the life of Jewish emigrants in America are especially noteworthy.

By the Waters of Manhattan. (Selected poems.) New Directions—San Francisco Review, 1962.
In Memoriam: 1933. The Objectivist Press, 1934.
Jerusalem the Golden. The Objectivist Press, 1934.
Testimony: the United States, 1885–1890. New Directions, 1965.

AFTER I HAD WORKED ALL DAY

After I had worked all day at what I earn my living,
I was tired. Now my own work has lost another day,
I thought, but began slowly,
and slowly my strength came back to me.
Surely, the tide comes in twice a day.

THE HEBREW OF YOUR POETS, ZION

The Hebrew of your poets, Zion,
is like oil upon a burn,
cool as oil;
after work,
the smell in the street at night
of the hedge in flower.
Like Solomon,
I have married and married the speech of strangers;
none are like you, Shulamite.

THESE DAYS THE PAPERS IN THE STREET

These days the papers in the street
leap into the air or burst across the lawns—
not a scrap but has the breath of life:
these in a gust of wind
play about,
those for a moment lie still and sun themselves.

ABOUT AN EXCAVATION

About an excavation
a flock of bright red lanterns
has settled.

LET OTHER PEOPLE COME AS STREAMS

Let other people come as streams
that overflow a valley
and leave dead bodies, uprooted trees and fields of sand;
we Jews are as the dew,
on every blade of grass,
trodden under foot today
and here tomorrow morning.

I WILL WRITE SONGS AGAINST YOU

I will write songs against you,
enemies of my people; I will pelt you
with the winged seeds of the dandelion;
I will marshall against you
the fireflies of the dusk.

I WILL GO INTO THE GHETTO

I will go into the ghetto: the sunlight
for only an hour or two at noon
on the pavement here is enough for me;

the smell of the fields in this street
for only a day or two in spring
is enough for me.
This peace is enough for me;
let the heathen rage.

They will take away
our cakes and delicacies,
the cheerful greetings, the hours of pleasant speech, the
    smiles,
and give us back
the sight of our eyes and our silent thoughts;
they will take away our groans and sighs
and give us—
merely breath.
Breathe deeply:
how good and sweet the air is.

NEW YEAR'S

The solid houses in the mist
are thin as tissue paper;
the water laps slowly at the rocks;
and the ducks from the north are here
at rest on the grey ripples.

The company in which we went
so free of care, so carelessly,
has scattered. Good-bye,
to you who lie behind in graves,
to you who galloped proudly off!
Pockets and heart are empty.

This is the autumn and our harvest—
such as it is, such as it is—
the beginnings of the end, bare trees and barren ground;
but for us only the beginning:
let the wild goat's horn
and the silver trumpet sound!

Reason upon reason
to be thankful:
for the fruit of the earth,

for the fruit of the tree,
for the light of the fire,
and to have come to this season.

The work of our hearts is dust
to be blown about in the winds
by the God of our dead in the dust
but our Lord delighting in life
(let the wild goat's horn
and the silver trumpet sound!)—
our God Who imprisons in coffin and grave
and unbinds the bound.

You have loved us greatly and given us
Your laws
for an inheritance,
Your sabbaths, holidays, and seasons of gladness,
distinguishing Israel
from other nations—
distinguishing us
above the shoals of men.
And yet why should we be remembered—
if at all—only for peace, if grief
is also for all? Our hopes,
if they blossom, if they blossom at all, the petals
and fruit fall.

You have given us the strength
to serve You,
but we may serve or not
as we please;
not for peace nor for prosperity,
not even for length of life, have we merited
remembrance; remember us
as the servants
You have inherited.

GENEVIEVE TAGGARD (1894–1948)

Hawaii, where Miss Taggard lived as a girl, furnishes a recurring motif in her metaphysically and traditionally oriented poems. She was a devoted craftsman whose work, though minor, remains taut, finished, and metrically alive; qualities she emphasized in her many years of teaching at Mount Holyoke and Sarah Lawrence, and in the pages of her magazine, *The Measure*, which she founded and edited during the twenties.

> Collected Poems, 1918–1938. Harper, 1938.
> Slow Music. Harper, 1946.

AMERICAN FARM, 1934

Space is too full. Did nothing happen here?
Skin of poor life cast off. These pods and shards
Rattle in the old house, rock with the old rocker,
Tick with the old clock, clutter the mantel.
Waste of disregarded trifles crooked as old crochet
On tabourets of wicker. Mute boredom of hoarding
Poor objects. These outlive water sluicing in cracks to
   join
The destroying river, the large Mississippi; or the tornado
Twisting dishes and beds and bird-cages into droppings
   of cloud.
The hard odd thing surviving precariously, once of some
   value
Brought home bright from the store in manila paper,
Now under the foot of the cow, caught in a crevice.
One old shoe, feminine, rotted with damp, one worn tire,
Crop of tin cans, torn harness, nails, links of a chain,—
Edge of a dress, wrappings of contraceptives, trinkets,
Fans spread, sick pink, and a skillet full of mould,
Bottles in cobwebs, butter-nuts—and the copperheads,
Night-feeders, who run their evil bellies in and out
Weaving a fabric of limbo for the devil of limbo;
Droppings of swallows, baked mud of wasps, confetti

Of the mouse nest, ancient cow-dung frozen,
Jumble of items, lost from use, with rusty tools,
Calendars, apple-cores, white sick grasses, gear from the
  stables,
Skull of a cow in the mud, with the stem of dead cabbage,
Part of the spine and the ribs, in the rot of swill mud. This
Array of limbo, once a part of swart labor, rusted now,
In every house, in every attic piled. Oh palsied people!
Under the weeds of the outhouse something one never
Picks up or burns; flung away. Let it lie; let it bleach.
Ironic and sinister junk filling a corner. If men vacate,
Prized or unprized, it jests with neglect.
Under the porch the kitten goes and returns,
Masked with small dirt. Odd objects in sheds and shelves,
And the stale air of bed-rooms, stink of stained bureaus,
Flies buzzing in bottles; vocal tone of no meaning.
No wonder our farms are dark and our dreams take these
  shapes.
Thistles mock all, growing out of rubbish
In a heap of broken glass with last year's soot.
Implacable divine rubbish prevails. Possessors of things
Look at the junk heap for an hour. Gnarled idle hands
Find ticks in the pelt of the dog, turn over a plank.
This parasite clutter invades sense and seems to breed
A like in our minds. Wind, water, sun;—it survives.
The whole sad place scales to the thistle and petty litter.
Neglect laughs in the fallen barns and the shutters broken
Hanging on a wailing hinge. Generations of wind
Owe you obeisance. You win. No man will war with you.
He has you in him; his hand trembles; he rights
The front acre while the wife tidies the parlour.
Economy, economy! Who'll till this land?

THE GERANIUMS

Even if the geraniums are artificial
Just the same,
In the rear of the Italian café
Under the nimbus of electric light
They are red; no less red
For how they were made. Above

The mirror and the napkins
In the little white pots . . .
. . . In the semi-clean café
Where they have good
Lasagne. . . . The red is a wonderful joy
Really, and so are the people
Who like and ignore it. In this place
They also have good bread.

THE LITTLE GIRL WITH BANDS ON HER TEETH

I was far forward on the plain, the burning swamp,
When the child called. And she was far behind.
She was not my child, my charge. By chance I heard.
She called from the first delusive fork. She cried her distress.
For me, much walking lay ahead, my stint, much walking.
The very gist of the problem. And nightfall. And I in a
swamp.
I heard, could not go on; she cried; she called me back.

Then my temper was short, for remember I split my duty
in two.
Any cry is the concern of all; we are all in a swamp . . .
this was discovered.
But the old fables of ruin decline. . . . I deserted myself.
Once to go back is nothing; one return matters not,
But daily to traverse the great gap of our ages,
Daily to go on, and daily return the triple mile!
And she less able to go . . . to see her less able.

Good Christopher, the saint! Bless the past for such pity.
The windows of pity shine, holy and vapid.
We need an essential plinth in the gap of that pity.
Farewell, Child. Try to hear my bleak meaning.
We will build a fine house, if we finish this journey.
My specious pride dies. If you wish, call me evil.
I travel the risk of the end. O perilous love.

IN THE TAIL OF THE SCORPION

A suave and paltry man, my enemy,
He encounters no spirit law to lay him low.
Thrives in his pose, lustrous where I wilt,
Pretender in a trivial charade.

Robs me and daunts me, to a meanness down.
Still there's no base to put my rage upon.
"No being is half so paltry. Search for depth."
O zero-hero of my hate and love!

Who in this splendid universe of smart
Summer equipment can make moral sense
Where men are folded down like garden chairs,
And whiffs of autumn fleck canary paint.

MARK VAN DOREN (1894–   )

Poet, dramatist, critic, scholar, and for many years a teacher at Columbia University, Van Doren is best known for his meditative lyrics in the tradition of English nature poetry, though his actual thematic range is broader than this may suggest. His home is in Connecticut.

Collected and New Poems, 1924–1963. Hill & Wang, 1963.
Narrative Poems. Hill & Wang, 1964.
Three Plays. Hill & Wang, 1966.
The Dialogues of Archibald MacLeish and Mark Van Doren. Ed. Warren V. Bush. Dutton, 1964.

FAMILY PRIME

Our golden age was then, when lamp and rug
Were one and warm, were globe against the indifferent
Million of cold things a world contains.
None there. A light shone inward, shutting out
All that was not corn yellow and love young.

Like winter bears we moved, our minds, our bodies
Jointed to fit the roundness of a room:
As sluggish, and as graceful, whether couch
Or table intercepted, or if marbles
Clicked on the floor and hunched us into play.

How long? I do not know. Before, a blank.
And after, all this oldness, them and me,
With the wind slicing in from everywhere,
And figures growing small. I may remember
Only a month of this. Or a God's hour.

Yet I remember, and my father said
He did: the moment spherical, that age
Fixes and gilds; eternity one evening
Perfect, such as maybe my own sons,
And yours, will know the taste of in their time.

THE ANCIENT COUPLE ON LU MOUNTAIN

Into the pool of silence our tears made,
Our secret tears when lord son went away—
How straight his back among the willows was!—
Into this lake of time whereon our house
Is a small hidden island, nevertheless
Sound falls: a single dropping of sweet words,
With every moon, into this upland sea
That no crane visits, for the shores are lost.

Lord son is faithful. With each full of the moon
A letter comes here from the capital:
Comes dripping, dripping its clear characters
Like raindrops, one by one, into soft water.
No silence then. Yet afterward! yet now,
When the moon wanes; when memory grows weaker
Of the few musical, pure drops. How deep this pool is
Only the dark cranes know that never come.

AND DID THE ANIMALS?

And did the animals in Noah's ark—
That was of oleander wood, with cabins
Cunningly bitumined in and out—
Did all those animals lie quietly?
For months and weeks and days, until the dove
Came home, and they were dry on Ararat,
Did every bird, with head beneath its wing,
Did every beast, with forepaws folded in,
Did every reptile, coiled upon itself,
Lie sleeping as no man did, patiently?
A man might think this tempest would not end,
Nor timbers cease to creak, nor the light come.
These did not know it rained, these did not know
Their kind survived in them if it survived.
A thinking man might doubt it, and in misery
Listen. Did they listen? But to what?
They did not know of time, they did not count
The waves. Then did they cry out in their dreams?
Or did they even dream, those specimen souls?

THOMAS HORNSBY FERRIL (1896–   )

A lifelong resident of the Colorado Rockies, Ferril is not only a scholar of his region's literature but our most distinguished contributor to it. Yet he is not primarily a regionalist: his dramatic and lyric poetry, though imbued with imagery of the high country, uses the materials basic to poetry anywhere. For many years he and his wife have published and edited the *Rocky Mountain Herald,* a weekly newspaper.

New and Selected Poems. Harper, 1952.
Words for Denver and Other Poems. Morrow, 1966.

WALTZ AGAINST THE MOUNTAINS

We are waltzing now into the moonlit morning
Of a city swung against the inland darkness
Of the prairie and the mountains and those lights
That stab from green to red and red to green.

The music ends. We lean against the sill
Feeling the mountains blowing over us.

What keeps on moving if your body stops?

I ask you this as if we were not new,
As if our city were an ancient city.
I ask you this in Denver, Colorado,
With a moon for the year's end over your naked shoulder.

Denver is younger than a white-haired man
Remembering yellow gold up to the grass roots.
They tell of eagles older than Denver is:
I search the crystal edges of the twilight
For birds still floating over these prairies and
These mountains that had floated over these prairies
And these mountains when there was no city here.

197

I walk alone down Blake Street and Wazee,
Looking for asters growing through the hub
Of a wheel that brought my city up from the prairie;
But a welder's mask with purple eyes is hanging
From a peg in a wall where a yellow ox was tied
The night the people came in a wagon to rivet
The steel of a set-back tower to a set-back tower.

I was pulling hair from the trunk of a cottonwood tree
The longhorn cattle rubbed when a sudden man
Started tossing red-hot rivets up through the leaves,
Scorching the amber varnish of the leaves.
He made the red-hot rivets stick to the sky.
I had to quiet the glowing clatter down
The frozen silence of a long long time;
I had to leave the tree and look for another.

The prairie twinkles up the Rocky Mountains.
Feel how the city sweeps against the mountains;
Some of those higher lights, I think, are stars.
Feel how the houses crowd and crack uphill.
The headlands buckle with too many houses.
They're trying to find a place where they can stand
Until the red lights turn to green again.

I'm only half as old as the city is.
I'm younger than an old box-elder tree;
I'm hardly older than the old cathedrals,
Yet I remember primroses and yucca
Out there where all those houses are tonight.
We children gathered primroses and yucca,
We gathered sand lilies and cactus blossoms.

But there's hardly a child in all the sleeping children
From here to where we think the stars begin
Who sleeps in a room where a child, his father, slumbered.

When you wake in the morning tracing a drowsy maze
In the wallpaper the sunrise trembles through,
The ceiling never whispers old directions
A ceiling learns from leading old men's eyes.
Off on that prairie frozen cattle flatten
With snow you cannot tell from moonlight on

Their shoulders and with darkness-clotted skulls
And darkness sagging in their hollow flanks;
And through those mountains black above this prairie
Are other animals alive and dead,
Some warmer than the rocks and some as cold,
And we are here, moving ourselves in music.

What keeps on moving if your body stops?

Mine is a city that has never known
A woman on a high wall looking down
Forever on the firelight of her kinsmen.
You're only a woman looking out of a window;
There are no ships, no smoking sacrifices,
And what we make, we are, and it is finished.

There's hardly time to speak beyond the flesh
In a city where the young men are always finding
A better place to start a cemetery.
Yet when this darkness cools the trembling tips
Of music in your breasts and earth has found
More certain use for me than waiting for
A woman on a wall, *what keeps on moving?*

We used to know, we don't know any more.
But I have seen enough of hills and blood,
And lovers and old men and windowsills,
The bones of churches and the bones of mountains,
To know how far we may have come together,
And where we're going for a little way.

So late you came up to these mountains from
A valley by the sea you hardly know
Yet where to gather blossoms of wild plums;
But part of what you are was here before
You came, and part of what you were is gone.
Already melting snow moves through your shoulder,
Atoms of hills are warm within your shoulder,
And somewhere in your fingers that press my fingers
Are particles of corn the bison made
When their bodies clogged the river in the spring.

You are a woman younger than the city,
You are a woman older than the city,
You are the mountains changing into woman,
You are a woman changing into prairie.

See how the moon goes down behind those mountains.
The hills with every waning moon are lower.
They cannot last. They go where we are going.
They wear away to feed our lips with words.

The moon's a sand lily petal floating down
Behind the blue wall of the Rocky Mountains.
I see you as a woman on that wall,
Stepping down crumbled distances forever,
One terrace of a mountain at a time,
One terrace of a prairie at a time,
Until you join your kinsmen at the sea.

What keeps on moving while the mountains linger?

It may be something spoken at a window
About the uses of some hill we've borrowed,
Or something a welder sings to a cottonwood tree,
Or something the seasons make the lovers say
When it's summer on the plains and spring on the
     ranges,
And we follow weeks of lilacs up from the prairie
Into lost towns of the mountains and return
With lilacs when the hay is being cut.

MORNING STAR

It is tomorrow now
In this black incredible grass.

The mountains with luminous discipline
Are coming out of the blackness
To take their places one in front of the other.

I know where you are and where the river is.

You are near enough to be a far horizon.
Your body breathing is a silver edge
Of a long black mountain rising and falling slowly
Against the morning and the morning star.

Before we cannot speak again
There will be time to use the morning star
For anything, like brushing it against
A pentstemon,
Or nearly closing the lashes of our lids
As children do to make the star come down.

Or I can say to myself as if I were
A wanderer being asked where he had been
Among the hills: "There was a range of mountains
Once I loved until I could not breathe."

ALWAYS BEGIN WHERE YOU ARE

Always begin right here where you are
And work out from here:
If adrift, feel the feel of the oar in the oarlock first,
If saddling a horse let your right knee slug
The belly of the horse like an uppercut,
Then cinch his suck,
Then mount and ride away
To any dream deserving the sensible world.

LOUISE BOGAN (1897–1970)

As poet, translator, and editor, and as poetry critic for *The New Yorker*, Miss Bogan was one of the most influential women of letters in America for thirty years. Her brief essays, perceptive and pointed, focus sharply on the virtues of the poets they celebrate, from both present and past. Similarly her own poems, brief formal lyrics, ironically define the situation of a woman in the modern world, with an insight more fundamental than that which most other women of her generation brought to the subject.

> *The Blue Estuaries: Poems, 1923–1968.* Farrar, Straus & Giroux, 1968.
> *Selected Criticism: Poetry and Prose.* Noonday Press, 1955.

MEN LOVED WHOLLY BEYOND WISDOM

Men loved wholly beyond wisdom
Have the staff without the banner.
Like a fire in a dry thicket
Rising within women's eyes
Is the love men must return.
Heart, so subtle now, and trembling,
What a marvel to be wise,
To love never in this manner!
To be quiet in the fern
Like a thing gone dead and still,
Listening to the prisoned cricket
Shake its terrible, dissembling
Music in the granite hill.

WOMEN

Women have no wilderness in them,
They are provident instead,
Content in the tight hot cell of their hearts
To eat dusty bread.

They do not see cattle cropping red winter grass,
They do not hear
Snow water going down under culverts
Shallow and clear.

They wait, when they should turn to journeys,
They stiffen, when they should bend.
They use against themselves that benevolence
To which no man is friend.

They cannot think of so many crops to a field
Or of clean wood cleft by an axe.
Their love is an eager meaninglessness
Too tense, or too lax.

They hear in every whisper that speaks to them
A shout and a cry.
As like as not, when they take life over their door-sills
They should let it go by.

CASSANDRA

To me, one silly task is like another.
I bare the shambling tricks of lust and pride.
This flesh will never give a child its mother,—
Song, like a wing, tears through my breast, my side,
And madness chooses out my voice again,
Again. I am the chosen no hand saves:
The shrieking heaven lifted over men,
Not the dumb earth, wherein they set their graves.

LATE

The cormorant still screams
Over cave and promontory.
Stony wings and bleak glory
Battle in your dreams.
Now sullen and deranged,
Not simply, as a child,
You look upon the earth
And find it harrowed and wild.

Now, only to mock
At the sterile cliff laid bare,
At the cold pure sky unchanged,
You look upon the rock,
You look upon the air.

TO BE SUNG ON THE WATER

Beautiful, my delight,
Pass, as we pass the wave.
Pass, as the mottled night
Leaves what it cannot save,
Scattering dark and bright.

Beautiful, pass and be
Less than the guiltless shade
To which our vows were said;
Less than the sound of the oar
To which our vows were made,—
Less than the sound of its blade
Dipping the stream once more.

JOHN WHEELWRIGHT (1897–1940)

Born into an old Back Bay family, Wheelwright was known affectionately in Boston during the twenties and thirties for his devotion to radical politics and his eccentric manner. Today his poems have been out of print for years; yet for their quirky style and forthrightness some deserve to be remembered.

Rock and Shell. Boston: Bruce Humphries, 1933.
Mirrors of Venus. Boston: Bruce Humphries, 1938.
Political Self-Portrait. Boston: Bruce Humphries, 1940.
Selected Poems. New Directions, 1941.

WHY MUST YOU KNOW?

—'What was that sound we heard
fall on the snow?'
—'It was a frozen bird.
Why must you know?
All the dull earth knows the good
that the air, with claws and wings
tears to the scattered questionings
which burn in fires of our blood.'
—'Let the air's beak and claws
    carry my deeds
far, where no springtime thaws
    the frost for their seeds.'
—'One could fathom every sound
that the circling blood can tell
who heard the diurnal syllable,
while lying close against the ground.'
—'My flesh, bone and sinew
    now would discern
hidden waters in you
    Earth, waters that burn.'
—'One who turns to earth again
finds solace in its weight; and deep
hears the blood forever keep
the silence between drops of rain.'

TRAIN RIDE

After rain, through afterglow, the unfolding fan
of railway landscape sidled on the pivot
of a larger arc into the green of evening;
I remembered that noon I saw a gradual bud
still white; though dead in its warm bloom;
always the enemy is the foe at home.

And I wondered what surgery could recover
our lost, long stride of indolence and leisure
which is labor in reverse; what physic recalls the smile
not of lips, but of eyes as of the sea bemused.

We, when we disperse from common sleep to several
tasks, we gather to despair; we, who assembled
once for hopes from common toil to dreams
or sickish and hurting or triumphal rapture;
always the enemy is our foe at home.

We, deafened with far scattered city rattles
to the hubbub of forest birds (never having
"had time" to grieve or to hear through vivid sleep
the sea knock on its cracked and hollow stones)
so that the stars, almost, and birds comply,
and the garden-wet; the trees retire; We are
a scared patrol, fearing the guns behind;
always the enemy is the foe at home.

What wonder that we fear our own eyes' look
and fidget to be at home alone, and pitifully
put off age by some change in brushing the hair and
stumble to our ends like smothered runners at their tape;

Then (as while the stars herd to the great trough
the blind, in the always-only-outward of their dismantled
archways, awake at the smell of warmed stone
or to the sound of reeds, lifting from the dim
into their segment of green dawn) *always
our enemy is our foe at home*, more
certainly than through spoken words or from grief-
twisted writing on paper, unblotted by tears
the thought came:

There is no physic
for the world's ill, nor surgery; it must
(hot smell of tar on wet salt air)
burn in a fever forever, an incense pierced
with arrows, whose name is Love and another name

Rebellion (the twinge, the gulf, split seconds,
the very raindrop, render, and instancy
of Love).

All Poetry to this not-to-be-looked-upon sun
of Passion is the moon's cupped light; all
Politics to this moon, a moon's reflected
cupped light, like the moon of Rome, after
the deep wells of Grecian light sank low;
always the enemy is the foe at home.

But these three are friends whose arms twine
without words; as, in a still air,
the great grove leans to wind, past and to come.

HORACE GREGORY (1898–   )

One of the most active poets and critics of the modern period, Gregory is known for his poems in dramatic forms, incorporating themes of social criticism and philosophical inquiry. As a translator, he has produced versions of Catullus and Ovid; as a critic, he has written studies of Whistler and D. H. Lawrence, among others.

Collected Poems. Holt, Rinehart & Winston, 1964.

LONGFACE MAHONEY DISCUSSES HEAVEN

If someone said, Escape,
let's get away from here,
you'd see snow mountains thrown
against the sky,
cold, and you'd draw your breath and feel
air like cold water going through your veins,
but you'd be free, up so high,
or you'd see a row of girls dancing on a beach
with tropic trees and a warm moon
and warm air floating under your clothes
and through your hair.
Then you'd think of heaven
where there's peace, away from here
and you'd go some place unreal
where everybody goes after something happens,
set up in the air, safe, a room in a hotel.
A brass bed, military hair brushes,
a couple of coats, trousers, maybe a dress
on a chair or draped on the floor.
This room is not on earth, feel the air,
warm like heaven and far away.

This is a place
where marriage nights are kept
and sometimes here you say, Hello

to a neat girl with you
and sometimes she laughs
because she thinks it's funny to be sitting here
for no reason at all, except perhaps
she likes you daddy.

Maybe this isn't heaven but near
to something like it,
more like love coming up in elevators
and nothing to think about except, O God,
you love her now and it makes no difference
if it isn't spring. All seasons are warm
in the warm air
and the brass bed is always there.

If you've done something
and the cops get you afterwards, you
can't remember the place again,
away from cops and streets—
it's all unreal—
the warm air, a dream
that couldn't save you now.
No one would care
to hear about it,
it would be heaven
far away, dark and no music,
not even a girl there.

"ASK NO RETURN"

Ask no return for love that's given
embracing mistress, wife or friend,
                              ask no return:
on this deep earth or in pale heaven,
awake and spend
hands, lips, and eyes in love,
in darkness burn,
                  the limbs entwined until the soul ascend.

Ask no return of seasons gone:
the fire of autumn and the first hour of spring,
the short bough blossoming

through city windows when night's done,
when fears adjourn
                    backward in memory where all loves end

in self again, again the inward tree
growing against the heart
and no heart free.
From love that sleeps behind each eye
in double symmetry
                    ask no return,
even in enmity, look! I shall take your hand;
nor can our limbs disjoin in separate ways again,
walking, even at night on foreign land
through houses open to the wind, through cold and rain,
waking alive, meet, kiss and understand.

THE REHEARSAL

Gentlemen, as we take our seats
In the darkened house, let us rehearse
The properties of the Western Theater;
Attention: this is item one,
Cloth of the Sun and Moon; it is
The Firmament, see how it glitters—
Life beyond life on earth, and
Beautiful. It has been praised,
Many regret to close their eyes
Upon it, the eternal skyscape
Which seems to wake at morning,
To burn at noon and to unveil
A silver mask at night. We do not
Hear it and yet its changes are
The Music of the Spheres—

                    so much for that.
What of the others? plant life,
Animal life, the earthly spirits?
Item: a Lock of Gilded Hair
From the Head of Venus, a Tree
Of Poisoned Apples, a Yellow Snake,
A Hebrew Maiden and a Naked Man—

We need not name them, they
Have walked out of the sight
Of God; they share our dark-
Ness. Here is a White Hot
Caldron for the Jew, a Chain
Of Dragons and Hell's Mouth,
And St. Sebastian with a weeping
Eye—tears? Four Glassy Tears,
Four Kingly Crowns: Russia,
France, Germany, Spain, a Wreath
Of Smoke, all painted on a curtain;
Behind the curtain, the West Wind,
And in the Wind, Three Cries of Beggars,
The Halt, the Maimed, the Blind.

Gentlemen, this is our Gold, our
Inheritance—even the Gibbet,
The Mask of Folly and the Stake,
The Fall from Grace, the Earthly Power—
We cannot sell it, and though
No actors come, we shall wear it
As tapestry is worn.

                         It is our Europe
To warm us in the cave, protect
Us from heat on the rocks, from
Dark, from flood, from moving mountains
Among ice, the fire of lightning,
The drifting wilderness of snow.

HART CRANE (1899–1932)

Crane's father, a well-to-do candy manufacturer in Cleveland, disapproved of his son's poetry. In consequence Crane, who had begun writing very early, left home at seventeen, and went to New York, where he plunged into a life of extreme disorder, broken by spells of guilt and despair. Only his poetry, written in apocalyptic fervor, held him together. His first book, *White Buildings* (1926), showed him combining diverse influences—Marlowe, Donne, Whitman, Eliot, and especially Rimbaud—into a style of great force and originality. His long poem, *The Bridge* (1930), which celebrates "the Myth of America," was written partly in answer to the "cultural pessimism" of Eliot's *Waste Land;* though structurally weak and at times incoherent or immature, it is still the finest poem of its kind in American literature. Shortly after completing *The Bridge,* Crane went to Mexico, where he hoped to write another long work, on themes from the life of Montezuma. He was able to produce only a few short poems, however. Finally he took ship for New York; but on the way leaped overboard, and disappeared before he could be rescued.

Complete Poems. Ed. Waldo Frank. Doubleday, 1958.
The Letters of Hart Crane. Ed. Brom Weber. Hermitage House, 1952.

CHAPLINESQUE

We make our meek adjustments,
Contented with such random consolations
As the wind deposits
In slithered and too ample pockets.

For we can still love the world, who find
A famished kitten on the step, and know
Recesses for it from the fury of the street,
Or warm torn elbow coverts.

We will sidestep, and to the final smirk
Dally the doom of that inevitable thumb
That slowly chafes its puckered index toward us,

Facing the dull squint with what innocence
And what surprise!

And yet these fine collapses are not lies
More than the pirouettes of any pliant cane;
Our obsequies are, in a way, no enterprise.
We can evade you, and all else but the heart:
What blame to us if the heart live on.

The game enforces smirks; but we have seen
The moon in lonely alleys make
A grail of laughter of an empty ash can,
And through all sound of gaiety and quest
Have heard a kitten in the wilderness.

THE WINE MENAGERIE

Invariably when wine redeems the sight,
Narrowing the mustard scansions of the eyes,
A leopard ranging always in the brow
Asserts a vision in the slumbering gaze.

Then glozening decanters that reflect the street
Wear me in crescents on their bellies. Slow
Applause flows into liquid cynosures:
—I am conscripted to their shadows' glow.

Against the imitation onyx wainscoting
(Painted emulsion of snow, eggs, yarn, coal, manure)
Regard the forceps of the smile that takes her.
Percussive sweat is spreading to his hair. Mallets,
Her eyes, unmake an instant of the world . . .

What is it in this heap the serpent pries—
Whose skin, facsimile of time, unskeins
Octagon, sapphire transepts round the eyes;
—From whom some whispered carillon assures
Speed to the arrow into feathered skies?

Sharp to the window-pane guile drags a face,
And as the alcove of her jealousy recedes

An urchin who has left the snow
Nudges a cannister across the bar
While August meadows somewhere clasp his brow.

Each chamber, transept, coins some squint,
Remorseless line, minting their separate wills—
Poor streaked bodies wreathing up and out,
Unwitting the stigma that each turn repeals:
Between black tusks the roses shine!

New thresholds, new anatomies! Wine talons
Build freedom up about me and distill
This competence—to travel in a tear
Sparkling alone, within another's will.

Until my blood dreams a receptive smile
Wherein new purities are snared; where chimes
Before some flame of gaunt repose a shell
Tolled once, perhaps, by every tongue in hell.
—Anguished, the wit that cries out of me:

"Alas,—these frozen billows of your skill!
Invent new dominoes of love and bile . . .
Ruddy, the tooth implicit of the world
Has followed you. Though in the end you know
And count some dim inheritance of sand,
How much yet meets the treason of the snow.

"Rise from the dates and crumbs. And walk away,
Stepping over Holofernes' shins—
Beyond the wall, whose severed head floats by
With Baptist John's. Their whispering begins.

"—And fold your exile on your back again;
Petrushka's valentine pivots on its pin."

AT MELVILLE'S TOMB

Often beneath the wave, wide from this ledge
The dice of drowned men's bones he saw bequeath
An embassy. Their numbers as he watched,
Beat on the dusty shore and were obscured.

And wrecks passed without sound of bells,
The calyx of death's bounty giving back
A scattered chapter, livid hieroglyph,
The portent wound in corridors of shells.

Then in the circuit calm of one vast coil,
Its lashings charmed and malice reconciled,
Frosted eyes there were that lifted altars;
And silent answers crept across the stars.

Compass, quadrant and sextant contrive
No farther tides . . . High in the azure steeps
Monody shall not wake the mariner.
This fabulous shadow only the sea keeps.

FROM *VOYAGES*

I

Above the fresh ruffles of the surf
Bright striped urchins flay each other with sand.
They have contrived a conquest for shell shucks,
And their fingers crumble fragments of baked weed
Gaily digging and scattering.

And in answer to their treble interjections
The sun beats lightning on the waves,
The waves fold thunder on the sand;
And could they hear me I would tell them:

O brilliant kids, frisk with your dog,
Fondle your shells and sticks, bleached
By time and the elements; but there is a line
Your must not cross nor ever trust beyond it
Spry cordage of your bodies to caresses
Too lichen-faithful from too wide a breast.
The bottom of the sea is cruel.

II

And yet this great wink of eternity,
Of rimless floods, unfettered leewardings,
Samite sheeted and processioned where
Her undinal vast belly moonward bends,
Laughing the wrapt inflections of our love;

Take this Sea, whose diapason knells
On scrolls of silver snowy sentences,
The sceptred terror of whose sessions rends
As her demeanors motion well or ill,
All but the pieties of lovers' hands.

And onward, as bells off San Salvador
Salute the crocus lustres of the stars,
In these poinsettia meadows of her tides,—
Adagios of islands, O my Prodigal,
Complete the dark confessions her veins spell.

Mark how her turning shoulders wind the hours,
And hasten while her penniless rich palms
Pass superscription of bent foam and wave,—
Hasten, while they are true,—sleep, death, desire,
Close round one instant in one floating flower.

Bind us in time, O Seasons clear, and awe.
O minstrel galleons of Carib fire,
Bequeath us to no earthly shore until
Is answered in the vortex of our grave
The seal's wide spindrift gaze toward paradise.

O CARIB ISLE!

The tarantula rattling at the lily's foot
Across the feet of the dead, laid in white sand
Near the coral beach—nor zigzag fiddler crabs
Side-stilting from the path (that shift, subvert
And anagrammatize your name)—No, nothing here
Below the palsy that one eucalyptus lifts
In wrinkled shadows—mourns.

And yet suppose
I count these nacreous frames of tropic death,
Brutal necklaces of shells around each grave
Squared off so carefully. Then

To the white sand I may speak a name, fertile
Albeit in a stranger tongue. Tree names, flower names
Deliberate, gainsay death's brittle crypt. Meanwhile
The wind that knots itself in one great death—
Coils and withdraws. So syllables want breath.

But where is the Captain of the doubloon isle
Without a turnstile? Who but catchword crabs
Patrols the dry groins of the underbrush?
What man, or What
Is Commissioner of the mildew throughout the ambushed
    senses?
His Carib mathematics web the eyes' baked lenses!

Under the poinciana, of a noon or afternoon
Let fiery blossoms clot the light, render my ghost
Sieved upward, white and black along the air
Until it meets the blue's comedian host.

Let not the pilgrim see himself again
For slow evisceration bound like those huge terrapin
Each daybreak on the wharf, their brine-caked eyes;
—Spiked, overturned; such thunder in their strain!

Slagged on the hurricane—I, cast within its flow,
Congeal by afternoons here, satin and vacant.
You have given me the shell, Satan,—carbonic amulet
Sere of the sun exploded in the sea.

A NAME FOR ALL

Moonmoth and grasshopper that flee our page
And still wing on, untarnished of the name
We pinion to your bodies to assuage
Our envy of your freedom—we must maim

Because we are usurpers, and chagrined—
And take the wing and scar it in the hand.
Names we have, even, to clap on the wind;
But we must die, as you, to understand.

I dreamed that all men dropped their names, and sang
As only they can praise, who build their days
With fin and hoof, with wing and sweetened fang
Struck free and holy in one Name always.

ALLEN TATE (1899–   )

A native of Kentucky and a graduate of Vanderbilt, where he was a founding member of the group called the Fugitives, Tate has won distinction of a high order for both his poetry and his criticism. His poems, though in the formal tradition, are uniquely his own; by turns elegant and angry; driven by intellectual fervor and deep moral feeling. They range over many themes, but chiefly the cultural predicament of the modern American, especially the modern southerner. Tate's essays, acute, learned, often polemical, have concentrated on Latin poetry, the Elizabethans, Edgar Allan Poe, the Victorians, and especially his own contemporaries; probably no other critic had as much to do with establishing standards of taste in American literature after 1925. He has taught at many universities, including Columbia, Princeton, and Minnesota, has been an editor of *The Sewanee Review*, has appeared on radio as a member of the cast of a popular educational series, and has always been a generous friend to younger poets. His one novel, *The Fathers* (1938), was widely translated and acclaimed abroad, and in a new edition (1958) continues a half-underground existence in the U.S.; it is a minor classic. Now retired, Tate lives in Sewanee, Tenn.

Poems. Scribner's, 1960.
Collected Essays. Denver: Alan Swallow, 1959.

THE MEDITERRANEAN

Quem das finem, rex magne, dolorum?

Where we went in the boat was a long bay
A slingshot wide, walled in by towering stone—
Peaked margin of antiquity's delay,
And we went there out of time's monotone:

Where we went in the black hull no light moved
But a gull white-winged along the feckless wave,
The breeze, unseen but fierce as a body loved,
That boat drove onward like a willing slave:

Where we went in the small ship the seaweed
Parted and gave to us the murmuring shore,
And we made feast and in our secret need
Devoured the very plates Aeneas bore:

Where derelict you see through the low twilight
The green coast that you, thunder-tossed, would win,
Drop sail, and hastening to drink all night
Eat dish and bowl to take that sweet land in!

Where we feasted and caroused on the sandless
Pebbles, affecting our day of piracy,
What prophecy of eaten plates could landless
Wanderers fulfil by the ancient sea?

We for that time might taste the famous age
Eternal here yet hidden from our eyes
When lust of power undid its stuffless rage;
They, in a wineskin, bore earth's paradise.

Let us lie down once more by the breathing side
Of Ocean, where our live forefathers sleep
As if the Known Sea still were a month wide—
Atlantis howls but is no longer steep!

What country shall we conquer, what fair land
Unman our conquest and locate our blood?
We've cracked the hemispheres with careless hand!
Now, from the Gates of Hercules we flood

Westward, westward till the barbarous brine
Whelms us to the tired land where tasseling corn,
Fat beans, grapes sweeter than muscadine
Rot on the vine: in that land were we born.

SONNETS AT CHRISTMAS

(1934)

I

This is the day His hour of life draws near,
Let me get ready from head to foot for it

Most handily with eyes to pick the year
For small feed to reward a feathered wit.
Some men would see it an epiphany
At ease, at food and drink, others at chase
Yet I, stung lassitude, with ecstasy
Unspent argue the season's difficult case
So: Man, dull critter of enormous head,
What would he look at in the coiling sky?
But I must kneel again unto the Dead
While Christmas bells of paper white and red,
Figured with boys and girls spilt from a sled,
Ring out the silence I am nourished by.

II

Ah, Christ, I love you rings to the wild sky
And I must think a little of the past:
When I was ten I told a stinking lie
That got a black boy whipped; but now at last
The going years, caught in an accurate glow,
Reverse like balls englished upon green baize—
Let them return, let the round trumpets blow
The ancient crackle of the Christ's deep gaze.
Deafened and blind, with senses yet unfound,
Am I, untutored to the after-wit
Of knowledge, knowing a nightmare has no sound;
Therefore with idle hands and head I sit
In late December before the fire's daze
Punished by crimes of which I would be quit.

THE OATH

It was near evening, the room was cold
Half dark; Uncle Ben's brass bullet-mould
And powder-horn and Major Bogan's face
Above the fire in the half-light plainly said:
There's naught to kill but the animated dead.
Horn nor mould nor major follows the chase.
Being cold I urged Lytle to the fire
In the blank twilight with not much left untold
By two old friends when neither's a great liar.
We sat down evenly in the smoky chill.

There's precious little to say between day and dark,
Perhaps a few words on the implacable will
Of time sailing like a magic barque
Or something as fine for the amenities,
Till dusk seals the window, the fire grows bright,
And the wind saws the hill with a swarm of bees.
Now meditating a little on the firelight
We heard the darkness grapple with the night
And give an old man's valedictory wheeze
From his westward breast between his polar jaws;
Then Lytle asked: Who are the dead?
Who are the living and the dead?
And nothing more was said.
So I, leaving Lytle to that dream,
Decided what it is in time that gnaws
The ageing fury of a mountain stream
When suddenly as an ignorant mind will do
I thought I heard the dark pounding its head
On a rock, crying: *Who are the dead?*
Then Lytle turned with an oath—By God it's true!

SHADOW AND SHADE

The shadow streamed into the wall—
The wall, break-shadow in the blast;
We lingered wordless while a tall
Shade enclouded the shadow's cast.

The torrent of the reaching shade
Broke shadow into all its parts,
What then had been of shadow made
Found exigence in fits and starts

Where nothing properly had name
Save that still element the air,
Burnt sea of universal frame
In which impounded now we were:

I took her hand, I shut her eyes
And all her shadow cleft with shade,
Shadow was crushed beyond disguise
But, being fear, was unafraid.

I asked fair shadow at my side:
What more shall fiery shade require?
We lay long in the immense tide
Of shade and shadowy desire

And saw the dusk assail the wall,
The black surge, mounting, crash the stone!
Companion of this lust, we fall,
I said, lest we should die alone.

MR. POPE

When Alexander Pope strolled in the city
Strict was the glint of pearl and gold sedans.
Ladies leaned out more out of fear than pity
For Pope's tight back was rather a goat's than man's.

Often one thinks the urn should have more bones
Than skeletons provide for speedy dust,
The urn gets hollow, cobwebs brittle as stones
Weave to the funeral shell a frivolous rust.

And he who dribbled couplets like a snake
Coiled to a lithe precision in the sun
Is missing. The jar is empty; you may break
It only to find that Mr. Pope is gone.

What requisitions of a verity
Prompted the wit and rage between his teeth
One cannot say. Around a crooked tree
A moral climbs whose name should be a wreath.

EMBLEMS

I

Maryland, Virginia, Caroline
Pent images in sleep
Clay valleys rocky hills old fields of pine
Unspeakable and deep

Out of that source of time my farthest blood
Runs strangely to this day
Unkempt the fathers waste in solitude
Under the hills of clay

Far from their woe fled to its thither side
To a river in Tennessee
In an alien house I will stay
Yet find their breath to be
All that my stars betide—
There some time to abide
Took wife and child with me.

II

When it is all over and the blood
Runs out, do not bury this man
By the far river (where never stood
His fathers) flowing to the West,
But take him East where life began.
O my brothers, there is rest
In the depths of an eastward river
That I can understand; only
Do not think the truth we hold
I hold the slighter for this lonely
Reservation of the heart:
Men cannot live forever
But they must die forever
So take this body at sunset
To the great stream whose pulses start
In the blue hills, and let
These ashes drift from the Long Bridge
Where only a late gull breaks
That deep and populous grave.

III

By the great river the forefathers to beguile
Them, being inconceivably young, carved out
Deep hollows of memory on a river isle
Now lost—their murmur the ghost of a shout

In the hollows where the forefathers
Without beards, their faces bright and long,

Lay down at sunset by the cool river
In the tall willows amid birdsong;

And the long sleep by the cool river
They've slept full and long, till now the air
Waits twilit for their echo; the burning shiver
Of August strikes like a hawk the crouching hare.

YVOR WINTERS (1900–1968)

During most of his life Winters was known primarily as a critic—a particularly irascible critic—and only secondarily as a poet. From a standpoint in stern rationalism, he kept up a steady attack on modern literary practice, condemning its symbolism as mere "pathetic fallacy" and its experimentalism as "the fallacy of affective form." He held traditional prosody to be the first, though by no means the last, rule of poetry. Today, although their vigor of expression and their sporadic brilliant insights, especially when he was writing about poets congenial to his temper, make his essays still well worth reading, their importance, next to that of his best poems, seems on the wane. Moreover, in spite of his traditionalism in the essays, his attitudes in poetry—social, cultural, metaphysical—are modern and often radical. Seldom has a poet's criticism seemed so at variance with his poetry, all the more in those poems which confess his humility before experience and his kinship in universal frailty—feelings which rarely found their way into his prose. Some of his poems have a bedrock genuineness of feeling that drives through their Ciceronian diction, and a spontaneity that makes their formalism as natural as a tree's. For many years Winters taught at Stanford, where his students, under his influence, constituted in effect a "school" of poets, distinct from any others in the country.

Collected Poems. Rev. ed. Denver: Alan Swallow, 1960.
In Defense of Reason. (Collected criticism.) Denver: Alan Swallow, 1947.
The Function of Criticism. Denver: Alan Swallow, 1957.

TO MY INFANT DAUGHTER (II)

Alas, that I should be
So old, and you so small!
You will think naught of me
When your dire hours befall.

Take few men to your heart!
Unstable, fierce, unkind,
The ways that men impart.
True love is slow to find.

True art is slow to grow.
Like a belated friend,
It comes to let one know
Of what has had an end.

ORPHEUS

In Memory of Hart Crane

Climbing from the Lethal dead,
Past the ruined waters' bed,
In the sleep his music cast
Tree and flesh and stone were fast—
As amid Dodona's wood
Wisdom never understood.

Till the shade his music won
Shuddered, by a pause undone—
Silence would not let her stay.
He could go one only way:
By the river, strong with grief,
Gave his flesh beyond belief.

Yet the fingers on the lyre
Spread like an avenging fire.
Crying loud, the immortal tongue,
From the empty body wrung,
Broken in a bloody dream,
Sang unmeaning down the stream.

THE MANZANITA

Under the forest, where the day is dark
And air is motionless throughout the day,
Rooted in leaf-mould and in rotting bark,
This old arbutus gathers strength to stay.

Tall as a man, and taller, but more old,
This is no shrub of some few years, but hard
Its smooth unbending trunk, oh, hard and cold!
Of earth and age the stony proof and guard!

The skin is rose: yet infinitely thin,
It is a color only. What one tells
Of ancient wood and softly glinting skin
Is less than are the tiny waxen bells.

This life is not our life; nor for our wit
The sweetness of these shades; these are alone.
There is no wisdom here; seek not for it!
This is the shadow of the vast madrone.

SIR GAWAINE AND THE GREEN KNIGHT

Reptilian green the wrinkled throat,
Green as a bough of yew the beard;
He bent his head, and so I smote;
Then for a thought my vision cleared.

The head dropped clean; he rose and walked;
He fixed his fingers in the hair;
The head was unabashed and talked;
I understood what I must dare.

His flesh, cut down, arose and grew.
He bade me wait the season's round,
And then, when he had strength anew,
To meet him on his native ground.

The year declined; and in his keep
I passed in joy a thriving yule;
And whether waking or in sleep,
I lived in riot like a fool.

He beat the woods to bring me meat.
His lady, like a forest vine,
Grew in my arms; the growth was sweet;
And yet what thoughtless force was mine!

By practice and conviction formed,
With ancient stubbornness ingrained,
Although her body clung and swarmed,
My own identity remained.

Her beauty, lithe, unholy, pure,
Took shapes that I had never known;
And had I once been insecure,
Had grafted laurel in my bone.

And then, since I had kept the trust,
Had loved the lady, yet was true,
The knight withheld his giant thrust
And let me go with what I knew.

I left the green bark and the shade,
Where growth was rapid, thick, and still;
I found a road that men had made
And rested on a drying hill.

AN ELEGY

for the U.S.N. Dirigible, Macon

The noon is beautiful: the perfect wheel
Now glides on perfect surface with a sound
Earth has not heard before; the polished ground
Trembles and whispers under rushing steel.

The polished ground, and prehistoric air!
Metal now plummets upward and there sways,
A loosened pendulum for summer days,
Fixing the eyeball in a limpid stare.

There was one symbol in especial, one
Great form of thoughtless beauty that arose
Above the mountains, to foretell the close
Of this deception, at meridian.

Steel-gray the shadow, than a storm more vast!
Its crowding engines, rapid, disciplined,
Shook the great valley like a rising wind.
This image, now, is conjured from the past.

Wind in the wind! O form more light than cloud!
Storm amid storms! And by the storms dispersed!

The brain-drawn metal rose until accursed
By its extension and the sky was loud!

Who will believe this thing in time to come?
I was a witness. I beheld the age
That seized upon a planet's heritage
Of steel and oil, the mind's viaticum:

Crowded the world with strong ingenious things,
Used the provision it could not replace,
To leave but Cretan myths, a sandy trace
Through the last stone age, for the pastoral kings

TIME AND THE GARDEN

The spring has darkened with activity.
The future gathers in vine, bush, and tree:
Persimmon, walnut, loquat, fig, and grape,
Degrees and kinds of color, taste, and shape.
These will advance in their due series, space
The season like a tranquil dwelling-place.
And yet excitement swells me, vein by vein:
I long to crowd the little garden, gain
Its sweetness in my hand and crush it small
And taste it in a moment, time and all!
These trees, whose slow growth measures off my years,
I would expand to greatness. No one hears,
And I am still retarded in duress!
And this is like that other restlessness
To seize the greatness not yet fairly earned,
One which the tougher poets have discerned—
Gascoigne, Ben Jonson, Greville, Raleigh, Donne,
Poets who wrote great poems, one by one,
And spaced by many years, each line an act
Through which few labor, which no men retract.
This passion is the scholar's heritage,
The imposition of a busy age,
The passion to condense from book to book
Unbroken wisdom in a single look,
Though we know well that when this fix the head,
The mind's immortal, but the man is dead.

TO THE HOLY SPIRIT

from a deserted graveyard
in the Salinas Valley

Immeasurable haze:
The desert valley spreads
Up golden river-beds
As if in other days.
Trees rise and thin away,
And past the trees, the hills,
Pure line and shade of dust,
Bear witness to our wills:
We see them, for we must;
Calm in deceit, they stay.

High noon returns the mind
Upon its local fact:
Dry grass and sand; we find
No vision to distract.
Low in the summer heat,
Naming old graves, are stones
Pushed here and there, the seat
Of nothing, and the bones
Beneath are similar:
Relics of lonely men,
Brutal and aimless, then
As now, irregular.

These are thy fallen sons,
Thou whom I try to reach.
Thou whom the quick eye shuns,
Thou dost elude my speech.
Yet when I go from sense
And trace thee down in thought,
I meet thee, then, intense,
And know thee as I ought.
But thou art mind alone,
And I, alas, am bound
Pure mind to flesh and bone,
And flesh and bone to ground.

These had no thought: at most
Dark faith and blinding earth.

Where is the trammeled ghost?
Was there another birth?
Only one certainty
Beside thine unfleshed eye,
Beside the spectral tree,
Can I discern: these die.
All of this stir of age,
Though it elude my sense
Into what heritage
I know not, seems to fall,
Quiet beyond recall
Into irrelevance.

A SONG IN PASSING

Where am I now? And what
Am I to say portends?
Death is but death, and not
The most obtuse of ends.

No matter how one leans
One yet fears not to know.
God knows what all this means!
The mortal mind is slow.

Eternity is here.
There is no other place.
The only thing I fear
Is the Almighty Face.

ROBERT FRANCIS (1901–   )

For much of his life Francis has lived alone in a woodland cabin near Amherst, Mass. As a poet he has worked, like all New England poets of his generation, under the shadow of Robert Frost; yet in tone and movement his poems are his own, written from an inner strength of compassion that Frost frequently lacked.

Stand with Me Here. Macmillan, 1936.
Valhalla and Other Poems. Macmillan, 1938.
The Sound I Listened For. Macmillan, 1944.
The Orb Weaver. Wesleyan University Press, 1960.
Come Out into the Sun. University of Massachusetts Press, 1965.

BY NIGHT

After midnight I heard a scream.
I was awake. It was no dream.
But whether it was bird of prey
Or prey of bird I could not say.
I never heard that sound by day.

FALL

Leave the bars lying in the grass.
Let all wanderers freely pass
Into the pasture now.

Gone are the fawn-shy heifers, gone
The little calf almost a fawn,
And the black two-year cow.

Leave the bars lying where they are.
Let each black-triangled birch bar
Be white and triple warning:

One for all tender things that go,
One for the near and ultimate snow,
One for frost by morning.

In that first snow a frightened deer,
Swifter than snowfall, swift as fear,
May pass here flying, flying.

What if no fence could foil his speed?
Spare him the leap, spare him one need
Of leaping. Leave the bars lying.

JUNIPER

From where I live, from windows on four sides
I see four common kinds of evergreen:
White pine, pitch pine, cedar, and juniper.
The last is less than tree. It hugs the ground.
It would be last for any wind to break
If wind could break the others. Pines would go first
As some of them have gone, and cedars next,
Though where is wind to blow a cedar down?
To overthrow a juniper a wind
Would have to blow the ground away beneath it.

Not wind but fire. I heard a farmer say
One lighted match dropped on a juniper
Would do the trick. And he had done the trick.
I try to picture how it would look: thin snow
Over the pasture and dark junipers
Over the snow and darker for the snow,
Each juniper swirl-shaped like flame itself.
Then from the slow green fire the swift hot fire
Flares, sputters with resin, roars, dies
While the next juniper goes next.

                              Poets
Are rich in points of view if they are rich
In anything. The farmer thinks one thing;
The poet can afford to think all things
Including what the farmer thinks, thinking

Around the farmer rather than above him,
Loving the evergreen the farmer hates,
And yet not hating him for hating it.

I know another fire in juniper,
Have felt its heat burn on my back, have breathed
Its invisible smoke, climbing New England hills
In summer. Have known the concentrated sun
Of hard blue berries, chewed them, and spit them out,
Their juice burning my throat. Juniper.

Its colors are the metals: tarnished bronze
And copper, violet of tarnished silver,
And if you turn it, white aluminum.
So many colors in so dull a green
And I so many years before I saw them.

I see those colors now, and far, far more
Than color. I see all that we have in common
Here where we live together on this hill.
And what I hope for is for more in common.

Here is my faith, my vision, my burning bush.
It will burn on and never be consumed.
It will be here long after I have gone,
Long after the last farmer sleeps. And since
I speak for it, its silence speaks for me.

FAIR AND UNFAIR

The beautiful is fair, the just is fair.
Yet one is commonplace and one is rare,
One everywhere, one scarcely anywhere.

So fair unfair a world. Had we the wit
To use the surplus for the deficit,
We'd make a fairer fairer world of it.

KENNETH FEARING (1902–1961)

Born in Oak Park, Ill., Fearing became in the thirties one of the most exuberant of the "proletarian poets," putting his radical criticism of society into rambling, witty, decidedly nonacademic poems. Only a few retain their vividness, but these few are among the best of their kind produced in America. Later Fearing wrote many novels, some pseudonymously, including several contributions to the hard-boiled school of crime fiction.

New and Selected Poems. Indiana University Press, 1956.

GREEN LIGHT

Bought at the drug store, very cheap; and later pawned.
After a while, heard on the street; seen in the park.
Familiar, but not quite recognized.
Followed and taken home and slept with.
Traded or sold. Or lost.

Bought again at the corner drug store,
At the green light, at the patient's demand, at nine o'clock.
Re-read and memorized and re-wound.
Found unsuitable.
Smashed, put together, and pawned.

Heard on the street, seen in a dream, heard in the park,
    seen by the light of day;
Carefully observed one night by a secret agent of the
    Greek Hydraulic Mining Commission, in plain clothes,
    off duty.
The agent, in broken English, took copious notes. Which
    he lost.
Strange, and yet not extraordinary.
Sad, but true.

True, or exaggerated, or true;
As it is true that the people laugh and the sparrows fly;

As it is exaggerated that the people change, and the sea
    stays;
As it is that the people go;
As the lights go on and it is night and it is serious, and just
    the same;
As some one dies and it is serious, and the same;
As a girl knows and it is small, and true;
As the corner hardware clerk might know and it is true,
    and pointless;
As an old man knows and it is grotesque, but true;
As the people laugh, as the people think, as the people
    change,
It is serious and the same, exaggerated or true.

Bought at the drug store down the street
Where the wind blows and the motors go by and it is
    always night, or day;
Bought to use as a last resort,
Bought to impress the statuary in the park.
Bought at a cut rate, at the green light, at nine o'clock.
Borrowed or bought. To look well. To ennoble. To prevent
    disease. To entertain. To have.
Broken or sold. Or given away. Or used and forgotten. Or
    lost.

OBITUARY

Take him away, he's as dead as they die,
Hear that ambulance bell, his eyes are staring straight at
    death;
Look at the fingers growing stiff, touch the face already
    cold, see the stars in the sky, look at the stains on the
    street,

Look at the ten-ton truck that came rolling along fast and
    stretched him out cold,

Then turn out his pockets and make the crowd move on.
Sergeant, what was his name? What's the driver's name?
    What's your name, sergeant?
Go through his clothes,

Take out the cigars, the money, the papers, the keys,
take everything there is,

And give a dollar and a half to the Standard Oil. It was
his true-blue friend.
Give the key of his flat to the D.A.R. They were friends
of his, the best a man ever had.
Take out the pawnticket, wrap it, seal it, send it along to
the People's Gas. They were life-long pals. It was more
than his brother. They were just like twins.

Give away the shoes,
Give his derby away. Donate his socks to the Guggenheim
fund,
Let the Morgans hold the priceless bills, and leaflets, and
racing tips under lock and key,
And give Mr. Hoover the pint of gin,
Because they're all good men. And they were friends of his.

Don't forget Gene Tunney. Don't forget Will Hays. Don't
forget Al Capone. Don't forget the I.R.T.
Give them his matches to remember him by.
They lived with him, in the same old world. And they're
good men, too.

That's all, sergeant. There's nothing else, lieutenant.
There's no more, captain.
Pick up the body, feed it, shave it, find it another job.

Have a cigar, driver?
Take two cigars—
You were his true-blue pal.

LANGSTON HUGHES (1902–1967)

Born in Joplin, Mo., Hughes settled, after a period of wandering, in Harlem. There he tried to create, by combining the forms of white poetry with elements of black sensibility and idiom, a folk poetry of the modern urban Negro, in much the way that Billie Holliday, Roy Eldridge, and other musicians of the thirties were creating an urban folk music from the crass materials of Tin Pan Alley. If, owing to music's greater amenability, he succeeded less well than his friends in jazz, he nevertheless accomplished, in his many books of poetry, fiction, drama, essays, autobiography, and journalism, more than other black writers of his generation, and exerted considerable influence on the coming generation.

The Langston Hughes Reader. Braziller, 1958.
Selected Poems. Knopf, 1959.

EPILOGUE

I, too, sing America.

I am the darker brother.
They send me to eat in the kitchen
When company comes,
But I laugh,
And eat well,
And grow strong.

Tomorrow,
I'll sit at the table
When company comes.
Nobody'll dare
Say to me,
"Eat in the kitchen,"
Then.

Besides,
They'll see how beautiful I am
And be ashamed,—

I, too, am America.

TODAY

This is earthquake
 Weather!
Honor and Hunger
 Walk lean
 Together.

NEGRO SERVANT

All day subdued, polite,
Kind, thoughtful to the faces that are white.
 O, tribal dance!
 O, drums!
 O, veldt at night!
Forgotten watch-fires on a hill somewhere!
 O, songs that do not care!
At six o'clock, or seven, or eight,
 You're through.
 You've worked all day.
 Dark Harlem waits for you.
 The bus, the sub—
 Pay-nights a taxi
 Through the park.
O, drums of life in Harlem after dark!
 O, dreams!
 O, songs!
 O, saxophones at night!
O, sweet relief from faces that are white!

COUNTEE CULLEN (1903–1946)

In his generation of black poets, Cullen stayed closer than most to the conventions of English literature, in a conscious attempt to transcend his role as the poet of a people and become a poet pure and simple. In addition to his poetry he wrote fiction and children's stories, and he edited an important early anthology of Negro verse, *Caroling Dusk* (1927). He was a native of Harlem and lived in New York City all his life, where he worked as a teacher in the public schools.

On These I Stand. (Selected poems.) Harper, 1947.

INCIDENT

Once riding in old Baltimore,
   Heart-filled, head-filled with glee,
I saw a Baltimorean
   Keep looking straight at me.

Now I was eight and very small,
   And he was no whit bigger,
And so I smiled, but he poked out
   His tongue, and called me, "Nigger."

I saw the whole of Baltimore
   From May until December;
Of all the things that happened there
   That's all that I remember.

FOR MY GRANDMOTHER

This lovely flower fell to seed;
   Work gently, sun and rain;
She held it as her dying creed
   That she would grow again.

BLACK MAJESTY

These men were kings, albeit they were black,
Christophe and Dessalines and L'Ouverture;
Their majesty has made me turn my back
Upon a plaint I once shaped to endure.
These men were black, I say, but they were crowned
And purple-clad, however brief their time.
Stifle your agony; let grief be drowned;
We know joy had a day once and a clime.

Dark gutter-snipe, black sprawler-in-the-mud,
A thing men did a man may do again.
What answer filters through your sluggish blood
To these dark ghosts who knew so bright a reign?
"Lo, I am dark, but comely," Sheba sings.
"And we were black," three shades reply, "but kings."

ONLY THE POLISHED SKELETON

The heart has need of some deceit
    To make its pistons rise and fall;
For less than this it would not beat,
    Nor flush the sluggish vein at all.

With subterfuge and fraud the mind
    Must fend and parry thrust for thrust,
With logic brutal and unkind
    Beat off the onslaughts of the dust.

Only the polished skeleton,
    Of flesh relieved and pauperized,
Can rest at ease and think upon
    The worth of all it so despised.

LORINE NIEDECKER (1903–)

Although she has been writing for more than three decades, generally in a mode associated with the objectivist poets of the thirties, Miss Niedecker has published little until recently. Many of her poems reflect her childhood in the Wisconsin river country, where her father was a carp seiner. She lives today in Milwaukee.

New Goose. Prairie City, Ill.: J. A. Decker, 1946.
My Friend Tree. Edinburgh: Wild Hawthorn Press, 1962.
T & G. Highlands, N.C.: Jonathan Williams, 1968.
North Central. London: Fulcrum Press, 1968.

SEVEN POEMS

1

As praiseworthy

the power of breathing (Epictetus)
while we sleep. Add:
to move the parts of the body
without sound

and to float
on a smooth green stream
in a silent boat

2

My mother saw the green tree toad
on the window sill
her first one
since she was young.
We saw it breathe

and swell up round.
My youth is no sure sign

I'll find this kind of thing
tho it does sing.
Let's take it in

I said so grandmother can see
but she could not
it changed to brown
and town
changed us, too.

3

For best work
you ought to put forth
        some effort
        to stand
in north woods
among birch

4

Young in Fall I said: the birds
are at their highest thoughts
of leaving

Middle life said nothing—
grounded
to a livelihood

Old age—a high gabbling gathering
before goodbye
of all we know

5

Smile
    to see the lake
        lay
    the still sky

And
    out for an easy
        make
    the dragonfly

6

Old man who seined
to educate his daughter
sees red Mars rise:
      What lies
behind it?

Cold water business
now starred in Fishes
of dipnet shape
      to ache
thru his arms.

7

You are my friend—
you bring me peaches
and the high bush cranberry
      you carry
my fishpole

you water my worms
you patch my boot
with your mending kit
      nothing in it
but my hand

RICHARD EBERHART (1904–   )

In his varied life Eberhart has been a tutor in the household of the king of Siam and the vice-president of a wax company; but chiefly a poet and teacher, one of the most prominent of the group which came to notice in the years before World War II. Until his recent retirement, he was poet in residence at Dartmouth College.

> Collected Poems, 1930–1960. Oxford University Press, 1960.
> Collected Verse Plays. University of North Carolina Press, 1962.
> Selected Poems, 1930–1965. New Directions, 1965.

"I WALKED OVER THE GRAVE OF HENRY JAMES"

I walked over the grave of Henry James
But recently, and one eye kept the dry stone.
The other leaned on boys at games away,
My soul was balanced in my body cold.

I am one of those prodigals of hell
Whom ten years have seen cram with battle;
Returns to what he canted from, grants it good,
As asthma makes itself a new resolution.

I crushed a knob of earth between my fingers,
This is a very ordinary experience.
A name may be glorious but death is death,
I thought, and took a street-car back to Harvard Square.

THE FURY OF AERIAL BOMBARDMENT

You would think the fury of aerial bombardment
Would rouse God to relent; the infinite spaces
Are still silent. He looks on shock-pried faces.
History, even, does not know what is meant.

You would feel that after so many centuries
God would give man to repent; yet he can kill
As Cain could, but with multitudinous will,
No farther advanced than in his ancient furies.

Was man made stupid to see his own stupidity?
Is God by definition indifferent, beyond us all?
Is the eternal truth man's fighting soul
Wherein the Beast ravens in its own avidity?

Of Van Wettering I speak, and Averill,
Names on a list, whose faces I do not recall
But they are gone to early death, who late in school
Distinguished the belt feed lever from the belt holding
   pawl.

FLUX

The old Penobscot Indian
Sells me a pair of moccasins
That stain my feet yellow.

The gods of this world
Have taken the daughter of my neighbor,
Who died this day of encephalitis.

The absentee landlord has taken over Tree Island
Where one now hesitates to go for picnics,
Off the wide beach to see Fiddle Head.

The fogs are as unpredictable as the winds.
The next generation comes surely on,
Their nonchalance baffles my intelligence.

Some are gone for folly, some by mischance,
Cruelty broods over the inexpressible,
The inexorable is ever believable.

The boy, in his first hour on his motorbike,
Met death in a head-on collision.
His dog stood silent by the young corpse.

Last week, the sea farmer off Stonington
Was tripped in the wake of a cruiser.
He went down in the cold waters of the summer.

Life is stranger than any of us expected,
There is a somber, imponderable fate.
Enigma rules, and the heart has no certainty.

LOUIS ZUKOFSKY (1904–   )

Although the scope and depth of his writing cannot be doubted, nor its integrity, originality, and in some passages sheer verbal fascination, Zukofsky has worked during most of his life in relative obscurity, a name—but scarcely more—associated with Pound, Williams, and Eliot. Born on Manhattan's Lower East Side, he has lived in New York nearly all his life, and has taught at Queens University and Brooklyn Polytechnic Institute. In the thirties he was a leader of the objectivists, and edited an anthology and an objectivist number of *Poetry*, both of which are now famous though difficult to find. In 1927 he began his still uncompleted long poem, entitled simply "A", which will have twenty-four sections when finished; twelve have been published in book form and seven more in magazines. Many elements unite in the substance of Zukofsky's poetry: music, science, the simplicities of common experience, a deeply felt commitment to family life. At the same time his warmly constructive criticism, particularly with respect to Shakespeare, has won an increasing audience. Indeed, thanks to recent efforts by younger poets, the importance of Zukofsky's work as a whole is now recognized, and most of it, but not all, is in print again.

ALL the Collected Short Poems, 1923–1958. Norton, 1965.
ALL the Collected Short Poems, 1956–1964. Norton, 1966.
"A" 1–12. Doubleday, 1967.
Bottom: on Shakespeare. University of Texas Ark Press, 1963.
Prepositions: The Collected Critical Essays. London: Rapp & Carroll, 1967.
An "Objectivists'" Anthology. Ed. Louis Zukofsky. Dijon, France: [Objectivist Press], 1932.

"CARS ONCE STEEL AND GREEN, NOW OLD"

Cars once steel and green, now old,
Find their grave at Cedar Manor.
They rust in a wind
The sky alone can hold.

For the wind
Flows heavily thru the mind like cold,
Drums in the ears
Till one knows its being which soon is not.

"IT'S HARD TO SEE BUT THINK OF A SEA"

It's hard to see but think of a sea
Condensed into a speck.
And there are waves—
Frequencies of light,
Others that may be heard.
The one is one sea, the other a second.
There are electric stresses across condensers
That wear them down till they can stand no strain,
Are of no force and as unreclaimed
      as the bottom of the sea
Unless the space the stresses cross be air,
      that can be patched.
Large and small condensers,
Passing in the one instance frequencies
      that can be turned to sound,
In the other, alternations that escape,
So many waves of a speck of sea or what,
Or a graph the curve of a wave beyond all sound,
An open circuit where no action—
Like that of the retina made human by light—
Is recorded otherwise
Than having taken a desired path a little way
And tho infinitely a mote to be uncontained for
      ever.
This science is then like gathering flowers of the
      weed
One who works with me calls birdseed
That are tiny and many on one stem
They shed to the touch tho on a par
      with the large flower
That picked will find a vase.
I see many things at one time
      the harder the concepts get,
Or nothing
Which is a forever become me over forty years.

I am like another, and another, who has
        finished learning
And has just begun to learn.
If I turn pages back
A child may as well be staring with me
Wondering at the meaning
I turn to last
Perhaps.

"I WALK IN THE OLD STREET"

I walk in the old street
to hear the beloved songs
afresh
this spring night.

Like the leaves—my loves wake—
not to be the same
or look tireless to the stars
and a ripped doorbell.

"THE LINES OF THIS NEW SONG ARE NOTHING"

The lines of this new song are nothing
But a tune making the nothing full
Stonelike become more hard than silent
The tune's image holding in the line.

"THE GREEN LEAF THAT WILL OUTLAST THE WINTER"

The green leaf that will outlast the winter
    because sheltered in the open:
the wall, transverse, and diagonal ribs
    of the privet that pocket air
        around the leaf inside them
    and cover but with walls of wind:
it happens wind colors like glass shelter,
        as the light's aire from a vault
        which has a knob of sun.

NON TI FIDAR

in opera poetry must be the obedient daughter of music
Mozart

The hand a shade of moonlight on the pillow
And that a shadowed white would seem above or below
Their heads ear to ear, hearing water
Not like the word, the flickflack of the eye opening on it
With what happiness
Where the word is the obedient daughter of music
And Don Giovanni's shapely seat and heart live in hell
Lovable as its fire
As all loves that breathe and kiss
Simply by life
Rocking to sleep and flame:
So frail is judgment
It must light up, an overseer
With some truckling in hell,
A song that lovers' heads
Ear to, and on ear foretell.

READING AND TALKING

Cauliflower-eared Spartan
Who go about
Your cestus bound to the hand
What are you hiding
The cestus girdle
Of Aphrodite
That sends love on the wind
Has not lifted?
What is the hurdle—
That you rule the world
By such wisdom?

And Plato said, not
Much better
Than a few things:
'Nor when love
Is disinterested
Is there any disgrace
In being deceived.

All creation into being
Is poetry or making.
But that
Made with music
Is named poetry
The same holds
Of love, only desire
Of good
Is the fire and light
Power of love.

They drawn towards
Love by the path of money-making,
Gymnastics, or philosophy,
Are not named lovers.
The simple truth is
That men love the good.

Would you like
The truth about love
In any order
That comes
Into my mind
At the time?"

Make music, Socrates,
The dream bids
Like the runner
Bid by eyes that see:
To run as he is
Already running

And Plato forgot to keep still
Building
A so-called good-for-all
With a cestus.

But I take it
          Too
He said—
Talk is a form of love
Let us talk.

The voice that first startled
        bodies
After they fail continues
To startle minds with abstractions
That hearts may pound again—
To a grammar
Aping a carved throw stick
Reindeer horn,
Tusks,
Lines, graves of lions,
The blood of old cave drawing

With new artifacts
Startling
A modern cave

            (Present?)

As a coda begins—
        Simple—

That year's
poem
will be
better

if tears
show him
to the
letter.

FROM "A"

4

    Giant sparkler,
    Lights of the river,

    (Horses turning)
    Tide,

    And pier lights
    Under a light of the hill,

A lamp on the leaf-green
Lampost seen by the light

Of a truck (a song)
Lanterns swing behind horses,

Their sides gleam
From levels of water—

Wherever we put our hats is our home
Our aged heads are our homes,
Eyes wink to their own phosphorescence,
No feast of Lights of Venice or The Last Supper light
Our beards' familiars; His
Stars of Deuteronomy are with us,
Always with us,
We had a speech, our children have
                              evolved a jargon.

We pray, Open, God, Gate of Psalmody,
That our Psalms may reach but
One shadow of Your light,
That you may see a minute over our waywardness.
Day You granted to Your seed, its promise, Its
                              Promise,
Do not turn away Your sun.
Let us rest, here,
        lightened
Of our tongues, hands, feet, eyes, ears and hearts.

        Fierce Ark!
        Gold lion stomach
        (Red hair in intaglio)
Dead loved stones of our Temple walls,
Ripped up pebble-stones of our tessellation,
Split cedar chest harboring our Law,
Even the Death has gone out of us—we are void.

        Hear—
    He calleth for Elias—
        A clavicembalo!

Deafen us, God, deafen us to their music,
Our own children have passed over to the ostracized,

They assail us—
'Religious, snarling monsters'—
And have mouthed a jargon:
"Rain blows, light, on quiet water
    I watch the rings spread and travel
Shimaunu-Sān, Samurai,
    When will you come home?—
        Shimaunu-Sān, my clear star.

To-day I gather all red flowers,
    Shed their petals on the paths,
Shimaunu-Sān, in the dawn,
    Red I go to meet him—
        Shimaunu-Sān, my clear star.

To-morrow I tear cherry sprays,
    Wreathe them in my hair and at my temples,
Shimaunu-Sān will see my head's white blossoms,
    In the dark run towards me
        Shimaunu-Sān, my clear star.

All turtle-doves have pledged
    To fly and search him:
Shimaunu-Sān, at my little windows
    Each night a tiny candle will be lighted—
        Shimaunu-Sān, my clear star."

—*Yehoash.*
        Song's kinship,
        The roots we strike.

        "Heavier from day to day
        Grow my limbs with sap of forests"

        "Deep roots hammer lower"

        "And to the Sun, I bow.
        On the gray mountains,
        Where multiply
        The stairs of crags, my prayer
        Will follow you, still Heir—
        Bestower—
        Of man and tree and sand,

256

When your face upon the land
Flames in last redness, allow me of your light—"

My father's precursors
Set masts in dinghies, chanted the Speech.

"Wider is the ash around the fire"
"Treasures turned to sand"

Yehoash,—
The courses we tide from.

Tree of the Bach family
Compiled by Sebastian himself.
'   Veit Bach, a miller in Wechmar,
Delighted most in his lute
Which he brought to the mill
And played while it was grinding.
A pretty noise the pair must have made,
Teaching him to keep time.
But, apparently, that is how
Music first came into our familyl'

A carousel—Flour runs.
Song drifts from the noises.

"My petted birds are dead."

"I will gather a chain
Of marguerites, pluck red anemone,
Till of every hostile see
Never a memory remain."

11

for Celia and Paul

River that must turn full after I stop dying
Song, my song, raise grief to music
Light as my loves' thought, the few sick
So sick of wrangling: thus weeping.
Sounds of light, stay in her keeping
And my son's face—this much for honor.

257

Freed by their praises who make honor dearer
Whose losses show them rich and you no poorer
Take care, song, that what stars' imprint you mirror
Grazes their tears; draw speech from their nature or
Love in you—faced to your outer stars—purer
Gold than tongues make without feeling
Art new, hurt old: revealing
The slackened bow as the stinging
Animal dies, thread gold stringing
The fingerboard pressed in my honor.

Honor, song, sang the blest is delight knowing
We overcome ills by love. Hurt, song, nourish
Eyes, think most of whom you hurt. For the flowing
River's poison where what rod blossoms. Flourish
By love's sweet lights and sing *in them I flourish.*
No, song, not any one power
May recall or forget, our
Love to see your love flows into
Us. If Venus lights, your words spin, to
Live our desires lead us to honor.

Graced, your heart in nothing less than in death, go—
I, dust—raise the great hem of the extended
World that nothing can leave; having had breath go
Face my son, say: 'If your father offended
You with mute wisdom, my words have not ended
His second paradise where
His love was in her eyes where
They turn, quick for you two—sick
Or gone cannot make music
You set less than all. Honor

His voice in me, the river's turn that finds the
Grace in you, four notes first too full for talk, leaf
Lighting stem, stems bound to the branch that binds the
Tree, and then as from the same root we talk, leaf
After leaf of your mind's music, page, walk leaf
Over leaf of his thought, sounding
His happiness: song sounding
The grace that comes from knowing
Things, her love our own showing
Her love in all her honor.'

STANLEY KUNITZ (1905–   )

Stanley Kunitz was educated at Harvard, where he received the Garrison Medal for Poetry. His first book of poems, *Intellectual Things*, appeared before he was twenty-five. Following military service in World War II, he taught at Bennington and the New School, and subsequently, as a visiting teacher of poetry, at the University of Washington, Queens College and Brandeis. He is currently associated with the graduate writing program at Columbia, and with Yale University as editor of the Yale Series of Younger Poets. His numerous awards and prizes include the Pulitzer Prize in 1959 for his *Selected Poems*.

> *Intellectual Things*. Doubleday, Doran, 1930.
> *Passport to the War*. Holt, 1944.
> *Selected Poems, 1928–1958*. Atlantic-Little, Brown, 1958.

BENEDICTION

God banish from your house
The fly, the roach, the mouse

That riots in the walls
Until the plaster falls;

Admonish from your door
The hypocrite and liar;

No shy, soft, tigrish fear
Permit upon your stair,

Nor agents of your doubt.
God drive them whistling out.

Let nothing touched with evil,
Let nothing that can shrivel

Heart's tenderest frond, intrude
Upon your still, deep blood.

Against the drip of night
God keep all windows tight,

Protect your mirrors from
Surprise, delirium,

Admit no trailing wind
Into your shuttered mind

To plume the lake of sleep
With dreams. If you must weep

God give you tears, but leave
You secrecy to grieve,

And islands for your pride,
And love to nest in your side.

God grant that, to the bone,
Yourself may be your own;

God grant that I may be
(My sweet) sweet company.

SHE WEPT, SHE RAILED

She wept, she railed, she spurned the meat
Men toss into a muslin cage
To make their spineless doxy bleat
For pleasure and for patronage,
As if she had no choice but eat
The lewd bait of a squalid age.

That moment when the lights go out
The years shape to the sprawling thing,
A marmoset with bloodied clout,
A pampered flank that learns to sing,
Without the grace, she cried, to doubt
The postures of the underling.

I thought of Judith in her tent,
Of Helen by the crackling wall,
Of Cressida, her bone-lust spent,
Of Catherine on the holy wheel:
I heard their woman-dust lament
The golden wound that does not heal.

What a wild air her small joints beat!
I only poured the raging wine
Until our bodies filled with light,
Mine with hers and hers with mine,
And we went out into the night
Where all the constellations shine.

THE THIEF

In a Roman tram, where the famous Roman mob,
Wrung from the bowels of the hippodrome,
Mauled into shape its many-elbowed god
To fight for exit through its civil wars,
Somebody Roman picked my pocket clean.
A pagan and a Christian curse on him!
Somebody Roman, may he find tonight
In the street of the serpents or the lion's mouth,
Strewn on a wine-soaked board,
More than he reached for, more than cash,
Green trumpeters, for whom the legions march
Through solid stone. (Meanwhile the Carthaginians
Play redskins in the ambush of the sea
To whom must be meted out the standard destruction:
It is a heavy responsibility.)

                        Let the *ladrone* sneer
As the leathered fold yields him my haunt of years,
The papers of a life I wanted lost,
Memos, addresses, the snapshot of a child,
To plague him through his alley nights until
He begs for mercy for the thing well-robbed.
Worlds in my pocket older than his own,
May they erupt on him like hissing gold,
Tooth of the pythoness, chimaera's scales,
Stones of the temple and Isaiah's beard—
Toss him, sweet furies, from Tarpeia's Rock!

More even than my purse,
And that's no laughing matter, it is my pride
That has been hurt: a fine Italian hand,
With its mimosa touch, has made me feel
Blind-skinned, indelicate, a fool Americano

Touring a culture like a grand museum,
People and statues interchangeable shows,
Perception blunted as one's syntax fails.
Why am I here? Some thirty years ago
A set of lantern slides I saw at school
Of these antiquities gave me an image
Of the rare serene that brimmed my eyes,
For nothing pleased me then in my legacy;
But the past that tempted me, the frozen pure,
Was a pedagogic lie. All's motion here,
And motion like emotion is impure,
A flower flawed by mutability,
Religion by its ruins, and yet thereby
More lovely and more graced, perhaps
More true. Still, still, the chariot wheels
Turn, the assassin motorcyclists charge,
Wolves prowl in the streets under arcades of bells,
Tiberius grovels through his dungeon halls
Dreaming of boy-sized fishes in his bath;
Behind the balcony of the Cardinal's palace,
Smelling the laureled Mamertine blood,
A baldpate awaits his rhetorical cue,
And the clouds drift
Through a triumph of broken columns.

Pick-pocket, pick-thank music plucks the strings
For the rag-madonna with perdurable babe
Most dolorously hallowing the square
Where Caesar walks three steps to meet Bernini,
Whose sumptuous art runs wild
From gate to gate, pausing in tiptoe-joy
Only to light a torch of fountains, to set
His tritons dancing, or at a blest façade
To cast up from his wrist a flight of angels,
Volute on volute, wing on climbing wing.
In the middle of my life I heard the waters playing.

Mater Cloaca, feast thee well, I pray,
On what has been subtracted from my fate—
Ten days of lectures, thirty days abroad:
In this excess that's Rome I'll not mope long,
Wearing my heart less Roman than baroque,
Though damn it all! I wish I'd lived in style,

Jogged in *carrozze* round and round the town,
Guzzled Spumante by the bucketful,
Bought wagons of daffodils to please my dear.
Now that I face the moment and the loss,
Driven to language on the Ides of March
Here in my blistered room
Where the wind flaps my ceiling like a sail
(A miracle, no doubt, to be left at that!)
I recognize the gods' capricious hand
And write this poem for money, rage, and love.

FOR THE WORD IS FLESH

O ruined father dead, long sweetly rotten
Under the dial, the time-dissolving urn,
Beware a second perishing, forgotten,
Heap fallen leaves of memory to burn
On the slippery rock, the black eroding heart,
Before the wedged frost splits it clean apart.

The nude hand drops no sacramentàl flower
Of blood among the tough upthrusting weeds.
Senior, in this commemorative hour,
What shall the quick commemorate, what deeds
Ephemeral, what dazzling words that flare
Like rockets from the mouth to burst in air?

Of hypochondriacs that gnawed their seasons
In search of proofs, Lessius found twenty-two
Fine arguments, Tolet gave sixty reasons
Why souls survive. And what are they to you?
And, father, what to me, who cannot blur
The mirrored brain with fantasies of Er,

Remembering such factual spikes as pierce
The supplicating palms, and by the sea,
Remembering the eyes, I hear the fierce
Wild cry of Jesus on the holy tree,
Yet have of you no syllable to keep,
Only the deep rock crumbling in the deep.

Observe the wisdom of the Florentine
Who, feeling death upon him, scribbled fast
To make revision of a deathbed scene,
Gloating that he was accurate at last.
Let sons learn from their lipless fathers how
Man enters hell without a golden bough.

END OF SUMMER

An agitation of the air,
A perturbation of the light
Admonished me the unloved year
Would turn on its hinge that night.

I stood in the disenchanted field
Amid the stubble and the stones,
Amazed, while a small worm lisped to me
The song of my marrow-bones.

Blue poured into summer blue,
A hawk broke from his cloudless tower,
The roof of the silo blazed, and I knew
That part of my life was over.

Already the iron door of the north
Clangs open: birds, leaves, snows
Order their populations forth,
And a cruel wind blows.

HE

He runs before the wise men: he
Is moving on the hills like snow.
No gifts, no tears, no company
He brings, but wind-rise and water-flow.

In meadows of descended day
His motion leans, dividing air:
He takes the unforgiving way
Beneath the apostolic star.

She who has known him calls him stranger.
Parting the night's long hair, he steals
Within the heart, that humble manger
Where the white, astonished spirit kneels.

His vertical inflicting pride,
Whose shadow cuts the nib of space,
Bends to this virtue fructified.
But though he kiss the little face

Like rapture breaking on the mind,
The necessary fierce details
Implacably he has designed.
Redemption hangs upon the nails.

WELCOME THE WRATH

Poor john, who joined in make of wrong
And guessed no guile, dare I complain?—
Or practice to endure the heart unstrung,
The waiting at the door too long,
Winter, wages, and self-disdain.

Endure? That is the dialect of love,
The greenhorn of the west, my late companion,
Now straggling crossfoot half-alive
Back to his country, with crazy sleeve
Flopping, like a shot pinion.

Let him endure. I'll not: not warp my vision
To square with odds; not scrape; not scamp my fiber,
Though pushed by spoilers of the nerves' precision,
Bothered by caterpillars of suspicion,
Hired by speculators in my gut and labor.

Wrath has come down from the hills to enlist
Me surely in his brindled generation,
The race of the tiger; come down at last
Has wrath to build a bonfire of my breast
With one wet match and all man's desolation.

VITA NUOVA

I abdicate my daily self that bled,
As others breathe, for porridge it might sup.
Henceforth apocalypse will get my bread
For me. I bit my tongue and gnawed my lip,
But now the visor of my name is up.

Giving to love my undivided nature,
Cherishing life, the only fire to keep,
I have been otherwise a part-time creature,
With many selves to fool myself with hope,
And in myself a gentler self to weep.

Now I will peel that vision from my brain
Of numbers wrangling in a common place,
And I will go, unburdened, on the quiet lane
Of my eternal kind, till shadowless
With inner light I wear my father's face.

Moon of the soul, accompany me now,
Shine on the colosseums of my sense,
Be in the tabernacles of my brow.
My dark will make, reflecting from your stones,
The single beam of all my life intense.

A CHOICE OF WEAPONS

Reviewing me without undue elation
A critic who has earned his reputation
By being always Johnny-on-the-spot
Where each contemporary starts to rot
Conceded me integrity and style
And stamina to walk a measured mile,
But wondered why a gang of personal devils
Need clank their jigging bones as public evils:

"The times are suited for the gay empiric,
The witty ironist, the casual lyric;
Apparently it's gristle-fare, not fat,
At certain tables: must we weep at that?
Though poets seem to rail at bourgeois ills

266

It is their lack of audience that kills.
Their metaphysics but reflects a folly:
'Read me or I'll be damned and melancholy.'
This poet suffers: that's his right, of course,
But we don't have to watch him beat his horse."

Sir, if appreciation be my lack,
You may appreciate me, front and back—
I won't deny that vaguely vulgar need:
But do not pity those whose motives bleed
Even while strolling in a formal garden.
Observe that tears are bullets when they harden;
The triggered poem's no water-pistol toy,
But shoots its cause, and is a source of joy.

KENNETH REXROTH (1905–)

Born in Indiana, mostly self-educated, Rexroth has been a painter, radio and television performer, editor, journalist, and librettist, as well as a poet. For many years he has lived in San Francisco, and has written extensively about the California mountains, especially the High Sierras; some of his mountain poems are among the best nature writing we have. In addition Rexroth has done translations from six languages, and has written three volumes of critical essays. His generous attitude toward younger poets, especially the Black Mountain poets and the Beats, has contributed largely toward making San Francisco a center of poetic activity in the past fifteen years.

The Collected Shorter Poems. New Directions, 1966.
The Collected Longer Poems. New Directions, 1968.
Beyond the Mountains. (Four plays.) San Francisco: City Lights Books, 1966.
100 Poems from the Chinese. New Directions, 1956.
100 Poems from the Japanese. New Directions, 1959.
Thirty Spanish Poems of Love and Exile. San Francisco: City Lights Books, n.d.

STRENGTH THROUGH JOY

Coming back over the col between
Isosceles Mountain and North Palisade,
I stop at the summit and look back
At the storm gathering over the white peaks
Of the Whitney group and the colored
Kaweahs. September, nineteen-thirty-nine.
This is the last trip in the mountains
This autumn, possibly the last trip ever.
The storm clouds rise up the mountainside,
Lightning batters the pinnacles above me,
The clouds beneath the pass are purple
And I see rising through them from the valleys
And cities a cold, murderous flood,
Spreading over the world, lapping at the last

Inviolate heights; mud streaked yellow
With gas, slimy and blotched with crimson.
Filled with broken bits of steel and flesh,
Moving slowly with the blind motion
Of lice, spreading inexorably
As bacteria spread in tissues,
Swirling with the precise rapacity of starved rats.
I loiter here like a condemned man
Lingers over his last breakfast, his last smoke;
Thinking of those heroes of the war
Of human skill, foresight, endurance and will;
The disinterested bravery,
The ideal combat of peace: Bauer
Crawling all night around his icecave
On snowbound Kanchenjunga, Tilman
And Shipton skylarking on Nanda Devi,
Smythe seeing visions on Everest,
The mad children of the Eigerwand—
What holidays will they keep this year?
Gun emplacements blasted in the rock;
No place for graves, the dead covered with quicklime
Or left in the snow till the spring thaw;
Machine gun duels between white robed ski troops,
The last screaming schusses marked with blood.
Was it for this we spent the years perfecting
The craft of courage? Better the corpse
Of the foolhardy, frozen on the Eiger
Accessible only to the storm,
Standing sentry for the avalanche.

ANDRÉE REXROTH

Mt. Tamalpais

The years have gone. It is spring
Again. Mars and Saturn will
Soon come on, low in the West,
In the dusk. Now the evening
Sunlight makes hazy girders
Over Steep Ravine above
The waterfalls. The winter
Birds from Oregon, robins

And varied thrushes, feast on
Ripe toyon and madrone
Berries. The robins sing as
The dense light falls.
                              Your ashes
Were scattered in this place. Here
I wrote you a farewell poem,
And long ago another,
A poem of peace and love,
Of the lassitude of a long
Spring evening in youth. Now
It is almost ten years since
You came here to stay. Once more,
The pussy willows that come
After the New Year in this
Outlandish land are blooming.
There are deer and raccoon tracks
In the same places. A few
New sand bars and cobble beds
Have been left where erosion
Has gnawed deep into the hills.
The rounds of life are narrow.
War and peace have past like ghosts.
The human race sinks towards
Oblivion. A bittern
Calls from the same rushes where
You heard one on our first year
In the West; and where I heard
One again in the year
Of your death.

Kings River Canyon

My sorrow is so wide
I cannot see across it;
And so deep I shall never
Reach the bottom of it.
The moon sinks through deep haze,
As though the Kings River Canyon
Were filled with fine, warm, damp gauze.
Saturn gleams through the thick light
Like a gold, wet eye; nearby,
Antares glows faintly,

Without sparkle. Far overhead,
Stone shines darkly in the moonlight—
Lookout Point, where we lay
In another full moon, and first
Peered down into this canyon.
Here we camped, by still autumnal
Pools, all one warm October.
I baked you a bannock birthday cake.
Here you did your best paintings—
Innocent, wondering landscapes.
Very few of them are left
Anywhere. You destroyed them
In the terrible trouble
Of your long sickness. Eighteen years
Have passed since that autumn.
There was no trail here then.
Only a few people knew
How to enter this canyon.
We were all alone, twenty
Miles from anybody;
A young husband and wife,
Closed in and wrapped about
In the quiet autumn,
In the sound of quiet water,
In the turning and falling leaves,
In the wavering of innumerable
Bats from the caves, dipping
Over the odorous pools
Where the great trout drowsed in the evenings.

Eighteen years have been ground
To pieces in the wheels of life.
You are dead. With a thousand
Convicts they have blown a highway
Through Horseshoe Bend. Youth is gone,
That only came once. My hair
Is turning grey and my body
Heavier. I too move on to death.
I think of Henry King's stilted
But desolated *Exequy*,
Of Yuan Chen's great poem,
Unbearably pitiful;
Alone by the Spring river

More alone than I had ever
Imagined I would ever be,
I think of Frieda Lawrence,
Sitting alone in New Mexico,
In the long drought, listening
For the hiss of the milky Isar,
Over the cobbles, in a lost Spring.

TIME IS THE MERCY OF ETERNITY

Time is divided into
Seconds, minutes, hours, years,
And centuries. Take any
One of them and add up its
Content, all the world over.
One division contains much
The same as any other.
What can you say in a poem?
Past forty, you've said it all.
The dwarf black oak grows out of
The cliff below my feet. It
May be two hundred years old,
Yet its trunk is no bigger
Than my wrist, its crown does not
Come to my shoulder. The late
Afternoon sun behind it
Fills its leaves with light like
A gem tree, like the wishing
Tree of jewels in the Eastern
Stories. Below it the cliff
Falls sheer away five hundred
Feet to a single burnt pine,
And then another thousand
Feet to a river, noisy
In spate. Off beyond it stretches
Shimmering space, then fold on
Dimmer fold of wooded hills,
Then, hardly visible in
The pulsating heat, the flat
Lands of the San Joaquin Valley,
Boiling with life and trouble.

The pale new green leaves twinkle
In the rising air. A blue
Black, sharp-beaked, sharp-crested jay
Rests for a moment amongst
Them and then plunges off, down
Through the hazy June afternoon.
Far away the writhing city
Burns in a fire of transcendence
And commodities. The bowels
Of men are wrung between the poles
Of meaningless antithesis.
The holiness of the real
Is always there, accessible
In total immanence. The nodes
Of transcendence coagulate
In you, the experiencer,
And in the other, the lover.
When the first blooms come on the
Apple trees, and the spring moon
Swims in immeasurable
Clear deeps of palpable light,
I sit by the waterfall.
The owls call, one beyond the
Other, indefinitely
Away into the warm night.
The moist black rocks gleam faintly.
The curling moss smells of wet life.
The waterfall is a rope
Of music, a black and white
Spotted snake in the moonlit
Forest. The thighs of the goddess
Close me in. The moon lifts into
The cleft of the mountains and a
Cloud of light pours around me like
Blazing perfume. When the moon has
Passed on and the owls are loud in
My ears again, I kneel and drink
The cold, sweet, twisting water.

All day clouds drift up the canyon.
By noon the high peaks are hidden.
Thunder mutters in the distance.
Suddenly the canyon is gone.

My camp on its narrow ledge is
Isolated in swirling mist.
Even the nearby pines grow dim,
And recede into the grayness.
Yellow lightning bursts, like fire through
Smoke, and sets all the mist aglow.
Thunder explodes under my feet.
The rain pours hissing through the
Pine needles. White hailstones fall
Awry between the red pine trunks.
They rattle on my tent. I catch
Some and watch them melt in my hand.
As evening comes, birds ruffle
Their feathers, and fly gingerly
From branch to branch, and sing a few
Notes, while through the orange twilight
Fall green, widely spaced drops of rain.

For three days the clouds have piled up,
And rain has circled the mountains.
For a while it will fall over
Black Rock Pass, and then move across
To the red Kaweahs, and then
On to the white Whitney Range. But
Here by the lake it does not fall,
And the air grows more oppressive.
I swim lazily. Even the
Water seems to be heavier.
The air is full of mosquitoes.
After a listless lunch, I sit
On the bank reading the wise poems
Of Charles Cros. Suddenly the wind
Rises. The tent flaps noisily.
Twigs and dust and pine needles fly
In all directions. Then the wind
Drops and the rain falls on the lake.
The drops chime against the ripples
Like the Japanese glass wind bells
I loved so much as a child.
The rain is gone in an hour.
In the clear evening freshness,
I hear the bell on my donkey,
In his meadow, a mile away.

Nighthawks cry overhead and dive,
Thrumming their wings as they turn.
A deer comes down to the water.
The high passes are closed with snow.
I am the first person in this season.
No one comes by. I am alone
In the midst of a hundred mountains.

Five o'clock, mid-August evening,
The long sunlight is golden
On the deep green grass and bright
Red flowers of the meadow.
I stop where a meander
Of the brook forms a deep pool.
The water is greenish brown,
But perfectly transparent.
A small dense cloud of hundreds
Of midges, no bigger than
My head, hovers over it.
On the bank are two small frogs.
In the water are beetles,
Hydras, water bugs, larvae
Of several insects. On
The surface are water boatmen.
I realize that the color
Of the water itself is
Due to millions of active
Green flecks of life. It is like
Peering into an inkspot,
And finding yourself staring
Out into the Milky Way.
The deep reverberation
Of my identity with
All this plentitude of life
Leaves me shaken and giddy.
I step softly across the
Meadows as the deer lift their
Antlers and idly watch me.

Here on this high plateau where
No one ever comes, beside
This lake filled with mirrored mountains,
The hours and days and weeks

Go by without variation.
Even the rare storms pass over
And empty themselves on the peaks.
There are no fish in the water.
There are few deer or bear in the woods.
Only the bright blue damsel flies
On the reeds in the daytime,
And the nighthawks overhead
In the evening. Suspended
In absolutely transparent
Air and water and time, I
Take on a kind of crystalline
Being. In this translucent
Immense here and now, if ever,
The form of the person should be
Visible, its geometry,
Its crystallography, and
Its astronomy. The good
And evil of my history
Go by. I can see them and
Weigh them. They go first, with all
The other personal facts,
And sensations, and desires.
At last there is nothing left
But knowledge, itself a vast
Crystal encompassing the
Limitless crystal of air
And rock and water. And the
Two crystals are perfectly
Silent. There is nothing to
Say about them. Nothing at all.

ROBERT PENN WARREN (1905–   )

Educated at Vanderbilt, where he was a member of the Fugitives, Warren became prominent among the southern writers who dominated American literature in the middle years of the century. In such novels as *At Heaven's Gate* (1943) and *All the King's Men* (1946), he produced popular studies of violence and corruption in southern politics, based on historical incidents, and his poems deal with similar themes of history, chance, tragedy, the enigma of existence. A college text, *Understanding Poetry* (1938), which he edited in collaboration with Cleanth Brooks, was the single most influential work of the New Criticism, popularizing its concepts of aesthetic autonomy and textual analysis.

> *Selected Poems: New & Old, 1923–1966.* Random House, 1966.
> *Brother to Dragons.* (Verse narrative.) Random House, 1953.

DEBATE: QUESTION, QUARRY, DREAM

Asking what, asking what?—all a boy's afternoon,
Squatting in the canebrake where the muskrat will come.
Muskrat, muskrat, please now, please, come soon.
He comes, stares, goes, lets the question resume.
He has taken whatever answer may be down to his mud-
   burrow gloom.

Seeking what, seeking what?—foot soft in cedar-shade.
Was that a deer-flag white past windfall and fern?
No, but by bluffside lurk powers and in the fern-glade
Tall presences, standing all night, like white fox-fire burn.
The small fox lays his head in your hand now and weeps
   that you go, not to return.

Dreaming what, dreaming what?—lying on the hill at
   twilight,
The still air stirred only by moth wing, and the last stain
   of sun

277

Fading to moth-sky, blood-red to moth-white and starlight,
And Time leans down to kiss the heart's ambition,
While far away, before moonrise, come the town lights,
    one by one.

Long since that time I have walked night streets, heel-iron
Clicking the stone, and in dark in windows have stared.
Question, quarry, dream—I have vented my ire on
My own heart that, ignorant and untoward,
Yearns for an absolute that Time would, I thought, have
    prepared,

But has not yet. Well, let us debate
The issue. But under a tight roof, clutching a toy,
My son now sleeps, and when the hour grows late,
I shall go forth where the cold constellations deploy
And lift up my eyes to consider more strictly the ap-
    palling logic of joy.

FALL COMES IN BACK-COUNTRY VERMONT

To William Meredith

(1 One Voter Out of Sixteen)

Deader they die here, or at least
Differently, deeper the hole, and after
The burying, at night, late, you
Are more apt to wonder about the drainage

Of the cemetery, but know that you needn't, for
Here's all hills anyway, or mountain, and the hole
Standard, but if no drainage problem, yet
You may still wake with a kind of psychic

Twitch, as when the nerves in the amputee's
Stump (a saw did it, no doubt) twitch and wonder
How that which has gone off and set up
As a separate self is making out, and whether

It repents of its rashness, and would like
To come back and crawl into bed and be
Forgiven, and even though you, like me,
May forget the name of the dead, in the dark you

Can't help but remember that if there are only
Sixteen voters and one dies, that leaves only
Fifteen, and no doubt you know the story
Of how it began, how he laid his axe down, then

Just sat on a log, not saying a word, till
The crew knocked off for the day, and never
Came back (it was cancer), and later you'd see him
Sit on the porch in the sun and throw bread

To the chipmunks, but that was last year, and now
There's the real-estate sign in the yard, and the grass
Not cut, and already one window knocked out,
For the widow's heartbroken and gone, and the bed

Is stripped to the mattress, and the bedpan
Washed with ammonia and put on a high shelf,
And the stuffed lynx he shot now all night glares
At the empty room with a feral vindication,

And does not forgive, and thinks with glee
How cancer is worse than a 30.30, and

(2 The Bear and the Last Person to Remember)

It is well the widow is gone, for here winter's
Not made for a woman lone, lorn, and slow-foot,
And summer already sinks southward, and soon
All over the state the summer people

Will put the lawn mower in the red barn, drain
The plumbing, deny the pain of that heart-pinch
They cannot define, and get out the suitcase
To pack, for last night, in moonlight and high

On the mountain, I heard the first bear-hoot,
As the bear that all day had stripped bushes of the last
Blueberries, felt that hot itch and heaved
Up his black, hairy man-height in moonlight,

Lifted the head and curled back the black lip
To show the white moon-gleam of tusk, and the throat
Pulsed in that call that is like the great owl's,
But more edged with anguish, and then far off,

From a ruined orchard, by the old cellar hole,
In the tang and tawny air-taste of the apple-
Night, the she bear, too, rises,
And the half-crushed apple, forgotten, falls

From the jaw gone slack in that moment before
Her utterance, and soon now, night after night,
On the mountain the moon-air will heave with that hunger,
So that, in that hour, the boys of the village

Come out, climb a ridge and reply, and when
Off on the mountain that hoot comes, and nearer,
The girls with them shiver and giggle, not quite
Daring to face that thought that from dark now,

Hot-breathed and hairy, earth-odored and foam-flecked,
Rises, and want to go home, all but one,
Who feels that the night cannot breathe, and who soon,
On the raw mattress, in that house, will cry

Out, but the house is empty, and
Through the window where once the lace curtains hung
And a green shade was but is not,
The moonlight now pours like God, and the sweat

Of her effort goes ice, for she remembers,
So struggles to thrust off that weight that chokes her,
Thrusts herself up on that mattress, and gasping
In that ice and ice-iron of moonlight, with

What breath in that dishevelment
Is possible, says: "But here—it was here—
On this bed that he died, and I'll catch it and die"—
But does not, comes back, comes back until snow flies,

And many years later will be the last person
To remember his name who there on that bed

(3 The Human Fabric)

Had died, but for now let us take some comfort
In the fact that the fifteen surviving voters,
Remembering his name, feel, in the heart,
Diminished, for in this section death

Is a window gone dark and a face not seen
Any more at the P. O., and in the act
Of rending irreparably the human fabric,
Death affirms the fact of that fabric, so what

If at night, in first snow, the hunters pass—
Pale clerks and mechanics from Springfield and Hartford
With red caps and rifles and their pitiful
Blood-lust and histrionic maleness—and passing,

Throw out from the car the empty bourbon
Bottle to lie in the snow by the For-
Sale sign, and snow covers the bottle, will cover
The sign itself, and then the snow plow

Will pile up the banks as high as the eaves,
So that skiers who sing past in sports cars at dusk
Cannot see it, nor singing, need yet to know
The truth which at last they will come to need,

That life is of life paradigm, and death
The legend of death, nor need ever to know

(4 Afterwards)

That all night, eaves-high, the snow will press
Its face to the black ice of glass, and by
The white light its own being sheds, stare
Into that trapped cubicle of emptiness which

Is that room, but by that time I
Will not be here, in another place be,
And in my bed, not asleep, will endeavor
To see in my mind the eagle that once,

Above sunset, above the mountain in Stratton,
I saw—on thinnest air, high, saw
Lounging—oh, look!—it turns, and turning,
Shoulders like spray that last light before

The whistling down-plunge to the mountain's shade.
I touch the hand there on the pillow.

RICHMOND LATTIMORE (1906–   )

Born in China, educated at Dartmouth and in Europe, Lattimore is a classicist known especially for his translations from Greek literature: the *Iliad* and *Odyssey*, Pindar, Hesiod, and the dramatists.

Poems. University of Michigan Press, 1957.
The Stride of Time. University of Michigan Press, 1966.
Sestina for a Far-off Summer. University of Michigan Press, 1967.

WITNESS TO DEATH

Disconsolate I
from the thinning line
have seen friends drop and die.
All I called mine
has gone or will go
from its place in the sun.
This we know,
and nothing can be done.

Villon, Nashe, Dunbar,
to your great testaments
I too assent from afar,
bestow my violence,
and throw my rhyme
and rage in the feeding face
of the great pig of time.
Beauty gone from her place

wit wasted and lost,
promise killed with blight,
McCarter and George Frost,
Dilys who was delight,
Gilly suddenly gone,
Cartwright killed in the air,

Forrester, Conklin undone
in their prime. Where, where

is the rose, and the great
heart, and the shine of wit?
I hate death. I hate
all who speak well of it.
Dunbar, Nashe, Villon,
we sang as best we could
for the sake of those who are gone,
and it does no good.

THEODORE ROETHKE (1908–1963)

Roethke's father was a flower grower in Saginaw, Mich. The poet's early experience in and around the greenhouse deeply influenced his writing, not only by furnishing him an imagery of root, soil, and flower, but by shaping his entire thematic view of reality. Roethke was interested in the primeval world, and in the mind which inhabited it, God-searching, unencumbered by doctrine; hence he was interested in children. Unlike most poets, he developed separate modes of writing. One was formal, lyrical, with stanzas modeled after such Elizabethans as Davies and Drayton (whom he reached by way of Yeats); and this was used for his metaphysical and erotic poetry, with intertwined themes of death and sexuality. The other mode was much freer, more strange and surrealistic, and was used for "psychological" poems, especially poems about children and old people. Toward the end of his life, Roethke began recombining his split poetic personality, in poems which expressed a more tranquil trust in nature than he had found earlier. But he died—of a heart attack suffered while swimming—before this final phase had reached its culmination. Roethke's work is primary nevertheless in his generation, and has greatly influenced other writers, particularly those of the Pacific Northwest, where he was poet in residence at the University of Washington before he died.

Collected Poems. Doubleday, 1966.
On the Poet and His Craft. (Selected prose.) Ed. Ralph J. Mills, Jr. University of Washington Press, 1965.

MOSS-GATHERING

To loosen with all ten fingers held wide and limber
And lift up a patch, dark-green, the kind for lining
    cemetery baskets,
Thick and cushiony, like an old-fashioned doormat,
The crumbling small hollow sticks on the underside mixed
    with roots,
And wintergreen berries and leaves still stuck to the top,—
That was moss-gathering.

But something always went out of me when I dug loose
    those carpets
Of green, or plunged to my elbows in the spongy yellow-
    ish moss of the marshes:
And afterwards I always felt mean, jogging back over the
    logging road,
As if I had broken the natural order of things in that
    swampland;
Disturbed some rhythm, old and of vast importance,
By pulling off flesh from the living planet;
As if I had committed, against the whole scheme of life, a
    desecration.

BIG WIND

Where were the greenhouses going,
Lunging into the lashing
Wind driving water
So far down the river
All the faucets stopped?—
So we drained the manure-machine
For the steam plant,
Pumping the stale mixture
Into the rusty boilers,
Watching the pressure gauge
Waver over to red,
As the seams hissed
And the live steam
Drove to the far
End of the rose-house,
Where the worst wind was,
Creaking the cypress window-frames,
Cracking so much thin glass
We stayed all night,
Stuffing the holes with burlap;
But she rode it out,
That old rose-house,
She hove into the teeth of it,
The core and pith of that ugly storm,
Ploughing with her stiff prow,
Bucking into the wind-waves

That broke over the whole of her,
Flailing her sides with spray,
Flinging long strings of wet across the roof-top,
Finally veering, wearing themselves out, merely
Whistling thinly under the wind-vents;
She sailed until the calm morning,
Carrying her full cargo of roses.

CHILD ON TOP OF A GREENHOUSE

The wind billowing out the seat of my britches,
My feet crackling splinters of glass and dried putty,
The half-grown chrysanthemums staring up like accusers,
Up through the streaked glass, flashing with sunlight,
A few white clouds all rushing eastward,
A line of elms plunging and tossing like horses,
And everyone, everyone pointing up and shouting!

MY PAPA'S WALTZ

The whiskey on your breath
Could make a small boy dizzy;
But I hung on like death:
Such waltzing was not easy.

We romped until the pans
Slid from the kitchen shelf;
My mother's countenance
Could not unfrown itself.

The hand that held my wrist
Was battered on one knuckle;
At every step you missed
My right ear scraped a buckle.

You beat time on my head
With a palm caked hard by dirt,
Then waltzed me off to bed
Still clinging to your shirt.

NIGHT CROW

When I saw that clumsy crow
Flap from a wasted tree,
A shape in the mind rose up:
Over the gulfs of dream
Flew a tremendous bird
Further and further away
Into a moonless black,
Deep in the brain, far back.

THE LOST SON

1. *The Flight*

At Woodlawn I heard the dead cry:
I was lulled by the slamming of iron,
A slow drip over stones,
Toads brooding wells.
All the leaves stuck out their tongues;
I shook the softening chalk of my bones,
Saying,
Snail, snail, glister me forward,
Bird, soft-sigh me home,
Worm, be with me.
This is my hard time.

Fished in an old wound,
The soft pond of repose;
Nothing nibbled my line,
Not even the minnows came.

Sat in an empty house
Watching shadows crawl,
Scratching.
There was one fly.

Voice, come out of the silence.
Say something.
Appear in the form of a spider
Or a moth beating the curtain.

Tell me:
Which is the way I take;
Out of what door do I go,
Where and to whom?

Dark hollows said, lee to the wind,
The moon said, back of an eel,
The salt said, look by the sea,
Your tears are not enough praise,
You will find no comfort here,
In the kingdom of bang and blab.

Running lightly over spongy ground,
Past the pasture of flat stones,
The three elms,
The sheep strewn on a field,
Over a rickety bridge
Toward the quick-water, wrinkling and rippling.

Hunting along the river,
Down among the rubbish, the bug-riddled foliage,
By the muddy pond-edge, by the bog-holes,
By the shrunken lake, hunting, in the heat of summer.

The shape of a rat?
It's bigger than that.
It's less than a leg
And more than a nose,
Just under the water
It usually goes.

Is it soft like a mouse?
Can it wrinkle its nose?
Could it come in the house
On the tips of its toes?

Take the skin of a cat
And the back of an eel,
Then roll them in grease,—
That's the way it would feel.

It's sleek as an otter
With wide webby toes

Just under the water
It usually goes.

2. *The Pit*

Where do the roots go?
   Look down under the leaves.
Who put the moss there?
   These stones have been here too long.
Who stunned the dirt into noise?
   Ask the mole, he knows.
I feel the slime of a wet nest.
   Beware Mother Mildew.
Nibble again, fish nerves.

3. *The Gibber*

At the wood's mouth,
By the cave's door,
I listened to something
I had heard before.

Dogs of the groin
Barked and howled,
The sun was against me,
The moon would not have me.

The weeds whined,
The snakes cried,
The cows and briars
Said to me: Die.

What a small song. What slow clouds. What dark water.
Hath the rain a father? All the caves are ice. Only the
   snow's here.
I'm cold. I'm cold all over. Rub me in father and
   mother.
Fear was my father, Father Fear.
His look drained the stones.

    What gliding shape
    Beckoning through halls,
    Stood poised on the stair,
    Fell dreamily down?

From the mouths of jugs
Perched on many shelves,
I saw substance flowing
That cold morning.

Like a slither of eels
That watery cheek
As my own tongue kissed
My lips awake.

Is this the storm's heart? The ground is unstilling itself.
My veins are running nowhere. Do the bones cast out
their fire?
Is the seed leaving the old bed? These buds are live as
birds.
Where, where are the tears of the world?
Let the kisses resound, flat like a butcher's palm;
Let the gestures freeze; our doom is already decided.
All the windows are burning! What's left of my life?
I want the old rage, the lash of primordial milk!
Goodbye, goodbye, old stones, the time-order is going,
I have married my hands to perpetual agitation,
I run, I run to the whistle of money.

Money money money
Water water water

How cool the grass is.
Has the bird left?
The stalk still sways.
Has the worm a shadow?
What do the clouds say?

These sweeps of light undo me.
Look, look, the ditch is running white!
I've more veins than a tree!
Kiss me, ashes, I'm falling through a dark swirl.

4. *The Return*

The way to the boiler was dark,
Dark all the way,
Over slippery cinders
Through the long greenhouse.

The roses kept breathing in the dark.
They had many mouths to breathe with.
My knees made little winds underneath
Where the weeds slept.

There was always a single light
Swinging by the fire-pit,
Where the fireman pulled out roses,
The big roses, the big bloody clinkers.

Once I stayed all night.
The light in the morning came slowly over the white
Snow.
There were many kinds of cool
Air.
Then came steam.

Pipe-knock.

Scurry of warm over small plants.
Ordnung! ordnung!
Papa is coming!

A fine haze moved off the leaves;
Frost melted on far panes;
The rose, the chrysanthemum turned toward the light.
Even the hushed forms, the bent yellowy weeds
Moved in a slow up-sway.

5. *"It was beginning winter"*

It was beginning winter,
An in-between time,
The landscape still partly brown:
The bones of weeds kept swinging in the wind,
Above the blue snow.

It was beginning winter,
The light moved slowly over the frozen field,
Over the dry seed-crowns,
The beautiful surviving bones
Swinging in the wind.

Light traveled over the wide field;
Stayed.
The weeds stopped swinging.
The mind moved, not alone,
Through the clear air, in the silence.

Was it light?
Was it light within?
Was it light within light?
Stillness becoming alive,
Yet still?

A lively understandable spirit
Once entertained you.
It will come again.
Be still.
Wait.

WHERE KNOCK IS OPEN WIDE

1

A kitten can
Bite with his feet;
Papa and Mamma
Have more teeth.

Sit and play
Under the rocker
Until the cows
All have puppies.

His ears haven't time.
Sing me a sleep-song, please.
A real hurt is soft.

Once upon a tree
I came across a time,
It wasn't even as
A ghoulie in a dream.

There was a mooly man
Who had a rubber hat
The funnier than that,—
He kept it in a can.

What's the time, papa-seed?
Everything has been twice.
My father is a fish.

2

I sing a small sing,
My uncle's away,
He's gone for always,
I don't care either.

I know who's got him,
They'll jump on his belly,
He won't be an angel,
I don't care either.

I know her noise.
Her neck has kittens.
I'll make a hole for her.
In the fire.

Winkie will yellow I sang.
Her eyes went kissing away
It was and it wasn't her there
I sang I sang all day.

3

I know it's an owl. He's making it darker.
Eat where you're at. I'm not a mouse.
Some stones are still warm.
I like soft paws.
Maybe I'm lost,
Or asleep.

A worm has a mouth.
Who keeps me last?
Fish me out.
Please.

God, give me a near. I hear flowers.
A ghost can't whistle.
I know! I know!
Hello happy hands.

4

We went by the river.
Water birds went ching. Went ching.
Stepped in wet. Over stones.
One, his nose had a frog,
But he slipped out.

I was sad for a fish.
Don't hit him on the boat, I said.
Look at him puff. He's trying to talk.
Papa threw him back.

Bullheads have whiskers.
And they bite.

    He watered the roses.
    His thumb had a rainbow.
    The stems said, Thank you.
    Dark came early.

That was before. I fell! I fell!
The worm has moved away.
My tears are tired.

Nowhere is out. I saw the cold.
Went to visit the wind. Where the birds die.
How high is have?
I'll be a bite. You be a wink.
Sing the snake to sleep.

5

Kisses come back,
I said to Papa;
He was all whitey bones
And skin like paper.

God's somewhere else,
I said to Mamma.
The evening came
A long long time.

I'm somebody else now.
Don't tell my hands.
Have I come to always? Not yet.
One father is enough.

Maybe God has a house.
But not here.

THE VOICE

One feather is a bird,
I claim; one tree, a wood;
In her low voice I heard
More than a mortal should;
And so I stood apart,
Hidden in my own heart.

And yet I roamed out where
Those notes went, like the bird,
Whose thin song hung in air,
Diminished, yet still heard:
I lived with open sound,
Aloft, and on the ground.

That ghost was my own choice,
The shy cerulean bird;
It sang with her true voice,
And it was I who heard
A slight voice reply;
I heard; and only I.

Desire exults the ear:
Bird, girl, and ghostly tree,
The earth, the solid air—
Their slow song sang in me;
The long noon pulsed away,
Like any summer day.

THE RENEWAL

1

What glories would we? Motions of the soul?
The centaur and the sibyl romp and sing
Within the reach of my imagining:
Such affirmations are perpetual.
I teach my sighs to lengthen into songs,
Yet, like a tree, endure the shift of things.

2

The night wind rises. Does my father live?
Dark hangs upon the waters of the soul;
My flesh is breathing slower than a wall.
Love alters all. Unblood my instinct, love.
These waters drowse me into sleep so kind
I walk as if my face would kiss the wind.

3

Sudden renewal of the self—from where?
A raw ghost drinks the fluid in my spine;
I know I love, yet know not where I am;
I paw the dark, the shifting midnight air.
Will the self, lost, be found again? In form?
I walk the night to keep my five wits warm.

4

Dry bones! Dry bones! I find my loving heart,
Illumination brought to such a pitch
I see the rubblestones begin to stretch
As if reality had split apart
And the whole motion of the soul lay bare:
I find that love, and I am everywhere.

THE SWAN

1

I study out a dark similitude:
Her image fades, yet does not disappear—
Must I stay tangled in that lively hair?

Is there no way out of that coursing blood?
A dry soul's wisest. O, I am not dry!
My darling does what I could never do:
She sighs me white, a Socrates of snow.

We think too long in terms of what to be;
I live, alive and certain as a bull;
A casual man, I keep my casual word,
Yet whistle back at every whistling bird.
A man alive, from all light I must fall.
I am my father's son, I am John Donne
Whenever I see her with nothing on.

2

The moon draws back its waters from the shore.
By the lake's edge, I see a silver swan,
And she is what I would. In this light air,
Lost opposites bend down—
Sing of that nothing of which all is made,
Or listen into silence, like a god.

THE HIPPO

A Head or Tail—which does he lack?
I think his Forward's coming back!
He lives on Carrots, Leeks and Hay;
He starts to yawn—it takes All Day—

Some time I think I'll live that way.

JOURNEY TO THE INTERIOR

1

In the long journey out of the self,
There are many detours, washed-out interrupted raw
    places
Where the shale slides dangerously
And the back wheels hang almost over the edge
At the sudden veering, the moment of turning.

Better to hug close, wary of rubble and falling stones.
The arroyo cracking the road, the wind-bitten buttes, the canyons,
Creeks swollen in midsummer from the flash-flood roaring into the narrow valley.
Reeds beaten flat by wind and rain,
Grey from the long winter, burnt at the base in late summer.
—Or the path narrowing,
Winding upward toward the stream with its sharp stones,
The upland of alder and birchtrees,
Through the swamp alive with quicksand,
The way blocked at last by a fallen fir-tree,
The thickets darkening,
The ravines ugly.

2

I remember how it was to drive in gravel,
Watching for dangerous down-hill places, where the wheels whined beyond eighty—
When you hit the deep pit at the bottom of the swale,
The trick was to throw the car sideways and charge over the hill, full of the throttle.
Grinding up and over the narrow road, spitting and roaring.
A chance? Perhaps. But the road was part of me, and its ditches,
And the dust lay thick on my eyelids,—Who ever wore goggles?—
Always a sharp turn to the left past a barn close to the roadside,
To a scurry of small dogs and a shriek of children,
The highway ribboning out in a straight thrust to the North,
To the sand dunes and fish flies, hanging, thicker than moths,
Dying brightly under the street lights sunk in coarse concrete,
The towns with their high pitted road-crowns and deep gutters,
Their wooden stores of silvery pine and weather-beaten red courthouses,

An old bridge below with a buckled iron railing, broken
by some idiot plunger;
Underneath, the sluggish water running between weeds,
broken wheels, tires, stones.
And all flows past—
The cemetery with two scrubby trees in the middle of the
prairie,
The dead snakes and muskrats, the turtles gasping in
the rubble,
The spikey purple bushes in the winding dry creek bed—
The floating hawks, the jackrabbits, the grazing cattle—
I am not moving but they are,
And the sun comes out of a blue cloud over the Tetons,
While, farther away, the heat-lightning flashes.
I rise and fall in the slow sea of a grassy plain,
The wind veering the car slightly to the right,
Whipping the line of white laundry, bending the cotton-
woods apart,
The scraggly wind-break of a dusty ranch-house.
I rise and fall, and time folds
Into a long moment;
And I hear the lichen speak,
And the ivy advance with its white lizard feet—
On the shimmering road,
On the dusty detour.

3

I see the flower of all water, above and below me, the
never receding,
Moving, unmoving in a parched land, white in the moon-
light:
The soul at a still-stand,
At ease after rocking the flesh to sleep,
Petals and reflections of petals mixed on the surface of a
glassy pool,
And the waves flattening out when the fishermen drag
their nets over the stones.

In the moment of time when the small drop forms, but
does not fall,
I have known the heart of the sun,—
In the dark and light of a dry place,

In a flicker of fire brisked by a dusty wind.
I have heard, in a drip of leaves,
A slight song,
After the midnight cries.
I rehearse myself for this:
The stand at the stretch in the face of death,
Delighting in surface change, the glitter of light on waves,
And I roam elsewhere, my body thinking,
Turning toward the other side of light,
In a tower of wind, a tree idling in air,
Beyond my own echo,
Neither forward nor backward,
Unperplexed, in a place leading nowhere.

As a blind man, lifting a curtain, knows it is morning,
I know this change:
On one side of silence there is no smile;
But when I breathe with the birds,
The spirit of wrath becomes the spirit of blessing,
And the dead begin from their dark to sing in my sleep.

THE DECISION

1

What shakes the eye but the invisible?
Running from God's the longest race of all.
A bird kept haunting me when I was young—
The phoebe's slow retreating from its song,
Nor could I put that sound out of my mind,
The sleepy sound of leaves in a light wind.

2

Rising or falling's all one discipline!
The line of my horizon's growing thin!
Which is the way? I cry to the dread black,
The shifting shade, the cinders at my back.
Which is the way? I ask, and turn to go,
As a man turns to face on-coming snow.

ROBERT FITZGERALD (1910–   )

Fitzgerald studied at Harvard and at Trinity College, Cambridge, then became a newspaperman in New York, where he joined the staff of *Time* in 1936. His first poems were published in 1931. He has done many translations from ancient and modern poetry, including especially the *Odyssey* and several long poems by St.-John Perse. In 1953 he moved to Italy, where he still lives part of each year, the rest being spent at Harvard; he is now Boylston Professor of Poetry and Rhetoric.

> *In the Rose of Time.* (Selected poems.) New Directions, 1956.

SONG FOR SEPTEMBER

Respect the dreams of old men, said the cricket,
Summer behind the song, the streams falling
Ledge to ledge in the mountains where clouds come.
Attend the old men who wander
Daylight and evening in the air grown cold,
Time thins, leaving their will to wind and whispers;
The bells are swallowed gently under ground.

Because in time the birds will leave this country,
Waning south, not to return again;
Because we walk in gardens among grasses,
Touching the garments of the wind that passes,
Dimming our eyes—

Give benches to the old men, said the cricket,
Listening by cool ways to the world that dies
Fainter than seas drawn off from mist and stone.
The rain that speaks at night is the prayer's answer.
What are dry phantoms to the old men
Lying at night alone?

They are not here whose gestures we have known,
Their hands in the dusk, their frail hair in the sun.

301

THE SHORE OF LIFE

I. I came then to the city of my brethren.
Not Carthage, not Alexandria, not London.

The wide blue river cutting through the stone
Arrowy and cool lay down beside her,
And the hazy and shining sea lay in the offing.

Ferries, pouring the foam before them, sliding
Into her groaning timbers, rang and rang;
And the chains tumbled taut in the winches.

Upstream the matted tugs in the heavy water,
Their soiling smoke unwrapped by the salt wind,
Footed with snowy trampling and snowy sound.

On tethers, pointing the way of the tide,
The crusted freighters swung with their sides gushing.

On evening's ship pointing northward,
A golden sailor at sunset stood at the bow,
As aloft in the strands a tramcar with tiny clanging
Slowly soared over, far upward and humming still.

II. Not Athens, Alexandria, Vienna or London.

And evening vast and clean above the city
Washed the high storeys with sea-light, with a silken
Sky-tint on the planes and the embrasures:

The clump of crags and glitter sinking eastward
With the slow world, the shadow-lipping shores,
Pale after-conflagration of the air.

On terraces, by windows of tiredness,
The eyes dropped from that glow to the dusk atremble,
Alive with its moving atomic monotone:

There the hot taxis at the pounding corner
Fitted their glossy flanks and shifted, waiting,
And the girls went by with wavering tall walking,
Their combed heads nodding in the evening:

302

The hour of shops closing, the cocktail hour,
Lighting desire and cigarettes and lighting
The strange lamps on the streaming avenue.

MISE EN SCÈNE

The last light muffles itseh in cloud and goes
Wildly in silence to the west
Beyond the rough ridge and the pasture snows.

How pale it turns away, like a madman's guest,
Or the queen in the tragedy drawn back
To her luminous height with sickness in her breast.

Leaving us weak as before to murmur "Alack"—
Though here is but Nature turning to night,
Nor angel nor fury glides in the planet's track.

We own no powers in heaven, though well we might
Crave such company of the air
To make majestic our harrowing and our fright.

By what grand eye were these images summoned there?

CHARLES OLSON (1910–1970)

Although he began publishing his poetry rather late in life, Olson exerted, through his poems, criticism, and personal connections with younger poets, a more profound influence than anyone else on the course of poetry in America during the fifteen years past. In the late forties he joined the staff of Black Mountain College, an experimental school in North Carolina, and soon after became its rector; under him, for a few years, many outstanding teachers gathered, especially, in poetry, Robert Creeley and Robert Duncan. This group, including as well a few students, became the nucleus of a movement which has expanded until it now encompasses an extraordinary number of young writers. It began as a revulsion against the New Criticism, or at least its late proliferations, and against the influence of Eliot and Ransom; it opposed the academic tendencies which had pervaded American writing in the late forties. The group's basic principles, adapted in part from the writings of Pound and Williams, were stated by Olson in his essay "Projective Verse" (1950), in which he advocated, among other things, a prosody based on breath units and an open, rather than terminal, poetic structure. Olson himself was born in Worcester, Mass., but lived most of his life in Gloucester, which is the locus of much of his poetry. His most important poem is an open sequence called the *Maximus Poems*, left unfinished at his death; but he composed other sequences, many individual poems, and a number of important critical works, including a revealing series of letters addressed to his friend Creeley from an extended archaeological holiday in Yucatan.

Selected Writings. (Poems and prose.) New Directions, 1966.

The Maximus Poems. New York: Jargon/Corinth, 1960.

Maximus from Dogtown I. San Francisco: Auerhahn Press, 1961.

The Distances. Grove Press, 1961.

O'Ryan, 1, 2, 3, 4, 5, 6, 7, 8, 9, 10. San Francisco: White Rabbit Press, 1965.

In Cold Hell, in Thicket. San Francisco: Four Seasons Foundation, 1967.

Mayan Letters. Ed. Robert Creeley. Palma, Mallorca: Divers Press, 1953.

Call Me Ishmael. San Francisco: City Lights Books, 1966.

Human Universe and Other Essays. Ed. Donald Allen. San Francisco: Auerhahn Press, 1965.

THE RING OF

it was the west wind caught her up, as
she rose
from the genital
wave, and bore her from the delicate
foam, home
to her isle

and those lovers
of the difficult, the hours
of the golden day welcomed her, clad her, were
as though they had made her, were wild
to bring this new thing born
of the ring of the sea pink
& naked, this girl, brought her
to the face of the gods, violets
in her hair

Beauty, and she
said no to zeus & them all, all were not or
was it she chose the ugliest
to bed with, or was it straight
and to expiate the nature of beauty, was it?

knowing hours, anyway,
she did not stay long, or the lame
was only one part, & the handsome
mars had her   And the child
had that name, the arrow of
as the flight of, the move of
his mother who adorneth

with myrtle the dolphin and words
they rise, they do who
are born of like
elements

THE PRAISES

She who was burned more than half her body
                                    skipped out of death

Observing
that there are five solid figures, the Master

(or so Aetius reports, in the *Placita*)
concluded that
the Sphere of the Universe arose from
the dodecahedron

       whence Alexander
       appearing in a dream to Antiochus,
       showed him
       And on the morrow, the enemy (the Galates)
       ran before it,
       before the sign, that is

1

By Filius Bonacci, his series, rediscovered Pisa 1202,
                           we shall attack,
for it, too, proceeds asymptotically toward the graphic
                      and tangible, the law
now determined to be
phi

       the ratios 5/8, 8/13
       in the seed-cones of fir-trees,
       the ratio 21/34
       in normal daisies

       Pendactylism is general in the animal kingdom.
       But crystals . . . there, pentagonal forms or lattices
       do not, can not appear

       So we have it: star and jelly fish, the sea urchin.
       And because there is an ideal and constant angle
         which,
       for leaves and branches on a stem, produces
       the maximum exposition to light, that light vertical,
       fruit blossoms   the briar rose   the passion
        flower
       But lilies   tulips   the hyacinth, like crys-
        tals . . .

       Here we must stop   And ponder   For nature,
       though she is, as you know (so far, that is

as it is allowed to a mortal to know) from all
points of view
similar to herself, yet minerals . . .

o, that's not fair, let
woman keep her jewels, odd man
his pleasure of her glow, let
your lady Nephritite
pumice her malachite, paint
her lids green against the light

Sd he:
to dream takes no effort
to think is easy
to act is more difficult
but for a man to act after he has taken thought, this!
is the most difficult thing of all

2

We turn now to Ammonius,
who was present when Nero was,
who is full of delights,
& who smiles quickly

The epiphanies, he says, in this case are four:
1st, to such as begin to learn & to inquire,
the Pythian response,
with flute

(2) when part of the truth is glimpsed, the sun
(a creature of four-fold eyes and heads,
of a ram   a bull   a snake   the bright-eyed
lion)
This is little, even though the drum
is added

When a person has got the knowledge, Ammonius
(and he does not mean to be ambiguous)
confers one overwhelming title:
he says a man may then call himself
OF THEBES. He may sing

The last, and triumphant mode, I leave, as he leaves
   it,
untranslated; when men are active, enjoy thought,
                              that is to say
when they talk, they are LESKENOI. They rage

Which is why what is related must remain enigmatic
And why Ammonius excepts, from these epiphanies,
those who are entirely brutish.

Which brings us to what concerns us in the present inquiry.

Avert, avert, avoid
pollution, to be clean
in a dirty time

          O Wheel, aid us
          to get the gurry off

You would have a sign. Look:
to fly? a fly can do that;
to try the moon? a moth
as well; to walk on water? a straw
precedes you

          O Wheel! draw
          that truth
          to my house

Like pa does, not like sis,
on all detractors, piss, o advertised earth!
And you, o lady Moon, observe my love,
whence it arose

Whence it arose,
and who it is who sits,
there at the base of the skull, locked
in his throne of bone, that mere pea of bone
where the axes meet, cross-roads of the system
god, converter, discloser, he will answer,
will look out, if you will look, look!

3

What has been lost
is the secret of secrecy, is
the value, viz., that the work get done, and quickly,
without the loss of due and profound respect for
the materials

which is not so easy as it sounds, nor
can it permit the dispersion which follows from
too many having too little
knowledge

> Says Iamblichus:
> by shipwreck, he perished (Hippasus, that is)
> the first to publish (write down, divulge)
> the secret,
> the construction of, from 12 pentagons,
> the sphere

"Thus was he punished for his impiety"

What is necessary is
containment,
that that which has been found out by work
$\qquad\qquad\qquad$ may, by work be passed on
(without undue loss of force)
for use
$\qquad$ USE

"And they took over power, political power,
$\qquad\qquad\qquad$ in Gr Greece, including
Sicily, and maintained themselves, even after the Master
$\qquad\qquad\qquad\qquad$ died, until,
at Metapontum, the mob

"Only Philalaos, and Lysis, did not perish in the fire. Later,
Archytas it was, pupil of Philalaos, who, friend to Plato,
$\qquad\qquad\qquad\qquad$ initiated him,
and, at Tarentum

4

Which is about what we had to say,
the clues, anyhow

What belongs to art and reason is
                          the knowledge of
                                consequences

L da V, in his notebook:

                    Every natural action obeys by
                    the straightest possible process

MAXIMUS, TO HIMSELF

I have had to learn the simplest things
last. Which made for difficulties.
Even at sea I was slow, to get the hand out, or to cross
a wet deck.

                    The sea was not, finally, my trade.
But even my trade, at it, I stood estranged
from that which was most familiar. Was delayed,
and not content with the man's argument
that such postponement
is now the nature of
obedience,

          that we are all late
          in a slow time,
          that we grow up many
          And the single
          is not easily
          known

It could be, though the sharpness (the *achiote*)
I note in others,
makes more sense
than my own distances. The agilities

they show daily
who do the world's
business
And who do nature's
as I have no sense
I have done either

I have made dialogues,
have discussed ancient texts,
have thrown what light I could, offered
what pleasures
doceat allows

        But the known?
This, I have had to be given,
a life, love, and from one man
the world.

        Tokens.
        But sitting here
        I look out as a wind
        and water man, testing
        And missing
        some proof

I know the quarters
of the weather, where it comes from,
where it goes. But the stem of me,
this I took from their welcome,
or their rejection, of me

        And my arrogance
        was neither diminished
        nor increased,
        by the communication

2

It is undone business
I speak of, this morning,
with the sea
stretching out
from my feet

311

WINFIELD TOWNLEY SCOTT (1910–1968)

Scott was born in Haverhill, Mass., and attended Brown University. Upon graduation, he went to work for the *Providence Journal*, which he served for many years as literary editor, giving the paper one of the best literary pages in the country. Meanwhile his own poetry became well known. Working in the New England tradition, he nevertheless avoided a Robinsonian or Frostean tone, particularly in his narrative poems, which are forthright yet complex, and in his love poems. In 1951 he resigned his newspaper job to devote himself to writing, and eventually moved to Santa Fe, N.M., where he spent his last years.

Collected Poems, 1937–1962. Macmillan, 1962.
New and Selected Poems. Ed. George P. Elliott. Doubleday, 1967.

FIVE FOR THE GRACE OF MAN

1

See this air, how empty it is of angels
Over O'Ryan's barroom. The bum thrown out
Shoulders the sidewalk, pushes it away,
His hat rolling and his baldspot gleaming
Under the rain and under O'Ryan's lights.

I watch from the opposite curb and do not know
Why the old boy was booted; he got the air
Maybe because his nickels were gone, maybe
Because he tried to cadge from those who now
Bar the door and laugh when he tries to enter.

See him there, arms at surrender pressing
Against the mucky glass, the jeering faces
He touches but cannot touch: they're in, he's out;
—Like a child's game: only he's sort of old,
And drunk and broke, alone, the game turned real.

2

A clock strikes midnight and the street lamp burps,
Calms and hums again and tries to light
This soot-clogged, rain-flecked, unangelic air.
I lean on the iron rails above the river
But stare at the emptied road: bar closed, whores home.

I am always waiting for something I do not know
And may as well wait here as any place.
Back streets are better than main streets for waiting
And night is better than day, being privater,
Vacated by all I am not looking for.

As the world pitches east I'm on a line
Between O'Ryan's darkened bar and the light
Storm-hid but drumming of the star Orion.
Romantic—Classic, and me in the middle:
Not much, but all there seems to be tonight.

3

I am getting the habit of hunting graveyards
In search of the living moments; as though the air
Emptied in fact of mortal flesh, the ground
That took it in might hold the germ of it
And I knowing it was here, know what was here.

See this air, how empty it is of angels,
And how the sunlight falling on the names,
Dates, new masonic emblems and old cherubs
Holds with the calm of daylight on the dead
The possible answer to all our separateness.

As though at the extremes of alienation,
My parenthetical hands training my face,
I peer into the house of this completion
To know my meaning, even to find whether
All men are brothers or all my enemies.

4

How shall I ever come to any good
And get my works in schoolbooks if I use
The rude word here and there, but how shall I
Let you know me if I bequeath you only
The several photographs, the family letters?

There is no image of a tired mind
Tired of its own vanity for fame.
I turn in the comfort of the midnight rain
And as much for pleasure as necessity
Piss in the river beyond O'Ryan's bar.

5

The night is common with fatigue and rain,
With one o'clock and far freights, then with trucks
Roaring toward the Post Road, then my walk
Resuming sound; trees shake out the shower,
I get a second wind, and the sky's clearing.

I know men happy drunk, some happy sober,
And some that, drunk or sober, are alone—
Rather, know they are alone. Myself,
I'm occupied investigating angels
Though there's a power of prose draining the air.

Poetry, I hear, is to be read aloud—
Like epitaphs by cemetery strollers
On Sunday afternoons? There's always Monday,
Which interests me more: I want an angel
Easy in the house on weekday mornings.

I want the separated hand and voice
Brought commonly together: flesh and word
Concerning whether stars or buttonholes
Only together can come through night and death
And move with morning light as with massed liberating
  wings.

MR. WHITTIER

It is so much easier to forget than to have been Mr.
   Whittier.
Though of course no one now remembers him when he
   was young.
A few old ladies who were little girls next door in Ames-
   bury,
Or practically next door, have reminiscences of pears and
   apples
Given them by the famous, tamed, white-bearded saint
   with the
Still inextinguishable dark Hebraic eyes; and
Of course there is the old man—and I for one am grate-
   ful—who
Recalls the seedy coat, the occasionally not so clean high
   collar,
And that like many another he read his paper by the hour
   in the privy.
Carl Schurz, finding him rained in by the stove at the
   village store,
Thought "So superior to those about him, and yet so
   like them"; and
His official biographer decided that Mr. Whittier's poetry
   was the kind
"Written first of all for the neighbors." There are lesser
   and worse.

In any case, here is a city, founded in 1630, present
   population somewhere about
55,000—has been more in boom times, and has been a
   lot less;—say,
In three hundred years has birthed a couple of hundred
   thousand people
And one poet. Not bad. And as proof of the title I shall
   only remark
It is easier to leave *Snow-Bound* and a dozen other items
   in or out of
The school curriculum than it is to have written them.
   Try it and see.

Born where the east wind brought the smell of the ocean
from Plum Island up-river,
At a brookside haunted in the foggy dark of autumn
nights
By six little witches in sky-blue capes—Uncle Moses had
seen them;—
Born on a farm to the *Bible, Pilgrim's Progress,* a weekly
paper, the Quaker meeting-house,
To hard poverty, obscure, and a few winters of country
school;
To die—though only after there were thirteen for dinner,
and the clock
Suddenly stopped—ancient with fame, with honorary de-
grees, and
One hundred thousand dollars all made out of poems—I
say
Even this was not easy, though also it is not
What I am talking about, but is really incidental along
with
Not liking Walt Whitman and never quite affording
marriage.

Neither, under the circumstances, could it have been easy,
and it was important,
To stand suddenly struck with wonder of old legends in
a young land,
To look up at last and see poetry driving a buckboard
around the bend,
And poetry all the time in the jays screeching at the cats
in the dooryard,
Climbing with the thrush into the August noon out of
the boy's sight
As he dawdled barefoot through poetry among the welts
of the goldenrod;
But nothing is hardest which treads on nobody else's
toes.

Let us not begrudge Mr. Whittier his white beard, his
saintliness, his other foibles;
Let us remember him when he was young, not to be-
grudge his rise
As a goddamn Abolitionist hated not only in the South,

316

Hated by manufacturers, politicians, the neighbors, our folk, all
Who hate the outspoken radical and know a safer way;
Denounced by the clergy—a serious matter in that time; by the good men who
Rotten-egged him in New Hampshire, burned him out in Pennsylvania,
Jailed those who read him, and twenty years later immortally froze
With Webster on whom he turned his scorn of compromise.
It is so much easier to forget than to have been Mr. Whittier.

He put the names of our places into his poems and he honored us with himself;
And is for us but not altogether, because larger than us.
When he was an old man, the Negroes came to him free to come and sang to him
"The Lord bless thee and keep thee;
The Lord make his face to shine upon thee and be gracious unto thee;
The Lord lift up his countenance upon thee, and give thee peace."
—No more begrudge their freedom than his tears.

O LYRIC LOVE

I swore I would go back
To that blossoming orchard
Where I had seen the girl
Leaning over a book.
(Dark, and rain in the air.)

The day I watched the girl
Was morning and the sun
Splattered across the grass
Flickered in her yellow hair.
(Dark, and rain in the air.)

Those years ago I told her
She might stay so forever:

317

Her little breasts downward
Her fallen-forward hair.
(Dark, and rain in the air.)

I did find the orchard
In a leafless season.
But she was not there.
And I was not there.
Dark, and rain in the air.

ELIZABETH BISHOP (1911–   )

Born in Worcester, Mass., Miss Bishop became one of the most popular of the New York "poets of wit" in the late forties. More recently, while her tone has softened, her metaphysical vision has become, on the contrary, more incisive than ever, and her grim humor more deeply imbued in the substance of her work. For some years she has lived in Brazil.

> Poems: North & South, A Cold Spring. Houghton, Mifflin, 1955.
> Questions of Travel. Farrar, Straus & Giroux, 1965.
> The Ballad of the Burglar of Babylon. Farrar, Straus & Giroux, 1968.

THE ARMADILLO

(For Robert Lowell)

This is the time of year
when almost every night
the frail, illegal fire balloons appear.
Climbing the mountain height,

rising toward a saint
still honored in these parts,
the paper chambers flush and fill with light
that comes and goes, like hearts.

Once up against the sky it's hard
to tell them from the stars—
planets, that is—the tinted ones:
Venus going down, or Mars,

or the pale green one. With a wind,
they flare and falter, wobble and toss;
but if it's still they steer between
the kite sticks of the Southern Cross,

receding, dwindling, solemnly
and steadily forsaking us,
or, in the downdraft from a peak,
suddenly turning dangerous.

Last night another big one fell.
It splattered like an egg of fire
against the cliff behind the house.
The flame ran down. We saw the pair

of owls who nest there flying up
and up, their whirling black-and-white
strained bright pink underneath, until
they shrieked up out of sight.

The ancient owls' nest must have burned.
Hastily, all alone,
a glistening armadillo left the scene,
rose-flecked, head down, tail down,

and then a baby rabbit jumped out,
short-eared, to our surprise.
So soft!—a handful of intangible ash
with fixed, ignited eyes.

Too pretty, dreamlike mimicry!
O falling fire and piercing cry
and panic, and a weak mailed fist
clenched ignorant against the sky!

VISITS TO ST. ELIZABETHS

1950

This is the house of Bedlam.

This is the man
that lies in the house of Bedlam.

This is the time
of the tragic man
that lies in the house of Bedlam.

This is a wristwatch
telling the time
of the talkative man
that lies in the house of Bedlam.

This is a sailor
wearing the watch
that tells the time
of the honored man
that lies in the house of Bedlam.

This is the roadstead all of board
reached by the sailor
wearing the watch
that tells the time
of the old, brave man
that lies in the house of Bedlam.

These are the years and the walls of the ward,
the winds and clouds of the sea of board
sailed by the sailor
wearing the watch
that tells the time
of the cranky man
that lies in the house of Bedlam.

This is a Jew in a newspaper hat
that dances weeping down the ward
over the creaking sea of board
beyond the sailor
winding his watch
that tells the time
of the cruel man
that lies in the house of Bedlam.

This is a world of books gone flat.
This is a Jew in a newspaper hat
that dances weeping down the ward
over the creaking sea of board
of the batty sailor
that winds his watch
that tells the time
of the busy man
that lies in the house of Bedlam.

This is a boy that pats the floor
to see if the world is there, is flat,
for the widowed Jew in the newspaper hat
that dances weeping down the ward
waltzing the length of a weaving board
by the silent sailor
that hears his watch
that ticks the time
of the tedious man
that lies in the house of Bedlam.

These are the years and the walls and the door
that shut on a boy that pats the floor
to feel if the world is there and flat.
This is a Jew in a newspaper hat
that dances joyfully down the ward
into the parting seas of board
past the staring sailor
that shakes his watch
that tells the time
of the poet, the man
that lies in the house of Bedlam.

This is the soldier home from the war.
These are the years and the walls and the door
that shut on a boy that pats the floor
to see if the world is round or flat.
This is a Jew in a newspaper hat
that dances carefully down the ward,
walking the plank of a coffin board
with the crazy sailor
that shows his watch
that tells the time
of the wretched man
that lies in the house of Bedlam.

J. V. CUNNINGHAM (1911–   )

Although he was born in Maryland, Cunningham considers himself a westerner; he grew up in Montana and then spent several years wandering in the western states, earning his living as he could. Later—"through the kindness," as he has written, "of Yvor Winters"—he entered Stanford, where he studied classics and mathematics, and began writing poems. His first book was published in 1942. If the resemblances between his work and Winters's are obvious, as they are, this has too often obscured, in critics' minds, Cunningham's own distinctiveness: his more lively metric and purer philosophical outlook. And his epigrams, virtually unique in modern poetry, owe nothing to anyone, unless it be Ben Jonson. In effect Cunningham's poetry and criticism run counter to every tendency of modern poetry except that of thematic candor; yet for liveliness and integrity and fidelity to experience his writing is as clearly indigenous to modern American literature as anyone's. He has taught at several universities, including Hawaii, Chicago, Virginia, and presently Brandeis.

The Exclusions of a Rhyme. (Collected poems.) Denver: Alan Swallow, 1960.

To What Strangers, What Welcome. Denver: Alan Swallow, 1964.

Some Salt. Madison, Wis.: The Perishable Press, 1967.

The Journal of John Cardan. (Selected prose.) Denver: Alan Swallow, 1962.

A MORAL POEM

Then leave old regret,
Ancestral remorse,
Which, though you forget,
Unseen keep their course;

Shaping what each says,
Weathered in his style,
They in his fond ways
Live on for a while.

But leave them at last
To find their own home.
Inured to the past,
Be what you become:

Nor ungrudgingly
Youth's hot hours dispense,
Nor live curiously,
Cheating providence.

CHOICE

Allegiance is assigned
Forever when the mind
Chooses and stamps the will.
Thus, I must love you still
Through good and ill.

But though we cannot part,
We may retract the heart,
And build such privacies
As self-regard agrees
Conduce to ease.

So manners will repair
The ravage of despair
Which generous love invites,
Rejecting vain delights
For quiet nights.

MONTANA PASTORAL

I am no shepherd of a child's surmises.
I have seen fear where the coiled serpent rises,

Thirst where the grasses burn in early May
And thistle, mustard, and the wild oat stay.

There is dust in this air. I saw in the heat
Grasshoppers busy in the threshing wheat.

So to this hour. Through the warm dusk I drove
To blizzards sifting on the hissing stove,

And found no images of pastoral will,
But fear, thirst, hunger, and this huddled chill.

COFFEE

When I awoke with cold
And looked for you, my dear,
And the dusk inward rolled,
Not light or dark, but drear,

Unabsolute, unshaped,
That no glass can oppose,
I fled not to escape
Myself, but to transpose.

I have so often fled
Wherever I could drink
Dark coffee and there read
More than a man would think

That I say I waste time
For contemplation's sake:
In an uncumbered clime
Minute inductions wake,

Insight flows in my pen.
I know nor fear nor haste.
Time is my own again.
I waste it for the waste.

TO A FRIEND, ON HER EXAMINATION
FOR THE DOCTORATE IN ENGLISH

After these years of lectures heard,
Of papers read, of hopes deferred,
Of days spent in the dark stacks
In learning the impervious facts

So well you can dispense with 'em,
Now that the final day has come
When you shall answer name and date
Where fool and scholar judge your fate
What have you gained?

                  A learnèd grace
And lines of knowledge on the face,
A spirit weary but composed
By true perceptions well-disposed,
A soft voice and historic phrase
Sounding the speech of Tudor days,
What ignorance cannot assail
Or daily novelty amaze,
Knowledge enforced by firm detail.

What revels will these trials entail!
What gentle wine confuse your head
While gossip lingers on the dead
Till all the questions wash away,
For you have learned, not what to say,
But how the saying must be said.

THE METAPHYSICAL AMORIST

You are the problem I propose,
My dear, the text my musings glose:
I call you for convenience love.
By definition you're a cause
Inferred by necessary laws—
You are so to the saints above.
But in this shadowy lower life
I sleep with a terrestrial wife
And earthy children I beget.
Love is a fiction I must use,
A privilege I can abuse,
And sometimes something I forget.

Now, in the heavenly other place
Love is in the eternal mind
The luminous form whose shade she is,

326

A ghost discarnate, thought defined.
She was so to my early bliss,
She is so while I comprehend
The forms my senses apprehend,
And in the end she will be so.

Her whom my hands embrace I kiss,
Her whom my mind infers I know.
The one exists in time and space
And as she was she will not be;
The other is in her own grace
And is *She is* eternally.

Plato! you shall not plague my life.
I married a terrestrial wife.
And Hume! she is not mere sensation
In sequence of observed relation.
She has two forms—ah, thank you, Duns!—,
I know her in both ways at once.
I knew her, yes, before I knew her,
And by both means I must construe her,
And none among you shall undo her.

ENVOI

Hear me, whom I betrayed
While in this spell I stayed,
Anger, cathartic aid,
Hear and approve my song!

See from this sheltered cove
The symbol of my spell
Calm for adventure move,
Wild in repose of love,
Sea-going on a shell
In a moist dream. How long—
Time to which years are vain—
I on this coastal plain,
Rain and rank weed, raw air,
Served that fey despair,
Far from the lands I knew!

Winds of my country blew
Not with such motion—keen,
Stinging, and I as lean,
Savage, direct, and bitten,
Not pitying and unclean.

Anger, my ode is written.

AGNOSCO VETERIS VESTIGIA FLAMMAE

I have been here. Dispersed in meditation,
I sense the traces of the old surmise—
Passion dense as fatigue, faithful as pain,
As joy foreboding. O my void, my being
In the suspended sources of experience,
Massive in promise, unhistorical
Being of unbeing, of all futures full,
Unrealised in none, how love betrays you,
Turns you to process and a fluid fact
Whose future specifies its past, whose past
Precedes it, and whose history is its being.

MEDITATION ON STATISTICAL METHOD

Plato, despair!
We prove by norms
How numbers bear
Empiric forms,

How random wrong
Will average right
If time be long
And error slight,

But in our hearts
Hyperbole
Curves and departs
To infinity.

Error is boundless.
Nor hope nor doubt,
Though both be groundless,
Will average out.

INTERVIEW WITH DOCTOR DRINK

I have a fifth of therapy
In the house, and transference there.
Doctor, there's not much wrong with me,
Only a sick rattlesnake somewhere

In the house, if it be there at all,
But the lithe mouth is coiled. The shapes
Of door and window move. I call.
What is it that pulls down the drapes,

Disheveled and exposed? Your rye
Twists in my throat: intimacy
Is like hard liquor. Who but I
Coil there and squat, and pay your fee?

EPIGRAMS

1.

Homer was poor. His scholars live at ease,
Making as many Homers as you please,
And every Homer furnishes a book.
Though guests be parasitic on the cook,
The moral is: *It is the guest who dines*.
I'll write a book to prove I wrote these lines.

2.

Time heals not: it extends a sorrow's scope
As goldsmiths gold, which we may wear like hope.

3.

Within this mindless vault
Lie *Tristan* and *Isolt*

Tranced in each other's beauties.
They had no other duties.

4.

Dear, if unsocial privacies obsess me,
If to my exaltations I be true,
If memories and images possess me,
Yes, if I love you, what is that to you?
My folly is no passion for collusion.
I cherish my illusions as illusion.

5.

After some years *Bohemian* came to this—
This Maenad with hair down and gaping kiss
Wild on the barren edge of·under fifty.
She would finance his art if he were thrifty.

6.

Dark thoughts are my companions. I have wined
With lewdness and with crudeness, and I find
Love is my enemy, dispassionate hate
Is my redemption though it come too late—
Though I come to it with a broken head
In the cat-house of the dishevelled dead.

7. *Motto for a sun dial*

I who by day am function of the light
Am constant and invariant by night.

8.

This *Humanist* whom no beliefs constrained
Grew so broad-minded he was scatter-brained.

9.

How we desire desire! Joy of surcease
In joy's fulfillment is bewildered peace,
And harsh renewal. Life in fear of death
Will trivialize the void with hurrying breath,
With harsh indrawal. Nor love nor lust impels us.
Time's hunger to be realised compels us.

330

10.

In whose will is our peace? Thou happiness,
Thou ghostly promise, to thee I confess
Neither in thine nor love's nor in that form
Disquiet hints at have I yet been warm;
And if I rest not till I rest in thee
Cold as thy grace, whose hand shall comfort me?

11. *Epitaph for someone or other*

Naked I came, naked I leave the scene,
And naked was my pastime in between.

12.

Life flows to death as rivers to the sea,
And life is fresh and death is salt to me.

PAUL GOODMAN (1911–   )

Truly a man of many talents, Goodman is a poet, novelist, playwright, critic, professor, psychoanalyst, sociologist, city planner, and in general his generation's most effective radical gadfly. His *Growing Up Absurd* (1960), about the problems of youth in urban society, had much to do with fixing the tone of New Left radicalism in recent years. His long novel, *The Empire City* (1959), upon which he worked for a decade, is a classic of panoramic fiction. But most readers probably feel that Goodman is first of all a poet. His work has an impromptu quality which is ingratiating; at the same time the best of it is informed by lyrical feeling and a sense of the inner tradition of poetry from Anacreon, whom Goodman has translated, to the present.

The Lordly Hudson. (Collected poems.) Macmillan, 1962.
Hawkweed. Random House, 1967.

THE LORDLY HUDSON

"Driver, what stream is it?" I asked, well knowing
it was our lordly Hudson hardly flowing,
"It is our lordly Hudson hardly flowing,"
he said, "under the green-grown cliffs."

Be still, heart! no one needs your passionate
suffrage to select this glory,
this is our lordly Hudson hardly flowing
under the green-grown cliffs.

"Driver! has this a peer in Europe or the East?"
"No no!" he said. Home! home!
be quiet, heart! this is our lordly Hudson
and has no peer in Europe or the East,

this is our lordly Hudson hardly flowing
under the green-grown cliffs
and has no peer in Europe or the East.
Be quiet, heart! home! home!

LONG LINES

The heavy glacier and the terrifying Alps
that simply I cannot, nor do I know the pass,
block me from Italy. As winter closes in,
just to survive I hole up in this hovel
with food that has no taste, no one to make love to
but fantasies and masturbating, sometimes sobbing
South! South! where white the torrent splashes down
past Lugano.
             Yes, I know
I cannot move these mountains, but how did I stray
by cunningly bad choices up among these snows?
Are most of men as miserable but only some
enough communicative to declare how much?
Balked! balked! the dreary snowflakes do not cease
drifting past my window in the demi-dark.

A CLASSICAL QUATRAIN

For rage and dignity no words compare
with the Atlantic Ocean lashed by winds;
the love-gestures of juveniles are sweeter
than any words of mine. But for alcaic

speed and in the end a pat surprise
you must read Horace. John, the fertile fields
and the repetitive factories produce,
though many other things, no metaphors.

Sure, many a labor is heavier to do
and profit by than stanzas, but these are
my skill, shall I ungratefully
my gift of formal speech disdain?

By literature Sheharazad a thousand
midnights his prone violence appeased,
the homicidal hurry in his soul
embarrassed into an uncertain smile.

THE *WEEPERS TOWER* IN AMSTERDAM

I see I've come a pilgrimage. I didn't
deliberately wander up this street
but here is Weepers Tower. It was hence
his *Half Moon* sailed away in Sixteen-Nine
and waxed into the full moon of New York,

my Captain Henry Hudson looking for
a shorter Passage—but there is no passage—
sailed to the maw of hope and the dead end
of the river broad whose other name is Lordly
and has no peer in Europe or the East.

Still here sits the squat bricken cylinder
oddly sheared off one side by the street
with a stubby steeple and a gilt *Half Moon*
weathervane. But why the "Tower of Tears"?
Upon this edge did women wave farewell

and wait and watch?—but *nothing* comes from watching,
not even tears. The number of whose hope
appears is null on the horizon. (Neither
are we who hustle happier by and large,
as I assay the fortunes of mankind!)

So. I remember how a lonely boy
I used to clamber up the Palisades
and, looking down across the lordly river,
to daydream the eroding centuries:
Offshore the *Half Moon* lies, and there my Captain

questions the Indians at Spuyten Duyvil
yonder under the monarch Tulip Tree,
now also dead and gone (like my desires
rotted away, as I squat here writing
at Schreiers-Tooren in a foreign port.)

He is sailing northward into Tappan Zeel
gloriously broad as the Pacific
Ocean not. The water has begun
to freshen, the saliva in his mouth
is saltier and bitter. This is not

either the Northwest Passage to the East.
Try elsewhere. Rapidly he is retreating
on the ebb-tide—but hanging from the cliff
in a slow agony the small boy watches
the lovely ship diminish.

                              He will rave
in the muffling ice, lost beyond Labrador,
the crosses of his spars stuck in the ice,
he will be lost, my Captain Henry Hudson
crazy my fearless navigator where
there is no passage, for there is no Passage.

He will have gone forth from this Weepers Tower
a one too many voyage to where crosses
of two masts and their spars are in the icebergs
stuck forever in the future perfect
that most bleak tense where winter comes on dark.

What do you want, my Captain? what you want
is impossible, therefore you must want nothing.
"I am looking for the Northwest Passage to
India; *if I had made the world
that would exist.*"

Oh many are the lovely northern rivers!
the Housatonic and Connecticut
and Charles and James and Thames and Roanoke
and the St. Lawrence and the Kennebec
and the Potomac and the sweet Delaware,

and not of them the least the lordly Hudson;
and all of them have made the fortunes
of famous towns as arteries of trade,
but all of them flow down into the sea,
all of them flow down into the sea.

SONNET 21

I start awake at night afraid of death
gasping for air, exclaiming O my God!
and sit up and my heart is beating hard.

But when I school my thoughts and catch my breath
and recollect myself my forty-fourth
year of discouragement, in this loveless bed
in this cold-moonlit lonely countryside
in America where my best has no worth,
why, it would be comfortable to be dead.
Death is like sleep that I often woo,
and cease to nag myself to try anew
where I have no resources; why do I
fight to wake up in panic, scream with dread,
and clutch at the bedclothes afraid to die?

APRIL 1962

My countrymen have now become too base,
I give them up. I cannot speak with men
not my equals. I was an American,
where now to drag my days out and erase
this awful memory of the United States?
how can I work? I hired out my pen
to make my country practical, but I can
no longer serve these people, they are worthless.

"*Resign! resign!*" the word rings in my soul
—is it for me? or shall I make a sign
and picket the White House blindly in the rain,
or hold it up on Madison Avenue
until I vomit, or trudge to and fro
gloomily in front of the public school?

"I PLANNED TO HAVE A BORDER OF LAVENDER"

I planned to have a border of lavender
but planted the bank too of lavender
and now my whole crazy garden
    is grown in lavender

it smells so sharp heady and musky
of lavender, and the hue of only

336

lavender is all my garden up
    into the gray rocks.

When forth I go from here the heedless lust
I squander—and in vain for I am stupid
and miss the moment—it has blest me silly
    when forth I go

and when, sitting as gray as these gray rocks
among the lavender, I breathe the lavender's
tireless squandering, I liken it
    to my silly lusting,

I liken my silly indefatigable
lusting to the lavender which has grown over
all my garden, banks and borders, up
    into the gray rocks.

"SAINT HARMONY MY PATRONESS"

Saint Harmony my patroness
    is slight and she has yellow hair
and she whispers to my loneliness
    in a whiskey-voice in my ear.

She moves in an idle way
    putting a foot here and there,
her counsel is nine parts dismay
    but softly ends, "Don't you care."

And people think the morals of
    my pug-nosed muse is carelessness
and so are mine, but we shall prove
    longer lasting than they guess.

So lightly I speak of her
    for love of whom my heart will break
now she is gone, there is a tear
    in my blue eyes for her sake.

JOSEPHINE MILES (1911-   )

A native Californian, Miss Miles has taught at the University of California in Berkeley for many years, and has been associated with the other Bay Area poets of her generation.

Poems, 1930-1960. Indiana University Press, 1960.
Civil Poems. Berkeley, Calif.: Oyez Press, 1966.
Kinds of Affection. Wesleyan University Press, 1967.

MERCHANT MARINE

Where is the world? not about.
The world is in the heart
And the heart is clogged in the sea lanes out of port.

Not in the work or the west,
Not in the will or the wriest
Task is the world. It is all seaward.

Chart is the world, a sheet
In the hand and a paper page,
A rendable tissue of sea lanes, there is the heart.

NONE

A nothing out of which to create a new
Was never nothing enough for a new, never
Empty lost lone nought enough
To come clean new in any morning light.

Always in that limbo wide as it was,
Deep, down, as it was, somebody lay
Qualifying any possible creation.
Toppled in that void tossed there, and woke.

THE DOCTOR WHO SITS AT THE BEDSIDE OF A RAT

The doctor who sits at the bedside of a rat
Obtains real answers—a paw twitch,
An ear tremor, a gain or loss of weight,
No problem as to which
Is temper and which is true.
What a rat feels, he will do.

Concomitantly then, the doctor who sits
At the bedside of a rat
Asks real questions, as befits
The place, like where did that potassium go, not what
Do you think of Willie Mays or the weather?
So rat and doctor may converse together.

KENNETH PATCHEN (1911–)

The outstanding biographical datum of Patchen's life, a spinal ill-
ness which has kept him immobilized for thirty years or more,
is never mentioned in his poems; the inference would be unmis-
takable even if Patchen hadn't stated it in a hundred other ways:
for him *life* means something else. His poems, spontaneously
surrealistic, veer among the poles of humor, protest, fantasy,
spiritual affirmation, and praise of Eros. He has published
twenty-three books of poetry, several novels and plays, and more
than a thousand "painted books"—unique booklets, individually
hand-lettered, specially bound, decorated with his own paintings.
Patchen was born in Ohio, the son of a steelworker, and lives now
on the West Coast.

The Collected Poems. New Directions, 1968.

THE CHARACTER OF LOVE SEEN AS A SEARCH FOR THE LOST

You, the woman; I, the man; this, the world:
And each is the work of all.

There is the muffled step in the snow; the stranger;
The crippled wren; the nun; the dancer; the Jesus-wing
Over the walkers in the village; and there are
Many beautiful arms about us and the things we know.

See how those stars tramp over heaven on their sticks
Of ancient light: with what simplicity that blue
Takes eternity into the quiet cave of God, where Caesar
And Socrates, like primitive paintings on a wall,
Look, with idiot eyes, on the world where we two are.

You, the sought for; I, the seeker; this, the search:
And each is the mission of all.

For greatness is only the drayhorse that coaxes
The built cart out; and where we go is reason.
But genius is an enormous littleness, a trickling
Of heart that covers alike the hare and the hunter.

How smoothly, like the sleep of a flower, love,
The grassy wind moves over night's tense meadow:
See how the great wooden eyes of the forest
Stare upon the architecture of our innocence.

You, the village; I, the stranger; this, the road:
And each is the work of all.

Then, not that man do more, or stop pity; but that he be
Wider in living; that all his cities fly a clean flag . . .
We have been alone too long, love; it is terribly late
For the pierced feet on the water and we must not die
now.

Have you wondered why all the windows in heaven were
broken?
Have you seen the homeless in the open grave of God's
hand?
Do you want to acquaint the larks with the fatuous
music of war?

There is the muffled step in the snow; the stranger;
The crippled wren; the nun; the dancer; the Jesus-wing
Over the walkers in the village; and there are
Many desperate arms about us and the things we know.

IN JUDGMENT OF THE LEAF

And we were speaking easily and all the light stayed low
Within your eyes; I think no equal glass has since been
ground:
My love was looking through the throng that gave you
mind.

We were quiet as the stars began to ride the billows;
And watching them we took any only mortal stair.
We wandered up the stable rays, were startled, lost
In a child's land whose stars are glory of jangling buoys,
Gunned by the froth of eternity and space.

Something snapped a twig at a distance from us:
it seemed real: a bird called its little bonfire of sound:
thickets flamed with the trial of a leaf in the night

Gentle hands were warm, scared within my hands; the
    moment's
Church wavered through Time's dripping tapers . . . was
    torn away.

        Suddenly
We knew that we could not belong again to simple love.
I saw your opening eyes reject the trade of tiny things
And I reasoned that the whole world might lie naked
In the earth of your eyes, in easy wonder building God.

BIOGRAPHY OF SOUTHERN RAIN

Rain's all right. The boys who physic
through town on freights won't kick
if it comes; they often laugh then, talking
about the girl who lived down the block,
and how her hair was corn-yellow gold
that God could use for money. But rain,
like memory, can come in filthy clothes too.

The whole upstairs of space caved in that night;
as though a drunken giant had stumbled over the sky—
and all the tears in the world came through.
It was that. Like everyone hurt crying at once.
Trees bent to it, their arms a gallows for all
who had ever died in pain, or were hungry, since
the first thief turned to Christ, cursing . . .

Then, out of the rain, a girl's voice—her hand
on my arm. "Buddy, help me get this train."
Her voice was soft . . . a cigarette after coffee.
I could hear the clickdamnitclick of the wheels;
saw the headlight writing something on the rain.
Then I saw her face—its bleeding sores—I didn't
ask her if she had ever been in love
or had ever heard of Magdalen and Mary
or why she wanted to leave that town.

Do you see what I mean about the rain?

"THE LIONS OF FIRE SHALL HAVE THEIR HUNTING"

The lions of fire
Shall have their hunting in this black land

Their teeth shall tear at your soft throats
Their claws kill

O the lions of fire shall awake
And the valleys steam with their fury

Because you are sick with the dirt of your money
Because you are pigs rooting in the swill of your war
Because you are mean and sly and full of the pus of
    your pious murder
Because you have turned your faces from God
Because you have spread your filth everywhere

O the lions of fire
Wait in the crawling shadows of your world
And their terrible eyes are watching you.

MIDNIGHT SPECIAL

There were no antelope on the balcony
And Thomas had not yet appeared
At the barred window above the precipice

A little snow had fallen since the afternoon
But it was warm in the thought
Of distant forests and I said: "God
Will not suffer if I run my hands
Out over these deeps and shy groves
Until I touch my own undertaking"

But Thomas was busy at his gruel
And when the antelope did come
The management had rigged up a loudspeaker
On the balcony and I was asked to say
A few words to the present George 6th
So I said: "Let the Midnight Special shine a light on me.
O let the Midnight Special shine its everlovin' light on me."

343

"O MY LOVE THE PRETTY TOWNS"

O my love
The pretty towns
All the blue tents of our nights together
And the lilies and the birds glad in our joy
The road through the forest
Where the surly wolf lived
And the snow at the top of the mountain
And the little
Rain falling on the roofs of the village
O my love my dear lady
The world is not very big
There is only room for our wonder
And the light leaning winds of heaven
Are not more sweet or pure
Than your mouth on my throat
O my love there are larks in our morning
And the finding flame of your hands
And the moss on the bank of the river
And the butterflies
And the whirling-mad
Butterflies!

THE VILLAGE TUDDA

Not all of them were human.
They laughed at me, hunting through
My coat for knives or contraceptives;
Running their hands up the front
And gently touching my hair.

*

Their house stood in a forest
Near the famous river.
Here all day the weather was cold,
Or warm; the sun or the unchanging stars
Put in their work.
Schoolboys piloted yachts on the same bay
Where dragons had been seen
Not twenty years before.
Plumbers sat on the meetinghouse roof

And fixed the pipes of heaven
So that it never rained on Tuesday,
Which was held to be in bad taste.
Plowgirls wandered in the verdant fields
Seeking the answer to the universe.
They were a gentle lot;
Their legends, too.

It is said that
Once, before the coming of man,
A hill caught fire, and the goddess Anna
Died, screaming in the flames, her womb
Burning like a sack of oil.
Next day the world split into four parts:
The place of water,
The place of heaven,
The place of mind,
And the place of air—
It is told that land did not exist at all,
Though many people knew nothing else.

On that hill strange things embraced
And their children hated the earth kind.

•

I believe that to deliver myself
Is to deliver you.
I seek only to have less.
It is not enough that my things strive;
Myself I lead.

•

The old women sat upon the couch
And made obscene gestures of love.
I did not fail my trust.

Three naked girls hung by their hair
From the pole of the roof.
When they cried, brightly-clad fools
Did hi-jinks at the door.

345

Dirty, torn and weary,
The day squatted on the town
Like a blind watchman, picking
His sun-pocked nose.

They brought the fairest then.
I had no rest.
She unbound her hair
And we lay down near the world.
I was drunk with her scent.
Coming back from that place of mystery,
She made me weep.

"O TERRIBLE IS THE HIGHEST THING"

O terrible is the highest thing . . .
So be death beautiful to my love.

His nearing wings disturb my sleep . . .
So be moon bright on her lonely way.

The acts of heaven hasten my pretty fair . . .
So be God bountiful to her sweet quality.

O beautiful is the highest thing . . .
So be the angels blinded in her new holiness.

"THE ANIMAL I WANTED"

The animal I wanted
Couldn't get into the world . . .
I can hear it crying
When I sit like this away from life.

HYAM PLUTZIK (1911–1962)

Plutzik grew up on a farm in rural New England, to which his parents moved shortly after emigrating from Russia; he could not speak English until he entered public school. He attended Trinity College and Yale, and became a teacher, with a special interest in relationships between science and literature; he wrote science fiction pseudonymously. His poetry, known for its unassertive reliance on Jewish lore and feeling, won many honors. At his death Plutzik was Deane Professor of Poetry and Rhetoric at the University of Rochester.

Aspects of Proteus. Harper, 1949.
Apples from Shinar. Wesleyan University Press, 1959.
Horatio. Atheneum, 1961.

I AM DISQUIETED WHEN I SEE MANY HILLS

I am disquieted when I see many hills,
As one who looks down on the backs of tremendous cattle,
Shoulder to shoulder, munching in silence the grass
    In a timeless region.

Where time is not, event and breath are nothing,
Yet we who are lost in time, growing and fading
In the shadow of majesty, cannot but dumbly yearn
    For its stronger oblivion.

Reject this archaic craving to be a herdsman
Of the immortals. Until they trample you down
Be still the herdsman's boy among these giants
    And the ridges of laurel.

JIM DESTERLAND

As I was fishing off Pondy Point
Between the tides, the sea so still—
Only a whisper against the boat—
No other sound but the scream of a gull,

I heard the voice you will never hear
Filling the crannies of the air.

The doors swung open, the little doors,
The door, the hatch within the brain,
And like the bellowing of ruin
The surf upon the thousand shores
Swept through me, and the thunder-noise
Of all the waves of all the seas.

The doors swung shut, the little doors,
The door, the hatch within the ear,
And I was fishing off Pondy Pier,
And all was as it was before,
With only the whisper of the swell
Against the boat, and the cry of a gull.

I draw a sight from tree to tree
Crossing this other from knoll to rock,
To mark the place. Into the sea
My line falls with an empty hook,
Yet fools the world. So day and night
I crouch upon the thwarts and wait.

There is a roaring in the skies
The great globes make, and there is the sound
Of all the atoms whirling round
That one can hear if one is wise—
Wiser than most—if one has heard
The doors, the little doors, swing wide.

OF OBJECTS CONSIDERED AS FORTRESSES IN A BALEFUL PLACE

I and the other intruders,
The oak and stone my brothers,
Stare at one another
Upon the plain of nothing.

As if to ask what wonder
By willing or by blunder
Could lead to this encounter
Upon the plain of nothing.

(As if to ask what meeting
Could overmatch the wonder
Of opaque hostile Being
Emergent out of nothing.)

The nothing is a glitter
Wicked, a frosty water,
Upon which no words scatter,
Not hallo, sob or laughter.

Upon their petty islands
The something and the something,
Knowing or blank, in silence
Await the will of nothing.

One, one, and one,
Mysteries of the moon,
And the always never-guests,
None, none.

BROTHER ANTONINUS (1912–   )

Born in Sacramento, William O. Everson was a conscientious objector during World War II, and not long after became converted to the Church of Rome. He joined the Dominican order as a lay brother, adopting the name Antoninus, and since 1951 has taught at St. Albert's College in Oakland.

> *The Residual Years.* New Directions, 1948.
> *The Crooked Lines of God.* University of Detroit Press, 1960.
> *Hazards of Holiness.* Doubleday, 1962.
> *Single Source.* Berkeley, Calif.: Oyez Press, 1966.
> *The Rose of Solitude.* Doubleday, 1967.
> *In the Fictive Wish.* Berkeley, Calif.: Oyez Press, 1967.

THE FLIGHT IN THE DESERT

The last settlement scraggled out with a barbed wire fence
And fell from sight. They crossed coyote country:
Mesquite, sage, the bunchgrass knotted in patches;
And there the prairie dog yapped in the valley;
And on the high plateau the short-armed badger
Delved his clay. But beyond that the desert,
Raw, unslakable, its perjured dominion wholly contained
In the sun's remorseless mandate, where the dim trail
Died ahead in the watery horizon: God knows where.

And there the failures: skull of the ox,
Where the animal terror trembled on in the hollowed eyes;
The catastrophic wheel, split, sandbedded;
And the sad jawbone of a horse. These the denials
Of the retributive tribes, fiercer than pestilence,
Whose scrupulous realm this was.

Only the burro took no notice: the forefoot
Placed with the nice particularity of one
To whom the evil of the day is wholly sufficient.
Even the jocular ears marked time.

But they, the man and the anxious woman,
Who stared pinch-eyed into the settling sun,
They went forward into its denseness
All apprehensive, and would many a time have turned
But for what they carried. That brought them on.
In the gritty blanket they bore the world's great risk,
And knew it; and kept it covered, near to the blind heart,
That hugs in a bad hour its sweetest need,
Possessed against the drawn night
That comes now, over the dead arroyos,
Cold and acrid and black.

This was the first of his goings forth into the wilderness
    of the world.
There was much to follow: much of portent, much of
    dread.
But what was so meek then and so mere, so slight and
    strengthless,
(Too tender, almost, to be touched)—what they nervously
    guarded
Guarded them. As we, each day, from the lifted chalice,
That strengthless Bread the mildest tongue subsumes,
To be taken out in the blatant kingdom,
Where Herod sweats, and his deft henchmen
Riffle the tabloids—that keeps us.

Over the campfire the desert moon
Slivers the west, too chaste and cleanly
To mean hard luck. The man rattles the skillet
To take the raw edge off the silence;
The woman lifts up her heart; the Infant
Knuckles the generous breast, and feeds.

THE MAKING OF THE CROSS

Rough fir, hauled from the hills. And the tree it had been,
Lithe-limbed, wherein the wren had nested,
Whereon the red hawk and the grey
Rested from flight, and the raw-head vulture
Shouldered to his feed—that tree went over
Bladed down with a double-bitted axe; was snaked with
    winches;

351

The wedge split it; hewn with the adze
It lay to season toward its use.

So too with the nails: millenniums under the earth,
Pure ore; chunked out with picks; the nail-shape
Struck in the pelt-lunged forge; tonged to a cask
And the wait against that work.

Even the thorn-bush flourished from afar,
As do the flourishing generations of its kind,
Filling the shallow soil no one wants;
Wind-sown, it cuts the cattle and the wild horse;
It tears the cloth of man, and hurts his hand.

Just as in life the good things of the earth
Are patiently assembled: some from here, some from
    there;
Wine from the hill and wheat from the valley;
Rain that comes blue-bellied out of the sopping sea;
Snow that keeps its drift on the gooseberry ridge,
Will melt with May, go down, take the egg of the salmon,
Serve the traffic of otters and fishes,
Be ditched to orchards . . .

So too are gathered up the possibles of evil.

And when the Cross was joined, quartered,
As is the earth; spoked, as is the Universal Wheel—
Those radials that led all unregenerate act
Inward to innocence—it met the thorn-wove Crown;
It found the Scourges and the Dice;
The Nail was given and the reed-lifted Sponge;
The Curse caught forward out of the heart corrupt;
The excoriate Foul, stoned with the thunder and the hail—
All these made up that miscellaneous wrath
And were assumed.

The evil and the wastage and the woe,
As if the earth's old cyst, back down the slough
To Adam's sin-burnt calcinated bones
Rushed out of time and clotted on the Cross.

Off there the cougar
Coughed in passion when the sun went out; the rattler
Filmed his glinty eye, and found his hole.

ZONE OF DEATH

Wind is not nigh.

No Holy Ghost,
Spirit outspilt,
Burnt this charred day.

What sin did this?
Could I?

Hot light blares.
Stars, outblistered now,
Mark time, extinct.

Night might bring
The seasonal constellations
In its sphere,
But night is nowhere.

Sun. Sand.
The noon-crazy jays
Cackle and gibber,
Jar on the gritted ear.

Dawn sneaked in unsmelt.
No wine, no water here.

Now the lance-riddled man
On yon pronged tree,
Stretched in the death-tread there,
Opens his executing eye
And gibbets me.

HY SOBILOFF (1912–)

Sobiloff's poems, with their affinities to the elegant, abstract modernism of painting, are personal, reflective, concise, and idiosyncratic, and give little hint of their author's role in the business world, where he is a prominent industrialist and investor.

Dinosaurs and Violins. Farrar, Straus & Young, 1954.
In Deepest Aquarium. Dial, 1959.
Breathing of First Things. Dial, 1963.

THE CHILD'S SIGHT

The child's wisdom is in saying
They say what they see when they see it
I am beginning to remember how
When I don't say it when I see it
I remember it differently

I am walking with the children
They have included me
None of us eavesdrops any more
We speak the same celestial gibberish
Our spirit ticks the same time
I feel again and am part of the inside world

The child is a little inspector when it crawls
It touches and tastes the earth
Rolls and stumbles toward the object
Zigzags like a sail
And outmaneuvers the room

I am learning the child's way
I pick up wood pieces from the ground
And see shapes into them
I notice a purple velvet bee resting on a flower
And stop to listen to its buzz

They have included me
And though I will not be put away to rock alone
And I don't roll down the plush hills
Nor spit for luck
I am learning their way
They have given me back the bliss of my senses

WISDOM

Wisdom has nothing to do with age
History has proved that
When men cannot prove themselves
On an aspen tree

Each person says to himself
Where am I
Am I in a jungle tree or am I a bongo jungle?
I am wood—I write I'm plastic
I write playing my piano
I'm wood I'm plastic
The scale—the scale
Like the scale of the fish

No more jungles and no more jangles
But for you the jangle
But to me the jungles
Under the aspen tree

I bring you my flowers
As my age increases in the plain fields
Speak to me child and
I will speak you back

I lost my hair but never lost my heart
I warmed the hedge and alarmed myself
With the hedge
The clover I see—the pine tree
And now worse than Wordsworth's Intimations
Or whoever was in the poet's blind sight
Like Keats searching
Or Father Hopkins

I would say as Shakespeare said
To thine own self be true

But what about me and the curate inside of me
Such a thing sings with humming feet
And the clover on the hedges
Will breathe you in
Prayers to be said
With no sacrifice

ROBERT HAYDEN (1913–)

Hayden, who was born in Detroit and educated at the University of Michigan, teaches today at Fisk University. Until 1966, when his *Selected Poems* was published, he was known to American readers only by a few poems in magazines, although a small book of his work had been published in England. A number of his poems deal with the history of the Bahai faith, others with the history of slavery in the U.S.

Selected Poems. New York: October House, 1966.

NIGHT, DEATH, MISSISSIPPI

1

A quavering cry. Screech-owl?
Or one of them?
The old man in his reek
and gauntness laughs—

One of them, I bet—
and turns out the kitchen lamp,
limping to the porch to listen
in the windowless night.

Be there with Boy and the rest
if I was well again.
Time was, Time was.
White robes like moonlight

In the sweetgum dark.
Unbucked that one then
and him squealing bloody Jesus
as we cut it off.

Time was. A cry?
A cry all right.
He hawks and spits,
fevered as by groinfire.

357

Have us a bottle,
Boy and me—
he's earned him a bottle—
when he gets home.

2

Then we beat them, he said,
beat them till our arms was tired
and the big old chains
messy and red.

O Jesus burning on the lily cross

Christ, it was better
than hunting bear
which don't know why
you want him dead.

O night, rawhead and bloodybones night

You kids fetch Paw
some water now so's he
can wash that blood
off him, she said.

O night betrayed by darkness not its own

THE BALLAD OF NAT TURNER

Then fled, O brethren, the wicked juba
    and wandered wandered far
from curfew joys in the Dismal's night.
    Fool of St. Elmo's fire

In scary night I wandered, praying,
    Lord God my harshener,
speak to me now or let me die;
    speak, Lord, to this mourner.

And came at length to livid trees
    where Ibo warriors
hung shadowless, turning in wind
    that moaned like Africa,

Their belltongue bodies dead, their eyes
    alive with the anger deep
in my own heart. Is this the sign,
    the sign forepromised me?

The spirits vanished. Afraid and lonely
    I wandered on in blackness.
Speak to me now or let me die.
    Die, whispered the blackness.

And wild things gasped and scuffled in
    the night; seething shapes
of evil frolicked upon the air.
    I reeled with fear, I prayed.

Sudden brightness clove the preying
    darkness, brightness that was
itself a golden darkness, brightness
    so bright that it was darkness.

And there were angels, their faces hidden
    from me, angels at war
with one another, angels in dazzling
    combat. And oh the splendor,

The fearful splendor of that warring.
    Hide me, I cried to rock and bramble.
Hide me, the rock, the bramble cried. . . .
    How tell you of that holy battle?

The shock of wing on wing and sword
    on sword was the tumult of
a taken city burning. I cannot
    say how long they strove,

For the wheel in a turning wheel which is time
    in eternity had ceased
its whirling, and owl and moccasin,
    panther and nameless beast

And I were held like creatures fixed
    in flaming, in fiery amber.
But I saw I saw oh many of
    those mighty beings waver,

Waver and fall, go streaking down
     into swamp water, and the water
hissed and steamed and bubbled and locked
     shuddering shuddering over

The fallen and soon was motionless.
     Then that massive light
began a-folding slowly in
     upon itself, and I

Beheld the conqueror faces and, lo,
     they were like mine, I saw
they were like mine and in joy and terror
     wept, praising praising Jehovah.

Oh praised my honer, harshener,
     till a sleep came over me,
a sleep heavy as death. And when
     I awoke at last free

And purified, I rose and prayed
     and returned after a time
to the blazing fields, to the humbleness.
     And bided my time.

MURIEL RUKEYSER (1913–)

Born in New York City, the daughter of a building contractor, Miss Rukeyser has based much of her poetry on technological imagery and on themes of building and unbuilding. Her writing has been vigorous and broad, including several studies in politics and scientific thought, and she has published more than a dozen books of verse. In addition she has made some notable translations, particularly of works by the Mexican poet Octavio Paz.

Waterlily Fire, Poems 1935–1962. Macmillan, 1962.
The Outer Banks. Santa Monica, Calif.: Unicorn Press, 1967.

BOY WITH HIS HAIR CUT SHORT

Sunday shuts down on this twentieth-century evening.
The El passes. Twilight and bulb define
the brown room, the overstuffed plum sofa,
the boy, and the girl's thin hands above his head.
A neighbor radio sings stocks, news, serenade.

He sits at the table, head down, the young clear neck
        exposed,
watching the drugstore sign from the tail of his eye;
tattoo, neon, until the eye blears, while his
solicitous tall sister, simple in blue, bending
behind him, cuts his hair with her cheap shears.

The arrow's electric red always reaches its mark,
successful neon! He coughs, impressed by that precision.
His child's forehead, forever protected by his cap,
is bleached against the lamplight as he turns head
and steadies to let the snippets drop.

Erasing the failure of weeks with level fingers,
she sleeks the fine hair, combing: "You'll look fine
        tomorrow!

You'll surely find something, they can't keep turning you
    down;
the finest gentleman's not so trim as you!" Smiling, he
    raises
the adolescent forehead wrinkling ironic now.

He sees his decent suit laid out, new-pressed,
his carfare on the shelf. He lets his head fall, meeting
her earnest hopeless look, seeing the sharp blades splitting,
the darkened room, the impersonal sign, her motion,
the blue vein, bright on her temple, pitifully beating.

EASTER EVE

Wary of time O it seizes the soul tonight
I wait for the great morning of the west
confessing with every breath mortality.
Moon of this wild sky struggles to stay whole
and on the water silvers the ships of war.
I go alone in the black-yellow light
all night waiting for day, while everywhere the sure
death of light, the leaf's sure return to the root
is repeated in million, death of all man to share.
Whatever world I know shines ritual death,
wide under this moon they stand gathering fire,
fighting with flame, stand fighting in their graves.
All shining with life as the leaf, as the wing shines,
the stone deep in the mountain, the drop in the green
    wave.
Lit by their energies, secretly, all things shine.
Nothing can black that glow of life;   although
    each part go crumbling down
    itself shall rise up whole.

Now I say there are new meanings;   now I name
death our black honor and feast of possibility
to celebrate casting of life on life. This earth-long day
between blood and resurrection where we wait
remembering sun, seed, fire;   remembering
that fierce Judaean Innocent who risked
every immortal meaning on one life.

Given to our year as sun and spirit are,
as seed we are blessed only in needing freedom.
Now I say that the peace the spirit needs is peace,
not lack of war, but fierce continual flame.
For all man : effort is freedom, effort's peace,
it fights. And along these truths the soul goes home,
 flies in its blazing to a place
 more safe and round than Paradise.

Night of the soul, our dreams in the arms of dreams
dissolving into eyes that look upon us.
Dreams the sources of action, the meeting and the end,
a resting-place among the flight of things.
And love which contains all human spirit, all wish,
the eyes and hands, sex, mouth, hair, the whole woman—
fierce peace I say at last, and the sense of the world.
In the time of conviction of mortality
whatever survive, I remember what I am.—
The nets of this night are on fire with sun and moon
pouring both lights into the open tomb.
Whatever arise, it comes in the shape of peace,
fierce peace which is love, in which move all the stars,
and the breathing of universes, filling, falling away,
and death on earth cast into the human dream.
 What fire survive forever
 myself is for my time.

THE SPEAKING TREE

Great Alexander sailing was from his true course turned
By a young wind from a cloud in Asia moving
Like a most recognizable most silvery woman;
Tall Alexander to the island came.
The small breeze blew behind his turning head.
He walked the foam of ripples into this scene.

The trunk of the speaking tree looks like a tree-trunk
Until you look again.   Then people and animals
Are ripening on the branches;   the broad leaves
Are leaves;   pale horses, sharp fine foxes
Blossom;   the red rabbit falls

Ready and running.   The trunk coils, turns,
Snakes, fishes.   Now the ripe people fall and run,
Three of them in their shore-dance, flames that stand
Where reeds are creatures and the foam is flame.

Stiff Alexander stands.   He cannot turn.
But he is free to turn :   this is the speaking tree,
It calls your name.   It tells us what we mean.

DELMORE SCHWARTZ (1913–1966)

Schwartz published his first poems while still a student, and within a short time found himself lionized. He was appointed poetry editor of *Partisan Review*, then the most influential magazine of its kind in the country, and his books began to appear in rapid succession. He became in effect a modern culture hero. But although he continued to write occasional poems of great power and to produce brilliant short stories and essays, and although he taught at several universities, including Princeton, Indiana, and Syracuse, his middle and later years were so disrupted by emotional illness and other adversities that his early promise was never fulfilled. When he died in an obscure New York hotel, for a time he was not even identified.

Selected Poems, 1938–1958. New Directions, 1967.
The World Is a Wedding. (Stories.) New Directions, 1948.
Successful Love. (Stories.) New York: Corinth, 1961.

IN THE NAKED BED, IN PLATO'S CAVE

In the naked bed, in Plato's cave,
Reflected headlights slowly slid the wall,
Carpenters hammered under the shaded window,
Wind troubled the window curtains all night long,
A fleet of trucks strained uphill, grinding,
Their freights covered, as usual.
The ceiling lightened again, the slanting diagram
Slid slowly forth.
           Hearing the milkman's chop,
His striving up the stair, the bottle's chink,
I rose from bed, lit a cigarette,
And walked to the window. The stony street
Displayed the stillness in which buildings stand,
The street-lamp's vigil and the horse's patience.
The winter sky's pure capital
Turned me back to bed with exhausted eyes.

Strangeness grew in the motionless air. The loose
Film grayed. Shaking wagons, hooves' waterfalls,

Sounded far off, increasing, louder and nearer.
A car coughed, starting. Morning, softly
Melting the air, lifted the half-covered chair
From underseas, kindled the looking-glass,
Distinguished the dresser and the white wall.
The bird called tentatively, whistled, called,
Bubbled and whistled, so! Perplexed, still wet
With sleep, affectionate, hungry and cold. So, so,
O son of man, the ignorant night, the travail
Of early morning, the mystery of beginning
Again and again,
                    while History is unforgiven.

THE BEAUTIFUL AMERICAN WORD, SURE

The beautiful American word, Sure,
As I have come into a room, and touch
The lamp's button, and the light blooms with such
Certainty where the darkness loomed before,

As I care for what I do not know, and care
Knowing for little she might not have been,
And for how little she would be unseen,
The intercourse of lives miraculous and dear.

Where the light is, and each thing clear,
Separate from all others, standing in its place,
I drink the time and touch whatever's near,

And hope for day when the whole world has that face:
For what assures her present every year?
In dark accidents the mind's sufficient grace.

FOR THE ONE WHO WOULD TAKE MAN'S
LIFE IN HIS HANDS

Tiger Christ unsheathed his sword,
Threw it down, became a lamb.
Swift spat upon the species, but
Took two women to his heart.

Samson who was strong as death
Paid his strength to kiss a slut.
Othello that stiff warrior
Was broken by a woman's heart.
Troy burned for a sea-tax, also for
Possession of a charming whore.
What do all examples show?
What must the finished murderer know?

You cannot sit on bayonets,
Nor can you eat among the dead.
When all are killed, you are alone,
A vacuum comes where hate has fed.
Murder's fruit is silent stone,
The gun increases poverty.
With what do these examples shine?
The soldier turned to girls and wine.
Love is the tact of every good,
The only warmth, the only peace.

"What have I said?" asked Socrates,
"Affirmed extremes, cried yes and no,
Taken all parts, denied myself,
Praised the caress, extolled the blow,
Soldier and lover quite deranged
Until their motions are exchanged.
—What do all examples show?
What can any actor know?
The contradiction in every act,
The infinite task of the human heart."

TIME'S DEDICATION

My heart beating, my blood running,
The light brimming,
My mind moving, the ground turning,
My eyes blinking, the air flowing,
The clock's quick-ticking,
Time moving, time dying,
Time perpetually perishing!
Time is farewell! Time is farewell!

Abide with me: do not go away,
But not as the dead who do not walk,
And not as the statue in the park,
And not as the rock which meets the wave,
But quit the dance from which is flowing
Wishes and turns, gestures and voices,
Angry desire and fallen tomorrow,
Quit the dance from which is flowing
Your blood and beauty: stand still with me.

We cannot stand still: time is dying,
We are dying: Time is farewell!

Stay then, stay! Wait now for me,
Deliberately, with care and circumspection,
Deliberately
Stop.
When we are in step, running together,
Our pace equal, our motion one,
Then we will be well, parallel and equal,
Running together down the macadam road,
Walking together,
Controlling our pace before we get old,
Walking together on the receding road,
Like Chaplin and his orphan sister,
Moving together through time to all good.

BAUDELAIRE

When I fall asleep, and even during sleep,
I hear, quite distinctly, voices speaking
Whole phrases, commonplace and trivial,
Having no relation to my affairs.

Dear Mother, is any time left to us
In which to be happy? My debts are immense.
My bank account is subject to the court's judgment.
I know nothing. I cannot know anything.
I have lost the ability to make an effort.
But now as before my love for you increases.
You are always armed to stone me, always:
It is true. It dates from childhood.

For the first time in my long life
I am almost happy. The book, almost finished,
Almost seems good. It will endure, a monument
To my obsessions, my hatred, my disgust.

Debts and inquietude persist and weaken me.
Satan glides before me, saying sweetly:
"Rest for a day! You can rest and play today.
Tonight you will work." When night comes,
My mind, terrified by the arrears,
Bored by sadness, paralyzed by impotence,
Promises: "Tomorrow: I will tomorrow."
Tomorrow the same comedy enacts itself
With the same resolution, the same weakness.

I am sick of this life of furnished rooms.
I am sick of having colds and headaches:
You know my strange life. Every day brings
Its quota of wrath. You little know
A poet's life, dear Mother: I must write poems,
The most fatiguing of occupations.

I am sad this morning. Do not reproach me.
I write from a café near the post office,
Amid the click of billiard balls, the clatter of dishes,
The pounding of my heart. I have been asked to write
"A History of Caricature." I have been asked to write
"A History of Sculpture." Shall I write a history
Of the caricatures of the sculptures of you in my heart?

Although it costs you countless agony,
Although you cannot believe it necessary,
And doubt that the sum is accurate,
Please send me money enough for at least three weeks.

KARL SHAPIRO (1913–   )

One of the most prominent poets of his generation, Shapiro, who was born in Baltimore and brought up partly in the South, has written some of his most moving poems about the social and cultural predicament of the Jew in America. His early poems, published just before and during World War II, quickly became popular. But Shapiro abandoned the formalistic manner in which they were written, and in a search for freer and more personal ways of writing has evolved progressively for twenty-five years in the direction of Whitmanian styles and attitudes. He has taught at several universities, and has edited two important literary magazines, *Poetry* and *The Prairie Schooner*. Today he lives in California.

> *Selected Poems.* Random House, 1968.
> *Poems 1940–1953.* Random House, 1953.
> *Essay on Rime.* Reynal & Hitchcock, 1945.
> *In Defense of Ignorance.* (Critical essays.) Random House, 1960.
> *White-haired Lover.* Random House, 1968.

HOSPITAL

Inside or out, the key is pain. It holds
The florist to your pink medicinal rose,
The nickname to the corpse. One wipes it from
Blue German blades or drops it down the drain;
The novelist with a red tube up his nose
Gingerly pets it. Nurse can turn it off.

This is the Oxford of all sicknesses.
Kings have lain here and fabulous small Jews
And actresses whose legs were always news.
In this black room the painter lost his sight,
The crippled dancer here put down her shoes,
And the scholar's memory broke, like an old clock.

These reached to heaven and inclined their heads
While starchy angels reached them into beds:

These stooped to hell to labor out their time,
Or choked to death in seas of glaucous slime:
All tasted fire, and then, their hate annealed,
Ate sad ice-cream and wept upon a child.

What church is this, what factory of souls
Makes the bad good and fashions a new nose,
And the doctors reel with Latin and even the dead
Expect the unexpected? For O the souls
Fly back like heavy homing-birds to roost
In long-racked limbs, filling the lonely boughs.

The dead cry *life* and stagger up the hill;
But is there still the incorrigible city where
The well enjoy their poverty and the young
Worship the gutter? Is Wednesday still alive
And Tuesday wanting terribly to sin?
Hush, there are many pressing the oak doors,

Saying, "Are boys and girls important fears?
Can you predict the elections by my guts?"
But the rubber gloves are deep in a deep wound,
Stitching a single heart. These far surpass
Themselves, their wives, and the removed goitre;
Are, for the most part, human but unbandaged.

AUTO WRECK

Its quick soft silver bell beating, beating,
And down the dark one ruby flare
Pulsing out red light like an artery,
The ambulance at top speed floating down
Past beacons and illuminated clocks
Wings in a heavy curve, dips down,
And brakes speed, entering the crowd.
The doors leap open, emptying light;
Stretchers are laid out, the mangled lifted
And stowed into the little hospital.
Then the bell, breaking the hush, tolls once,
And the ambulance with its terrible cargo
Rocking, slightly rocking, moves away,
As the doors, an afterthought, are closed.

We are deranged, walking among the cops
Who sweep glass and are large and composed.
One is still making notes under the light.
One with a bucket douches ponds of blood
Into the street and gutter.
One hangs lanterns on the wrecks that cling,
Empty husks of locusts, to iron poles.

Our throats were tight as tourniquets,
Our feet were bound with splints, but now,
Like convalescents intimate and gauche,
We speak through sickly smiles and warn
With the stubborn saw of common sense,
The grim joke and the banal resolution.
The traffic moves around with care,
But we remain, touching a wound
That opens to our richest horror.
Already old, the question Who shall die?
Becomes unspoken Who is innocent?
For death in war is done by hands;
Suicide has cause and stillbirth, logic;
And cancer, simple as a flower, blooms.
But this invites the occult mind,
Cancels our physics with a sneer,
And spatters all we knew of denouement
Across the expedient and wicked stones.

MY GRANDMOTHER

My grandmother moves to my mind in context of sorrow
And, as if apprehensive of near death, in black;
Whether erect in chair, her dry and corded throat
    harangued by grief,
Or at ragged book bent in Hebrew prayer,
Or gentle, submissive, and in tears to strangers;
Whether in sunny parlor or back of drawn blinds.

Though time and tongue make any love disparate,
On daguerreotype with classic perspective
Beauty I sigh and soften at is hers.
I pity her life of deaths, the agony of her own,

But most that history moved her through
Stranger lands and many houses,
Taking her exile for granted, confusing
The tongues and tasks of her children's children.

THE JEW AT CHRISTMAS EVE

I see the thin bell-ringer standing at corners
Fine as a breath, in cloth of red,
With eyes afar and long arm of a reed
Weakly waving a religious bell,
Under the boom of caroling hours
I see the thin bell-ringer standing still,
Breasting the prosperous tide on the Christmas pave.

I see the thin bell-ringer repeating himself
From corner to corner, year to year,
Struggling to stand beneath the windy blare
Of horns that carol out of walls.
He would attract a crying waif
Or garrulous old woman down-at-heels
Or a pair of lovers on the icy pave.

Whom do you summon, Santa of the spare?
Whom do you summon, arm of a reed?
Whom do you cheer with ringing and whom chide,
And who stops at the tripod at your side
And wishes you the time of year?
A few who feed the cauldron of the unfed,
The iron cauldron on the fireless pave.

I see the thin bell-ringer as a flame
Of scarlet, trying to throw the flame
With each sweep of the bell. The tide pours on
And wets the ringer in cloth of red
And parts around the ringer of flame
With eyes afar and long arm of a reed
Who shakes the fire on the snowy pave.

THE FIRST TIME

Behind shut doors, in shadowy quarantine,
There shines the lamp of iodine and rose
That stains all love with its medicinal bloom.
This boy, who is no more than seventeen,
Not knowing what to do, takes off his clothes
As one might in a doctor's anteroom.

Then in a cross-draft of fear and shame
Feels love hysterically burn away,
A candle swimming down to nothingness
Put out by its own wetter gusts of flame,
And he stands smooth as uncarved ivory
Heavily curved for some expert caress.

And finally sees the always open door
That is invisible till the time has come,
And half falls through as through a rotten wall
To where chairs twist with dragons from the floor
And the great bed drugged with its own perfume
Spreads its carnivorous flower-mouth for all.

The girl is sitting with her back to him;
She wears a black thing and she rakes her hair,
Hauling her round face upward like moonrise;
She is younger than he, her angled arms are slim
And like a country girl her feet are bare.
She watches him behind her with old eyes,

Transfixing him in space like some grotesque,
Far, far from her where he is still alone
And being here is more and more untrue.
Then she turns round, as one turns at a desk,
And looks at him, too naked and too soon,
And almost gently asks: *Are you a Jew?*

QUINTANA LAY IN THE
SHALLOW GRAVE OF CORAL

Quintana lay in the shallow grave of coral. The guns
   boomed stupidly fifty yards away. The plasma
   trickled into his arm. Naked and filthy, covered

374

with mosquitoes, he looked at me as I read his white cloth tag. How do you feel, Quintana? He looks away from my gaze. I lie: we'll get you out of here sometime today.

I never saw him again, dead or alive. Skin and bones, with eyes as soft as soot, neck long as a thigh, a cross on his breastbone not far from the dog tags. El Greco was all I could think of. Quintana lying in his shallow foxhole waiting to be evacuated. A dying man with a Spanish name equals El Greco. A truck driver from Dallas probably.

When the Japs were making the banzai charge, to add insult to death, they came at us screaming the supreme insult: *Babe Ruth, go to hell!* The Americans, on the other hand, when the Japs flew over dropping sticks of explosives, shouted into the air, as if they could hear: *Tojo eat shit!*

Soldiers fall in love with the enemy all too easily. It's the allies they hate. Every war is its own cause. That's why they're all surrounded with ideals. That's why they're all crusades.

ALL TROPIC PLACES SMELL OF MOLD

All tropic places smell of mold. A letter from Karachi smells of mold. A book I had in New Guinea twenty years ago smells of mold. Cities in India smell of mold and dung. After a while you begin to like it. The curry dishes in the fine Bombay restaurant add the dung flavor. In the villages dung patties plastered to the walls, the leavings of the cows the only cooking fuel. The smell rubs into the blood.

Paris in the winter smells of wood smoke and fruit. Near the Gare St. Lazare in the freezing dusk the crowds pour slowly down the streets in every direction. A police van the size of a Pullman car goes at a walking pace. The gendarme keeps jumping down from

the rear like a streetcar conductor in the old days.
He is examining identity cards of pedestrians, es-
pecially the females. A girl comes swinging along,
her pocketbook in rhythm with her behind. She is
bareheaded and wears a raincoat. The gendarme
examines her identity card. She is motioned into the
paddy wagon.

Salzburg, the castle smells of snow and peat. Baltimore,
old oaken bucket. Portsmouth, Virginia, roses and
diesel oil. Dublin, coal dust, saccharine whiskey,
bitter bodies. Damp gusts of Siena doorways. Ware-
houses of Papeete, acrid smell of copra, frangipani,
salt water and mold. Smell of rotting water in Hol-
landia.

Unbreathable jungles, parks subtle and cool. Backstage
the ballet dancers wipe their sweat; "the entire stage
stinks like a stable." Sewer gas of beauty parlors.
Electric smell of hair in rut. Talcum powder, earliest
recollection. Rome, the armpit of the universe.

AUBADE

What dawn is it?
The morning star stands at the end of your street as you
watch me turn to laugh a kind of goodbye, with
love-crazed head like a white satyr moving through
wet bushes.
The morning star bursts in my eye like a hemorrhage as
I enter my car in a dream surrounded by your
heavenly-earthly smell.
The steering wheel is sticky with dew,
The golf course is empty, husbands stir in their sleep
desiring, and though no cocks crow in suburbia, the
birds are making a hell of a racket.
Into the newspaper dawn as sweet as your arms that
hold the old new world, dawn of green lights that
smear the empty streets with come and go.
It is always dawn when I say goodnight to you,
Dawn of wrecked hair and devastated beds,

Dawn when protective blackness turns to blue and lovers
    drive sunward with peripheral vision.
To improvise a little on Villon
Dawn is the end for which we are together.

My house of loaded ashtrays and unwashed glasses, tulip
    petals and columbine that spill on the table and
    splash on the floor,
My house full of your dawns,
My house where your absence is presence,
My slum that loves you, my bedroom of dustmice and
    cobwebs, of local paintings and eclectic posters, my
    bedroom of rust neckties and divorced mattresses,
    and of two of your postcards, *Pierrot with Flowers*
    and *Young Girl with Cat,*
My bed where you have thrown your body down like a
    king's ransom or a boa constrictor.

But I forgot to say: May passed away last night,
May died in her sleep,
That May that blessed and kept our love in fields and
    motels.
I erect a priapic statue to that May for lovers to kiss as
    long as I'm in print, and polish as smooth as the
    Pope's toe.
This morning came June of spirea and platitudes,
This morning came June discreetly dressed in gray,
June of terrific promises and lawsuits.

And where are the poems that got lost in the shuffle of
    spring?
Where is the poem about the eleventh of March, when
    we raised the battleflag of dawn?
Where is the poem about the coral necklace that whipped
    your naked breasts in leaps of love?
The poem concerning the ancient lover we followed
    through your beautiful sleeping head?
The fire-fountain of your earthquake thighs and your
    electric mouth?
Where is the poem about the little one who says my
    name and watches us almost kissing in the sun?
The vellum stretchmarks of your learned belly,
Your rosy-fingered nightgown of nylon and popcorn,

377

Your razor that caresses your calves like my hands?
Where are the poems that are already obsolete, leaves of
    last month, a very historical month?
Maybe I'll write them, maybe I won't, no matter,
And this is the end for which we are together.
Et c'est la fin pour quoy sommes ensemble.

JOHN BERRYMAN (1914–   )

Berryman's most important works are long poems or sequences, too long for reprinting in toto and not readily excerptible; of the major poets of his generation, he is the one least likely to be well represented in an anthology. But it should be noted that two of his poems, *Homage to Mistress Bradstreet* (1956) and the sequence called *Dream Songs* (still in progress), are among the most highly regarded in recent American literature. His mature, somewhat eccentric style, with its abrupt cadence and syntax, evolved slowly from more conventional early poems, published in the thirties. Berryman was born in McAlester, Okla., and educated at Columbia and Cambridge. In addition to his poems, he has written short stories and an important biography of Stephen Crane (1950).

> *Homage to Mistress Bradstreet.* Farrar, Straus & Cudahy, 1956.
> *77 Dream Songs.* Farrar, Straus & Giroux, 1964.
> *Berryman's Sonnets.* Farrar, Straus & Giroux, 1967.
> *Short Poems.* (Collected.) Farrar, Straus & Giroux, 1967.
> *The Dream Songs.* Farrar, Straus & Giroux, 1969.

THE TRAVELLER

They pointed me out on the highway, and they said
'That man has a curious way of holding his head.'

They pointed me out on the beach; they said 'That man
Will never become as we are, try as he can.'

They pointed me out at the station, and the guard
Looked at me twice, thrice, thoughtfully & hard.

I took the same train that the others took,
To the same place. Were it not for that look
And those words, we were all of us the same.
I studied merely maps. I tried to name
The effects of motion on the travellers,

I watched the couple I could see, the curse
And blessings of that couple, their destination,
The deception practised on them at the station,
Their courage. When the train stopped and they knew
The end of their journey, I descended too.

THE MOON AND THE NIGHT AND THE MEN

On the night of the Belgian surrender the moon rose
Late, a delayed moon, and a violent moon
For the English or the American beholder;
The French beholder. It was a cold night,
People put on their wraps, the troops were cold
No doubt, despite the calendar, no doubt
Numbers of refugees coughed, and the sight
Or sound of some killed others. A cold night.

On Outer Drive there was an accident:
A stupid well-intentioned man turned sharp
Right and abruptly he became an angel
Fingering an unfamiliar harp,
Or screamed in hell, or was nothing at all.
Do not imagine this is unimportant.
He was a part of the night, part of the land,
Part of the bitter and exhausted ground
Out of which memory grows.

                              Michael and I
Stared at each other over chess, and spoke
As little as possible, and drank and played.
The chessmen caught in the European eye,
Neither of us I think had a free look
Although the game was fair. The move one made
It was difficult at last to keep one's mind on.
'Hurt and unhappy' said the man in London.
We said to each other, The time is coming near
When none shall have books or music, none his dear,
And only a fool will speak aloud his mind.
History is approaching a speechless end,
As Henry Adams said. Adams was right.

All this occurred on the night when Leopold
Fulfilled the treachery four years before
Begun—or was he well-intentioned, more
Roadmaker to hell than king? At any rate,
The moon came up late and the night was cold,
Many men died—although we know the fate
Of none, nor of anyone, and the war
Goes on, and the moon in the breast of man is cold.

CANTO AMOR

Dream in a dream the heavy soul somewhere
struck suddenly & dark down to its knees.
A griffin sighs off in the orphic air.

If (Unknown Mystery) I not confess
praise for the wrack the rock the live sailor
under the blue sea,—yet I may You bless

always for hér, in fear & joy for hér
whose gesture summons ever when I grieve
me back and is my mage and minister.

—Muses: whose worship I may never leave
but for this pensive woman, now I dare,
teach me her praise! with her my praise receive.—

Three years already of the round world's war
had rolled by stoned & disappointed eyes
when she and I came where we were made for.

Pale as a star lost in returning skies,
more beautiful than midnight stars more frail
she moved towards me like chords, a sacrifice;

entombed in body trembling through the veil
arm upon arm, learning our ancient wound,
we see our one soul heal, recovering pale.

Then priestly sanction, then the drop of sound.
Quickly part to the cavern ever warm
deep from the march, body to body bound,

descend (my soul) out of dismantling storm
into the darkness where the world is made.
.. Come back to the bright air. Love is multiform.

Heartmating hesitating unafraid
although incredulous, she seemed to fill
the lilac shadow with light wherein she played,

whom sorry childhood had made sit quite still,
an orphan silence, unregarded sheen,
listening for any small soft note, not hopeful:

caricature: as once a maiden Queen,
flowering power comeliness kindness grace,
shattered her mirror, wept, would not be seen.

These pities moved. Also above her face
serious or flushed, swayed her fire-gold
not earthly hair, now moonless to unlace,

resistless flame, now in a sun more cold
great shells to whorl about each secret ear,
mysterious histories, white shores, unfold.

New musics! One the music that we hear,
this is the music which the masters make
out of their minds, profound solemn & clear.

And then the other music, in whose sake
all men perceive a gladness but we are drawn
less for that joy than utterly to take

our trial, naked in the music's vision,
the flowing ceremony of trouble and light,
all Loves becoming, none to flag upon.

Such Mozart made,—an ear so delicate
he fainted at a trumpet-call, a child
so delicate. So merciful that sight,

so stern, we follow rapt who ran a-wild.
Marriage is the second music, and thereof
we hear what we can bear, faithful & mild.

Therefore the streaming torches in the grove
through dark or bright, swiftly & now more near
cherish a festival of anxious love.

Dance for this music, Mistress to music dear,
more, that storm worries the disordered wood
grieving the midnight of my thirtieth year

and only the trial of our music should
still this irresolute air, only your voice
spelling the tempest may compel our good:

Sigh then beyond my song: whirl & rejoice!

THE DISPOSSESSED

'and something that . . that is theirs—no longer ours'
stammered to me the Italian page. A wood
seeded & towered suddenly. I understood.—

The Leading Man's especially, and the Juvenile Lead's,
and the Leading Lady's thigh that switches & warms,
and their grimaces, and their flying arms:

our arms, our story. Every seat was sold.
A crone met in a clearing sprouts a beard
and has a tirade. Not a word we heard.

Movement of stone within a woman's heart,
abrupt & dominant. They gesture how
fings really are. Rarely a child sings now.

My harpsichord weird as a koto drums
adagio for twilight, for the storm-worn dove
no more de-iced, and the spidery business of love.

The Juvenile Lead's the Leader's arm, one arm
running the whole bole, branches, roots, (O watch)
and the faceless fellow waving from her crotch,

Stalin-unanimous! who procured a vote
and care not use it, who have kept an eye
and care not use it, percussive vote, clear eye.

That which a captain and a weaponeer
one day and one more day did, we did, *ach*
we did not, *They* did . . cam slid, the great lock

lodged, and no soul of us all was near was near,—
an evil sky (where the umbrella bloomed)
twirled its mustaches, hissed, the ingenue fumed,

poor virgin, and no hero rides. The race
is done. Drifts through, between the cold black trunks,
the peachblow glory of the perishing sun

in empty houses where old things take place.

THE POET'S FINAL INSTRUCTIONS

Dog-tired, suisired, will now my body down
near Cedar Avenue in Minneap,
when my crime comes. I am blazing with hope.
Do me glory, come the whole way across town.

I couldn't rest from hell just anywhere,
in commonplaces. Choiring & strange my pall!
I might not lie still in the waste of St Paul
or buy DAD's root beer; good signs I forgive.

Drop here, with honour due, my trunk & brain
among the passioning of my countrymen
unable to read, rich, proud of their tags
and proud of me. Assemble all my bags!
Bury me in a hole, and give a cheer,
near Cedar on Lake Street, where the used cars live.

FROM *THE BLACK BOOK*

I

Grandfather, sleepless in a room upstairs,
seldom came down; so when they tript him down
we wept. The blind light sang about his ears,

later we heard. Brother had pull. In pairs
he, some, slept upon stone.
Later they stamped him down in mud.
The windlass drew him silly & odd-eyed, blood
broke from his ears before they quit.
Before they trucked him home they cleaned him up some-
    what.

Only the loose eyes' glaze they could not clean
and soon he died. He howled a night and shook
our teeth before the end; we breathed again
when he stopt. Abraham, what we have seen
write, I beg, in your Book.
No more the solemn and high bells
call to our pall; we call or gibber; Hell's
irritable & treacherous
despairs here here (not him) reach now to shatter us.

II

Luftmenschen dream, the men who live on air,
of other values, in the blackness watching
peaceful for gangs or a quick raid,
the ghetto nods a mortal head
soundless but for a scurry, a sigh, retching,—
no moan of generation fear.
Hands hold each other limper
while the moon lengthens on the sliding river.

Prolong the woolen night—Solomon sang—
and never the soul with its own revenge encumber
but like a cry of cranes dies out,
ecstatic, faint, a moment float-
ing, flying soul, or flares like August timber
in wild woe vanishing.
Blue grows from grey, towards slaughter.
(An Ashkenazi genius stoned Ivan; a sculptor.)

"Boleslaus brought us here, surnamed the Good,
whose dust rolls nearly seven hundred years
towards Sirius; we thank that King
as for the ledge whereto we cling,
night in the caves under the ruins; stars,

armbands come off, for which we could
be glad but the black troops gather."
So those who kneel in the paling sky & shiver.

Dawn like a rose unfolds—flower of parks—
alleys of limetrees, villas, ponds, a palace
down a deserted riverbed,
the Lazienki Gardens' pride,
monument to a king able and callous
who far Vienna from the Turks
bloodily did deliver.
For foreigners, now, a sort of theatre.

One officer in black demarches here
cupshot, torn collar by a girl unwilling
native & blond through the debauch
that kept him all night from his couch,
hurts his head and from the others' howling
drove him out for morning air.
Brooding over the water
he reddens suddenly. He went back & shot her.

III

Lover & child, a little sing.
From long-lockt cattle-cars who grope
who near a place of showers come
foul no more, whose murmuring
grows in a hiss of gas will clear them home:
Away from & toward me: a little soap,
disrobing. *Achtung!* in a dirty hope,
they shuffle with their haircuts in to die.
Lift them an elegy, poor you and I,
fair & strengthless as seafoam
under a deserted sky.

OWEN DODSON (1914–   )

Though primarily a dramatist, Dodson has published one book of sharply sardonic poems, mostly on racial themes, as well as more recent work in magazines. He was born in Brooklyn, and is now head of the department of drama at Howard University.

Powerful Long Ladder. Farrar, Straus & Giroux, 1946.

YARDBIRD'S SKULL

for Charlie Parker

The bird is lost,
Dead, with all the music:
Whole sunsets heard the brain's music
Faded to last horizon notes.
I do not know why I hold
This skull, smaller than a walnut's,
Against my ear,
Expecting to hear
The smashed fear
Of childhood from . . . bone;
Expecting to see
Wind nosing red and purple,
Strange gold and magic
On bubbled windowpanes
Of childhood. Shall I hear?
I should hear: this skull
Has been with violets
Not Yorick, or the gravedigger,
Yapping his yelling story,
This skull has been in air,
Sensed his brother, the swallow,
(Its talent for snow and crumbs).
Flown to lost Atlantis islands,
Places of dreaming, swimming lemmings.
O I shall hear skull skull,

Hear your lame music,
Believe music rejects undertaking,
Limps back.
Remember tiny lasting, we get lonely:
Come sing, come sing, come sing sing
And sing.

JEAN GARRIGUE (1914-   )

Miss Garrigue has been prominent among New York poets for some years, though she was born in Indiana; her work has appeared in many magazines and anthologies, and in six books of her own. Her early poems were richly intense, with complex sound patterns and highly colored diction. Recently she has simplified her style, but her themes remain chiefly psychological and cultural, often originating in her travels.

New and Selected Poems. Macmillan, 1968.

CATCH WHAT YOU CAN

The thing to do is try for that sweet skin
One gets by staying deep inside a thing.
The image that I have is that of fruit—
The stone within the plum or some such pith
As keeps the slender sphere both firm and sound.

Stay with me, mountain flowers I saw
And battering moth against a wind-dark rock,
Stay with me till you build me all around
The honey and the clove I thought to taste
If lingering long enough I lived and got
Your intangible wild essence in my heart.
And whether that's by sight or thought
Or staying deep inside an aerial shed
Till imagination makes the heart-leaf vine
Out of damned bald rock, I cannot guess.
The game is worth the candle if there's flame.

REMEMBER THAT COUNTRY

My dear, do you remember that country
Of abandoned stone houses with their roofs toppled in,
Eyes of their windows blank sockets,

Great nest-holes for birds and ways for the wind?
Steps to them crumbling, the grasses grown wild,
Half hay and half weed in the gardens?
And the ascensions and erosions of mountains
Sharply arising from the river's deep basin
Where the hilltowns sat in their jagged nests,
Abandoned as well, and dying.
Ancient, so ancient, built
In the times of the Saracens
When the only defense was retreat
And triple-made bastions of walls out of rock,
So old, who had been driven so far
Up to such verges, to live at all.
Do you remember, and the deep gorges,
Those long gashes in earth the river had cut,
Very fantasias of concentric circles of rock
Up which the stream's bed went?
And the joy of the day, the way the birds sang,
The sun on the river, the rosemary and lavender,
Do you remember the fête and the danceband
To which the nightingales sang?
And the women washing clothes
In the brimmed stone tubs on the turns of the way
Up to the first of those towns so crookedly set
On crazy needles of rock?
And the goat bleating in a shut-in stable?
Do you remember? It was you set the pace,
You would take every zigzag path,
Given up to the vigils of knowing and seeking,
Intolerably wanting to touch every crest,
Go back of each mountain into the stilled
Frozen seas of their wilderness.
That day when we were parched with thirst
It was you who discovered the medlar.
How we robbed that tree of its fruit
For the taste of its happiness!
Do you remember? Such distances!
Such echoes! So many towers!
And the great river we walked by
So many miles! All that had happened!
Such thickness of leaves should you turn to the legends,
The Sieges, the Plague, the Wars of Religion,
The countships, the courts of love

And the olives and lizards by the clamorous river
Drowning our voices as it drowned theirs
That had their eyes once and their bodies,
Stones that they threw, songs that they sang,
And their kisses.
Do you remember those discarded old bridges
Still sustaining substantially
Spans for mere marguerites to take,
In such slow travel, along with the poppies,
Where wagons and horsemen once went?
And that army of sheep back from some grassland,
And their heat, so close-pressed, though they
Were new-shaven, the tremolo of their baas
And their dogs, the donkeys, and shepherds?
Then there was that yellow wild flower
Casting up such fresh gusts of fragrance
That it, broken by the night-singing of birds,
Shall sum up for the rest of my days
An unsullied country, almost beyond the stars.

GEORGE HITCHCOCK (1914–)

A native of the Pacific Northwest, especially the lumber towns of Oregon, Hitchcock has been a longstanding radical activist and surrealist poet. In recent years he has lived in San Francisco. He is founder and editor of the important magazine *Kayak*.

Poems & Prints. San Francisco Review, 1962.
Tactics of Survival. San Francisco: Bindweed Press, 1964.
The Dolphin with the Revolver in Its Teeth. Santa Barbara, Calif.: Unicorn Press, 1967.

THREE PORTRAITS

1. The Peddler

In the zócalo
a one-eyed salesman
offers me a gourd
wrinkled
dried
with the face of God
painted on it
in cochineal & indigo

God is dead,
I tell him.

You are right,
he answers,
but it is only one peso.

I shake the gourd;
the seeds rattle
like thoughts in a dry brain.

O unfortunate country!

2. An Old Man

An old man with
tears on his cheeks
spoke to me in the park.
"Where can I buy shingles?"
is what I thought he said.

But I must have been
mistaken
because
his teeth were gone
his green eyes homeless
and his hands
cupped about some tiny animal—
a moth, perhaps.

3. Student

In her mind
peach blossom
and the Villa
Farnese
on her breast
the deuce of diamonds
and firm/oh firm
in her white hand
the Palo
Alto
bus schedule.

FIGURES IN A RUINED BALLROOM

The chandeliers hemorrhage, Tritons
weep for the plaster dolphins, the pheasant
in its glass room feeds on candle-droppings:

apothecaries cannot heal the wax dogs,
sutures will no longer save Apollo
nor violins awake the stuffed ospreys.

Roses in this carpet grow from a soil
of forgotten shoe-laces and those eyes
which gleamed at cotillions now jostle

393

the glands of mendicants. Dust is king.
Neptune burns in the sea, on a sepia cliff
Aphrodite sits, plaiting a braid of tears.

These statues turn by concealed levers:
their hinges fold in on mortality.

MAY ALL EARTH BE CLOTHED IN LIGHT

Morning spreads over
the beaches like lava;
the waves lie still, they
glitter with pieces of light.

I stand at the window
& watch a heron on one leg,
its plumage white in the green banks
of mint. Behind me
smoke rises from a nest
of bricks, the brass clock
on the kitchen shelf
judges & spares.

Slowly the bird
opens its dazzling wings.
I am filled with joy.
The fields are awake!
the fields with their hidden lizards
& fire of new iris.

DAVID IGNATOW (1914–   )

Ignatow was born in Brooklyn. During the thirties he worked on
a WPA writers' project in Manhattan; later he turned to teaching,
especially at Vassar.

> *Say Pardon.* Wesleyan University Press, 1961.
> *Figures of the Human.* Wesleyan University Press, 1964.
> *Rescue the Dead.* Wesleyan University Press, 1968.

DILEMMA

Whatever we do, whether we light
strangers' cigarettes—it may turn out
to be a detective wanting to know who is free
with a light on a lonely street nights—
or whether we turn away and get a knife
planted between our shoulders for our discourtesy;
whatever we do—whether we marry for love
and wake up to find love is a task,
or whether for convenience, to find love
must be won over or we are desperate—
whatever we do; save by dying,
and there too we are caught,
by being planted too close to our parents.

HE PUTS ME TO REST

I am unhappy that I am not God,
I talk to myself and listen,
hoping to find in this dialogue
a hint of Him. I do things
and measure them to find
God there, or, if not,
that this would prove
the opposite is true.

I would do this opposite
to become God. I think of it,
and when I must sleep
He puts me to rest.

LAST NIGHT

Last night I spoke to a dead woman with green face.
She told me of her good life among the living,
with a faithful man. He was right there
beside her as tall as I, and moving
like me, with kind motions. If she did breathe,
it was just to talk and tell her life
in their basement smelling moist
like freshly opened earth. He was good to her
and she had worked as a typist
every day and came home to cook.
It was a good life with her husband,
he was kind; and she took hold of his hand
and said, "In this basement we've made a home,
with me working as typist and he studying
his music." She was dead, that much she understood
herself by her tone; and she looked at me
with green eyes.

RESCUE THE DEAD

Finally, to forgo love is to kiss a leaf,
is to let rain fall nakedly upon your head,
is to respect fire,
is to study man's eyes and his gestures
as he talks,
is to set bread upon the table
and a knife discreetly by,
is to pass through crowds
like a crowd of oneself.
Not to love is to live.

To love is to be led away
into a forest where the secret grave

is dug, singing, praising darkness
under the trees.

To live is to sign your name,
is to ignore the dead,
is to carry a wallet
and shake hands.

To love is to be a fish.
My boat wallows in the sea.
You who are free,
rescue the dead.

AN ALLEGORY

I offer my back to the silken net
to keep it from falling to the ground—
the smooth part of me,
silk would catch on my nails,
the skein spread as far as I can see
across humped backs like mine.
Those straightening up
through a rip and looking about
say, "How everything shines."

RANDALL JARRELL (1914–1965)

Although Jarrell was born in Nashville and attended Vanderbilt, his outlook was unmarked by the social conservatism of his forerunners there, the Fugitives. His writing, like that of his New York friends after World War II when he was literary editor of the *Nation*, was in the style of urban radicalism. His early poems, written during the war, were stark and bitter; but his later work, often dramatic in structure and phantasmal in effect, became more complex. He was, as one critic has said, a "self-divided southern Romantic." Always an active writer, he turned out many influential reviews and essays, and also one novel, *Pictures from an Institution* (1954), and one children's book, *The Bat-Poet* (1964). During his last years he taught at the Women's College of the University of North Carolina. His death came when he walked onto a highway at night amid speeding traffic.

Poetry and the Age. (Criticism.) Knopf, 1953.
The Complete Poems. Farrar, Straus & Giroux, 1969.

PROTOCOLS

(Birkenau, Odessa; the children speak alternately.)

We went there on the train. *They had big barges that
they towed,
We stood up, there were so many I was squashed.*
There was a smoke-stack, then they made me wash.
It was a factory, I think. *My mother held me up
And I could see the ship that made the smoke.*

When I was tired my mother carried me.
She said, "Don't be afraid." But I was only tired.
Where we went there is no more Odessa.
They had water in a pipe—like rain, but hot;
The water there is deeper than the world

*And I was tired and fell in in my sleep
And the water drank me. That is what I think.*

And I said to my mother, "Now I'm washed and dried,"
My mother hugged me, and it smelled like hay
And that is how you die. And that is how you die.

COME TO THE STONE . . .

The child saw the bombers skate like stones across the
   fields
As he trudged down the ways the summer strewed
With its reluctant foliage; how many giants
Rose and peered down and vanished, by the road
The ants had littered with their crumbs and dead.

"That man is white and red like my clown doll,"
He says to his mother, who has gone away.
"I didn't cry, I didn't cry."
In the sky the planes are angry like the wind.
The people are punishing the people—why?

He answers easily, his foolish eyes
Brightening at that long simile, the world.
The angels sway above his story like balloons.
A child makes everything—except his death—a child's.
Come to the stone and tell me why I died.

A FRONT

Fog over the base: the beams ranging
From the five towers pull home from the night
The crews cold in fur, the bombers banging
Like lost trucks down the levels of the ice.
A glow drifts in like mist (how many tons of it?),
Bounces to a roll, turns suddenly to steel
And tires and turrets, huge in the trembling light.
The next is high, and pulls up with a wail,
Comes round again—no use. And no use for the rest
In drifting circles out along the range;
Holding no longer, changed to a kinder course,
The flights drone southward through the steady rain.
The base is closed. . . . But one voice keeps on calling,

The lowering pattern of the engines grows;
The roar gropes downward in its shaky orbit
For the lives the season quenches. Here below
They beg, order, are not heard; and hear the darker
Voice rising: *Can't you hear me? Over. Over—*
All the air quivers, and the east sky glows.

THE DEATH OF THE BALL TURRET GUNNER

From my mother's sleep I fell into the State,
And I hunched in its belly till my wet fur froze.
Six miles from earth, loosed from its dream of life,
I woke to black flak and the nightmare fighters.
When I died they washed me out of the turret with a
    hose.

VARIATIONS

I

"I lived with Mr. Punch, they said my name was Judy,
I beat him with my rolling-pin, he hit me with his cane.
I ran off with a soldier, he followed in a carriage,
And he drew a big revolver and he shot me through the
    brain.
But that was his duty, he only did his duty—"

Said Judy, said the Judy, said poor Judy to the string.

"O hear her, just hear her!" the string said softly.
And the string and Judy, they said no more.
Yes, string or Judy, it said no more.
But they hanged Mr. Punch with a six-inch rope,
And "Clap," said the manager; "the play is over."

II

"I lay like a swan upon the down of Heaven.
When the clouds came the rain grew
Into the rice of my palaces, the great wits

400

Were the zithers of my garden, I stood among sedge
And held to the peoples the gold staff of God."

Said Grace, said Good, O said the son of God.

The wives and wise, the summer's willows
Nodded and were fed by the wind; when the snow fell
And the wind's steps were pink in the pure winter,
Who spared his charcoal for the son of God,
The vain wind failing at the pass to Hell?

III

"I lived in a room full of bears and porridge,
My mother was dead and my nurse was horrid.
I sat all day on a white china chamber
And I lay all night in my trundle bed.
And she wasn't, she wasn't, O not a bit dead!"

The boy said, the girl said—and Nurse she said:

"I'll stew your ears all day, little hare,
Just as God ate your mother, for you are bad,
Are bad, are bad—" and the nurse is the night
To wake to, to die in: and the day I live,
The world and its life are her dream.

IV

"I was born in a hut, my wit is heavy.
My sister died, they killed my father.
There is no time I was not hungry.
They used me, I am dying.
I stand here among graves."

The white, the yellow, the black man said.

And the world said: Child, you will not be missed.
You are cheaper than a wrench, your back is a road;
Your death is a table in a book.
You had our wit, our heart was sealed to you:
Man is the judgment of the world.

A SICK CHILD

The postman comes when I am still in bed.
"Postman, what do you have for me today?"
I say to him. (But really I'm in bed.)
Then he says—what shall I have him say?

"This letter says that you are president
Of—this word here; it's a republic."
Tell them I can't answer right away.
"It's your duty." No, I'd rather just be sick.

Then he tells me there are letters saying everything
That I can think of that I want for them to say.
I say, "Well, thank you very much. Good-bye."
He is ashamed, and turns and walks away.

If I can think of it, it isn't what I want.
I want . . . I want a ship from some near star
To land in the yard, and beings to come out
And think to me: "So this is where you are!

Come." Except that they won't do,
I thought of them. . . . And yet somewhere there must be
Something that's different from everything.
All that I've never thought of—think of me!

IN MONTECITO

In a fashionable suburb of Santa Barbara,
Montecito, there visited me one night at midnight
A scream with breasts. As it hung there in the sweet air
That was always the right temperature, the contractors
Who had undertaken to dismantle it, stripped off
The lips, let the air out of the breasts.
                                        People disappear
Even in Montecito. Greenie Taliaferro,
In her white maillot, her good figure almost firm,
Her old pepper-and-salt hair stripped by the hairdresser
To nothing and dyed platinum—Greenie has left her Bent-
ley.
They have thrown away her electric toothbrush, someone
    else slips
The key into the lock of her safety-deposit box

402

At the Crocker-Anglo Bank; her seat at the cricket matches
Is warmed by buttocks less delectable than hers.
Greenie's girdle is empty.

                        A scream hangs there in the night:
They strip off the lips, let the air out of the breasts,
And Greenie has gone into the Greater Montecito
That surrounds Montecito like the echo of a scream.

WELL WATER

What a girl called "the dailiness of life"
(Adding an errand to your errand. Saying,
"Since you're up . . ." Making you a means to
A means to a means to) is well water
Pumped from an old well at the bottom of the world.
The pump you pump the water from is rusty
And hard to move and absurd, a squirrel-wheel
A sick squirrel turns slowly, through the sunny
Inexorable hours. And yet sometimes
The wheel turns of its own weight, the rusty
Pump pumps over your sweating face the clear
Water, cold, so cold! you cup your hands
And gulp from them the dailiness of life.

FIELD AND FOREST

When you look down from the airplane you see lines,
Roads, ruts, braided into a net or web—
Where people go, what people do: the ways of life.

Heaven says to the farmer: "What's your field?"
And he answers: "Farming," with a field,
Or: "Dairy-farming," with a herd of cows.
They seem a boy's toy cows, seen from this high.

Seen from this high,
The fields have a terrible monotony.

But between the lighter patches there are dark ones.
A farmer is separated from a farmer
By what farmers have in common: forests,

Those dark things—what the fields were to begin with.
At night a fox comes out of the forest, eats his chickens.
At night the deer come out of the forest, eat his crops.

If he could he'd make farm out of all the forest,
But it isn't worth it: some of it's marsh, some rocks,
There are things there you couldn't get rid of
With a bulldozer, even—not with dynamite.
Besides, he likes it. He had a cave there, as a boy;
He hunts there now. It's a waste of land,
But it would be a waste of time, a waste of money,
To make it into anything but what it is.

At night, from the airplane, all you see is lights,
A few lights, the lights of houses, headlights,
And darkness. Somewhere below, beside a light,
The farmer, naked, takes out his false teeth:
He doesn't eat now. Takes off his spectacles:
He doesn't see now. Shuts his eyes.
If he were able to he'd shut his ears,
And as it is, he doesn't hear with them.
Plainly, he's taken out his tongue: he doesn't talk.
His arms and legs: at least, he doesn't move them.
They are knotted together, curled up, like a child's.
And after he has taken off the thoughts
It has taken him his life to learn,
He takes off, last of all, the world.

When you take off everything what's left? A wish,
A blind wish; and yet the wish isn't blind,
What the wish wants to see, it sees.

There in the middle of the forest is the cave
And there, curled up inside it, is the fox.

He stands looking at it.
Around him the fields are sleeping: the fields dream.
At night there are no more farmers, no more farms.
At night the fields dream, the fields *are* the forest.
The boy stands looking at the fox
As if, if he looked long enough—

                                     he looks at it.
Or is it the fox that's looking at the boy?
The trees can't tell the two of them apart.

WELDON KEES (1914–1955)

Kees was a poet, fiction writer, critic, composer (chiefly in jazz), photographer and film maker, and a painter associated with Willem de Kooning and Hans Hoffman. Born in Nebraska, he worked in New York until 1951, when he moved to San Francisco. In 1955 he disappeared. His car was found near the Golden Gate Bridge; but because he had spoken both of suicide and of retiring abroad under an assumed name, his fate remains conjectural.

Collected Poems. Ed. Donald Justice. Iowa City, Iowa: Stone Wall Press, 1960.

GUIDE TO THE SYMPHONY

Three flutes, two oboes, English horn, violins,
Two clarinets, snare, tuba, tambourine,
And a contra-bassoon played by a worn-looking blonde.

The work is classical in form. *Mit Kraft*:.
A wayward dance proceeds; the woodwind voices and
    the strings
Unite in *agitato* passages that state,

Some critics believe, "Man's long revolt against the Higher
    Will."
Staccato notes, *fortissimo*, engage the clarinets.
The work is dissonant, "though not excessively."

An agitated, almost angry theme ensues, in F.
(Trombones.) A struggle. (Flutes.) And then the scherzo
    movement,
Lachrymose, so often thought to deal

With Western Man's religious hopes gone dim.
Drums; and the famous "Wailing of the Damned" motif.
    (Bassoons.)
A horn sounds yearningly. A short ejaculation from the
    fifes.

Man's nature sweetens (key of B flat); and the reeds,
Augmented by an alto sax, pick up
A hopeful theme (*allegro moderato*), though

Baumgarten writes that Koussevitsky used instead
A *moderato* beat.—But now the gloom
Has deepened once again; the heckelphone implores

In ¾ time, the cellos. Morning. Pan awakes.
Sunrise. Entrance of the false Messiahs. Here
A surging countertheme, in E flat minor, and the oboes
    shrill.

The specter of a dead waltz drifts
In sleep. Bass flutes, violas, and the English horn
Repeat the second theme, in fifths. Sad

Pizzicati of the strings. A bell sounds, and the violins
Lash furiously, subside, diminishing.
(All this in E flat major.) Clarinets sing plaintively.

The last stroke of the hammer. (Tympani.) The sacred
    stag
Is dead. Long anguished *tuttis* by the brass. A final roll
    of drums.
It ends. The concertmaster rubs a little resin on his bow.

LA VITA NUOVA

Last summer, in the blue heat,
Over the beach, in the burning air,
A legless beggar lurched on calloused fists
To where I waited with the sun-dazed birds.
He said, "The summer boils away. My life
Joins to another life; this parched skin
Dries and dies and flakes away,
Becomes your costume when the torn leaves blow."

—Thus in the losing autumn,
Over the streets, I now lurch
Legless to your side and speak your name
Under a gray sky ripped apart
By thunder and the changing wind.

THE BEACH IN AUGUST

The day the fat woman
In the bright blue bathing suit
Walked into the water and died,
I thought about the human
Condition. Pieces of old fruit
Came in and were left by the tide.

What I thought about the human
Condition was this: old fruit
Comes in and is left, and dries
In the sun. Another fat woman
In a dull green bathing suit
Dives into the water and dies.
The pulmotors glisten. It is noon.

We dry and die in the sun
While the seascape arranges old fruit,
Coming in with the tide, glistening
At noon. A woman, moderately stout,
In a nondescript bathing suit,
Swims to a pier. A tall woman
Steps toward the sea. One thinks about the human
Condition. The tide goes in and goes out.

THE COMING OF THE PLAGUE

September was when it began.
Locusts dying in the fields; our dogs
Silent, moving like shadows on a wall;
And strange worms crawling; flies of a kind
We had never seen before; huge vineyard moths;
Badgers and snakes, abandoning
Their holes in the field; the fruit gone rotten;
Queer fungi sprouting; the fields and woods
Covered with spiderwebs; black vapors
Rising from the earth—all these,
And more, began that fall. Ravens flew round
The hospital in pairs. Where there was water,
We could hear the sound of beating clothes
All through the night. We could not count
All the miscarriages, the quarrels, the jealousies.

And one day in a field I saw
A swarm of frogs, swollen and hideous,
Hundreds upon hundreds, sitting on each other,
Huddled together, silent, ominous,
And heard the sound of rushing wind.

SMALL PRAYER

Change, move, dead clock, that this fresh day
May break with dazzling light to these sick eyes.
Burn, glare, old sun, so long unseen,
That time may find its sound again, and cleanse
Whatever it is that a wound remembers
After the healing ends.

JAMES LAUGHLIN (1914–   )

Laughlin established his publishing company, New Directions, while still a student at Harvard in 1936, in order to publish work, then neglected and out of print, by important American avant-garde writers, notably Pound and Williams. Since then, New Directions has been paramount, and sometimes virtually alone, in its friendliness to serious writing of all kinds, especially experimental poetry and fiction. Laughlin's own poetry has been published in several small volumes, but so reticently that few people, except his friends and associates, know it. He lives in Connecticut.

Selected Poems. New Directions, 1959.

THE MOUNTAIN AFTERGLOW

Afterglow goldens the
peak its rock beak glows

like raw blood and red
red is the snowfield

beneath it inevitably my
thoughts go to Christ's

blood which our weakness
drinks and to the blood

of another useless hope-
less war then from its

blackness the heart cries
to the peak O give us a

sign make us a sign
but back to our valley

comes only the sun's
dying glow as so softly

so delicately the bright
rock and snow fade into

night and night clouds
fold dark on the stars.

THE SWARMING BEES

I remember the evening
that Uncle Willy's bees

swarmed in the neigh-
bor's yard high up in

an old box elder tree
that gravid cluster hung

swelled with so many
thousand bees it al-

most broke the branch
and Uncle Willy sent

his boy Peter up the
trunk with a garbage

pail but of course the
pail fell and the whole

big cluster came down
right on top of Uncle

Willy's head but he
stood still and never

got a sting though he
was black with bees so

for the next two weeks
he was quoting Horace

how a wolf won't bite
so virtuous a man and

after he'd coaxed and
smoked the bees into a

new hive he sat out on
the front porch with his

shoes off and drank 3
highballs down one for

the bees & one for the
dead departed soul of

President Heber Grant
& one to the health

of that dauntless war-
rior General Principles

this all happened just
when the Russians were

blasting Berlin and for
a long time that livid

cluster hung in my mind
the black & burned and

crawling deathshead of
my youth's Old Europe.

STEP ON HIS HEAD

Let's step on daddy's head shout
the children my dear children as
we walk in the country on a sunny

summer day my shadow bobs dark on
the road as we walk and they jump
on its head and my love of them

fills me all full of soft feelings
now I duck with my head so they'll
miss when they jump they screech

with delight and I moan oh you're
hurting you're hurting me stop and
they jump all the harder and love

fills the whole road but I see it run
on through the years and I know
how some day they must jump when

it won't be this shadow but really
my head (as I stepped on my own
father's head) it will hurt really

hurt and I wonder if then I will
have love enough will I have love
enough when it's not just a game?

WILLIAM STAFFORD (1914–   )

Stafford's early years were spent in a succession of small Kansan towns, where he absorbed the imagery of prairie and farm that suffuses much of his poetry. A long-standing peace activist, he has served four years in confinement for his conscientious objection to war. Today he teaches at Lewis and Clark College in Oregon.

> *West of Your City*. Los Gatos, Calif.: Talisman Press, 1960.
> *Traveling Through the Dark*. Harper & Row, 1962.
> *The Rescued Year*. Harper & Row, 1966.

ONE HOME

Mine was a Midwest home—you can keep your world.
Plain black hats rode the thoughts that made our code.
We sang hymns in the house; the roof was near God.

The light bulb that hung in the pantry made a wan light,
but we could read by it the names of preserves—
outside, the buffalo grass, and the wind in the night.

A wildcat sprang at Grandpa on the Fourth of July
when he was cutting plum bushes for fuel,
before Indians pulled the West over the edge of the sky.

To anyone who looked at us we said, "My friend";
liking the cut of a thought, we could say, "Hello."
(But plain black hats rode the thoughts that made our code.)

The sun was over our town; it was like a blade.
Kicking cottonwood leaves we ran toward storms.
Wherever we looked the land would hold us up.

413

THE FARM ON THE GREAT PLAINS

A telephone line goes cold;
birds tread it wherever it goes.
A farm back of a great plain
tugs an end of the line.

I call that farm every year,
ringing it, listening, still;
no one is home at the farm,
the line gives only a hum.

Some year I will ring the line
on a night at last the right one,
and with an eye tapered for braille
from the phone on the wall

I will see the tenant who waits—
the last one left at the place;
through the dark my braille eye
will lovingly touch his face.

"Hello, is Mother at home?"
No one is home today.
"But Father—he should be there."
No one—no one is here.

"But you—are you the one . . .?"
Then the line will be gone
because both ends will be home:
no space, no birds, no farm.

My self will be the plain,
wise as winter is gray,
pure as cold posts go
pacing toward what I know.

THE ANIMAL THAT DRANK UP SOUND

1

One day across the lake where echoes come now
an animal that needed sound came down. He gazed
enormously, and instead of making any, he took

away from, sound: the lake and all the land
went dumb. A fish that jumped went back like a knife,
and the water died. In all the wilderness around he
drained the rustle from the leaves into the mountainside
and folded a quilt over the rocks, getting ready
to store everything the place had known; he buried—
thousands of autumns deep—the noise that used to come
    there.

Then that animal wandered on and began to drink
the sound out of all the valleys—the croak of toads,
and all the little shiny noise grass blades make.
He drank till winter, and then looked out one night
at the stilled places guaranteed around by frozen
peaks and held in the shallow pools of starlight.
It was finally tall and still, and he stopped on the highest
ridge, just where the cold sky fell away
like a perpetual curve, and from there he walked on
   silently, and began to starve.

When the moon drifted over that night the whole world
   lay
just like the moon, shining back that still
silver, and the moon saw its own animal dead
on the snow, its dark absorbent paws and quiet
muzzle, and thick, velvet, deep fur.

2

After the animal that drank sound died, the world
lay still and cold for months, and the moon yearned
and explored, letting its dead light float down
the west walls of canyons and then climb its delighted
soundless way up the east side. The moon
owned the earth its animal had faithfully explored.
The sun disregarded the life it used to warm.

But on the north side of a mountain, deep in some rocks,
a cricket slept. It had been hiding when that animal
passed, and as spring came again this cricket waited,
afraid to crawl out into the heavy stillness.
Think how deep the cricket felt, lost there
in such a silence—the grass, the leaves, the water,
the stilled animals all depending on such a little
thing. But softly it tried—"Cricket!"—and back like a river

from one act flowed the kind of world we know,
first whisperings, then moves in the grass and leaves;
the water splashed, and a big night bird screamed.

It all returned, our precious world with its life and sound,
where sometimes loud over the hill the moon,
wild again, looks for its animal to roam, still,
down out of the hills, any time.
But somewhere a cricket waits.

It listens now, and practices at night.

THOMAS MERTON (1915–1968)

Merton's father was an English painter, his mother an American Quaker; he was born in France, educated at French and English schools, then at Cambridge University, then Columbia. In 1938 he became converted to Catholicism. Three years later he entered the Cistercian order as a novice at the Trappist monastery near Gethsemani, Ky., where he lived thereafter. His early work, mystical and apocalyptic, was followed by a period of protest writing, socially and pacifistically oriented. More recently his writing has become philosophical and experimental; he describes his belief as "an eschatological Christian-Zen type radicalism, with no hang-ups on any movement or party, a strictly independent position. . . ." His early autobiographical account of his conversion, *Seven Storey Mountain* (1948), was a great popular success, leading to several other books of catechetical or homiletic intent. But in general Merton concentrated on poetry, speculative essays, and translations, published in more than a score of volumes. He lived in a hermit's cabin on the monastery grounds, where he edited a quarterly magazine, *Monk's Pond*.

> *Selected Poems.* Rev. ed. New Directions, 1967.
> *Cables to the Ace.* New Directions, 1968.
> *Geography of Lograire.* New Directions, 1969.

ST. MALACHY

In November, in the days to remember the dead
When air smells cold as earth,
St. Malachy, who is very old, gets up,
Parts the thin curtains of trees and dawns upon our land.

His coat is filled with drops of rain, and he is bearded
With all the seas of Poseidon.
(Is it a crozier, or a trident in his hand?)
He weeps against the gothic window, and the empty
    cloister
Mourns like an ocean shell.

Two bells in the steeple
Talk faintly to the old stranger
And the tower considers his waters.
"I have been sent to see my festival," (his cavern speaks!)
"For I am the saint of the day.
Shall I shake the drops from my locks and stand in your
    transept,
Or, leaving you, rest in the silence of my history?"

So the bells rang and we opened the antiphoners
And the wrens and larks flew up out of the pages.
Our thoughts became lambs. Our hearts swam like seas.
One monk believed that we should sing to him
Some stone-age hymn
Or something in the giant language.
So we played to him in the plainsong of the giant
    Gregory:
Oceans of Scripture sang upon bony Eire.

Then the last salvage of flowers
(Fostered under glass after the gardens foundered)
Held up their little lamps on Malachy's altar
To peer into his wooden eyes before the Mass began.

Rain sighed down the sides of the stone church.
Storms sailed by all day in battle fleets.
At five o'clock, when we tried to see the sun, the speech-
    less visitor
Sighed and arose and shook the humus from his feet
And with his trident stirred our trees
And left down-wood, shaking some drops upon the ground.

Thus copper flames fall, tongues of fire fall
The leaves in hundreds fall upon his passing
While night sends down her dreadnought darkness
Upon this spurious Pentecost.

And the Melchisedec of our year's end
Who came without a parent, leaves without a trace,
And rain comes rattling down upon our forest
Like the doors of a country jail.

A RESPONSORY, 1948

Suppose the dead could crown their wit
With some intemperate exercise,
Spring wine from their ivory
Or roses from their eyes?

Or if the wise could understand
And the world without heart
That the dead are not yet dead
And that the living live apart

And the wounded are healing,
Though in a place of flame.
The sick in a great ship
Are riding. They are riding home.

Suppose the dead could crown their wit
With some intemperate exercise,
Spring wine from their ivory
Or roses from their eyes?

Two cities sailed together
For many thousand years.
And now they drift asunder.
The tides of new wars

Sweep the sad heavens,
Divide the massed stars,
The black and white universe
The blooming spheres.

Down, down, down
The white armies fall
Moving their ordered snows
Toward the jaws of hell.

Suppose the dead could crown their wit
With some intemperate exercise,
Spring wine from their ivory
Or roses from their eyes?

ELEGY FOR THE MONASTERY BARN

As though an aged person were to wear
Too gay a dress
And walk about the neighborhood
Announcing the hour of her death,

So now, one summer day's end,
At suppertime, when wheels are still,
The long barn suddenly puts on the traitor, beauty,
And hails us with a dangerous cry,
For: "Look!" she calls to the country,
"Look how fast I dress myself in fire!"

Had we half guessed how long her spacious shadows
Harbored a woman's vanity
We would be less surprised to see her now
So loved, and so attended, and so feared.
She, in whose airless heart
We burst our veins to fill her full of hay,
Now stands apart.
She will not have us near her. Terribly,
Sweet Christ, how terribly her beauty burns us now!

And yet she has another legacy,
More delicate, to leave us, and more rare.

Who knew her solitude?
Who heard the peace downstairs
While flames ran whispering among the rafters?
Who felt the silence, there,
The long, hushed gallery
Clean and resigned and waiting for the fire?

Look! They have all come back to speak their summary:
Fifty invisible cattle, the past years
Assume their solemn places one by one.
This is the little minute of their destiny.
Here is their meaning found. Here is their end.

Laved in the flame as in a Sacrament
The brilliant walls are holy
In their first-last hour of joy.

Fly from within the barn! Fly from the silence
Of this creature sanctified by fire!
Let no man stay inside to look upon the Lord!
Let no man wait within and see the Holy
One sitting in the presence of disaster
Thinking upon this barn His gentle doom!

THERE HAS TO BE A JAIL FOR LADIES

There has to be a jail where ladies go
When they are poor, without nice things, and with their
    hair down.
When their beauty is taken from them, when their hearts
    are broken
There is a jail where they must go.

There has to be a jail for ladies, says the Government,
When they are ugly because they are wrong.
It is good for them to stay there a long time
Until the wrong is forgotten.

When no one wants to kiss them any more,
Or only wants to kiss them for money
And take their beauty away
It is right for the wrong to be unheard for a long time
Until the ladies are not remembered.

But I remember one favorite song,
And you ladies may not have forgotten:
"Poor broken blossom, poor faded flower," says my song.

Poor ladies, you are jailed roses:
When you speak you curse, when you curse
God and Hell are rusted together in one red voice
Coming as sweet as dust out of a little hollow heart.
Is there no child, then, in that empty heart?

Poor ladies, if you ever sang
It would be brown notes and sad, from understanding too
    much
No amount of soapsy sudsy supersuds will make you

Dainty again and not guilty
Until the very end, when you are all forgotten.
There is a jail, where guilt is not forgotten.

Not many days, or many years of that stale wall, that
    smell of disinfectant
Trying, without wanting, to kill your sin
Can make you innocent again:
So I come with this sad song
I love you, dusty and sore,
I love you, unhappy ones.

You are jailed buttercups, you are small field flowers,
To me your voice is not brown
Nor is God rusted together with Hell.
Tell me, darlings, can God be in Hell?
You may curse; but He makes your dry voice turn to
    butter
(Though for the policeman it is still brown)
God becomes your heart's prisoner, He will laugh at
    judges.
He will laugh at the jail.
He will make me write this song.

Keep me in your pocket if you have one. Keep me in
    your heart if you have no pocket.
It is not right for your sorrow to be unknown forever.
Therefore I come with these voices:

Poor ladies, do not despair—
God will come to your window with skylarks
And pluck each year like a white rose.

HENRY RAGO (1915–1969)

A lifelong Chicagoan, Rago edited *Poetry* from 1955 until his sudden death in 1969, and brought the magazine to a level of distinction it had never consistently held before. He also was professor of literature and theology in the Divinity School of the University of Chicago. His own meticulously crafted poems are informed by philosophical concern and religious feeling, and are precise yet lyrical definitions of personal spiritual awareness.

The Travelers. Cleveland: Golden Goose Press, 1949.
A Sky of Late Summer. Macmillan, 1963.

THE KNOWLEDGE OF LIGHT

I

The willow shining
From the quick rain,
Leaf, cloud, early star
Are shaken light in this water:
The tremolo of their brightness: light
Sung back in light.

II

The deep shines with the deep.
A deeper sky utters the sky.
These words waver
Between sky and sky.

III

A tree laced of many rivers
Flows into a wide slow darkness
And below the darkness, flowers again
To many rivers, that are a tree.

IV

Wrung from silence
Sung in lightning
From stone sprung

423

The quickening signs
Lines quivered
Numbers flew

Darkness beheld
Darkness and told
Each in each
The depths not darkness.

V

To know
Meaning to celebrate:
Meaning
To become "in some way"
Another; to come
To a becoming:
To have come well.

VI

Earth wakens to the word it wakens.

These dancers turn half-dreaming
Each to the other, glide
Each from a pool of light on either side
Below the dark wings
And flutter slowly, come slowly
Or drift farther again,
Turn to the single note, lifted,
And leap, their whirling lines
Astonished into one lucidity:
Multiples of the arc.

Shapes of the heart!

VII

The year waits at the depth of summer.
The air, the island, and the water
Are drawn to evening. The long month
Is lost in the long evening.

If words could hold this world
They would bend themselves to one

Transparency; if this
Depth of the year, arch of the hour
Came perfect to
The curving of one word
The sound would widen, quietly as from crystal,
Sphere into sphere: candor
Answering a child's candor
Beyond the child's question.

THE SUMMER COUNTRIES

Opened, clear as a child's geography,
The summer countries, the hills
Folding and unfolding. Sunlight
Stretched long upon the beach, hung
Folded and unfolded in the nets:
The land a long morning, the morning
A land, its hours clear and still
As pebbles, corals, blue shells.

As for the first time opened

And the whole sky caught among
Its nets and pebbles, the country never
And always open, and time burst
Into the first time, fell
Cadenzas of first light along
The long beach. It was
Both land and morning, and the light
Was loud and everywhere, like bells.

THE GREEN AFTERNOON

Translucent green on the wall, a dance of leaves,
    Of hands weaving
Peace like a vine on the bedroom wall,

And the white gauze curtains blown
    Of wind or light
Suspend the green afternoon

As the room suspends
   And is the whole house, is the day
Or the one clarity of the day

Asserting its clear furniture,
   Confirming
The definition of itself

Like a choice
   Returned to and returned to, like
A luminous choice.

THOMAS MCGRATH (1916–   )

McGrath's early years were spent, he writes, "on a badly beat up North Dakota farm." He began writing in the thirties, turning quickly to themes of revolutionary politics, and continued during the war and after, producing some of the most authentic poems in the native American radical-labor movement. He has taught at several colleges, and has worked as a film writer. Today he lives in North Dakota.

New and Selected Poems. Denver: Alan Swallow, 1964.

JIG TUNE: NOT FOR LOVE

Where are you going? asked Manny the Mayor.
What are you doing? asked President Jane.
I'll bet you're a bastard, said Daniel the Deacon;
We'll put you away where you'll never be seen.

There won't be no pardon, said Manny the Murderer.
There won't be no stay, said Tommygun Jane.
Said Daniel McBedlam, You won't go no farther;
My father won't even declare you insane.

For a Madman's Way, intoned Manny the Magnate.
The Public Good, shouted Editor Jane.
I think he's a Commie, cried Danny O'Garrote;
If he won't do murder, I call it a crime.

It's not a long drop, sang Manny the Hangman.
The rope will stop you, crooned Juryman Jane.
In a box long and black, chanted Danny Le Flack,
We'll suit you warm to keep out the rain.

All flesh is grass, sighed Manny the Mourner.
The handsome young man, wept Sob-sister Jane.
R.I.P., prayed Capital Daniel;
If he were alive we could kill him again.

A LONG WAY OUTSIDE YELLOWSTONE

Cheyenne, Wyoming, 1940

Across the tracks in Cheyenne, behind the biggest billboard,
Are a couple of human beings who aren't in for the Rodeo.
A week out of Sacramento, Jack, who was once a choir boy,
And Judy, a jail-bird's daughter, make love against the cold.
He gets the night freight for Denver. She hitches out for
    Billings.
But now under one blanket they go about their business.
Suppose you go about yours. Their business is being human,
And because they travel naked they are fifty jumps ahead
    of you
And running with all their lights on while half the world is
    blacked out.

Poverty of all but spirit turns up love like aces
That weren't in the deck at all.
                        Meanwhile the cold
Is scattered like petals of flowers down from the mountains
    of exile
And makes comradeship essential, though perhaps you
    choose not to believe it.
That doesn't matter at all, for their hands touching deny
    you,
Becoming, poor blinded beggars, pilgrims on the road to
    heaven.

Back in the Park, at the best hotel, it is true
The mountains are higher, and the food oftener, and love
As phony as a nine-dollar bill. Though perhaps
When the millionaire kisses the Princess farewell (he's
    going nowhere)
She weeps attractively in the expensive dark, moving—
O delicately—among the broken hearts, perhaps haunted,
Wondering if hers is among them. Or perhaps not.

DEATH FOR THE DARK STRANGER

The knave of darkness, limber in the leaves
Where the blue water blues the green of willows
And the blue geese tamely admire the wild mallows

428

In that always summer where memory grieves and lives,
Was a childhood friend perhaps, but now has other loves.

Or he posed as an uncle maybe, wise,
An old head among the winds of that region,
An impartial umpire while the wars were raging—
Or he was the enchanting stranger with Spartan ways
Whose judgments were always final. But whoever the
    Presence was

He was cop in your county—and nothing ever less—
(Though always, in your private legend, one you knew)
Saying "keep off the grass" and "no, no,"
Infecting all your hopes with sense of loss
And to all new settings-forth crying "alas, alas."

For he is the heart's head-keeper, the bland
Insane director of a rich asylum
Where sanity is poisoned. He is king on that island,
Society's hangman, super-ego, he was born blind;
His loves are like Hitler's: upperclass and blond.

He is the keeper of what we never had,
And in order to arrive where we have never been
He must be numbered with the enemy slain—
His voice be loud with those we never heed:
His death alone unites the warring heart and head.

And wakes the proud blood of those fierce birds—
Else bewitched by their image in the dead still water
Of that enchanted summer where their wild hearts wither
(As our will is weakened by a crutch of words)—
So again the miraculous thunder of discovering wings is
    heard.

A LETTER FOR MARIAN

I sit musing, ten minutes from the Jap,
Six hours by sun from where my heart is,
Forty-three years into the hangman's century,
Half of them signed with the difficult homage
Of personal existence.

My candle is burning at both ends and the middle,
And my halo is blazing, but I'm blind as a bat.
If fortune knocks twice, no one will answer.
Am going on instruments, my private weather
Socked in zero zero.

Sorely troubled by the need for identity
And its best expression, communication.
But the lights fail on the hills, the voice is lost in
The night of the army, or even in death, its
Big fog.

When the telephone rings there's a war on each end.
The message arrives, but there's no one to sign for it.
No one can translate the songs of the birds or
The words on the radio where the ignorant enemy
Is jamming all frequencies.

The need is definition of private boundaries:
This hill is my heart: and these worn mountains
What honor remains: this forest, what courage:
Bounded by love and by need, my frontiers
Extend to include you;

Or the need to say: this is the word and this
Its easiest meaning—for the brave words are all now
Devoured by the small souls from within:
Politicos offer the embroidered noose:
"See if this fits you."

Needed between all men and all peoples
For history to turn on the pimp and the slaver
The eyes of the poor and their terrible judgment.
Simple as the lover says "I am yours."
But not so easy.

SONG

Lovers in ladies' magazines
(Tragedies hinted on the cover)
Avoid Time's nets and part no more
Than from one slick page to another.

430

Romeo and Juliet
Died for Shakespeare, and do again;
Yet, when the last-act curtain falls,
Survive to take love home with them.

We are less lucky whom the miles
And stratagems of sullen war
Divide; for whom Time's snipers lie
In ambush on the calendar.

As in farewell, you stand on the deck and wave
To one on the ship, and over and over say
"Love does not change for time, nor the heart ever—"
But the face at the rail is farther and farther away.

ODE FOR THE AMERICAN DEAD IN KOREA

1

God love you now, if no one else will ever,
Corpse in the paddy, or dead on a high hill
In the fine and ruinous summer of a war
You never wanted. All your false flags were
Of bravery and ignorance, like grade school maps:
Colors of countries you would never see—
Until that weekend in eternity
When, laughing, well armed, perfectly ready to kill
The world and your brother, the safe commanders sent
You into your future. Oh, dead on a hill,
Dead in a paddy, leeched and tumbled to
A tomb of footnotes. We mourn a changeling: you:
Handselled to poverty and drummed to war
By distinguished masters whom you never knew.

2

The bee that spins his metal from the sun,
The shy mole drifting like a miner ghost
Through midnight earth—all happy creatures run
As strict as trains on rails the circuits of
Blind instinct. Happy in your summer follies,
You mined a culture that was mined for war:

The state to mold you, church to bless, and always
The elders to confirm you in your ignorance.
No scholar put your thinking cap on nor
Warned that in dead seas fishes died in schools
Before inventing legs to walk the land.
The rulers stuck a tennis racket in your hand,
An Ark against the flood. In time of change
Courage is not enough: the blind mole dies,
And you on your hill, who did not know the rules.

3

Wet in the windy counties of the dawn
The lone crow skirls his draggled passage home:
And God (whose sparrows fall aslant his gaze,
Like grace or confetti) blinks and he is gone,
And you are gone. Your scarecrow valor grows
And rusts like early lilac while the rose
Blooms in Dakota and the stock exchange
Flowers. Roses, rents, all things conspire
To crown your death with wreaths of living fire.
And the public mourners come: the politic tear
Is cast in the Forum. But, in another year,
We will mourn you, whose fossil courage fills
The limestone histories: brave: ignorant: amazed:
Dead in the rice paddies, dead on the nameless hills.

THEODORE WEISS (1916–   )

Twenty-five years ago Weiss and his wife Renée founded *The Quarterly Review of Literature*, which they have edited since then from various addresses, making it one of the most distinguished and responsive little magazines of the period. Weiss's own poems are introspective, taut, sometimes elliptical; tense with the effort of their own search for simplifications within exactnesses. He teaches now at Princeton.

> *The Catch.* Twayne, 1951.
> *Outlanders.* Macmillan, 1960.
> *Gunsight.* (A long poem.) New York University Press, 1962.
> *The Medium.* Macmillan, 1965.
> *The Last Day and the First.* Macmillan, 1968.

PREFACE

"Sonja Henie," the young girl,
looking out of the evening paper,
cries, "just got married!"

"I don't care if she did,"
the mother replies. "She's been
married before; it's nothing new."

      Darnel, Ragweed, Wortle

And turning to me, the young poet
tries to say once more what weeds
mean to him—
          luscious weeds
riding high, wholly personal:
"O go ahead, hack away as much
as you like; I've been thrown out
of better places than this"—

his face just come back from staring
out the window into a day
wandering somewhere in early fall
and a long quiet contented rain,

the sky still on his face, the barn
out there, green-roofed and shiny,
gay in a wet way with its red
wet-streaked sides.
                        I read his poem,
mainly about how much it likes weeds,
how definite they are, yet how hard
to come by.
                        I say, "Like all the rest
only their own face will do, each
a star squinting through 30,000 years
of storm for its particular sky."

And as though a dream should try
to recollect its dreamer, we look out
across the long highways of rain,
look out

                Darnel, Ragweed, Wortle

I do not say what we both are thinking
as we see it flicker in that rain-
soaked day: the face exceeding
face, name, and memory,
yet clinging to our thoughts.
                                        Black
against the sky, a flock of cranes
shimmers, one unbroken prickly rhythm,
wave on wave, keeping summer jaunty
in its midst.
                And Sonja Henie,
The star, the thin-ice skater,
after many tries, tries once more.

"The poem's not right, I know,
though I worked at it again and again,
I didn't get those old weeds through.
I'm not satisfied, but I'm not done
with it yet."

There in that wheatfield
of failures, beside all manner
of barns, frost already experimenting,
the slant of weather definitely
fall, lovely scratchy

Darnel, Ragweed, Wortle

A DAB OF COLOR

for Ralph Ellison

By dint of color
in his skin
that nature, unrelenting
innovator, dabbled in
(it marked him

off better than fences
can) a wind began,
a winter that companion-
ately and forever
went with him.
O never
twit the artist, never
call him ivory-tower
scholar, bent
on anything but sense.

He knows—for he has
learned from nature—
that a little dab
of color, aptly mixed,
makes all the difference.

THE LAST DAY AND THE FIRST

The stocky woman at the door,
with her young daughter "Linda" looking
down, as she pulls out several copies
of *The Watchtower* from her canvas bag,

in a heavy German accent asks me:
"Have you ever thought that these
may be the last days of the world?"

And to my nodding "Yes, I have,"
she and the delicate, blonde girl
without a further word, turning tail,
sheepishly walk away.
         And I feel
for them, as for us all, this world
in what may be its last days.
And yet this day itself is full
of unbelief, that or marvelously
convincing ignorance.
         Its young light
O so tentative, those first steps
as of a beginning dance (snowdrops
have already started up, and crocuses
we heard about last night the teller's
children quickly trampled in play)

make it hard not to believe that we are
teetering on creation's brink all over
again. And I almost thrill with fear
to think of what will soon be asked
of us, of you and me;
         am I at least
not a little old now (like the world)
to be trembling on the edge
of nakedness, a love, as Stendhal
knew it, "as people love for the first
time at nineteen and in Italy"?

Ah well, until I have to crawl
on hands and knees and then can crawl
no more, so may it every Italian-
returning season be, ever the last
day of this world about to burst
and ever for blossoming the first.

A LETTER FROM THE PYGMIES

Dear Whoever-You-Are-That-You-Are,

Whatever chance this has of reaching You,
I write to bring You up to date.

I cannot, little as I join them
in their skills at hunting,
undertake Your tigers. Rarely
do Your dotty auks invite me
to the confabs of their aeries.
Pastimes Leviathan delights in
never has he offered to share
with me; never has he proffered
island back or cove-snug belly.

Still there is the cat Hoppy
who, whatever our blandishments,
as he cannot drop his creaturehood,
claws flying in his pleasure, takes me
some good distance into Your creation;
dew starlit on his fur, the fields
wherein Your wonders grow he smells of.
And when, unblinkingly, he fixes me
as though he were upon the scent

of rabbit, mouse, or other friend,
I know the instantaneous delight
of terror. So elation finds me
in the chickadee that bobs
upon our thrashing window-bush,
skullcap awry like any plucky Jew's,
a Job in synagogue of ashes, cries;
as Hoppy bats the pane, it never
budges from our fat-packed rind.

In short, though there's a scheme
afoot to blow Your ark and all in it

to smithereens, to pitch a cloudy,
climbing tower will convert the earth
into one tomb, I know by feelings
craning, preening deep inside
the ark's still riding, riding high.

So from time to time, what time remains,
I'll do my best to keep in touch with You.

Faithfully yours,
Theodore

GWENDOLYN BROOKS (1917–)

Although born in Topeka, Miss Brooks grew up on Chicago's
South Side, where she still lives, and her poetry has consistently
dealt with the stresses of individual and neighborhood life in that
milieu. She has also written a novel, *Maud Martha* (1953).

Selected Poems. Harper & Row, 1963.
In the Mecca. Harper & Row, 1968.

A STREET IN BRONZEVILLE:
SOUTHEAST CORNER

The School of Beauty's a tavern now.
The Madam is underground.
Out at Lincoln, among the graves
Her own is early found.
Where the thickest, tallest monument
Cuts grandly into the air
The Madam lies, contentedly.
Her fortune, too, lies there,
Converted into cool hard steel
And right red velvet lining;
While over her tan impassivity
Shot silk is shining.

BEVERLY HILLS, CHICAGO

"and the people live till they have white hair"
E. M. Price

The dry brown coughing beneath their feet,
(Only a while, for the handyman is on his way)
These people walk their golden gardens.
We say ourselves fortunate to be driving by today.

That we may look at them, in their gardens where
The summer ripeness rots. But not raggedly.
Even the leaves fall down in lovelier patterns here.
And the refuse, the refuse is a neat brilliancy.

When they flow sweetly into their houses
With softness and slowness touched by that everlasting
  gold,
We know what they go to. To tea. But that does not mean
They will throw some little black dots into some water and
  add sugar and the juice of the cheapest lemons that are
  sold,

While downstairs that woman's vague phonograph bleats,
  "Knock me a kiss."
And the living all to be made again in the sweatingest phys-
  ical manner
Tomorrow.... Not that anybody is saying that these people
  have no trouble.
Merely that it is trouble with a gold-flecked beautiful
  banner.

Nobody is saying that these people do not ultimately cease
  to be. And
Sometimes their passings are even more painful than ours.
It is just that so often they live till their hair is white.
They make excellent corpses, among the expensive
  flowers. . . .

Nobody is furious. Nobody hates these people.
At least, nobody driving by in this car.
It is only natural, however, that it should occur to us
How much more fortunate they are than we are.

It is only natural that we should look and look
At their wood and brick and stone
And think, while a breath of pine blows,
How different these are from our own.

We do not want them to have less.
But it is only natural that we should think we have not
  enough.
We drive on, we drive on.
When we speak to each other our voices are a little gruff.

BIG BESSIE THROWS HER SON INTO THE STREET

A day of sunny face and temper.
The winter trees
Are musical.

Bright lameness from my beautiful disease,
You have your destiny to chip and eat.

Be precise.
With something better than candles in the eyes.
(Candles are not enough.)

At the root of the will, a wild inflammable stuff.

New pioneer of days and ways, be gone.
Hunt out your own or make your own alone.

Go down the street.

ROBERT LOWELL (1917–   )

Lowell belongs to the famous Bostonian family which has also produced James Russell Lowell, Percival Lowell, and a number of other distinguished writers and scholars. A graduate of Kenyon College, where he studied under John Crowe Ransom, Lowell began writing poetry, chiefly devotional poems on historical themes, in a highly formalistic manner, which he later modified considerably in his more expressly autobiographical work. The toughness and artistic sincerity of his work have made him one of the most influential poets of his generation. Jailed for draft resistance during World War II, he has been associated closely with recent movements for peace and civil rights in the U.S.

Lord Weary's Castle. Harcourt, Brace, 1946.
The Mills of the Kavanaughs. Harcourt, Brace, 1951.
Life Studies. Farrar, Straus & Cudahy, 1959.
Imitations. (Translations.) Farrar, Straus & Cudahy, 1961.
For the Union Dead. Farrar, Straus & Giroux, 1964.
The Old Glory. (Plays.) Farrar, Straus & Giroux, 1965.
Near the Ocean. Farrar, Straus & Giroux, 1967.
Notebook. Farrar, Straus & Giroux, 1969.

THE DRUNKEN FISHERMAN

Wallowing in this bloody sty,
I cast for fish that pleased my eye
(Truly Jehovah's bow suspends
No pots of gold to weight its ends);
Only the blood-mouthed rainbow trout
Rose to my bait. They flopped about
My canvas creel until the moth
Corrupted its unstable cloth.

A calendar to tell the day;
A handkerchief to wave away
The gnats; a couch unstuffed with storm
Pouching a bottle in one arm;
A whiskey bottle full of worms;

And bedroom slacks: are these fit terms
To mete the worm whose molten rage
Boils in the belly of old age?

Once fishing was a rabbit's foot—
O wind blow cold, O wind blow hot,
Let suns stay in or suns step out:
Life danced a jig on the sperm-whale's spout—
The fisher's fluent and obscene
Catches kept his conscience clean.
Children, the raging memory drools
Over the glory of past pools.

Now the hot river, ebbing, hauls
Its bloody waters into holes;
A grain of sand inside my shoe
Mimics the moon that might undo
Man and Creation too; remorse,
Stinking, has puddled up its source;
Here tantrums thrash to a whale's rage.
This is the pot-hole of old age.

Is there no way to cast my hook
Out of this dynamited brook?
The Fisher's sons must cast about
When shallow waters peter out.
I will catch Christ with a greased worm,
And when the Prince of Darkness stalks
My bloodstream to its Stygian term . . .
On water the Man-Fisher walks.

AT THE INDIAN KILLER'S GRAVE

> *"Here, also, are the veterans of King Philip's War,
> who burned villages and slaughtered young and old,
> with pious fierceness, while the godly souls through-
> out the land were helping them with prayer."*
>   Hawthorne.

Behind King's Chapel what the earth has kept
Whole from the jerking noose of time extends
Its dark enigma to Jehoshaphat;

Or will King Philip plait
The just man's scalp in the wailing valley! Friends,
Blacker than these black stones the subway bends
About the dirty elm roots and the well
For the unchristened infants in the waste
Of the great garden rotten to its root;
Death, the engraver, puts forward his bone foot
And Grace-with-wings and Time-on-wings compel
All this antique abandon of the disgraced
To face Jehovah's buffets and his ends.

The dusty leaves and frizzled lilacs gear
This garden of the elders with baroque
And prodigal embellishments but smoke,
Settling upon the pilgrims and their grounds,
Espouses and confounds
Their dust with the off-scourings of the town;
The libertarian crown
Of England built their mausoleum. Here
A clutter of Bible and weeping willows guards
The stern Colonial magistrates and wards
Of Charles the Second, and the clouds
Weep on the just and unjust as they will,—
For the poor dead cannot see Easter crowds
On Boston Common or the Beacon Hill
Where strangers hold the golden Statehouse dome
For good and always. Where they live is home:
A common with an iron railing: here
Frayed cables wreathe the spreading cenotaph
Of John and Mary Winslow and the laugh
Of Death is hacked in sandstone, in their year.

A green train grinds along its buried tracks
And screeches. When the great mutation racks
The Pilgrim Fathers' relics, will these placques
Harness the spare-ribbed persons of the dead
To battle with the dragon? Philip's head
Grins on the platter, fouls in pantomime
The fingers of kept time:
"Surely, this people is but grass,"
He whispers, "this will pass;
But, Sirs, the trollop dances on your skulls
And breaks the hollow noddle like an egg

That thought the world an eggshell. Sirs, the gulls
Scream from the squelching wharf-piles, beg a leg
To crack their crops. The Judgment is at hand;
Only the dead are poorer in this world
Where State and elders thundered *raca*, hurled
Anathemas at nature and the land
That fed the hunter's gashed and green perfection—
Its settled mass concedes no outlets for your puns
And verbal Paradises. Your election,
Hawking above this slime
For souls as single as their skeletons,
Flutters and claws in the dead hand of time."

When you go down this man-hole to the drains,
The doorman barricades you in and out;
You wait upon his pleasure. All about
The pale, sand-colored, treeless chains
Of T-squared buildings strain
To curb the spreading of the braced terrain;
When you go down this hole, perhaps your pains
Will be rewarded well; no rough-cast house
Will bed and board you in King's Chapel. Here
A public servant putters with a knife
And paints the railing red
Forever, as a mouse
Cracks walnuts by the headstones of the dead
Whose chiselled angels peer
At you, as if their art were long as life.

I ponder on the railing at this park:
Who was the man who sowed the dragon's teeth,
That fabulous or fancied patriarch
Who sowed so ill for his descent, beneath
King's Chapel in this underworld and dark?
John, Matthew, Luke and Mark,
Gospel me to the Garden, let me come
Where Mary twists the warlock with her flowers—
Her soul a bridal chamber fresh with flowers
And her whole body an ecstatic womb,
As through the trellis peers the sudden Bridegroom.

FOR GEORGE SANTAYANA

1863–1952

In the heydays of 'forty-five,
bus-loads of souvenir-deranged
G.I.'s and officer-professors of philosophy
came crashing through your cell,
puzzled to find you still alive,
free-thinking Catholic infidel,
stray spirit, who'd found
the Church too good to be believed.
Later I used to dawdle
past Circus and Mithraic Temple
to *Santo Stefano* grown paper-thin
like you from waiting. . . .
There at the monastery hospital,
you wished those geese-girl sisters wouldn't bother
their heads and yours by praying for your soul:
"There is no God and Mary is His Mother."

Lying outside the consecrated ground
forever now, you smile
like Ser Brunetto running for the green
cloth at Verona—not like one
who loses, but like one who'd won . . .
as if your long pursuit of Socrates'
demon, man-slaying Alcibiades,
the demon of philosophy, at last had changed
those fleeting virgins into friendly laurel trees
at *Santo Stefano Rotondo*, when you died
near ninety,
still unbelieving, unconfessed and unreceived,
true to your boyish shyness of the Bride.

Old trooper, I see your child's red crayon pass,
bleeding deletions on the galleys you hold
under your throbbing magnifying glass,
that worn arena, where the whirling sand
and broken-hearted lions lick your hand
refined by bile as yellow as a lump of gold.

MY LAST AFTERNOON WITH UNCLE DEVEREUX WINSLOW

1922: the stone porch of my Grandfather's summer house

I

"I won't go with you. I want to stay with Grandpa!"
That's how I threw cold water
on my Mother and Father's
watery martini pipe dreams at Sunday dinner.
. . . Fontainebleau, Mattapoisett, Puget Sound. . . .
Nowhere was anywhere after a summer
at my Grandfather's farm.
Diamond-pointed, athirst and Norman,
its alley of poplars
paraded from Grandmother's rose garden
to a scarey stand of virgin pine,
scrub, and paths forever pioneering.

One afternoon in 1922,
I sat on the stone porch, looking through
screens as black-grained as drifting coal.
Tockytock, tockytock
clumped our Alpine, Edwardian cuckoo clock,
slung with strangled, wooden game.
Our farmer was cementing a root-house under the hill.
One of my hands was cool on a pile
of black earth, the other warm
on a pile of lime. All about me
were the works of my Grandfather's hands:
snapshots of his *Liberty Bell* silver mine;
his high school at *Stukkert am Neckar;*
stogie-brown beams; fool's-gold nuggets;
octagonal red tiles,
sweaty with a secret dank, crummy with ant-stale;
a Rocky Mountain chaise longue,
its legs, shellacked saplings.
A pastel-pale Huckleberry Finn
fished with a broom straw in a basin
hollowed out of a millstone.
Like my Grandfather, the décor
was manly, comfortable,
overbearing, disproportioned.

What were those sunflowers? Pumpkins floating shoulder-
   high?
It was sunset, Sadie and Nellie
bearing pitchers of ice-tea,
oranges, lemons, mint, and peppermints,
and the jug of shandygaff,
which Grandpa made by blending half and half
yeasty, wheezing homemade sarsaparilla with beer.
The farm, entitled *Char-de-sa*
in the Social Register,
was named for my Grandfather's children:
Charlotte, Devereux, and Sarah.
No one had died there in my lifetime . . .
Only Cinder, our Scottie puppy
paralysed from gobbling toads.
I sat mixing black earth and lime.

II

I was five and a half.
My formal pearl gray shorts
had been worn for three minutes.
My perfection was the Olympian
poise of my models in the imperishable autumn
display windows
of Rogers Peet's boys' store below the State House
in Boston. Distorting drops of water
pinpricked my face in the basin's mirror.
I was a stuffed toucan
with a bibulous multicolored beak.

III

Up in the air
by the lakeview window in the billiards-room,
lurid in the doldrums of the sunset hour,
my Great Aunt Sarah
was learning *Samson and Delilah*.
She thundered on the keyboard of her dummy piano,
with gauze curtains like a boudoir table,
accordionlike yet soundless.
It had been bought to spare the nerves
of my Grandmother,
tone-deaf, quick as a cricket,

now needing a fourth for "Auction,"
and casting a thirsty eye
on Aunt Sarah, risen like the phoenix
from her bed of troublesome snacks and Tauchnitz classics.
Forty years earlier,
twenty, auburn headed,
grasshopper notes of genius!
Family gossip says Aunt Sarah
tilted her archaic Athenian nose
and jilted an Astor.
Each morning she practiced
on the grand piano at Symphony Hall,
deathlike in the off-season summer—
its naked Greek statues draped with purple
like the saints in Holy Week. . . .
On the recital day, she failed to appear.

IV

I picked with a clean finger nail at the blue anchor
on my sailor blouse washed white as a spinnaker.
What in the world was I wishing?
. . . A sail-colored horse browsing in the bullrushes . . .
A fluff of the west wind puffing
my blouse, kiting me over our seven chimneys,
troubling the waters. . . .
As small as sapphires were the ponds: *Quittacus, Snip-
    pituit,*
and *Assawompset,* halved by "the Island,"
where my Uncle's duck blind
floated in a barrage of smoke-clouds.
Double-barrelled shotguns
stuck out like bundles of baby crow-bars.
A single sculler in a camouflaged kayak
was quacking to the decoys. . . .
At the cabin between the waters,
the nearest windows were already boarded.
Uncle Devereux was closing camp for the winter.
As if posed for "the engagement photograph,"
he was wearing his severe
war-uniform of a volunteer Canadian officer.
Daylight from the doorway riddled his student posters,
tacked helter-skelter on walls as raw as a board-walk.

Mr. Punch, a water melon in hockey tights,
was tossing off a decanter of Scotch.
La Belle France in a red, white and blue toga
was accepting the arm of her "protector,"
the ingenu and porcine Edward VII.
The pre-war music hall belles
had goose necks, glorious signatures, beauty-moles,
and coils of hair like rooster tails.
The finest poster was two or three young men in khaki
    kilts
being bushwhacked on the veldt—
They were almost life-size. . . .

My Uncle was dying at twenty-nine.
"You are behaving like children,"
said my Grandfather,
when my Uncle and Aunt left their three baby daughters,
and sailed for Europe on a last honeymoon . . .
I cowered in terror.
I wasn't a child at all—
unseen and all-seeing, I was Agrippina
in the Golden House of Nero. . . .
Near me was the white measuring-door
my Grandfather had pencilled with my Uncle's heights.
In 1911, he had stopped growing at just six feet.
While I sat on the tiles,
and dug at the anchor on my sailor blouse,
Uncle Devereux stood behind me.
He was as brushed as Bayard, our riding horse.
His face was putty.
His blue coat and white trousers
grew sharper and straighter.
His coat was a blue jay's tail,
his trousers were solid cream from the top of the bottle.
He was animated, hierarchical,
like a ginger snap man in a clothes-press.
He was dying of the incurable Hodgkin's disease. . . .
My hands were warm, then cool, on the piles
of earth and lime,
a black pile and a white pile. . . .
Come winter,
Uncle Devereux would blend to the one color.

COMMANDER LOWELL

1887–1950

There were no undesirables or girls in my set,
when I was a boy at Mattapoisett—
only Mother, still her Father's daughter.
Her voice was still electric
with a hysterical, unmarried panic,
when she read to me from the Napoleon book.
Long-nosed Marie Louise
Hapsburg in the frontispiece
had a downright Boston bashfulness,
where she grovelled to Bonaparte, who scratched his
    navel,
and bolted his food—just my seven years tall!
And I, bristling and manic,
skulked in the attic,
and got two hundred French generals by name,
from *A* to *V*—from Augereau to Vandamme.
I used to dope myself asleep,
naming those unpronounceables like sheep.

Having a naval officer
for my Father was nothing to shout
about to the summer colony at "Matt."
He wasn't at all "serious,"
when he showed up on the golf course,
wearing a blue serge jacket and numbly cut
white ducks he'd bought
at a Pearl Harbor commissariat. . . .
and took four shots with his putter to sink his putt.
"Bob," they said, "golf's a game you really ought to
    know how to play,
if you play at all."
They wrote him off as "naval,"
naturally supposed his sport was sailing.
Poor Father, his training was engineering!
Cheerful and cowed
among the seadogs at the Sunday yacht club,
he was never one of the crowd.

"Anchors aweigh," Daddy boomed in his bathtub,
"Anchors aweigh,"
when Lever Brothers offered to pay
him double what the Navy paid.
I nagged for his dress sword with gold braid,
and cringed because Mother, new
caps on all her teeth, was born anew
at forty. With seamanlike celerity,
Father left the Navy,
and deeded Mother his property.

He was soon fired. Year after year,
he still hummed "Anchors aweigh" in the tub—
whenever he left a job,
he bought a smarter car.
Father's last employer
was Scudder, Stevens and Clark, Investment Advisors,
himself his only client.
While Mother dragged to bed alone,
read Menninger,
and grew more and more suspicious,
he grew defiant.
Night after night,
à la clarté déserte de sa lampe,
he slid his ivory Annapolis slide rule
across a pad of graphs—
piker speculation! In three years
he squandered sixty thousand dollars.

Smiling on all,
Father was once successful enough to be lost
in the mob of ruling-class Bostonians.
As early as 1928,
he owned a house converted to oil,
and redecorated by the architect
of St. Mark's School. . . . Its main effect
was a drawing room, "longitudinal as Versailles,"
its ceiling, roughened with oatmeal, was blue as the sea.
And once
nineteen, the youngest ensign in his class,
he was "the old man" of a gunboat on the Yangtze.

FALL 1961

Back and forth, back and forth
goes the tock, tock, tock
of the orange, bland, ambassadorial
face of the moon
on the grandfather clock.

All autumn, the chafe and jar
of nuclear war;
we have talked our extinction to death.
I swim like a minnow
behind my studio window.

Our end drifts nearer,
the moon lifts,
radiant with terror.
The state
is a diver under a glass bell.

A father's no shield
for his child.
We are like a lot of wild
spiders crying together,
but without tears.

Nature holds up a mirror.
One swallow makes a summer.
It's easy to tick
off the minutes,
but the clockhands stick.

Back and forth!
Back and forth, back and forth—
my one point of rest
is the orange and black
oriole's swinging nest!

NIGHT SWEAT

Work-table, litter, books and standing lamp,
plain things, my stalled equipment, the old broom—
but I am living in a tidied room,
for ten nights now I've felt the creeping damp
float over my pajamas' wilted white . . .
Sweet salt embalms me and my head is wet,
everything streams and tells me this is right;
my life's fever is soaking in night sweat—
one life, one writing! But the downward glide
and bias of existing wrings us dry—
always inside me is the child who died,
always inside me is his will to die—
one universe, one body . . . in this urn
the animal night sweats of the spirit burn.
Behind me! You! Again I feel the light
lighten my leaded eyelids, while the gray
skulled horses whinny for the soot of night.
I dabble in the dapple of the day,
a heap of wet clothes, seamy, shivering,
I see my flesh and bedding washed with light,
my child exploding into dynamite,
my wife . . . your lightness alters everything,
and tears the black web from the spider's sack,
as your heart hops and flutters like a hare.
Poor turtle, tortoise, if I cannot clear
the surface of these troubled waters here,
absolve me, help me, Dear Heart, as you bear
this world's dead weight and cycle on your back.

WILLIAM BRONK (1918–   )

Bronk, who did not begin publishing his witty, pessimistic, and philosophically acute poems until he was forty-five, is a business-man in Hudson Falls, N.Y.

The World, the Worldless. New Directions, 1964.

METONYMY AS AN APPROACH TO A REAL WORLD

Whether what we sense of this world
is the what of this world only, or the what
of which of several possible worlds
—which what?—something of what we sense
may be true, may be the world, what it is, what we sense.
For the rest, a truce is possible, the tolerance
of travelers, eating foreign foods, trying words
that twist the tongue, to feel that time and place,
not thinking that this is the real world.

Conceded, that all the clocks tell local time;
conceded, that "here" is anywhere we bound
and fill a space; conceded, we make a world:
is something caught there, contained there,
something real, something which we can sense?
Once in a city blocked and filled, I saw
the light lie deep in the chasm of a street,
palpable and blue, as though it had drifted in
from, say, the sea, a purity of space.

THE FEELING

One has a feeling it is all coming to an end;
no, not that. One has a feeling it is like
that war whose last battle was fought long
after the treaty was signed. The imminence
relates to a past doom. We look back

to one time, some time, something that already has
happened. Look, we are still here, but note
that nothing of moment has happened for an age, an age,
for as long as we can piece together, not
since the time it happened. Was there that time?
Once, there must have been. When will it end?

A POSTCARD TO SEND TO SUMER

Something you said—I found it written down—
and your picture yesterday, brought back old times.
We are here in another country now. It's hard.
(When was it ever different?) The language is odd;
we have to grope for words for what we mean.
And we hardly ever really feel at home
as though we might be happier somewhere else.
Companion, brother, (this is funny) I look
for you among the faces as if I might find
you here, or find you somewhere, and problems would
   then
be solved. What problems are ever solved?
Brother, the stars are almost all the same
and in good weathers—here it is summer now—
when the airs are kind, it seems the world and we
might last unchanged forever. Brother, I think
you would like it here in spite of everything.
I don't know where to send this to you. Perhaps
I'll be able to find it before the mails have closed.

ASPECTS OF THE WORLD LIKE CORAL REEFS

In the spring woods, how good it is to see
again the trees, old company,
how they have withstood the winter, their girth.

By gradual actions, how the gross earth
gathers around us and grows real, is there,
as though it were really there, and is good.

Certain stars, of stupendous size, are said
to be such and such distances away,—
oh, farther than the eyes alone would ever see.

Thus magnified, the whole evidence
of our senses is belied. For it is not
possible for miles to add miles to miles

forever, not even if expressed as the speed of light.
The fault lies partly in the idea of miles.
It is absurd to describe the world in sensible terms.

How good that even so, aspects of the world
that are real, or seem to be real, should rise like reefs
whose rough agglomerate smashes the sea.

THE BODY

Watch it. That's the body: what goes on
next door. Here, you can see it. Turn out the light;
their luminousness will show more in our dark.
What are they doing? We seldom know for sure,
but what a pleasure it is to watch. Look now!
I think he hit her, did he? We can't hear
what they say. Sometimes in summer a little. Then,
when the windows are open. But most of the time we
    guess.
It's like a play: he said. . . ., she said. . . . Write
your own lines as you will. Or leave them blank.
Blank as they are. Or are they? You look at a back
sometimes and know it's talking. There are even times
it's almost all we want to do, to go
right over and move right in; but after all,
we live here, not there, and have, as you know,
for a long time. These people, they come and go.
But it's fascinating. There's always something new.

ROBERT DUNCAN (1919–   )

Although Duncan began to write and publish poems in an experimental manner during the thirties, he reckons the beginning of his mature work from the late forties, the years of Pound's *Pisan Cantos*, Williams's *Paterson*, and Olson's essay on "Projective Verse." Since then, he has produced work that is more than impressive for its scope, depth of feeling, and variety of verbal effect. His writing includes several open sequences, verse dramas, translations, modern re-creations of poems from past English literature, and many individual lyrics. In addition, for some years he has been at work on an extended critical appreciation of the poetry of H.D., parts of which have appeared in magazines. Duncan has lived on Mallorca and has taught at eastern colleges, but California has been his real home from birth, including a period of five years in childhood spent in Yosemite Valley.

> *Roots and Branches*. Scribner's, 1964.
> *Bending the Bow*. New Directions, 1968.
> *Faust Foutu, a Comic Mask*. San Francisco: White Rabbit Press, 1958.
> *From the Mabinogion*. University of North Carolina Press, 1963.
> *Medea at Kolchic*. Berkeley, Calif.: Oyez Press, 1965.
> *The Sweetness and Greatness of Dante's Divine Comedy, 1265–1965*. San Francisco: Open Space, 1965.
> *The Years as Catches: First Poems (1939–1946)*. Berkeley, Calif.: Oyez Press, 1966.
> *Epilogos*. Los Angeles: Black Sparrow Press, 1967.

ROOTS AND BRANCHES

    Sail, Monarchs, rising and falling
orange merchants in spring's flowery markets!
messengers of March in warm currents of news floating,
    flitting into areas of aroma,
tracing out of air unseen roots and branches of sense
    I share in thought,
filaments woven and broken where the world might light
    casual certainties of me. There are

echoes of what I am in what you perform
this morning. How you perfect my spirit!
    almost restore
an imaginary tree of the living in all its doctrines
    by fluttering about,
intent and easy as you are, the profusion of you!
awakening transports of an inner view of things.

NIGHT SCENES

1

The moon's up-riding makes a line
    flowing out into lion's mane
of traffic, of speeding lights.

And in the nest of neon-glow and shadows
the nets of the city's merchants and magickers
restless move towards deserted streets where morning
    breaks,
holding back heaviness, emptiness, night,
    with a hand of light fingers tapping,
obscuring the drift of stars,   waiting . . .

    The whale-shark dark with the universe
pushes up a blunt nose of loneliness
    against the thin strands, shakes
the all-night glare of the street lamps,
    so that for a moment terror
touches my heart, our hearts, all hearts
    that have come in along these sexual avenues
seeking to release Eros from our mistrust.

    Our nerves respond to the police-cars cruising,
a part of the old divine threat. How in each
    time the design is still moving. The city roars
and is a lion. But it is a deep element,
    a treacherous leviathan.

The moon climbs the scale of souls.
O, to release the first music somewhere again,
    for a moment
to touch the design of the first melody!

and in what tempers restore that current
    which forth-flowing goes
a wholeness green lovers know
    as each in each a fearful happiness
sees the resolute eye in which
    opposites
spring twined forthright.

A light toward the knotted tides of dark,
into the tenderness of the crown, night's dominion,
I saw the Prince of Morning fall,
                 opening in fucking a door of Eros.

And from the Beast a man that was Day came
shaking my heart like a storm in old trees.

      Attendant, the maiden hours dance
      with tambourines and tiny bells clustering,
      circling to slow down ecstasy.

      Time in the folds of their skirts' motion
      sways as if from a center
        that is female
      —there being to four o'clock in the morning
        breasts, undulating belly, thighs,
        an inner temple of durations.

          The charme dissolves apace
And as the morning steales upon the night
(Melting the darkness) so their rising scenes
Begin to chace the ignorant fumes that mantle
Their cleerer reason

               sweet Ariel-song the body hears
in the mother-tides of the first magic—

Where the Bee sucks, there, the airy spirit sings, *suck I!*
Where does the bee sip? harvest what honey
    in what beehive?
In a Cowslips bell, I lie   —at the ledge

youth spurts, at the lip the flower
    lifts lifewards, at the
four o'clock in the morning, stumbling,
    into whose arms, at whose

mouth out of slumber sweetening,
    so that I know I am not I
but a spirit of the hour descending into body
    whose tongue touches
        myrrh of the morgenrot,

as in a cowslip's bell that is a moment comes Ariel
    to joy all round,
but we see one lover take his lover in his mouth,
    leaping.   Swift flame of
abiding sweetness is in this flesh.

    Fatigue spreading back, a grand chorale
of who I am, who he is, where we are,
    in which a thin spire of longing
perishes,   this single up-fountain of a
    single note around which

        the throat shapes!

3

La lampe du coeur Breton qui file et bientôt
    hoquète à l'approche des parvis
smokes, raises a music out of the light, a lamp of notes
that runs through the opening in Paradise
    into the meat from the dream the heart knows.

Flashes seize the eye's grey, forcing
    out of whose pits night's images of what day desired
    montaient vers moi
soulevées par les vapeurs d'un abîme
—figures of women passing through the strings of the harp
of the sun,
    fingers that flash chains we are signals
    of protest, of assent, of longing, of anger.

O Breton, poet, we too—

where from the muscles of men working in fields see
cathedrals rise　—fume and sing out,

the early markets spreading round anthems,
the torsos of men and trucks in their own light, steaming,
by the raised lamp that surrounds the sleeping men,
circulations of food and rays!

These gates are not breasts or lions of the Queen of
　　Byzantium,
but men working.　These grails
have men's arms and eyes, from which lamps like women
　　fume

　　at the approach of the Outer Court,
　　half-naked the men mounting and dismounting,

　　when I come into whose environs my heart smokes,
　　la belle, la violée, la soumise, l'accablante.

She is at work in her sleep.
She draws in food from the country around her.
She compels me wandering from Breton and towards him
　　by the plan of her streets.
She makes a temple of produce, in her buying and selling,
　　a place of transport and litanies.
She surrounds her priests and appears in their place at
　　the tips time has before falling.

Pelagius, Eckhardt, Joachim de Flore, Novalis are arms
　　of her desire
　　where she hungers for us and feeds us.

Out of André Breton
—these things translated from her savor into the savor of
　　men's bodies
　　we return to her parvis.

FOURTH SONG THE NIGHT NURSE SANG

Let sleep take her, let sleep take her, let sleep
        take her away!
The cold tears of her father
have made a hill of ice.
        Let sleep take her.

Her mother's fear has made a feyrie.
        Let sleep take her.
Now all of the kingdom lies down to die.
        Let sleep take her.

Let dawn wake her, if dawn can find her.
    Let the prince of day take her
from sleep's dominion at the touch of his finger,
    if he can touch her.

The weather will hide her, the spider will bind her

    : so the wind sang.

O, there she lay
in an egg hanging from an invisible thread
spinning out I cannot tell whether

from a grave or a bed, from a grave or a bed.

A PART-SEQUENCE FOR CHANGE

1

If they had cursed the man,
dried back the water in the spring
by boiling water in a frying pan
until the thirsty sun
feard for the songs that he once sang
and burnd to sing,

over *them* the cursed image
over *them* the blackend thing.

2

I shall draw back
and among my sacred objects
gather the animal power back,
the force that in solitude
works in me its leases,
the night-bird's voice
in the day's verses.

The flame in the body of the lamp
fumes upon the surface of the glass.
The boy I was watches
not without fear
black places in the darkening room
where animal faces
appear and pass away

and reappear.

3

Estranged. Deeply estranged.
Fish caught in no net,
hand at the harp without strings
striking the dark air for music,
having no more than the need
to go by.

Deeply estranged.
For I have been let go from what
I felt in the music.
I have been deserted by the words spoken
in the rapture of being deserted,

of the rising meshes, the escaping waters,
        the writhing and
therein thriving catch of fishes
raised by the Fisher out of my solitude
into the acclaiming throng without me.

But say they take this song up
and in the threads of their voices
these words appear (mine) (theirs).
Estranged. Deeply estranged.

Once more tne young days of the year
find out the invisible ranges
and break from the tree
changes and turnings of the heart,
the swarm of too many buds
for melody

and the ascendancy of the shadow
in the blossoming mass.

AT THE LOOM   PASSAGES 2

                    A cat's purr
in the hwirr thkk   *"thgk, thkk"*
of Kirke's loom on Pound's Cantos
        "I heard a song of that kind . . ."

my mind a shuttle among
            set strings of the music
lets a weft of dream grow in the day time,
            an increment of associations,
    luminous soft threads,
the thrown glamour, crossing and recrossing,
        the twisted sinews underlying the work.

Back of the images, the few cords that bind
    meaning in the word-flow,
            the rivering web
    rises among wits and senses
gathering the wool into its full cloth.

The secret!   the secret!   It's hid
    in its showing forth.
The white cat kneads his paws
        and sheathes his eyes in ecstasy against the light,
    the light bounding from his fur as from a shield
            held high in the midst of a battle.

What does the Worm work in His cocoon?

    There was such a want in the old ways
        when craft came into our elements,
    the art shall never be free of that forge,
        that loom, that lyre—

the fire, the images, the voice.

Why, even in the room where we are,
        reading to ourselves, or I am reading aloud,
sounding the music,
                    the stuff
                    vanishes upon the air,
                            line after line thrown.

Let there be the clack of the shuttle flying
        forward and back,   forward and
            back,

warp, *wearp, varp*: *"cast of a net, a laying of eggs"*
from °warp- *"to throw"*

        the threads twisted for strength
            that can be a warp of the will.

    "O weaver, weaver, work no more,"
        Gascoyne is quoted:
    "thy warp hath done me wrong."

And the shuttle carrying the woof I find
    was *skutill* *"harpoon"* —a dart, an arrow
        or a little ship,

    navicula   *weberschiff,*

crossing and recrossing from shore to shore—

    prehistoric °*skutil* °*skut-*
    "a bolt, a bar, as of a door"
    "a flood-gate"   •

                    but the battle I saw
was on a wide plain,   for the
    sake of valor,
the hand traind to the bow,
    the man's frame
withstanding,   each side

466

facing its foe for the sake of
    the alliance,
allegiance, the legion, that the
    vow that makes a nation
one body not be broken.

Yet it is all, we know, a mêlée,
    a medley of mistaken themes
    grown dreadful and surmounting dread,

so that Achilles may have his wrath
    and throw down
    the heroic Hektor who raised
that reflection of the heroic

    in his shield . . .

Feb. 4–11 1964

ENVOY   PASSAGES 7

    Good Night,   at last

the light of the sun is gone

    under Earth's rim

        and we

can see the dark   interstices

        Day's lord erases.

467

jump   stone   hand   leaf   shadow   sun

day   plash   coin   light   downstream   fish

first   loosen   under   boat   harbor   circle

old   earth   bronze   dark   wall   waver

new   smell   purl   close   wet   green

now   rise   foot   warm   hold   cool

blood   disk

horizon   flame

The day at the window
the rain at the window
the night and the star at the window

Do you know the old language?
I do not know the old language.
Do you know the language of the old belief?

From the wood we thought burning
our animal spirits flee,   seeking refuge wherever,

as if in Eden,   in this   panic

lion and lamb lie down,   quail

heed not the eagle in flight before the flames high

over head go.

We see at last the man-faced roe and his

gentle mate;   the wild boar too

turns a human face.   In whose visages no terror

but a philosophic sorrow shows.   The ox

is fierce with terror, his thick tongue

slavers and sticks out panting

to make the gorgoneion face.

(This is Piero di Cosimo's great painting *A Forest Fire*, dated 1490–1500, preserved in the Ashmolean Museum at Oxford)

He inherits the *sfumato* of Leonardo da Vinci—

there is a softening of outline,   his color fuses.

A glow at the old borders makes

magic Pletho, Ficino, Pico della Mirandola prepared,

reviving in David's song,

Saul in his flaming rage heard,   music

Orpheus first playd,

chords and melodies of the spell that binds

the many in conflict in contrasts of one mind:

"For, since song and sound arise from the cognition of the mind, and the impetus of the phantasy, and the feeling of the heart, and, together with the air they have broken up and temperd, strike the aerial spirit of the hearer, which is the junction of the soul and the body, they easily move the phantasy, affect the heart and penetrate into the deep recesses of the mind"

Di Cosimo's   featherd, furrd, leafy

boundaries where   even the Furies are birds

and blur   in higher harmonies Eumenides;

whose animals, entering a charmd field

in the light of his vision, a stillness,

have their dreamy glades and pastures.

The flames, the smoke.   The curious

sharp focus in a glow   sight

in the Anima Mundi has.

Where in the North (1500) shown in Bosch's illumination:

Hell breaks out   an opposing music.

The faces of the deluded   leer, faint, in lewd praise,

close their eyes in voluptuous torment,

enthralld by fear,   avidly

following the daily news: the earthquakes, eruptions,
flaming automobiles, enraged lovers, wars against communism,
heroin addicts, police raids, race riots . . .

caught in the *lascivia animi* of this vain sound.

And we see at last the faces of evil openly

over us,

bestial extrusions no true animal face knows.

There are rats, snakes, toads, Boehme tells us,

that are the Devil's creatures.   There is

a Devil's mimic of man, a Devil's chemistry.

The Christ closes His eyes,   bearing the Cross

as if dreaming.   Is His Kingdom

not of this world, but a dream of the Anima Mundi,

the World-Ensouling?

The painter's *sfumato* gives His face

pastoral stillness amidst terror,   sorrow

that has an echo in the stag's face we saw before.

About Him, as if to drown   sweet music out,

Satan looks forth from
men's faces:
Eisenhower's idiot grin, Nixon's
black jaw, the sly stare in Goldwater's eye, or
the look of Stevenson lying in the U.N. that our
Nation save face   •

His face multiplies from the time of Roosevelt, Stalin,
Churchill, Hitler, Mussolini;   from the dream
of Oppenheimer, Fermi, Teller, Vannevar Bush,

brooding the nightmare formulae—to win the war!   the

inevitable   •   at Los Alamos

plotting the holocaust of Hiroshima　　　　•

　　　Teller openly for the Anti-Christ

•　　　glints of the evil that one sees in the power of this
world,

"In the North and East, swarms of dough-faces, office-
vermin, kept editors, clerks, attaches of ten thousand
officers and their parties, aware of nothing further
than the drip and spoil of politics—ignorant of princi-
ples . . . In the South, no end of blusterers, braggarts,
windy, melodramatic, continually screaming, in fal-
setto, a nuisance to These States, their own just as
much as any . . . and with the most incredible succes-
ses, having pistol'd, bludgeoned, yelled and threatend
America, these past twenty years, into one long train
of cowardly concessions, and still not through but
rather at the commencement. Their cherished secret
scheme is to dissolve the union of These States . . ."
　　　　　　　　　　　　　　　　(Whitman, 1856)

faces of Princes, Popes, Prime Usurers, Presidents,
　　Gang Leaders of whatever Clubs, Nations, Legions
　　meet

　　　to conspire, to coerce, to cut down　　　•

Now, the City, impoverisht, swollen, dreams again

the great plagues—typhus, syphilis, the black buboes

epidemics,　manias.

My name is Legion　and in every nation　I multiply.

　　　Over those who would be Great Nations　Great
　　Evils.

They are burning the woods, the brushlands, the

472

grassy fields razed;   their

profitable suburbs spread.

Pan's land, the pagan countryside, they'd

lay waste.

cool	green	waver	circle	fish	sun
hold	wet	wall	harbor	downstream	shadow
warm	close	dark	boat	light	leaf
foot	purl	bronze	under	coin	hand
rise	smell	earth	loosen	plash	stone
now	new	old	first	day	jump

LAWRENCE FERLINGHETTI (1919–   )

Not only was Ferlinghetti an originator of the Beat movement
during the fifties, together with Allen Ginsberg and Jack Kerouac,
but through his City Lights Books, which quickly expanded from
a bookshop into a publishing company, he became its chief im-
presario as well; and he still is. The numbers of his early mimeo-
graphed magazine, *Beatitude*, are now collectors' items. His own
popularity is very great: his first major book of poems, *A
Coney Island of the Mind* (1958), has been the best seller of all
American poetry for more than a decade, and his effective public
readings have made him the poet most in demand on the reading
circuits. Though an easterner by birth, he has lived and worked
in San Francisco for the past fifteen years.

> *Pictures of the Gone World.* San Francisco: City Lights
> Books, 1955.
> *A Coney Island of the Mind.* New Directions, 1958.
> *Her.* (Novel.) New Directions, 1960.
> *Unfair Arguments with Existence.* (Plays.) New Direc-
> tions, 1963.
> *Routines.* New Directions, 1964.
> *Starting from San Francisco.* Rev. ed. New Directions,
> 1967.
> *After the Cries of the Birds.* San Francisco: D. Haselwood,
> 1967.

CHRIST CLIMBED DOWN

Christ climbed down
from His bare Tree
this year
and ran away to where
there were no rootless Christmas trees
hung with candycanes and breakable stars

Christ climbed down
from His bare Tree
this year
and ran away to where

there were no gilded Christmas trees
and no tinsel Christmas trees
and no tinfoil Christmas trees
and no pink plastic Christmas trees
and no gold Christmas trees
and no black Christmas trees
and no powderblue Christmas trees
hung with electric candles
and encircled by tin electric trains
and clever cornball relatives

Christ climbed down
from His bare Tree
this year
and ran away to where
no intrepid Bible salesmen
covered the territory
in two-tone cadillacs
and where no Sears Roebuck creches
complete with plastic babe in manger
arrived by parcel post
the babe by special delivery
and where no televised Wise Men
praised the Lord Calvert Whiskey

Christ climbed down
from His bare Tree
this year
and ran away to where
no fat handshaking stranger
in a red flannel suit
and a fake white beard
went around passing himself off
as some sort of North Pole saint
crossing the desert to Bethlehem
Pennsylvania
in a Volkswagen sled
drawn by rollicking Adirondack reindeer
with German names
and bearing sacks of Humble Gifts
from Saks Fifth Avenue
for everybody's imagined Christ child

Christ climbed down
from His bare Tree
this year
and ran away to where
no Bing Crosby carollers
groaned of a tight Christmas
and where no Radio City angels
iceskated wingless
thru a winter wonderland
into a jinglebell heaven
daily at 8:30
with Midnight Mass matinees

Christ climbed down
from His bare Tree
this year
and softly stole away into
some anonymous Mary's womb again
where in the darkest night
of everybody's anonymous soul
He awaits again
an unimaginable
and impossibly
Immaculate Reconception
the very craziest
of Second Comings

ONE THOUSAND FEARFUL WORDS
FOR FIDEL CASTRO

I am sitting in Mike's Place trying to figure out
                what's going to happen
                without Fidel Castro
Among the salami sandwiches and spittoons
                I see no solution
                It's going to be a tragedy
                I see no way out
among the admen and slumming models
and the brilliant snooping columnists
who are qualified to call Castro psychotic
        because they no doubt are doctors
        and have examined him personally

and know a paranoid hysterical tyrant when they see one
because they have it on first hand
from personal observation by the CIA
and the great disinterested news services
And Hearst is dead but his great Cuban wire still stands:
"You get the pictures, I'll make the War"
I see no answer
I see no way out
among the paisanos playing pool
it looks like Curtains for Fidel
They're going to fix his wagon
in the course of human events

In the back of Mike's the pinball machines
shudder and leap from the floor
when Cuban Charlie shakes them
and tries to work his will
on one named "Independence Sweepstakes"
Each pinball wandered lonely as a man
siphons thru and sinks
no matter how he twists and turns
A billiardball falls in a felt pocket
like a peasant in a green landscape
You're whirling around in your little hole
Fidel
and you'll soon sink
in the course of human events

On the nickelodeon a cowboy ballad groans
"Got myself a Cadillac" the cowhand moans
He didn't get it in Cuba, baby
Outside in the night of North Beach America
the new North American cars flick by
from Motorama
their headlights never bright enough
to dispel this night
in the course of human events

Three creepy men come in
One is Chinese
One is Negro
One is some kind of crazy Indian
They look like they may have been
walking up and down in Cuba

477

but they haven't
All three have hearing aids
It's a little deaf brotherhood of Americans
The skinny one screws his hearing aid
in his skinny ear
He's also got a little transistor radio
the same size as his hearing aid box
For a moment I confuse the two

The radio squawks
some kind of memorial program
"When in the course of human events
it becomes necessary for one people
to dissolve the political bonds
which have connected them with another—"
I see no way out
no escape
He's tuned in on your frequency, Fidel
but can't hear it
There's interference
It's going to be
a big evil tragedy
They're going to fix you, Fidel
with your big Cuban cigar
which you stole from us
and your army surplus hat
which you probably also stole
and your Beat beard

History may absolve you, Fidel
but we'll dissolve you first, Fidel
You'll be dissolved in history
We've got the solvent
We've got the chaser
and we'll have a little party
somewhere down your way, Fidel
It's going to be a Gas
As they say in Guatemala

Outside of Mike's Place now
an ambulance sirens up
It's a midnight murder or something
Some young bearded guy stretched on the sidewalk

with blood sticking out
Here's your little tragedy, Fidel
They're coming to pick you up
and stretch you on their Stretcher
That's what happens, Fidel
when in the course of human events
it becomes necessary for one people to dissolve
the bonds of International Tel & Tel
and United Fruit
Fidel
How come you don't answer anymore
Fidel
Did they cut you off our frequency
We've closed down our station anyway
We've turned you off, Fidel

I was sitting in Mike's Place, Fidel
waiting for someone else to act
like a good Liberal
I hadn't quite finished reading Camus' *Rebel*
So I couldn't quite recognize you, Fidel
walking up and down your island
when they came for you, Fidel
"My Country or Death" you told them
Well you've got your little death, Fidel
like old Honest Abe
one of your boyhood heroes
who also had his little Civil War
and was a different kind of Liberator
(since no one was shot in his war)
and also was murdered
in the course of human events

Fidel . . . Fidel . . .
your coffin passes by
thru lanes and streets you never knew
thru day and night, Fidel
While lilacs last in the dooryard bloom, Fidel
your futile trip is done
yet is not done
and is not futile
I give you my sprig of laurel

San Francisco, January, 1961

479

MAY SWENSON (1919–   )

Born in Logan, Utah, in a Mormon family, Miss Swenson has
worked in New York for the past twenty years, much of the time
as an editorial reader specializing in poetry. Her own poems are
noted for their experimental forms and their crisp view of ob-
jective details.

A Cage of Spines. Rinehart, 1958.
To Mix with Time. Scribner's, 1963.
Half Sun, Half Sleep. Scribner's, 1967.

QUESTION

Body my house
my horse my hound
what will I do
when you are fallen

Where will I sleep
How will I ride
What will I hunt

Where can I go
without my mount
all eager and quick
How will I know
in thicket ahead
is danger or treasure
when Body my good
bright dog is dead

How will it be
to lie in the sky
without roof or door
and wind for an eye

With cloud for shift
how will I hide?

GREEN RED BROWN AND WHITE

Bit an apple on its red
side   Smelled like snow
Between white halves broken open
brown winks slept in sockets of green

Stroked a birch white as a thigh
scar-flecked smooth as the neck
of a horse   On mossy pallets green
the pines dropped down
their perfect carvings brown

Lost in the hairy wood
followed berries red
to the fork   Had to choose
between green and green   High

in a sunwhite dome a brown bird
sneezed   Took the path least likely
and it led me home   For

each path leads both out and in
I come while going   No to and from
There is only here   And here
is as well as there   Wherever
I am led I move within the care
of the season
hidden in the creases of her skirts
of green or brown or beaded red

And when they are white
I am not lost   I am not lost then
only covered for the night

HAYDEN CARRUTH (1921–   )

The editor of this anthology has become, in the course of his work on it, more convinced than ever of the futility of "final judgments" in the arts, and of their danger when made by the artist about his own work. Hence he limits his presentation to a few of the "short-shorts" he wrote while engrossed in his editorial reading; to be arbitrary about it, the last five of the several hundred so composed. They are offered simply as a token—but no less earnestly for that—of fellowship with all poets, those who are here and those who are not.

The Crow and the Heart. Macmillan, 1959.
Journey to a Known Place. New Directions, 1961.
The Norfolk Poems. Iowa City, Iowa: Prairie Press, 1962.
North Winter. Iowa City, Iowa: Prairie Press, 1964.
Nothing for Tigers. Macmillan, 1965.
Contra Mortem. Johnson, Vt.: Crow's Mark Press, 1967.

FIVE SHORT-SHORTS

Why speak of the use
of poetry? Poetry
is what uses us.

*

Ah, you beast of love,
my cat, my dove, my spider!
—too late I'm natured.

*

A hard journey. Yes,
it must be. At the end they
always fall asleep.

*

Your tears, Niobe,
are your children now. See how
we have multiplied.

*

So be it. I am
a wholeness I'll never know.
Maybe that's the best.

RICHARD WILBUR (1921-   )

Wilbur, who is Professor of English at Wesleyan in Connecticut, has made a number of notable translations for the stage from works by neo-classical French dramatists, and in his own poems has developed a similar courtly tone of respect for order to mask fundamental metaphysical uncertainty.

The Poems of Richard Wilbur. Harcourt, Brace & World, 1963.

LOVE CALLS US TO THE THINGS OF THIS WORLD

The eyes open to a cry of pulleys,
And spirited from sleep, the astounded soul
Hangs for a moment bodiless and simple
As false dawn.
              Outside the open window
The morning air is all awash with angels.

Some are in bed-sheets, some are in blouses,
Some are in smocks: but truly there they are.
Now they are rising together in calm swells
Of halcyon feeling, filling whatever they wear
With the deep joy of their impersonal breathing;

Now they are flying in place, conveying
The terrible speed of their omnipresence, moving
And staying like white water; and now of a sudden
They swoon down into so rapt a quiet
That nobody seems to be there.
                  The soul shrinks

From all that it is about to remember,
From the punctual rape of every blessèd day,
And cries,
        "Oh, let there be nothing on earth but laundry,

Nothing but rosy hands in the rising steam
And clear dances done in the sight of heaven."

Yet, as the sun acknowledges
With a warm look the world's hunks and colors,
The soul descends once more in bitter love
To accept the waking body, saying now
In a changed voice as the man yawns and rises,

"Bring them down from their ruddy gallows;
Let there be clean linen for the backs of thieves;
Let lovers go fresh and sweet to be undone,
And the heaviest nuns walk in a pure floating
Of dark habits,
                    keeping their difficult balance."

PIAZZA DI SPAGNA, EARLY MORNING

            I can't forget
How she stood at the top of that long marble stair
Amazed, and then with a sleepy pirouette
Went dancing slowly down to the fountain-quieted square;

            Nothing upon her face
But some impersonal loneliness,—not then a girl,
    But as it were a reverie of the place,
            A called-for falling glide and whirl;

    As when a leaf, petal, or thin chip
Is drawn to the falls of a pool and, circling a moment above
    it,
            Rides on over the lip—
    Perfectly beautiful, perfectly ignorant of it.

LOOKING INTO HISTORY

        Five soldiers fixed by Mathew Brady's eye
        Stand in a land subdued beyond belief.
        Belief might lend them life again. I try
I.   Like orphaned Hamlet working up his grief

To see my spellbound fathers in these men
Who, breathless in their amber atmosphere,
Show but the postures men affected then
And the hermit faces of a finished year.

The guns and gear and all are strange until
Beyond the tents I glimpse a file of trees
Verging a road that struggles up a hill.
They're sycamores.
               The long-abated breeze

Flares in those boughs I know, and hauls the sound
Of guns and a great forest in distress.
Fathers, I know my cause, and we are bound
Beyond that hill to fight at Wilderness.

II.   But trick your eyes with Birnam Wood, or think
How fire-cast shadows of the bankside trees
Rode on the back of Simois to sink
In the wide waters. Reflect how history's

Changes are like the sea's, which mauls and mulls
Its salvage of the world in shifty waves,
Shrouding in evergreen the oldest hulls
And yielding views of its confounded graves

To the new moon, the sun, or any eye
That in its shallow shoreward version sees
The pebbles charging with a deathless cry
And carageen memorials of trees.

III.   Now, old man of the sea,
I start to understand:
The will will find no stillness
Back in a stilled land.

The dead give no command
And shall not find their voice
Till they be mustered by
Some present fatal choice.

Let me now rejoice
In all impostures, take

486

The shape of lion or leopard,
Boar, or watery snake,

Or like the comber break,
Yet in the end stand fast
And by some fervent fraud
Father the waiting past,

Resembling at the last
The self-established tree
That draws all waters toward
Its live formality.

MARIE PONSOT (1922-)

Mrs. Ponsot, who is bilingual in French and English, has lived in Europe and North Africa, and has made many translations, both of poetry and of children's literature. She has also worked in television and radio, and now teaches at Queens College in New York.

True Minds. San Francisco: City Lights Books, 1956.

POSSESSION

You are right. In dreams I might well dance before the
    Ark.
Coming out of ether I might cry on reed and rood of
    sacredness.
Yet you should not for that reason suspect altars between
    us
Nor scent a fear of incense in the cruciform caress.
Marriage is blessed but does not bless.

I warned you before this smoked ground struck your knees,
Saying Be holy, see where the whipped top spins;
Saying This world is that world's mimesis, bloodless
But sensual and we do not even contain our sins.
I said, Betray it and the bedraggled cockerel wins.

Listen. Do you hear? Now he crows.
Now we are going where God knows.

MULTIPARA: GRAVIDA 5

Come to term the started child shocks
Peace upon me; I am great with peace;
Pain teaches primal cause; my bones unlock
To learn my final end. The formal increase

Of passionate patience breaks into a storm of heat
Where calling on you love my heart's hopes rise
With violence to seize as prayer this sweet
Submitting act. I pray. Loud with surprise
Thrown sprung back wide the blithe body lies
Exultant and wise. The born child cries.

COMMUNION OF SAINTS:
THE POOR BASTARD UNDER THE BRIDGE

The arrows of the narrow moon flock down direct
Into that looking heart by Seine walls unprotected.
Moonward the eyes of that hurt head still will
Stare and scarcely see the moonlight spill
Because black Notre Dame between her towers
Strikes home to him the third of this day's hours
And he, now man, heaped cold afaint
Below the Pont Marie will, with a shout,
Enlist among the triumphant when Poor Saint
Julien's bells will clock out
Four.
      In his rags, unchapleted, almost astray
Among the dead packed all immaculate away
Under the city, he awaits his sentry
The four o'clock moon to warrant for his entry
          o and pure
The pure in children's ranks by bells immured
In gowns of light will singing telling rise
Unfold their arms impelled without surprise
Will lift up flowered laurel, will walk out
Among their golden singing like a victor's shout
To their triumphant heaven's golden ringing brim
And welcome welcome welcome him.

SUBJECT

We but begin to hope to know, having known
The no-man's echo of your knowing voice;
We barely claim we have chosen,
Naming our choice.

To feast your coming it is you who must prepare;
Given your love we dare not not care;
Wherefore spare not spare us not
Do not spare.

TO THE AGE'S INSANITIES

Shriek said the saw smile said the mice
Come said the tall crowfooted bright
Bareheaded boy I won't call twice.

Twist said the tongue leap said the toe
Leave said the seaman arched in fright
One of this crew has got to go.

Spit said the thorn kiss said the tree
But Peace cried I loud in the night
You are my freedom. And they let me be.

JAMES DICKEY (1923–   )

In both his poetry and his criticism, which have been equally influential, Dickey has sought to avoid the formalism of poetry in the postwar years—what he calls "the suspect"—but at the same time to preserve the poem's substantial unity. His work turns often on themes of the war or of rural life in his native Georgia, usually cast against an implicit acknowledgment of the world of natural force. Today Dickey lives in Columbia, S.C.

Poems 1957–1967. Wesleyan University Press, 1967.
The Suspect in Poetry. (Collected reviews.) Madison, Minn.: The Sixties Press, 1964.

THE MOVEMENT OF FISH

No water is still, on top.
Without wind, even, it is full
Of a chill, superficial agitation.
It is easy to forget,
Or not to know at all

That fish do not move
By means of this rippling
Along the outside of water, or
By anything touching on air.
Where they are, it is still,

Under a wooden bridge,
Under the poised oar
Of a boat, while the rower leans
And blows his mistaken breath
To make the surface shake,

Or yells at it, or sings,
Half believing the brilliant scan
Of ripples will carry the fish away
On his voice like a buried wind.
Or it may be that a fish

Is simply lying under
The ocean-broad sun
Which comes down onto him
Like a tremendous, suffusing
Open shadow

Of gold, where nothing is,
Sinking into the water,
Becoming dark around
His body. Where he is now
Could be gold mixed

With absolute blackness.
The surface at mid-sea shivers,
But he does not feel it
Like a breath, or like anything.
Yet suddenly his frame shakes,

Convulses the whole ocean
Under the trivial, quivering
Surface, and he is
Hundreds of feet away,
Still picking up speed, still shooting

Through half-gold,
Going nowhere. Nothing sees him.
One must think of this to understand
The instinct of fear and trembling,
And, of its one movement, the depth.

FENCE WIRE

Too tight, it is running over
Too much of this ground to be still
Or to do anything but tremble
And disappear left and right
As far as the eye can see

Over hills, through woods,
Down roads, to arrive at last
Again where it connects,
Coming back from the other side
Of animals, defining their earthly estate

492

As the grass becomes snow
While they are standing and dreaming
Of grass and snow.
The winter hawk that sits upon its post,
Feeling the airy current of the wires,

Turns into a robin, sees that this is wrong,
Then into a boy, and into a man who holds
His palm on the top tense strand
With the whole farm feeding slowly
And nervously into his hand.

If the wire were cut anywhere
All his blood would fall to the ground
And leave him standing and staring
With a face as white as a Hereford's.
From years of surrounding grain,

Cows, horses, machinery trying to turn
To rust, the humming arrives each second,
A sound that arranges these acres
And holds them highstrung and enthralled.
Because of the light, chilled hand

On the top thread tuned to an E
Like the low string of a guitar,
The dead corn is more
Balanced in death than it was,
The animals more aware

Within the huge human embrace
Held up and borne out of sight
Upon short, unbreakable poles
Wherethrough the ruled land intones
Like a psalm: properly,

With its eyes closed,
Whether on the side of the animals
Or not, whether disappearing
Right, left, through trees or down roads,
Whether outside, around, or in.

THE DRIVER

At the end of the war I arose
From my bed in the tent and walked
Where the island fell through white stones
Until it became the green sea.
Into light that dazzled my brain
Like the new thought of peace, I walked
Until I was swimming and singing.

Over the foundered landing craft
That took the island, I floated,
And then like a thistle came
On the deep wind of water to rest
Far out, my long legs of shadow down-
pointing to ground where my soul
Could take root and spring as it must.

Below me a rusted halftrack
Moved in the depths with the movement
One sees a thing take through tears
Of joy, or terrible sorrow;
A thing which in quietness lies
Beyond both. Slowly I sank
And slid into the driver's shattered seat.

Driving through the country of the drowned
On a sealed secret-keeping breath,
Ten feet under water, I sat still,
Getting used to the burning stare
Of the wide-eyed dead after battle.
I saw, through the sensitive roof—
The uneasy, lyrical skin that lies

Between death and life, trembling always—
An airplane come over, perfectly
Soundless, but could not tell
Why I lived, or why I was sitting,
With my lungs being shaped like two bells,
At the wheel of a craft in a wave
Of attack that broke upon coral.

"I become pure spirit," I tried
To say, in a bright smoke of bubbles,

But I was becoming no more
Than haunted, for to be so
Is to sink out of sight, and to lose
The power of speech in the presence
Of the dead, with the eyes turning green,

And to leap at last for the sky
Very nearly too late, where another
Leapt and could not break into
His breath, where it lay, in battle
As in peace, available, secret,
Dazzling and huge, filled with sunlight,
For thousands of miles on the water.

THE CELEBRATION

All wheels; a man breathed fire,
Exhaling like a blowtorch down the road
And burnt the stripper's gown
Above her moving-barely feet.
A condemned train climbed from the earth
Up stilted nightlights zooming in a track.
I ambled along in that crowd

Between the gambling wheels
At carnival time with the others
Where the dodgem cars shuddered, sparking
On grillwire, each in his vehicle half
In control, half helplessly power-mad
As he was in the traffic that brought him.
No one blazed at me; then I saw

My mother and my father, he leaning
On a dog-chewed cane, she wrapped to the nose
In the fur of exhausted weasels.
I believed them buried miles back
In the country, in the faint sleep
Of the old, and had not thought to be
On this of all nights compelled

To follow where they led, not losing
Sight, with my heart enlarging whenever

I saw his crippled Stetson bob, saw her
With the teddy bear won on the waning
Whip of his right arm. They laughed;
She clung to him; then suddenly
The Wheel of wheels was turning

The colored night around.
They climbed aboard. My God, they rose
Above me, stopped themselves and swayed
Fifty feet up; he pointed
With his toothed cane, and took in
The whole Midway till they dropped,
Came down, went from me, came and went

Faster and faster, going up backward,
Cresting, out-topping, falling roundly.
From the crowd I watched them,
Their gold teeth flashing,
Until my eyes blurred with their riding
Lights, and I turned from the standing
To the moving mob, and went on:

Stepped upon sparking shocks
Of recognition when I saw my feet
Among the others, knowing them given,
Understanding the whirling impulse
From which I had been born,
The great gift of shaken lights,
The being wholly lifted with another,

All this having all and nothing
To do with me. Believers, I have seen
The wheel in the middle of the air
Where old age rises and laughs,
And on Lakewood Midway became
In five strides a kind of loving,
A mortal, a dutiful son.

MITCHELL GOODMAN (1923–   )

Goodman is a novelist who has only recently begun to write poems; until now none has been published, except privately. He is also a leader in the anti-Vietnam resistance, and in 1968 was arrested and convicted, with Dr. Benjamin Spock and several others, on charges arising from his political activities; the case was successfully appealed. Born in Brooklyn, Goodman lives today in Maine.

COMING AND GOING

Buy the paper, take it home,
turn away   from the world
to the obituaries: A simple
truth, black and white: DEATHS
it says, column after column,
today's deaths: Dalton, Dasch,
Domenick, Dubins—all
dead, no story, no need
to explain, the simple
fact of Mr. Death, black
and white He comes,
They go: *Stella, beloved*
wife of Leon, dear Sister-
in-Law of Esther
Vogel: so it is, from
Star to Lion to Bird in
any language; *darling Aunt*
of Carrie, Laura and
Pierre. Services Tues.
Feb. 14 1:30 P.M. at
The Riverside. Please omit
flowers.

MAN AND WIFE

It was late, we
talked   it all
came out   words
fell   we stuffed them
in each other's ears

I talked, she listened
and agreed. Not
enough. Don't shout
she yelled, Don't—I'm
not—. Quietly: In other
words, I said—There are
no other words
she said. *Think.* I
(thought) can't think.
Words she could not say
I said, then she
spoke for me.

Be a woman, I said.
What is a woman,
she asked, nakedly,
taking off her clothes. That
ended it. The next night
we began again, as if
there were someone
who knew
the answer.

ARTHUR GREGOR (1923–   )

Gregor was born in Vienna, and lived there until 1939, when he came to the U.S. After the war he worked for a while as an engineer, but then entered the publishing business; today he is a senior editor at Macmillan in New York.

Octavian Shooting Targets. Dodd, Mead, 1954.
Declensions of a Refrain. New York: Poetry London-New York, 1957.
Basic Movements. New York: Gyre Press, 1966.
Figure in the Door. Doubleday, 1968.

POEM

So many pigeons at Columbus
Circle in America; go, Tierra,
go; it is past the wars and
the nuns are waiting at sea-
ports, at the entrance to the
park. The fountains in the
Villa d'Este are the most
beautiful fountains in all

of Italy, was a statement in
a survey on Western Civili-
zation, and on the Piazza della
Signoria, Perseus is slaying
the Medusa to this day. When
I was 12, I said: Patria
nostra olim provincia Romana
erat and landed, riding on

seahorses of gold, on centuries
and Cellini, bumps in front of
the Doge's palace holding hands
with Beatrice, what an inter-
minable link, I thought, with

499

many orators and many merchants
and Punchinello, Punchinello,
the idiot of the circus, he

whom we have wronged too
much, Lisa's delight when
she was 4, he who sits on
church steps bleeding out
endless harps from his
nailed down fingers, O Tierra,
O witches in a reddening
forest, O whoever, whatever

recalls this all; like certain
young men who turn on an
elegant street, who go on
past cathedrals jittery as
swans and princes who have
missed their cue, who have no
other chance and have no
other chance. So many dead,

so many murdered, Tierra, and
there was the singer in the
valley of oranges, and there
were the snows, the emerald
crowns on fishes in der Arls-
bergergrotte, and there was
the silence, and there were
the madonnas at noon. . . .

SPIRITS, DANCING

Having put yourself on the way,
it is inevitable that you
should reach here. If in
your thoughts you've had
the notion of reward
as you fought to come this far,
banish them. And,
as penalty for entering,
shed the attitudes of worldly men

regarding us and this
celestial sphere where now
your spirit begs to enter.

From the extremity
to which you've come, you see
us sway as in a dance.
It is no sign that we
are happy. To be happy
is being a step removed
from happiness. Which we
never are. Nor are we sad.
Sorrow is man in the world,
and we, the total expression
and awareness of his state,
are sorrowful.

What seems to you,
who were taught to feel
we must fulfill
where the world has failed,
must turn to good the bad,
must invoke permanence
for material whose law
and will it is to die—
what seems to you, driven here
by urgency, a dance
is nothing but the pain in the world
which we like a mirror contain.

To sway is to depart
as branches from a stem,
as shadows from foliage
thick and dark—
and to depart is what is pain.
What you must know before
you enter this domain
and learn the ways of which
we shall not speak is this
first truth of what you are:
a sorrow, a sorrow
begging for home. Or you
would not have come this far.

THE LIKENESS

How can you live, how exist
without assurance of
or at least the memory of
someone, something
fantastic, marvelous
always behind you,
a hand, grip on your shoulder,
a presence surrounding you
as a shell surrounds what lives inside?
Song closer to you than flutter to wing!
Word more antique than age!

Without it—call it intimacy,
your intimate connection—
how do you stand vis-à-vis
the multiplicity of things,
a tree, fence, grass, person in your path?
Unless you find in them
that quality no one defines,
how do you love, what do you
whisper, what song
do you share in the dark?

Without it I am as someone
lost from his caravan
a sandstorm whipping him;
someone out to find help on a frozen sea,
man alone on a waste of ice
imagining as the vast and hazy
emptiness absorbs him
a tattered though victorious
humanity coming toward him,
soldiers linking arms,
a populace with banners
singing and beating drums.

Without it
I am cut off.
I await its sound.
I ravage memory
for sight of it, its melody.

I shape with bare
and desperate hands
its likeness in myself.

LATE LAST NIGHT

Late last night we drove through fog:
nothing but a vague onslaught at
the window: vapors, or was it breath?

the clouds of the earth coming at us
all along the road. In the watery
substance all turned the same:

lights around corners, dreams behind
rooms, the country wide as oceans,
the singleness in every name.

ANTHONY HECHT (1923-   )

Born in New York City, Hecht served in the American infantry during World War II, in France, Germany, Czechoslovakia, and Japan—an experience which has marked much of his poetry. He has taught at Bard College and the University of Rochester.

The Hard Hours. (New and selected poems.) Atheneum, 1967.

THE DOVER BITCH: A CRITICISM OF LIFE

So there stood Matthew Arnold and this girl
With the cliffs of England crumbling away behind them,
And he said to her, "Try to be true to me,
And I'll do the same for you, for things are bad
All over, etc., etc."
Well now, I knew this girl. It's true she had read
Sophocles in a fairly good translation
And caught that bitter allusion to the sea,
But all the time he was talking she had in mind
The notion of what his whiskers would feel like
On the back of her neck. She told me later on
That after a while she got to looking out
At the lights across the channel, and really felt sad,
Thinking of all the wine and enormous beds
And blandishments in French and the perfumes.
And then she got really angry. To have been brought
All the way down from London, and then be addressed
As a sort of mournful cosmic last resort
Is really tough on a girl, and she was pretty.
Anyway, she watched him pace the room
And finger his watch-chain and seem to sweat a bit,
And then she said one or two unprintable things.
But you mustn't judge her by that. What I mean to say is,
She's really all right. I still see her once in a while
And she always treats me right. We have a drink
And I give her a good time, and perhaps it's a year
Before I see her again, but there she is,
Running to fat, but dependable as they come.
And sometimes I bring her a bottle of *Nuit d'Amour.*

"MORE LIGHT! MORE LIGHT!"

Composed in the Tower before his execution
These moving verses, and being brought at that time
Painfully to the stake, submitted, declaring thus:
"I implore my God to witness that I have made no crime."

Nor was he forsaken of courage, but the death was
    horrible,
The sack of gunpowder failing to ignite.
His legs were blistered sticks on which the black sap
Bubbled and burst as he howled for the Kindly Light.

And that was but one, and by no means one of the worst;
Permitted at least his pitiful dignity;
And such as were by made prayers in the name of
    Christ,
That shall judge all men, for his soul's tranquillity.

We move now to outside a German wood.
Three men are there commanded to dig a hole
In which the two Jews are ordered to lie down
And be buried alive by the third, who is a Pole.

Not light from the shrine at Weimar beyond the hill
Nor light from heaven appeared. But he did refuse.
A Lüger settled back deeply in its glove.
He was ordered to change places with the Jews.

Much casual death had drained away their souls.
The thick dirt mounted toward the quivering chin.
When only the head was exposed the order came
To dig him out again and to get back in.

No light, no light in the blue Polish eye.
When he finished a riding boot packed down the earth.
The Lüger hovered lightly in its glove.
He was shot in the belly and in three hours bled to death.

No prayers or incense rose up in those hours
Which grew to be years, and every day came mute
Ghosts from the ovens, sifting through crisp air,
And settled upon his eyes in a black soot.

DANIEL HOFFMAN (1923–   )

Hoffman teaches in the English department at the University of
Pennsylvania. In addition to his poems, he has published a num-
ber of volumes of criticism, chiefly in the areas of American
literature and folklore.

An Armada of Thirty Whales. Yale University Press, 1954.
A Little Geste and Other Poems. Oxford University
Press, 1960.
The City of Satisfactions. Oxford University Press, 1963.
Striking the Stones. Oxford University Press, 1968.

È, THE FEASTING FLORENTINES

stared, astonied all,
As the raging lion
   (archangelicall)
Adown the table where they sate
   strode with golden growl
That Michelangelo in butter
   carved, a spoon his trowel.

   Florentians, being men of sense,
when time melted their wonder
   Passed around the fresh tall staves
and ate them thick with butter.

SIGNATURES

Wings outstretched, a horned owl
Nailed beneath a crown
Of antlers on the barn door

Shrivels in the wind,
And in the swale
Among black pellets,

Signatures of deer,
The wild roses of the field
—*Rosa Virginiana*—sway

As tall as trees. Each leafy bough
Beneath the deepest center of the sky
Is scented crimson as it's green with thorns.

There, on the sky's brim, floats
One lone jet too high
To break the day's long stillnesses.

Its white breath
Splits the sky.
The halves of heaven

Are bluer than each other.
All they cover leans to sign
Bequests of their significance,

Urgent as the center of the sun,
Yet silent
And invisible

As those fixed stars
We drift beneath
In the confusions of our light.

DENISE LEVERTOV (1923–   )

Miss Levertov was born in England, and her first poems, showing the influence of Herbert Read, were published there; but she came to the U.S. after World War II, and entered so quickly and completely into the American scene that there can be no question about the national locus of her work since then. Although she had no direct connection with Black Mountain College, her poetry is usually associated with the movement which began there. Indeed, she, Robert Creeley, and Robert Duncan are the three poets most centrally identified with the "Black Mountain" movement. Miss Levertov has taught at many universities, and has lectured and read widely. Her strongly musical and sensuous poems have been extremely influential in the recent work of younger writers. She lives today in Maine.

Here and Now. San Francisco: City Lights Books, 1956.
Overland to the Islands. Highlands, N.C.: Jonathan Williams, 1958.
With Eyes at the Back of Our Heads. New Directions, 1959.
The Jacob's Ladder. New Directions, 1961.
O Taste and See. New Directions, 1964.
Sorrow Dance. New Directions, 1967.
A Tree Telling of Orpheus. Los Angeles: Black Sparrow Press, 1968.

BEYOND THE END

In 'nature' there's no choice—
                    flowers
swing their heads in the wind, sun & moon
    are as they are. But we seem
almost to have it (not just
    available death)

It's energy: a spider's thread: not to
'go on living' but to quicken, to activate: extend:
    Some have it, they force it—
with work or laughter or even
    the act of buying, if that's
all they can lay hands on—

the girls crowding the stores, where light,
   color, solid dreams are—what gay
desire! It's their festival,
    ring game, wassail, mystery.

It has no grace like that of
the grass, the humble rhythms, the
falling & rising of leaf and star;
it's barely
a constant. Like salt:
take it or leave it

The 'hewers of wood' & so on; every damn
craftsman has it while he's working
     but it's not
a question of work: some
shine with it, in repose. Maybe it is
response, the will to respond—('reason
can give nothing at all/like
the response to desire') maybe
a gritting of the teeth, to go
just that much further, beyond the end
beyond whatever ends: to begin, to be, to defy.

THE RECOGNITION

Since the storm two nights ago
the air
is water-clear, the mountains
tranquil and clear.
       Have you seen
an intelligent invalid—that look
about the eyes and temples?—one who
knows damn well
death is coming—in the guise let's say
of a carpenter, coming
to fix him for good
with his big hammer and
sharp nails.
       The air and the horizon.
Clouds make
     gestures of flight but

remain suspended. The builders
continue to build the
house next door.
                    Nothing
will happen. A transparence
of the flesh, revealing
not bones but the shape of bones.

ILLUSTRIOUS ANCESTORS

The Rav
of Northern White Russia declined,
in his youth, to learn the
language of birds, because
the extraneous did not interest him; nevertheless
when he grew old it was found
he understood them anyway, having
listened well, and as it is said, 'prayed
            with the bench and the floor.' He used
what was at hand—as did
Angel Jones of Mold, whose meditations
were sewn into coats and britches.
            Well, I would like to make,
thinking some line still taut between me and them,
poems direct as what the birds said,
hard as a floor, sound as a bench,
mysterious as the silence when the tailor
would pause with his needle in the air.

THE QUARRY POOL

Between town and the
old house, an inn—
the Half-Way House.
So far one could ride, I remember,

the rest was an uphill walk,
a mountain lane with
steep banks and sweet
hedges, half walls of

gray rock. Looking
again at this looking-glass face
unaccountably changed in a week,
three weeks, a month,

I think without thinking of
Half-Way House. Is it
the thought that this far
I've driven at ease, as in a bus,

a country bus where one could talk to the driver?
Now on foot towards the village;
the dust clears, silence
draws in around one. I hear
the rustle and hum of the fields: alone.

It must be the sense
of essential solitude that chills me
looking into my eyes.
I should remember

the old house at the walk's ending,
a square place with a courtyard,
granaries, netted strawberry-beds,
a garden that was many

gardens, each one
a world hidden from the
next by leaves, enlaced trees,
fern-hairy walls, gilly-flowers.

I should see, making
a strange face at myself,
nothing to fear in the thought of
Half-Way House—

the place one got down
to walk—. What is
this shudder, this
dry mouth?

Think, please, of the quarry pool,
the garden's furthest
garden, of your childhood's
joy in its solitude.

TO THE READER

As you read, a white bear leisurely
pees, dyeing the snow
saffron,

and as you read, many gods
lie among lianas: eyes of obsidian
are watching the generations of leaves,

and as you read
the sea is turning its dark pages,
turning
its dark pages.

"...ELSE A GREAT PRINCE IN PRISON LIES"

All that blesses the step of the antelope
all the grace a giraffe lifts to the highest leaves
all steadfastness and pleasant gazing, alien to ennui,
dwell secretly behind man's misery.

Animal face, when the lines
of human fear, knots of a net, become transparent
and your brilliant eyes and velvet muzzle
are revealed, who shall say you are not the face of a man?

In the dense light of wakened flesh
animal man is a prince. As from alabaster
a lucency animates him from heel to forehead.
Then his shadows are deep and not gray.

CLARITAS

i

The All-Day Bird, the artist,
whitethroated sparrow,
striving
in hope and
good faith to make his notes
ever more precise, closer
to what he knows.

ii

There is the proposition
and the development.
The way
one grows from the other.
The All-Day Bird
ponders.

iii

May the first note
be round enough
and those that follow
fine, fine as
sweetgrass,
               prays
the All-Day Bird.

iv

Fine
as the tail of a lizard,
as a leaf of
chives—
the *shadow of a difference*
falling between
note and note,
a *hair's breadth*
defining them.

v

The dew is on the vineleaves.
My tree
is lit with the
break of day.

vi

Sun
light.
       Light
light light light.

ABEL'S BRIDE

Woman fears for man, he goes
out alone to his labors. No mirror
nests in his pocket. His face
opens and shuts with his hopes.
His sex hangs unhidden
or rises before him
blind and questing.

She thinks herself
lucky. But sad. When she goes out
she looks in the glass, she remembers
herself. Stones, coal,
the hiss of water upon the kindled
branches—her being
is a cave, there are bones at the hearth.

STEPPING WESTWARD

What is green in me
darkens, muscadine.

If woman is inconstant,
good, I am faithful to

ebb and flow, I fall
in season and now

is a time of ripening.
If her part

is to be true,
a north star,

good, I hold steady
in the black sky

and vanish by day,
yet burn there

in blue or above
quilts of cloud.

There is no savor
more sweet, more salt

than to be glad to be
what, woman,

and who, myself,
I am, a shadow

that grows longer as the sun
moves, drawn out

on a thread of wonder.
If I bear burdens

they begin to be remembered
as gifts, goods, a basket

of bread that hurts
my shoulders but closes me

in fragrance. I can
eat as I go.

LIFE AT WAR

The disasters numb within us
caught in the chest, rolling
in the brain like pebbles. The feeling
resembles lumps of raw dough

weighing down a child's stomach on baking day.
Or Rilke said it, 'My heart . . .
Could I say of it, it overflows
with bitterness . . . but no, as though

its contents were simply balled into
formless lumps, thus
do I carry it about.'
The same war

continues.
We have breathed the grits of it in, all our lives,
our lungs are pocked with it,
the mucous membrane of our dreams
coated with it, the imagination
filmed over with the gray filth of it:

the knowledge that humankind,
delicate Man, whose flesh
responds to a caress, whose eyes
are flowers that perceive the stars,

whose music excels the music of birds,
whose laughter matches the laughter of dogs,
whose understanding manifests designs
fairer than the spider's most intricate web,

still turns without surprise, with mere regret
to the scheduled breaking open of breasts whose milk
runs out over the entrails of still-alive babies,
transformation of witnessing eyes to pulp-fragments,
implosion of skinned penises into carcass-gulleys.

We are the humans, men who can make;
whose language imagines *mercy*,
lovingkindness; we have believed one another
mirrored forms of a God we felt as good—

who do these acts, who convince ourselves
it is necessary; these acts are done
to our own flesh; burned human flesh
is smelling in Viet Nam as I write.

Yes, this is the knowledge that jostles for space
in our bodies along with all we
go on knowing of joy, of love;

our nerve filaments twitch with its presence
day and night,
nothing we say has not the husky phlegm of it in the
    saying,
nothing we do has the quickness, the sureness,
the deep intelligence living at peace would have.

WHAT WERE THEY LIKE?

1) Did the people of Viet Nam
   use lanterns of stone?
2) Did they hold ceremonies
   to reverence the opening of buds?
3) Were they inclined to quiet laughter?
4) Did they use bone and ivory,
   jade and silver, for ornament?
5) Had they an epic poem?
6) Did they distinguish between speech and singing?

1) Sir, their light hearts turned to stone.
   It is not remembered whether in gardens
   stone lanterns illumined pleasant ways.
2) Perhaps they gathered once to delight in blossom,
   but after the children were killed
   there were no more buds.
3) Sir, laughter is bitter to the burned mouth.
4) A dream ago, perhaps. Ornament is for joy.
   All the bones were charred.
5) It is not remembered. Remember,
   most were peasants; their life
   was in rice and bamboo.
   When peaceful clouds were reflected in the paddies
   and the water buffalo stepped surely along terraces,
   maybe fathers told their sons old tales.
   When bombs smashed those mirrors
   there was time only to scream.
6) There is an echo yet
   of their speech which was like a song.
   It was reported their singing resembled
   the flight of moths in moonlight.
   Who can say? It is silent now.

LIVING

The fire in leaf and grass
so green it seems
each summer the last summer.

The wind blowing, the leaves
shivering in the sun,
each day the last day.

A red salamander
so cold and so
easy to catch, dreamily

moves his delicate feet
and long tail. I hold
my hand open for him to go.

Each minute the last minute.

LOUIS SIMPSON (1923–   )

Born on Jamaica, B.W.I., Simpson attended Columbia University, and has taught there and at the University of California in Berkeley. In addition to his poems he has written short stories, criticism, and a novel, *Riverside Drive* (1962).

Selected Poems. Harcourt, Brace & World, 1965.

MEMORIES OF A LOST WAR

The guns know what is what, but underneath
In fearful file
We go around burst boots and packs and teeth
That seem to smile.

The scene jags like a strip of celluloid,
A mortar fires,
Cinzano falls, Michelin is destroyed,
The man of tires.

As darkness drifts like fog in from the sea
Somebody says
"We're digging in." Look well, for this may be
The last of days.

Hot lightnings stitch the blind eye of the moon,
The thunder's blunt.
We sleep. Our dreams pass in a faint platoon
Toward the front.

Sleep well, for you are young. Each tree and bush
Drips with sweet dew,
And earlier than morning June's cool hush
Will waken you.

The riflemen will wake and hold their breath.
Though they may bleed
They will be proud a while of something death
Still seems to need.

MY FATHER IN THE NIGHT COMMANDING NO

My father in the night commanding No
Has work to do. Smoke issues from his lips;
 He reads in silence.
The frogs are croaking and the streetlamps glow.

And then my mother winds the gramophone;
The Bride of Lammermoor begins to shriek—
 Or reads a story
About a prince, a castle, and a dragon.

The moon is glittering above the hill.
I stand before the gateposts of the King—
 So runs the story—
Of Thule, at midnight when the mice are still.

And I have been in Thule! It has come true—
The journey and the danger of the world,
 All that there is
To bear and to enjoy, endure and do.

Landscapes, seascapes . . . where have I been led?
The names of cities—Paris, Venice, Rome—
 Held out their arms.
A feathered god, seductive, went ahead.

Here is my house. Under a red rose tree
A child is swinging; another gravely plays.
 They are not surprised
That I am here; they were expecting me.

And yet my father sits and reads in silence,
My mother sheds a tear, the moon is still,
 And the dark wind
Is murmuring that nothing ever happens.

Beyond his jurisdiction as I move
Do I not prove him wrong? And yet, it's true
 They will not change
There, on the stage of terror and of love.

The actors in that playhouse always sit
In fixed positions—father, mother, child
 With painted eyes.
How sad it is to be a little puppet!

Their heads are wooden. And you once pretended
To understand them! Shake them as you will,
    They cannot speak.
Do what you will, the comedy is ended.

Father, why did you work? Why did you weep,
Mother? Was the story so important?
    "Listen!" the wind
Said to the children, and they fell asleep.

STUMPFOOT ON 42ND STREET

A Negro sprouts from the pavement like an asparagus.
One hand beats a drum and cymbal;
He plays a trumpet with the other.

He flies the American flag;
When he goes walking, from stump to stump,
It twitches, and swoops, and flaps.

Also, he has a tin cup which he rattles;
He shoves it right in your face.
These freaks are alive in earnest.

He is not embarrassed.
It is for you to feel embarrassed,
Or God, the way things are.

Therefore he plays the trumpet
And therefore he beats the drum.

2

I can see myself in Venezuela,
With flowers, and clouds in the distance.
The mind tends to drift.

But Stumpfoot stands near a window
Advertising cameras, trusses, household utensils.
The billboards twinkle. The time
Is 12:26.

O why don't angels speak in the infinite
To each other? Why this confusion,
These particular bodies—
Eros with clenched fists, sobbing and cursing?

The time is 12:26.
The streets lead on in burning lines
And giants tremble in electric chains.

3

I can see myself in the middle of Venezuela
Stepping in a nest of ants.
I can see myself being eaten by ants.

My ribs are caught in a thorn bush
And thought has no reality.
But he has furnished his room

With a chair and table.
A chair is like a dog, it waits for man.
He unstraps his apparatus,

And now he is taking off his boots.
He is easing his stumps,
And now he is lighting a cigar.

It seems that a man exists
Only to say, Here I am in person.

PHILIP WHALEN (1923–)

Born in Oregon, Whalen attended Reed College, where he was a fellow student of Gary Snyder. He has lived in San Francisco for some years.

Memoirs of an Interglacial Age. San Francisco: Auerhahn Press, 1960.
Like I Say. New York: Totem Press, 1960.
Every Day. Eugene, Ore.: Coyote's Journal, 1965.
Highgrade. Eugene, Ore.: Coyote's Journal, 1966.

FOR C.

I wanted to bring you this Jap iris
Orchid-white with yellow blazons
But I couldn't face carrying it down the street
Afraid everyone would laugh
And now they're dying of my cowardice.

Abstract beauty in the garden
In my hand, in the street it is a sign
A whole procession of ithyphallic satyrs
Through a town whose people like to believe:
"I was made like Jesus, out of Love; my daddy was a
    spook."

The upright flower would scare them. "What's shot,"
They think, "from the big flesh cannon will decay."
Not being there I can't say that being born is a chance
To learn, to love and to save each other from ourselves:
Live ignorance rots us worse than any grave.

And lacking the courage to tell you, "I'm here,
Such as I am; I need you and you need me"
Planning to give you this flower instead—
Intending it to mean "This is really I, tall, slender,
Perfectly formed"—is uglier than their holy fantasies,

Worse to look at than my own gross shape.
After all this fuss about flowers I walked out
Just to walk, not going to see you (I had nothing to
  bring—
This poem wasn't finished, didn't say
What was on my mind; I'd given up)

I saw bushes of crimson rhododendron, sparkling wet
Beside the hospital walk—I had to see you.
If you were out, I'd leave these flowers.
Even if I couldn't write or speak
At least I broke and stole that branch with love.

FURTHER NOTICE

I can't live in this world
And I refuse to kill myself
Or let you kill me

The dill plant lives, the airplane
My alarm clock, this ink
I won't go away

I shall be myself—
Free, a genius, an embarrassment
Like the Indian, the buffalo

Like Yellowstone National Park.

CID CORMAN (1924–   )

As poet and critic Corman has contributed a strong individual voice to American poetry of the past twenty years, and as editor and publisher he has sponsored much of the best of it: in *Origin* and the Origin Press. His own writing has often derived from his experiences in living abroad, particularly in France, southern Italy, and recently in Japan.

> *Sun Rock Man.* Kyoto, Japan: Origin Press, 1962.
> *In Good Time.* Kyoto, Japan: Origin Press, 1964.
> *Words for Each Other.* London: Rapp & Whiting, 1967.
> *& Without End.* New Rochelle, N.Y.: Elizabeth Press, 1968.

THE CONTAINER

I found a
hummingbird
on the sill

by the books
before the
hollyhocks

dying. I
urged the beak
a drop but

its breath had
migrated.
What remained

made of my
palm a nest
for the dead.

DECEASED

it comes back
unopened

why open
to see what I said

there was
much to tell you

now there is nothing
to say

THE DESK

a god's head for a paperweight
and nothing to write

the large window open upon
an inner garden

harbored from heat
and the swamping dust of July

a dachshund romps among roses
and yaps at a yawn

the edge of the sky above the wall
the laurel tree tipping it in

it is hard to be anywhere once
and twice is a dream

LA SELVA

The soul is lonely
like the gift I was once given

of a hundred sheets of white paper
and a jar of peanut butter.

526

Time is no solution, it
evaporates.

And love
locked nakedly in the dark

fears to cry. Headlights
peer to the end of the street

where the trees march firmly
out of rank into the woods.

THE TORTOISE

Always to want to
go back, to correct
an error, ease a

guilt, see how a friend
is doing. And yet
one doesn't, except

in memory, in
dreams. The land remains
desolate. Always

the feeling is of
terrible slowness
overtaking haste.

"I HAVE COME FAR TO HAVE FOUND NOTHING"

I have come far to have found nothing
or to have found that what was found
was only to be lost, lost finally
in that absence whose trace is silence.

"THERE ARE THINGS TO BE SAID"

There are things to be said. No doubt.
And in one way or another
they will be said. But to whom tell

the silences? With whom share them
now? For a moment the sky is
empty and then there was a bird.

"CALL IT A LOUSE"

Call it a louse—I'm
not so fussy about
the nomenclature

of small insects. This one,
crushed, at any rate,
between pages, looks

more like a period
than a former creature—
but its pause has legs.

THE LOCUS

Why say the idiot is not
a genius? He at least
knows nothing he does not
feel. The poorest fool
provides intelligence
a case of birth. And animal
is not the beast of scorn.
Consider the simple horse
ambling down the macadamized
Appian Way, under
the arch of flowering acacia,
not at all deterred
by notions of propriety,
slowing to drop dung

528

where other dung provided
precedent, as other time
other dung with earth.
Nor does the thoroughly-stained
sweatband of the contadino's
broad hat contradict
the brain concealed within.
Behind the small black eyes
more insistent than
mosquitoes in aimless aim,
amended by a gold halo
hung from the right lobe
signalling where angels may
fear to tread, no thought
has wormed its way except
through withered speech. OK.
One does not ask for more
when one sees always less.
We know too much and not
enough to touch place.
As the olive in ground so barbered
and rock-gutted, splits
upon its trunk, swallowing
pride, to spit up seed
in season, to purge the earth
of a little death. Oil
from the limbs for the limbs of life.
Genius? Nothing not
native to the soil—
indigenous even if indigent.
Each day a day's work,
an ideal the wisest man
has not yet formulated
into truth,
        as the earth has.

HARVEY SHAPIRO (1924-   )

Shapiro's poems reflect the tension between his orthodox religious
background and his experiences in war and in modern city living.
Today he lives in New York, where he works for the *New York
Times*.

The Eye. Denver: Alan Swallow, 1953.
Mountain, Fire, Thornbush. Denver: Alan Swallow, 1961.
Battle Report. Wesleyan University Press, 1966.

MOUNTAIN, FIRE, THORNBUSH

How everything gets tamed.
The pronominal outcry, as if uttered in ecstasy,
Is turned to syntax. We are
Only a step from discursive prose
When the voice speaks from the thornbush.
Mountain, fire, and thornbush.
Supplied only with these, even that aniconic Jew
Could spell mystery. But there must be
Narrative. The people must get to the mountain.
Doors must open and close.
How to savor the savagery of Egyptians,
Who betrayed the names of their gods
To demons, and tore the hair
From their godheads
As lotus blossoms are pulled out of the pool.

FEAST OF THE RAM'S HORN

As seventh sign, the antique heavens show
A pair of scales. And Jews, no less antique,
Hear the ram-rod summons beat their heels,
Until they stand together in mock show
As if they meant to recognize a king.

For they are come again to this good turning:
That from the mountain where their leader goes,
In ten days' time they greet the Law descending.
And these are ancient stories from a book
That circulates, and for them has no ending.

All stand as witness to the great event.
Ezra, their scribe, before the water gate
Takes up the book, and the people rise.
And those who weep upon the word are bid
To hold their peace because the day is holy.

Feast of the ram's horn. Let the player rise.
And may the sound of that bent instrument,
In the seventh month, before the seventh gate,
Speak for all the living and the dead,
And tell creation it is memorized.

Let Isaac be remembered in the ram
That when the great horn sounds, and all are come,
These who now are gathered as one man
Shall be gathered again. Set the bright
Scales in the sky until that judgment's done.

NATIONAL COLD STORAGE COMPANY

The National Cold Storage Company contains
More things than you can dream of.
Hard by the Brooklyn Bridge it stands
In a litter of freight cars,
Tugs to one side; the other, the traffic
Of the Long Island Expressway.
I myself have dropped into it in seven years
Midnight tossings, plans for escape, the shakes.
Add this to the national total—
Grant's tomb, the Civil War, Arlington,
The young President dead.
Above the warehouse and beneath the stars
The poets creep on the harp of the Bridge.
But see,
They fall into the National Cold Storage Company

One by one. The wind off the river is too cold,
Or the times too rough, or the Bridge
Is not a harp at all. Or maybe
A monstrous birth inside the warehouse
Must be fed by everything—ships, poems,
Stars, all the years of our lives.

PHILIP BOOTH (1925–   )

Booth spent much of his childhood on the Maine coast; life there, i.e., life on the edge or margin, has shaped much of his poetry. Today he teaches at Syracuse University.

> *Letter from a Distant Land.* Viking, 1957.
> *The Islanders.* Viking, 1961.
> *Weathers and Edges.* Viking, 1966.

WAS A MAN

Was a man, was a two-
faced man, pretended
he wasn't who he was,
who, in a men's room,
faced his hung-over
face in a mirror hung
over the towel rack.
The mirror was cracked.
Shaving close in that
looking glass, he nicked
his throat, bled blue
blood, grabbed a new
towel to patch the wrong
scratch, knocked off
the mirror and, facing
himself, almost intact,
in final terror hung
the wrong face back.

ONE MAN'S WIFE

Not that he promised not to windowshop,
or refuse free samples; but he gave up
exploring warehouse bargains, and forgot
the trial offers he used to mail away for.

After, that is, she laid on the counter what
she'd long kept hidden under the penny-candy,
and demonstrated (one up-country Sunday)
the total inventory of one wife's general store.

DEER ISLE

Out-island once, on a South slope
bare in March, I saw a buck
limp out of the spruce and snow
to ease his gut in a hummocky meadow.

He fed two rooted hours on the hope
of spring, browsed, and flicked back
into the trees, a big ghost
of what hunters tracked at first frost.

That was six winters ago. Today,
three hundred miles South, a commuter
trapped by a detour sign
at dusk, I trailed a reflecting line

of red arrows that took me the long way
home. Late, caught in the neuter
traffic, driven beyond where I wanted
to go, I braked by a slanted

orchard where six cars were stopped.
There were six does there, feeding on frozen
winesaps, fat and white-rumped
as the drivers who sat in their cars. One limped,

and I thought of that buck, equipped
to survive, on the island he'd chosen
to swim to. That coast, about now,
would lie gray: the raw salt snow

topping a man's hauled lobsterpots,
and sifting down through thick spruce
where the sweat on a run buck
would freeze. A man with no luck

534

but a gun would be hunting home cross-lots.
I was parked miles beyond choice,
miles from home on a blocked curve
in the dead mist of a thick suburban preserve.

My guts clamped. I honked my way clear,
tramping the gas toward nowhere
but where home was. My wife understood.
If I didn't go now, I never would.

DONALD JUSTICE (1925–)

As a child in Miami during the depression—"that half-alive resort," he calls it—Justice suffered from osteomyelitis, an experience which may have been responsible for the inward, sardonic eloquence of his poetry. He teaches at Syracuse.

The Summer Anniversaries. Wesleyan University Press, 1960.
A Local Storm. Iowa City, Iowa: Stone Wall Press, 1963.
Night Light. Wesleyan University Press, 1967.

THE SNOWFALL

The classic landscapes of dreams are not
More pathless, though footprints leading nowhere
Would seem to prove that a people once
Survived for a little even here.

Fragments of a pathetic culture
Remain, the lost mittens of children,
And a single, bright, detasseled snow-cap,
Evidence of some frantic migration.

The landmarks are gone. Nevertheless
There is something familiar about this country.
Slowly now we begin to recall

The terrible whispers of our elders
Falling softly about our ears
In childhood, never believed till now.

ANOTHER SONG

Merry the green, the green hill shall be merry.
Hungry, the owlet shall seek out the mouse,
And Jack his Joan, but they shall never marry.

And snows shall fly, the big flakes fat and furry.
Lonely, the traveler shall seek out the house,
And Jack his Joan, but they shall never marry.

Weary the soldiers go, and come back weary,
Up a green hill and down the withered hill,
And Jack from Joan, and they shall never marry.

IN BERTRAM'S GARDEN

Jane looks down at her organdy skirt
As if *it* somehow were the thing disgraced,
For being there, on the floor, in the dirt,
And she catches it up about her waist,
Smooths it out along one hip,
And pulls it over the crumpled slip.

On the porch, green-shuttered, cool,
Asleep is Bertram, that bronze boy,
Who, having wound her around a spool,
Sends her spinning like a toy
Out to the garden, all alone,
To sit and weep on a bench of stone.

Soon the purple dark will bruise
Lily and bleeding-heart and rose,
And the little Cupid lose
Eyes and ears and chin and nose,
And Jane lie down with others soon
Naked to the naked moon.

BOB KAUFMAN (1925–   )

Kaufman's boyhood in New Orleans was deeply influenced by the Orthodox Judaism of his father, a German Jew, and the devout Roman Catholicism of his mother, a Martinique Negress. At thirteen he went to sea, and remained in the merchant service for twenty years, acquiring a taste for literature from older crewmen. During the fifties, in Los Angeles, he met Allen Ginsberg and other poets of the new California "renaissance," and soon he was in the midst of it, writing, giving public readings, helping to edit the magazine *Beatitude*. Currently he lives in San Francisco.

Solitudes Crowded with Loneliness. New Directions, 1965.

AFTERWARDS, THEY SHALL DANCE

In the city of St. Francis they have taken down the
    statue of St. Francis,
And the hummingbirds all fly forward to protest, hum-
    ming feather poems.

Bodenheim denounced everyone and wrote. Bodenheim
    had no sweet marijuana dreams,
Patriotic muscateleer, did not die seriously, no poet love
    to end with, gone.

Dylan took the stone cat's nap at St. Vincent's, vaticaned
    beer, no defense;
That poem shouted from his nun-filled room, an insult to
    the brain, nerves,
Save now from Swansea, white horses, beer birds, snore
    poems, Wales-bird.

Billie Holliday got lost on the subway and stayed there
    forever,
Raised little peace-of-mind gardens in out of the way
    stations,
And will go on living in wrappers of jazz silence forever,
    loved.

My face feels like a living emotional relief map, forever wet.
My hair is curling in anticipation of my own wild gardening.

Poor Edgar Allan Poe died translated, in unpressed pants, ended in light,
Surrounded by ecstatic gold bugs, his hegira blessed by Baudelaire's orgy.

Whether I am a poet or not, I use fifty dollars' worth of air every day, cool.
In order to exist I hide behind stacks of red and blue poems
And open little sensuous parasols, singing the nail-in-the-foot song, drinking cool beatitudes.

TO MY SON PARKER, ASLEEP IN THE NEXT ROOM

On ochre walls in ice-formed caves shaggy Neanderthals marked their place in time.
On germinal trees in equatorial stands embryonic giants carved beginnings.
On Tasmanian flatlands mud-clothed first men hacked rock, still soft.
On Melanesian mountain peaks barked heads were reared in pride and beauty.
On steamy Java's cooling lava stooped humans raised stones to altar height.
On newborn China's plain mythless sons of Han acquired peaked gods with teak faces.
On holy India's sacred soil future gods carved worshipped reflections.
On Coptic Ethiopia's pimple rock pyramid builders tore volcanoes from earth.
On death-loving Egypt's godly sands living sacrifices carved naked power.
On Sumeria's cliffs speechless artists gouged messages to men yet uncreated.
On glorious Assyria's earthen dens art priests chipped figures of awe and hidden dimensions.

On splendored Peru's gold-stained body filigreed temples were torn from severed hands.

On perfect Greece's bloody sites marble stirred under hands of men.

On degenerate Rome's trembling sod imitators sculpted lies into beauty.

On slave Europe's prostrate form chained souls shaped free men.

On wild America's green torso original men painted glacial languages.

On cold Arctica's snowy surface leathery men raised totems in frozen air.

On this shore, you are all men, before, forever, eternally free in all things.

On this shore, we shall raise our monuments of stones, of wood, of mud, of color, of belief, of being, of life, of love, of self, of man expressed
in self-determined compliance, or willful revolt,
secure in this avowed truth, that no man is our master, nor can any ever be, at any time in time to come.

CAROLYN KIZER (1925–   )

Vachel Lindsay, who lived with Miss Kizer's family in Spokane when she was a child, encouraged her early interest in poetry, especially oriental poetry. Later she lived in China for a year. She has translated from the classical Chinese, and the influence of Chinese poets, particularly Tu Fu, on her own poems, some of which she modestly calls "Chinese imitations," is pervasive, though her work is free of the sentimentality of most oriental imitations. Miss Kizer has served as poet in residence at the U.S. Embassy in Pakistan, and was Director of Literary Programs at the National Endowment for the Arts, in Washington. She founded, and for some years edited, *Poetry Northwest*, a quarterly published in Seattle.

The Ungrateful Garden. Indiana University Press, 1961.
Knock upon Silence. Doubleday, 1965.

FOR JAN, IN BAR MARIA

Though it's true we were young girls when we met,
We have been friends for twenty-five years.
But we still swim strongly, run up the hill from the
    beach without getting too winded.
Here we idle in Ischia, a world away from our birth-
    place—
That colorless town!—drinking together, sisters of sum-
    mer.
Now we like to have groups of young men gathered around
    us.
We are trivial-hearted. We don't want to die any more.

Remember, fifteen years ago, in our twin pinafores
We danced on the boards of the ferry deck at Mukilteo
Mad as yearling mares in the full moon?
Here in the morning moonlight we climbed on a work-
    man's cart

And three young men, shouting and laughing, dragged
    it up through the streets of the village.
It is said we have shocked the people of Forio.
They call us Janna and Carolina, those two mad *straniere*.

AMUSING OUR DAUGHTERS

for Robert Creeley

We don't lack people here on the Northern coast,
But they are people one meets, not people one cares for.
So I bundle my daughters into the car
And with my brother poets, go to visit you, brother.

Here come your guests! A swarm of strangers and chil-
    dren;
But the strangers write verses, the children are daugh-
    ters like yours.
We bed down on mattresses, cots, roll up on the floor;
Outside, burly old fruit trees in mist and rain;
In every room, bundles asleep like larvae.

We waken and count our daughters. Otherwise, nothing
    happens.
You feed them sweet rolls and melon, drive them all to
    the zoo;
Patiently, patiently, ever the father, you answer their
    questions.
Later we eat again, drink, listen to poems.
Nothing occurs, though we are aware you have three
    daughters
Who last year had four. But even death becomes part
    of our ease:
Poems, parenthood, sorrow, all we have learned
From these, of tenderness, holds us together
In the center of life, entertaining daughters
By firelight, with cake and songs.

You, my brother, are a good and violent drinker,
Good at reciting short-line or long-line poems.
In time we will lose all our daughters, you and I,
Be temperate, venerable, content to stay in one place,
Sending our messages over the mountains and waters.

SUMMER NEAR THE RIVER

I have carried my pillow to the windowsill
And try to sleep, with my damp arms crossed upon it
But no breeze stirs the tepid morning.
Only I stir. . . . Come, tease me a little!
With such cold passion, so little teasing play,
How long can we endure our life together?

No use. I put on your long dressing-gown;
The untied sash trails over the dusty floor.
I kneel by the window, prop up your shaving mirror
And pluck my eyebrows.
I don't care if the robe slides open
Revealing a crescent of belly, a tan thigh.
I can accuse that non-existent breeze. . . .

I am as monogamous as the North Star
But I don't want you to know it. You'd only take advantage.
While you are as fickle as spring sunlight.
All right, sleep! The cat means more to you than I.
I can rouse you, but then you swagger out.
I glimpse you from the window, striding towards the
    river.

When you return, reeking of fish and beer,
There is salt dew in your hair. Where have you been?
Your clothes weren't that wrinkled hours ago, when you
    left.
You couldn't have loved someone else, after loving me!
I sulk and sigh, dawdling by the window.
Later, when you hold me in your arms
It seems, for a moment, the river ceases flowing.

THE SKEIN

Moonlight through my gauze curtains
Turns them to nets for snaring wild birds,
Turns them into woven traps, into shrouds.
The old, restless grief keeps me awake.
I wander around, holding a scarf or shawl;
In the muffled moonlight I wander around

Folding it carefully, shaking it out again.
Everyone says my old lover is happy.
I wish they said he was coming back to me.
I hesitate here, my scarf like a skein of yarn
Binding my two hands loosely
          that would reach for paper and pen.

So I memorize these lines,
Dew on the scarf, dappling my nightdress also.
O love long gone, it is raining in our room!
So I memorize these lines,
         without salutation, without close.

KENNETH KOCH (1925–   )

Koch attended Harvard, where he was associated with John
Ashbery and Frank O'Hara. In the early fifties the three moved
to New York, where they continued their experimental writing,
using techniques derived from surrealism and from the painting
of the "New York School." Today Koch teaches at Columbia.

Poems New York. New York: Tibor de Nagy Gallery,
1953.
Ko; or, A Season on Earth. Grove, 1960.
Guinevere; or, The Death of the Kangaroo. (Drama.)
New York: American Theatre for Poets, 1961.
Thank You and Other Poems. Grove, 1962.
Bertha and Other Plays. Grove, 1966.
Poems, from 1952 and 1953. Los Angeles: Black Sparrow
Press, 1968.

THANKSGIVING

What's sweeter than at the end of a summer's day
To suddenly drift away
From the green match-wrappers in an opened pocket-
book
And be part of the boards in a tavern?

A tavern made of new wood.
There's an orange-red sun in the sky
And a redskin is hunting for you underneath ladders of
timber.
I will buy this tavern. Will you buy this tavern? I do.

In the Indian camp there's awful dismay.
Do they know us as we know they
Know us or will know us, I mean a—
I mean a hostile force, the month of May.

How whitely the springtime is blossoming,
Ugh! all around us!
It is the brilliant Indian time of year
When the sweetest Indians mate with the sweetest others.

But I fear the white men, I fear
The rent apple blossoms and discarded feathers
And the scalp lying secretly on the ground
Like an unoffending nose!

But we've destroyed all that. With shocking guns.
Peter Stuyvesant, Johnny Appleseed,
We've destroyed all that. Come,
Do you believe right was on either side?

How would you like to be living in an Indian America,
With feathers dressing every head? We'd eat buffalo
    hump
For Thanksgiving dinner. Everyone is in a tribe.
A girl from the Bep Tribe can't marry a brave from the
    Bab Tribe. Is that democracy?

And then those dreary evenings around the campfires
Listening to the Chief! If there were a New York
It would be a city of tents, and what do you suppose
Our art and poetry would be like? For the community!
    the tribe!
No beautiful modern abstract pictures, no mad incom-
    prehensible
Free lovable poems! And our moral sense! tribal.
If you would like to be living in an Indian America
Why not subscribe to this newspaper, *Indian America*?

In Wisconsin, Ben, I stand, I walk up and down and try
    to decide.

Is this country getting any better or has it gotten?
If the Indian New York is bad, what about our white
    New York?
Dirty, unwholesome, the filthy appendage to a vast am-
    munition works, I hate it!
Disgusting rectangular garbage dump sending its fumes
    up to suffocate the sky—
Foo, what fumes! and the scaly white complexion of her
    citizens.
There's hell in every firm handshake, and stifled rage in
    every look.
If you do find somewhere to lie down, it's a dirty in-
    spected corner,

And there are newspapers and forums and the stinking
   breath of Broadway
To investigate what it feels like to be a source of stench
And nothing else. And if one does go away,
It is always here, waiting, for one to come back. And one
   does come back,
As one comes back to the bathroom, and to a time of
   suffering.

Where else would I find such ardent and graceful spirits
Inspired and wasted and using and used by this horrible
   city,
New York, New York? Can the Pilgrims' Thanksgiving
   dinner really compare to it?
And the Puritans? And the single-minded ankle-divided
   Indians?
No, nothing can compare to it! So it's here we speak from
   the heart,
And it's rotting so fast that what we say
Fades like the last of a summer's day,
Rot which makes us prolific as the sun on white unfastened
   clouds.

DOWN AT THE DOCKS

Down at the docks
Where everything is sweet and inclines
At night
To the sound of canoes
I planted a maple tree
And every night
Beneath it I studied the cosmos
Down at the docks.

Sweet ladies, listen to me.
The dock is made of wood
The maple tree's not made of wood
It is wood
Wood comes from it
As music comes from me
And from this mandolin I've made
Out of the maple tree.

Jealous gentlemen, study how
Wood comes from the maple
Then devise your love
So that it seems
To come from where
All is it yet something more
White spring flowers and leafy bough
Jealous gentlemen.

Arrogant little waves
Knocking at the dock
It's for you I've made this chanson
For you and that big dark blue.

JACK SPICER (1925–1965)

Born in Hollywood, Spicer became a professional linguist and served for several years on a project to make a linguistic map of the U.S. His poems reflect his interest in cosmology, a view of poetry he shares with several other Bay Area poets. Among his deepest concerns was his belief in the magical elements of poetry, and the record of his participation in such a world is found in the later works: "Things fit together. We knew that—it is the principle of magic. Two inconsequential things can combine together to become a consequence. This is true of poems too. A poem is never to be judged by itself alone. A poem is never by itself alone" (quoted from his unpublished book *Admonitions*, 1958). His books are composed of poems, which after 1961 he came to call serial poems. He was living in San Francisco when he died.

> *After Lorca.* San Francisco: White Rabbit Press, 1957.
> *Billy the Kid.* Stinson Beach, Calif.: Enkidu Surrogate, 1959.
> *The Heads of the Town up to the Aether.* San Francisco: Auerhahn Press, 1962.
> *Lament for the Makers.* Oakland: White Rabbit Press, 1962.
> *The Holy Grail.* San Francisco: White Rabbit Press, 1964.
> *Language.* San Francisco: White Rabbit Press, 1965.
> *Book of Magazine Verse.* San Francisco: White Rabbit Press, 1966.

FROM THE SEQUENCE CALLED "GRAPHEMICS"

1

Like a scared rabbit running over and
      over again his tracks in the snow
We spent this Halloween together, forty
      miles apart.
The tracks are there and the rabbit's
      feeling of death is there.   And the
      children no longer masquerading
      themselves as ghosts but as
      businessmen, yelled "Trick or treat,"
      maybe even in Stinson

The tracks in the snow and rabbit's
          motion which writes it is quite
          legible.   The children
Not even pretending to be souls of the
          dead are not.   Forty miles.   Nothing
          really restored
We
And the dead are not really on the frozen field.
          (The children don't even wear masks)   This
Is another poem about the death of John F. Kennedy.

7

Walden Pond
All those noxious gases rising from it
          in the summer.   In the winter ice
Dirty now.   Almost as dirty as the snow in Boston.
W.P.A. swimming hole.   Erected
By the Commonwealth of Massachusetts.
We saw the lights across the pond
          They said that there was some sort
          of being across the pond, drinking
          dry martinis like we were.
We made tapes.   They were probably
          erased like we were.   Figures
          on the pond's surface.
And yet the water like a piece of paper
          moved and moves
Restlessly while memory gives the light
From the other side.

10

Love is not mocked whatever use
          you put to it.   Words are also not mocked.
The soup of real turtles flows through
          our veins. Being a [poet] a
          disyllable in a world of monosyllables
          Awakened by the distance between
          the [o] and the [e].

The earth quakes.   John F. Kennedy
          is assassinated.   The dark forest
          of words lets in some light from
          its branches.   Mocking them,
          the deep leaves
That time leaves us
Words, loves.

A. R. AMMONS (1926–   )

The speech and country lore of his native Carolina figure in some of Ammons's poems; others deal with the intricacies of science, especially zoology. One long poem was written entirely on a roll of adding-machine tape. He teaches at Cornell.

Selected Poems. Cornell University Press, 1968.
Tape for the Turn of the Year. Cornell University Press, 1965.

HARDWEED PATH GOING

Every evening, down into the hardweed
going,
the slop bucket heavy, held-out, wire handle
freezing in the hand, put it down a minute, the jerky
smooth unspilling levelness of the knees,
meditation of a bucket rim,
lest the wheat meal,
floating on clear greasewater, spill,
down the grown-up path:

don't forget to slop the hogs,
feed the chickens,
water the mule,
cut the kindling,
build the fire,
call up the cow:

supper is over, it's starting to get
dark early,
better get the scraps together, mix a little meal in,
nothing but swill.

The dead-purple woods hover on the west.
I know those woods.
Under the tall, ceiling-solid pines, beyond the edge of
field and brush, where the wild myrtle grows,
I let my jo-reet loose.

552

A jo-reet is a bird. Nine weeks of summer he
sat on the well bench in a screened box,
a stick inside to walk on,
>"jo-reet," he said, "jo-reet."
>and I
would come up to the well and draw the bucket down
deep into the cold place where red and white marbled
clay oozed the purest water, water celebrated
throughout the county:
>"Grits all gone?"
>"jo-reet."
Throw a dipper of cold water on him. Reddish-black
flutter
>"reet, reet, reet!"

>Better turn him loose before
cold weather comes on.
>Doom caving in
>inside
>any pleasure, pure
>attachment
>of love.

Beyond the wild myrtle away from cats I turned him
>loose
and his eye asked me what to do, where to go;
he hopped around, scratched a little, but looked up at me.
Don't look at me. Winter is coming.
Disappear in the bushes. I'm tired of you and will
be alone hereafter. I will go dry in my well.
>I will turn still.
Go south. Grits is not available in any natural form.
Look under leaves, try mushy logs, the floors of piny-
>woods.
South into the dominion of bugs.

>They're good woods.
But lay me out if a mourning dove far off in the dusky
>pines starts.

>Down the hardweed path going,
leaning, balancing, away from the bucket, to
Sparkle, my favorite hog, sparse, fine black hair,

grunted while feeding if rubbed,
scratched against the hair, or if talked to gently:
got the bottom of the slop bucket:
                    "Sparkle..."
                    "grunt, grunt..."
                    "You hungry?"
                    "grunt, grunt..."
                    "Hungry, girly?"
                    "grunt, grunt, grunt...."
blowing, bubbling in the trough.

          Waiting for the first freeze:
"Think it's going to freeze tonight?" say the neighbors,
the neighbors, going by.

          Hog-killing.

Oh, Sparkle, when the axe tomorrow morning falls
and the rush is made to open your throat,
I will sing, watching dry-eyed as a man, sing my
          love for you in the tender feedings.

          She's nothing but a hog, boy.

Bleed out, Sparkle, the moon-chilled bleaches
          of your body hanging upside-down
hardening through the mind and night of the first freeze.

PAUL BLACKBURN (1926–   )

Though he was born in St. Albans, Vt., Blackburn is decidedly a big-city poet, concerned with the urban phenomenon both in the U.S. and abroad. He has taught for two years at the University of Toulouse, and in addition to his own poetry has done many translations from the medieval literature of Provence.

> *The Dissolving Fabric.* Palma de Mallorca: Divers Press, 1955.
> *Brooklyn-Manhattan Transit: A Bouquet for Flatbush.* New York: Totem Press, 1960.
> *The Nets.* New York: Trobar, 1961.
> *The Cities.* Grove, 1967.
> *The Reardon Poems.* Madison, Wis.: The Perishable Press, 1967.

HOT AFTERNOONS HAVE BEEN IN WEST 15TH STREET

Here, in late spring, the summer is on us already
                    Clouds and sun,
            a haze over the city.   Outside my
window the ailanthus nods sleepily under
            a hot wind, under
            wetness in the air, the brightness
of day even with overcast.   The chair on the next roof
            sits by itself and waits
for someone to come stretch his length in it.   Suddenly

thunder cracks to the south over the ocean, one can
                    shuteye see
the waves' grey wife, the storm, implacably stride
rain nipplings on the surface of the sea, the waves
            powerfully starting to rise, raise their
            powers before the hot wind
The endless stretchout to Europe disappears, the
rainsweep moving toward the city rising caught in the
      haze-
            hot island atmosphere

Hate anger powers whip toward the towers rising
from the hum of slugbedded traffic clogging avenues, the
    trees
            of heaven gracing their backyards crazily
            waving under the strengthening wind

            sun brighter
            more thunder
            birdsong
            rises shrilly announcing the
storm in advance in encroach in abstruse syllables of pure
    SOUND   .   SONG   .   SOME-
    ONE
comes to the porched roof to cover the chair from the
            thunderfilled wet atmosphere,   there is
nothing clearly defined wrong I can see except
I must go uptown and see what other storms there
        be, there

And paint the inside of my wife's white filing cabinet red
that all things may be resolved   correct   and dead .

INVITATION STANDING

BRING a leaf to me
just a leaf just a
spring leaf, an
april leaf
just
    come

Blue sky
never mind
Spring rain
never mind
Reach up and
take a leaf and
    come
just come

ROBERT BLY (1926–)

Bly lives on a farm in Madison, Minn., where he was born. There he conducts *The Sixties*; an influential magazine, and earns his living chiefly as a translator of Scandinavian and Spanish literature; in recent years he has been particularly active in the peace movement, has organized a series of poetry readings "against the Vietnam war," and with David Ray has edited two books of antiwar poems. In 1968, when his second book of poems was awarded the National Book Award, he turned his acceptance speech into a public castigation of the American publishing industry for its failure to oppose militarism, and gave his prize to the Resistance movement.

> *Silence in the Snowy Fields*. Wesleyan University Press, 1962.
> *The Light Around the Body*. Harper & Row, 1967.

SURPRISED BY EVENING

There is unknown dust that is near us,
Waves breaking on shores just over the hill,
Trees full of birds that we have never seen,
Nets drawn down with dark fish.

The evening arrives; we look up and it is there,
It has come through the nets of the stars,
Through the tissues of the grass,
Walking quietly over the asylums of the waters.

The day shall never end, we think:
We have hair that seems born for the daylight;
But, at last, the quiet waters of the night will rise,
And our skin shall see far off, as it does under water.

DRIVING TO TOWN LATE TO MAIL A LETTER

It is a cold and snowy night. The main street is deserted.
The only things moving are swirls of snow.
As I lift the mailbox door, I feel its cold iron.
There is a privacy I love in this snowy night.
Driving around, I will waste more time.

SOLITUDE LATE AT NIGHT IN THE WOODS

I

The body is like a November birch facing the full moon
And reaching into the cold heavens.
In these trees there is no ambition, no sodden body, no
    leaves,
Nothing but bare trunks climbing like cold fire!

II

My last walk in the trees has come. At dawn
I must return to the trapped fields,
To the obedient earth.
The trees shall be reaching all the winter.

III

It is a joy to walk in the bare woods.
The moonlight is not broken by the heavy leaves.
The leaves are down, and touching the soaked earth,
Giving off the odor that partridges love.

ROBERT CREELEY (1926–   )

Creeley, who taught briefly at Black Mountain College and is one of the leaders of the "Black Mountain movement," has extended William Carlos Williams's statement that there are "no ideas but in things" to say that "things are made of words." The poet's involvement in this making is, for him, the root of his creative endeavor. Though Creeley's poems are decidedly anticonventional, they have a more formal movement than the work of most of his associates, an inner decorum which is even courtly at times, especially in his many poems on erotic themes. Creeley was born in New England, and has lived on Mallorca, where he established the Divers Press, and in Mexico. Today his permanent home is in New Mexico, but he spends part of each year in western New York, where he teaches at the University of Buffalo.

> *For Love, Poems 1950–1960.* Scribner's, 1962.
> *Words.* Scribner's, 1967.
> *A Form of Women.* Highlands, N.C.: Jargon Books, 1959.
> *The Finger.* Los Angeles: Black Sparrow Press, 1968.
> *5 Numbers.* New York: Poets Press, 1968.
> *Divisions & Other Early Poems.* Madison, Wis.: The Perishable Press, 1968.
> *The Island.* (Novel.) Scribner's, 1963.

THE WARNING

For love—I would
split open your head and put
a candle in
behind the eyes.

Love is dead in us
if we forget
the virtues of an amulet
and quick surprise.

THE INVOICE

I once wrote a letter as follows:
dear Jim, I would like to borrow
200 dollars from you
to see me through.

I also wrote another: dearest M/,
please come.
There is no one
here at all.

I got word today,
viz: hey
sport, how are you making it?
And, why don't you get with it.

THE DOOR

for Robert Duncan

It is hard going to the door
cut so small in the wall where
the vision which echoes loneliness
brings a scent of wild flowers in a wood.

What I understood, I understand.
My mind is sometime torment,
sometimes good and filled with livelihood,
and feels the ground.

But I see the door,
and knew the wall, and wanted the wood,
and would get there if I could
with my feet and hands and mind.

Lady, do not banish me
for digressions. My nature
is a quagmire of unresolved
confessions. Lady, I follow.

I walked away from myself,
I left the room, I found the garden,

I knew the woman
in it, together we lay down.

Dead night remembers. In December
we change, not multiplied but dispersed,
sneaked out of childhood,
the ritual of dismemberment.

Mighty magic is a mother,
in her there is another issue
of fixture, repeated form, the race renewal,
the charge of the command.

The garden echoes across the room.
It is fixed in the wall like a mirror
that faces a window behind you
and reflects the shadows.

May I go now?
Am I allowed to bow myself down
in the ridiculous posture of renewal,
of the insistence of which I am the virtue?

Nothing for You is untoward.
Inside You would also be tall,
more tall, more beautiful.
Come toward me from the wall, I want to be with You.

So I screamed to You,
who hears as the wind, and changes
multiply, invariably,
changes in the mind.

Running to the door, I ran down
as a clock runs down. Walked backwards,
stumbled, sat down
hard on the floor near the wall.

Where were You.
How absurd, how vicious.
There is nothing to do but get up.
My knees were iron, I rusted in worship, of You.

For that one sings, one
writes the spring poem, one goes on walking.
The Lady has always moved to the next town
and you stumble on after Her.

The door in the wall leads to the garden
where in the sunlight sit
the Graces in long Victorian dresses,
of which my grandmother had spoken.

History sings in their faces.
They are young, they are obtainable,
and you follow after them also
in the service of God and Truth.

But the Lady is indefinable,
she will be the door in the wall
to the garden in sunlight.
I will go on talking forever.

I will never get there.
Oh Lady, remember me
who in Your service grows older
not wiser, no more than before.

How can I die alone.
Where will I be then who am now alone,
what groans so pathetically
in this room where I am alone?

I will go to the garden.
I will be a romantic. I will sell
myself in hell,
in heaven also I will be.

In my mind I see the door,
I see the sunlight before me across the floor
beckon to me, as the Lady's skirt
moves small beyond it.

THE RAIN

All night the sound had
come back again,
and again falls
this quiet, persistent rain.

What am I to myself
that must be remembered,
insisted upon
so often? Is it

that never the ease,
even the hardness,
of rain falling
will have for me

something other than this,
something not so insistent—
am I to be locked in this
final uneasiness.

Love, if you love me,
lie next to me.
Be for me, like rain,
the getting out

of the tiredness, the fatuousness, the semi-
lust of intentional indifference.
Be wet
with a decent happiness.

A TOKEN

My lady
fair with
soft
arms, what

can I say to
you—words, words
as if all
worlds were there.

THE MEMORY

Like a river she was,
huge roily mass of water
carrying tree trunks
and divers drunks.

Like a Priscilla, a feminine Benjamin,
a whore gone right over
the falls,
she was.

Did you know her.
Did you love her, brother.
Did wonder pour down
on the whole goddamn town.

SONG

Those rivers run from that land
to sea. The wind
finds trees to move,
then goes again.

And me, why me
on any day might be
favored with kind prosperity
or sunk in wretched misery.

I cannot stop the weather
by putting together
myself and another
to stop those rivers.

Or hold the wind
with my hand from the tree,
the mind from the thing,
love from her or me.

Be natural, while alive.
Dead, we die to that
also, and go another
course, I hope.

And me, why me
on any day might be
favored with kind prosperity
or sunk in wretched misery.

You I want back of me
in the life we have here,
waiting to see
what becomes of it.

Call, call loud,
I will hear you, or if
not me, the wind will
for the sake of the tree.

AIR: "THE LOVE OF A WOMAN"

The love of a woman
is the possibility which
surrounds her as hair
her head, as the love of her

follows and describes
her. But what if
they die, then there is
still the aura

left, left sadly, but
hovers in the air, surely,
where this had taken place?
Then sing, of her, of whom

it will be said, he
sang of her, it was the
song he made which made her
happy, so she lived.

THE PEOPLE

Wistful,
they speak of
satis-
faction, love

and divers
other
things. It
comforts,

it surprises
them, the
old
remembrances,

like hands to
hold them
safe and
warm. So

must it be, then,
some god looks
truly down
upon them.

THE WIFE

I know two women
        and the one
is tangible substance,
        flesh and bone.

The other in my mind
        occurs.
She keeps her strict
        proportion there.

But how should I
        propose to live
with two such creatures
        in my bed—

or how shall he
   who has a wife
yield two to one
   and watch the other die.

WAITING

He pushes behind the words
which, awkward, catch
and turn him to a disturbed
and fumbling man.

What if it all stops.
Then silence
is as silence was
again.

What if the last time
he was moved to touch,
work out in his own mind,
such limits was the last—

and then a quiet, a dull
space of hanging actions, all
depending on some time
has come and gone.

God help him then
if such things can.
That risk
is all there is.

FOR NO CLEAR REASON

I dreamt last night
the fright was over, that
the dust came, and then water,
and women and men, together
again, and all was quiet
in the dim moon's light.

A paean of such patience—
laughing, laughing at me,
and the days extend over
the earth's great cover,
grass, trees, and flower-
ing season, for no clear reason.

THE WINDOW

Position is where you
put it, where it is,
did you, for example, that

large tank there, silvered,
with the white church along-
side, lift

all that, to what
purpose? How
heavy the slow

world is with
everything put
in place. Some

man walks by, a
car beside him on
the dropped

road, a leaf of
yellow color is
going to

fall. It
all drops into
place. My

face is heavy
with the sight. I can
feel my eye breaking.

QUICK-STEP

More gaily, dance
with such ladies make
a circumstance of dancing.

Let them lead
around and around, all
awkwardness apart.

There is
an easy grace gained
from falling forward

in time, in
simple time to
all their graces.

THE MOON

Earlier in the evening the moon
was clear to the east,
over the snow of the yard
and fields—a lovely

bright clarity and perfect
roundness, isolate,
riding as they say the
black sky. Then we went

about our businesses of the
evening, eating supper, talking,
watching television, then
going to bed, making love,

and then to sleep. But before
we did I asked her to look
out the window at the moon
now straight up, so that

she bent her head and looked
sharply up, to see it.

Through the night it must
have shone on, in that

fact of things—another
moon, another night—a
full moon in the winter's
space, a white loneliness.

I came awake to the blue
white light in the darkness,
and felt as if someone
were there, waiting, alone.

ALLEN GINSBERG (1926–   )

Ginsberg was born in New Jersey and attended Columbia, where his early poems were written, it is said, in the manner of Sir Thomas Wyatt; but he soon broke with European conventions, and began writing in a free, highly wrought style. His poem "Howl," published by Lawrence Ferlinghetti in 1955, is generally regarded as the first manifestation of the "Beat" movement in American poetry; the entire first edition was confiscated, but was later cleared of obscenity charges in San Francisco Municipal Court. Through his flowing cadences and charged diction, Ginsberg works with great sympathetic perception toward the inner being of his poetic feeling, usually in poems too long to be anthologized. His best-known to date is probably a long eulogy for his mother, "Kaddish" (1960). Ginsberg has lived in Europe and the Far East, but makes his home today in New York City.

> *Howl and Other Poems.* San Francisco: City Lights Books, 1956.
> *Kaddish and Other Poems.* San Francisco: City Lights Books, 1960.
> *Empty Mirror: Early Poems.* New York: Totem Press, 1961.
> *Reality Sandwiches, 1953–1960.* San Francisco: City Lights Books, 1963.
> *TV Baby Poems.* London: Cape Goliard Press, 1967.
> *Planet News.* San Francisco: City Lights Books, 1968.

```
        *

     *     *

POEM
Rocket

    •         •

    •         •

    •         •

    •         •

    •         •

      •     •

        •

  •••••••••••••
```

'Be a Star-screwer!'
Gregory Corso

Old moon my eyes are new moon with human footprint
no longer Romeo Sadface in drunken river Loony Pierre
  eyebrow, goof moon
O possible moon in Heaven we get to first of ageless
  constellations of names
as God is possible as All is possible so we'll reach another
  life.

Moon politicians earth weeping and warring in eternity
tho not one star disturbed by screaming madmen from
  Hollywood
oil tycoons from Romania making secret deals with flabby
  green Plutonians—
slave camps on Saturn Cuban revolutions on Mars?
Old life and new side by side, will Catholic church find
  Christ on Jupiter
Mohammed rave in Uranus will Buddha be acceptable on
  the stolid planets
or will we find Zoroastrian temples flowering on Neptune?
What monstrous new ecclesiastical design on the entire
  universe unfolds in the dying Pope's brain?

Scientist alone is true poet he gives us the moon
he promises the stars he'll make us a new universe if it
    comes to that
O Einstein I should have sent you my flaming mss.
O Einstein I should have pilgrimaged to your white
    hair!

O fellow travellers I write you a poem in Amsterdam in
    the Cosmos
where Spinoza ground his magic lenses long ago
I write you a poem long ago
already my feet are washed in death
Here I am naked without identity
with no more body than the fine black tracery of pen
    mark on soft paper
as star talks to star multiple beams of sunlight all the same
    myriad thought
in one fold of the universe where Whitman was
and Blake and Shelley saw Milton dwelling as in a starry
    temple
brooding in his blindness seeing all—
Now at last I can speak to you beloved brothers of an
    unknown moon
real Yous squatting in whatever form amidst Platonic
    Vapors of Eternity
I am another Star.
Will you eat my poems or read them
or gaze with aluminum blind plates on sunless pages?
do you dream or translate & accept data with indifferent
    droopings of antennae?
do I make sense to your flowery green receptor eyesockets?
    do you have visions of God?
Which way will the sunflower turn surrounded by mil-
    lions of suns?

This is my rocket my personal rocket I send up my message
    Beyond
Someone to hear me there
My immortality
without steel or cobalt basalt or diamond gold or mercurial
    fire
without passports filing cabinets bits of paper warheads
without myself finally

pure thought
message all and everywhere the same
I send up my rocket to land on whatever planet awaits it
preferably religious sweet planets no money
fourth dimensional planets where Death shows movies
plants speak (courteously) of ancient physics and poetry
    itself is manufactured by the trees
the final Planet where the Great Brain of the Universe
    sits waiting for a poem to land in His golden pocket
joining the other notes mash-notes love-sighs complaints-
    musical shrieks of despair and the million unutterable
    thoughts of frogs
I send you my rocket of amazing chemical
more than my hair my sperm or the cells of my body
the speeding thought that flies upward with my desire
    as instantaneous as the universe and faster than light
and leave all other questions unfinished for the moment
    to turn back to sleep in my dark bed on earth.

Amsterdam 1958

MESSAGE

Since we had changed
rogered spun worked
wept and pissed together
I wake up in the morning
with a dream in my eyes
but you are gone in NY
remembering me Good
I love you I love you
& your brothers are crazy
I accept their drunk cases
It's too long that I have been alone
it's too long that I've sat up in bed
without anyone to touch on the knee, man
or woman I don't care what anymore, I
want love I was born for I want you with me now
Ocean liners boiling over the Atlantic
Delicate steelwork of unfinished skyscrapers
Back end of the dirigible roaring over Lakehurst

574

Six women dancing together on a red stage naked
The leaves are green on all the trees in Paris now
I will be home in two months and look you in the eyes

1958

TO AUNT ROSE

Aunt Rose—now—might I see you
with your thin face and buck tooth smile and pain
            of rheumatism—and a long black heavy shoe
                for your bony left leg
    limping down the long hall in Newark on the running
    carpet
            past the black grand piano
                in the day room
                    where the parties were
        and I sang Spanish loyalist songs
            in a high squeaky voice
                (hysterical) the committee listening
            while you limped around the room
                collected the money—
    Aunt Honey, Uncle Sam, a stranger with a cloth arm
    in his pocket
            and huge young bald head
                of Abraham Lincoln Brigade

—your long sad face
    your tears of sexual frustration
            (what smothered sobs and bony hips
                under the pillows of Osborne Terrace)
    —the time I stood on the toilet seat naked
    and you powdered my thighs with Calomine
            against the poison ivy—my tender
                and shamed first black curled hairs
    what were you thinking in secret heart then
            knowing me a man already—
    and I an ignorant girl of family silence on the thin
    pedestal
            of my legs in the bathroom—Museum of Newark.

                                        Aunt Rose

Hitler is dead, Hitler is in Eternity; Hitler is with
        Tamburlane and Emily Brontë

Though I see you walking still, a ghost on Osborne Terrace
        down the long dark hall to the front door
        limping a little with a pinched smile
        in what must have been a silken
                                        flower dress
welcoming my father, the Poet, on his visit to Newark
        —see you arriving in the living room
        dancing on your crippled leg
        and clapping hands his book
        had been accepted by Liveright

Hitler is dead and Liveright's gone out of business
The Attic of the Past and Everlasting Minute are out of
    print
        Uncle Harry sold his last silk stocking
        Claire quit interpretive dancing school
        Buba sits a wrinkled monument in Old
        Ladies Home blinking at new babies

last time I saw you was the hospital
        pale skull protruding under ashen skin
        blue veined unconscious girl
        in an oxygen tent
        the war in Spain has ended long ago
        Aunt Rose

                                        Paris 1958

DEATH TO VAN GOGH'S EAR!

Poet is Priest
Money has reckoned the soul of America
Congress broken thru to the precipice of Eternity
the President built a War machine which will vomit and
    rear up Russia out of Kansas
The American Century betrayed by a mad Senate which
    no longer sleeps with its wife
Franco has murdered Lorca the fairy son of Whitman
just as Mayakovsky committed suicide to avoid Russia

                    576

Hart Crane distinguished Platonist committed suicide to cave in the wrong America

just as millions of tons of human wheat were burned in secret caverns under the White House

while India starved and screamed and ate mad dogs full of rain

and mountains of eggs were reduced to white powder in the halls of Congress

no godfearing man will walk there again because of the stink of the rotten eggs of America

and the Indians of Chiapas continue to gnaw their vitaminless tortillas

aborigines of Australia perhaps gibber in the eggless wilderness

and I rarely have an egg for breakfast tho my work requires infinite eggs to come to birth in Eternity

eggs should be eaten or given to their mothers

and the grief of the countless chickens of America is expressed in the screaming of her comedians over the radio

Detroit has built a million automobiles of rubber trees and phantoms

but I walk, I walk, and the Orient walks with me, and all Africa walks

and sooner or later North America will walk

for as we have driven the Chinese Angel from our door he will drive us from the Golden Door of the future

we have not cherished pity on Tanganyika

Einstein alive was mocked for his heavenly politics

Bertrand Russell driven from New York for getting laid

and the immortal Chaplin has been driven from our shores with the rose in his teeth

a secret conspiracy by Catholic Church in the lavatories of Congress has denied contraceptives to the unceasing masses of India.

Nobody publishes a word that is not the cowardly robot ravings of a depraved mentality

the day of the publication of the true literature of the American body will be day of Revolution

the revolution of the sexy lamb

the only bloodless revolution that gives away corn

poor Genet will illuminate the harvesters of Ohio

Marijuana is a benevolent narcotic but J. Edgar Hoover prefers his deathly scotch

And the heroin of Lao-Tze & the Sixth Patriarch is punished by the electric chair

but the poor sick junkies have nowhere to lay their heads

fiends in our government have invented a cold-turkey cure for addiction as obsolete as the Defense Early Warning Radar System.

I am the defense early warning radar system

I see nothing but bombs

I am not interested in preventing Asia from being Asia

and the governments of Russia and Asia will rise and fall but Asia and Russia will not fall

the government of America also will fall but how can America fall

I doubt if anyone will ever fall anymore except governments

fortunately all the governments will fall

the only ones which won't fall are the good ones

and the good ones don't yet exist

But they have to begin existing they exist in my poems

they exist in the death of the Russian and American governments

they exist in the death of Hart Crane & Mayakovsky

Now is the time for prophecy without death as a consequence

the universe will ultimately disappear

Hollywood will rot on the windmills of Eternity

Hollywood whose movies stick in the throat of God

Yes Hollywood will get what it deserves

Time

Seepage or nerve-gas over the radio

History will make this poem prophetic and its awful silliness a hideous spiritual music

I have the moan of doves and the feather of ecstasy

Man cannot long endure the hunger of the cannibal abstract

War is abstract

the world will be destroyed

but I will die only for poetry, that will save the world

Monument to Sacco & Vanzetti not yet financed to ennoble Boston

natives of Kenya tormented by idiot con-men from England

South Africa in the grip of the white fool

Vachel Lindsay Secretary of the Interior
Poe Secretary of Imagination
Pound Secty. of Economics
and Kra belongs to Kra, and Pukti to Pukti
crossfertilization of Blok and Artaud
Van Gogh's Ear on the currency
no more propaganda for monsters
and poets should stay out of politics or become monsters
I have become monstrous with politics
the Russian poet undoubtedly monstrous in his secret
    notebook
Tibet should be left alone
These are obvious prophecies
America will be destroyed
Russian poets will struggle with Russia
Whitman warned against this 'fabled Damned of nations'
Where was Theodore Roosevelt when he sent out ultima-
    tums from his castle in Camden
Where was the House of Representatives when Crane
    read aloud from his prophetic books
What was Wall Street scheming when Lindsay announced
    the doom of Money
Were they listening to my ravings in the locker rooms of
    Bickfords Employment Offices?
Did they bend their ears to the moans of my soul when I
    struggled with market research statistics in the Forum
    at Rome?
No they were fighting in fiery offices, on carpets of heart-
    failure, screaming and bargaining with Destiny
fighting the Skeleton with sabres, muskets, buck teeth,
    indigestion, bombs of larceny, whoredom, rockets, ped-
    erasty,
back to the wall to build up their wives and apartments,
    lawns, suburbs, fairydoms,
Puerto Ricans crowded for massacre on 114th St. for the
    sake of an imitation Chinese-Moderne refrigerator
Elephants of mercy murdered for the sake of an Eliza-
    bethan birdcage
millions of agitated fanatics in the bughouse for the sake
    of the screaming soprano of industry
Money-chant of soapers—toothpaste apes in television
    sets—deodorizers on hypnotic chairs—
petroleum mongers in Texas—jet plane streaks among the
    clouds—

sky writers liars in the face of Divinity—fanged butchers
of hats and shoes, all Owners! Owners! Owners! with
obsession on property and vanishing Selfhood!
and their long editorials on the fence of the screaming
negro attacked by ants crawled out of the front page!
Machinery of a mass electrical dream! A war-creating
Whore of Babylon bellowing over Capitols and Acade-
mies!
Money! Money! Money! shrieking mad celestial money
of illusion! Money made of nothing, starvation, suicide!
Money of failure! Money of death!
Money against Eternity! and eternity's strong mills grind
out vast paper of Illusion!

Paris 1958

JAMES MERRILL (1926–   )

Widely traveled, Merrill has put his observations not only into witty and colorful poems, but into a number of novels and plays as well. He lives in New York City.

> *The Black Swan and Other Poems.* Athens: Icaros, 1946.
> *First Poems.* Knopf, 1951.
> *The Country of a Thousand Years of Peace.* Knopf, 1959.
> *Selected Poems.* London: Chatto & Windus, 1961.
> *Water Street.* Atheneum, 1962.
> *Nights and Days.* Atheneum, 1966.

FOLIAGE OF VISION

As landscapes richen after rain, the eye
Atones, turns fresh after a fit of tears.
When all the foliage of vision stirs
I glimpse the plump fruit hanging, falling, fallen
Where wasps are sputtering. In the full sky
Time, a lean wasp, sucks at the afternoon.

The tiny black and yellow agent of rot
Assaults the plum, stinging and singing. What
A marvel is the machinery of decay!
How rare the day's wrack! What fine violence
Went to inject its gall in the glad eye!
The plum lies all brocaded with corruption.

There is no wit in weeping, yet I wept
To head the insect wrath and rhythm of time,
Surround the plum that fell like a leper's thumb.
The hours, my friend, are felicitous imagery,
Yet I became their image to watch the sun
Dragging with it a scarlet palace down.

The eye attunes, pastoral warbler, always.
Joy in the cradle of calamity
Wakes though dim voices work at lullaby.
Triumph of vision: the act by which we see

Is both the landscape-gardening of our dreams
And the root's long revel under the clipped lawn.

I think of saints with hands pierced and wrenched eyes
Sensational beyond the art of sense,
As though whatever they saw was about to be
While feeling alters in its imminence
To palpable joy; of Dante's ascent in hell
To greet with a cleansed gaze the petaled shores;

Of Darwin's articulate ecstasy as he stood
Before a tangled bank and watched the creatures
Of air and earth noble among much leafage
Dancing an order rooted not only in him
But in themselves, bird, fruit, wasp, limber vine,
Time and disaster and the limping blood.

SWIMMING BY NIGHT

A light going out in the forehead
Of the house by the ocean,
Into warm black its feints of diamond fade.
Without clothes, without caution

Plunging past gravity—
Wait! Where before
Had been floating nothing, is a gradual body
Half remembered, astral with phosphor,

Yours, risen from its tomb
In your own mind,
Haunting nimbleness, glimmerings a random
Spell had kindled. So that, new-limned

By this weak lamp
The evening's alcohol will feed
Until the genie chilling bids you limp
Heavily over stones to bed,

You wear your master's robe
One last time, the far break
Of waves, their length and sparkle, the spinning globe
You wear, and the star running down his cheek.

STANLEY MOSS (1926–   )

Educated at Yale and abroad, Moss has served on the editorial staffs of *Botteghe Oscure* and *New Directions*, and is now poetry editor of the *New American Review*.

The Wrong Angel. Macmillan, 1966.

SAILING FROM THE UNITED STATES

In this country I planted not one seed,
Moved from address to address, did not plead
For justice in its courts, fell in love and out,
Thrust my arm into the sea and could not pull it out;
I did not see the summer lose its balance,
Or organize the lonely in a gang, by chance
I did not build a city or a ship, or burn
The leaves that fell last autumn, in my turn
Built by the numb city building noise,
I learned the morning and the night are decoys
To catch a life and heap the profits of the grave.

I have lost a country, its hills and heroes;
In a country that taught me to talk, confined
To the city of myself, I oppose
The market place and thoroughfares, my mind
Shaping this history, my mouth to a zero.
The wind in my house is not a wind through olive trees,
I hear no music in the janitor's keys,
I fashion no reed, no pipe, have not the wind for it,
Gold and violent death prove counterfeit.
Through the villages of New England and the free country,
I will my unconditional mutiny,
I leave this crockery heaped on a shelf,
For an old regime, to work myself
As a mine, subject to explosions and cave-in.

THE HANGMAN'S LOVE SONG

In the house of the hangman
do not talk of rope,
or use death, half death,
little death; the victim
always hangs himself,
trap sprung, tongue ripped
like love in the house.
Despite the world's
regalia, I want
a useful funeral.
High, on tip-toe,
swinging back
and forth, the victim,
who cannot speak,
mimics the bell,
such things as bait
for wild game, and love.
Brain hung and heart,
hope swings, sun creaks,
rope in the wind,
and the hangman sings.

GOD POEM

I

Especially he loves
His space and the parochial darkness.
They are his family, from them grow his kind:
Idols with many arms and suns that fathered
The earth, among his many mirrors, and some
That do not break:
Rain kept sacred by faithful summer grasses,
Fat Buddha and lean Christ, bull and ram,
Horns thrusting up his temple and cathedral;
Mirrors—but he is beyond such vanities.
Easy to outlive
The moment's death having him on your knees;
Grunting and warm he prefers wild positions:
He mouths the moon and sun, brings his body

Into insects that receive him beneath stone,
Into fish that leap as he chases,
Or silent stones that receive his silence.
Chivalrous and polite the dead take
His caress, and the sea rolling under him
Takes his fish as payment and his heaps of shells.

II

As he will,
He throws the wind arch-backed on the highway,
Lures the cat into moonlit alleys,
Mountains and fields with wild strawberries.
He is animal,
His tail drags uncomfortably, he trifles
With the suck of bees and lovers, so simple
With commonplace tongues; his eyes ripple
Melancholy iron and carefree tin,
His thighs are raw from rubbing, cruel as pine,
He can wing an eagle off a hare's spine,
Crouch with the Sphinx, push bishops down
In chilly chapels, a wafer in their mouths;
Old men cry out his passage through their bowels.

III

No word, none of these, no name, "Red Worm! Snake!"
What name makes him leave his hiding place?
Out of the null and void,
No name and no meaning: God, Jahweh, the Lord,
Not to be spoken to, he never said a word
Or took the power of death: the inconspicuous
Plunge from air into sea he gave to us,
Winds that wear away our towns . . . Who breathes
Comes to nothing: absence, a world.

FRANK O'HARA (1926–1966)

O'Hara was associated with John Ashbery and Kenneth Koch
in New York during the fifties, where the three were leaders
of a group generally called the "New York poets." O'Hara
worked for *Art News* and the Museum of Modern Art. Later
he moved to San Francisco. He was killed by an automobile
on Fire Island, N.Y.

> *Meditations in an Emergency.* Grove, 1957.
> *Second Ave.* New York: Totem Press, 1960.
> *Awake in Spain.* (Drama.) New York: American Theatre
> for Poets, 1960.
> *Lunch Poems.* San Francisco: City Lights Books, 1964.
> *Love's Labor, an Eclogue.* American Theatre for Poets,
> 1964.
> *Love Poems.* New York: Tibor de Nagy Editions, 1965.
> *In Memory of My Feelings.* (Selected poems.) Museum
> of Modern Art, 1967.

A STEP AWAY FROM THEM

It's my lunch hour, so I go
for a walk among the hum-colored
cabs. First, down the sidewalk
where laborers feed their dirty
glistening torsos sandwiches
and Coca-Cola, with yellow helmets
on. They protect them from falling
bricks, I guess. Then onto the
avenue where skirts are flipping
above heels and blow up over
grates. The sun is hot, but the
cabs stir up the air. I look
at bargains in wristwatches. There
are cats playing in sawdust.

                      On
to Times Square, where the sign
blows smoke over my head, and higher

the waterfall pours lightly. A
Negro stands in a doorway with a
toothpick, languorously agitating.
A blonde chorus girl clicks: he
smiles and rubs his chin. Everything
suddenly honks: it is 12:40 of
a Thursday.
        Neon in daylight is a
great pleasure, as Edwin Denby would
write, as are light bulbs in daylight.
I stop for a cheeseburger at JULIET'S
CORNER. Giulietta Masina, wife of
Federico Fellini, *è bell' attrice.*
And chocolate malted. A lady in
foxes on such a day puts her poodle
in a cab.
        There are several Puerto
Ricans on the avenue today, which
makes it beautiful and warm. First
Bunny died, then John Latouche,
then Jackson Pollock. But is the
earth as full as life was full, of them?
And one has eaten and one walks,
past the magazines with nudes
and the posters for BULLFIGHT and
the Manhattan Storage Warehouse,
which they'll soon tear down. I
used to think they had the Armory
Show there.
        A glass of papaya juice
and back to work. My heart is in my
pocket, it is Poems by Pierre Reverdy.

POEM

Lana Turner has collapsed!
I was trotting along and suddenly
it started raining and snowing
and you said it was hailing
but hailing hits you on the head
hard so it was really snowing and

raining and I was in such a hurry
to meet you but the traffic
was acting exactly like the sky
and suddenly I see a headline
LANA TURNER HAS COLLAPSED!
there is no snow in Hollywood
there is no rain in California
I have been to lots of parties
and acted perfectly disgraceful
but I never actually collapsed
oh Lana Turner we love you get up

DAVID WAGONER (1926–)

Wagoner often writes in the flat, fluent idiom of his native Mid-west, especially in his narrative and dramatic poems. Like many former students of Theodore Roethke, he pays his teacher tribute, not in an imitative style, but in seriousness and breadth of poetic attitude. Today he lives in Seattle, where he teaches at the University of Washington and edits *Poetry Northwest*. He has also written four novels.

> *Dry Sun, Dry Wind*. Indiana University Press, 1953.
> *A Place to Stand*. Indiana University Press, 1958.
> *The Nesting Ground*. Indiana University Press, 1963.
> *Staying Alive*. Indiana University Press, 1966.

THE POETS AGREE TO BE QUIET BY THE SWAMP

They hold their hands over their mouths
And stare at the stretch of water.
What can be said has been said before:
Strokes of light like herons' legs in the cattails,
Mud underneath, frogs lying even deeper.
Therefore, the poets may keep quiet.
But the corners of their mouths grin past their hands.
They stick their elbows out into the evening,
Stoop, and begin the ancient croaking.

LOOKING FOR MOUNTAIN BEAVERS

The man in the feed store called them mountain beavers
When I asked about the burrows riddling the slope
Behind our house. "Sometimes you see dirt moving,

But nothing else," he said. "They eat at night.
My tomcat ate one once, and now he's missing."
He gummed his snuff like a liar. "One ate *him*."

That night my wife and I, carrying flashlights,
Went up the hill to look through brush and bracken
Under the crossfire of the moon for beavers

And, keeping quiet, knelt at pairs of holes
And shone our lights as far as we could reach
Down the smooth runways, finding nothing home,

No brown bushwhacker's prints straddling a cat's paw,
Not even each other's lights around the corners.
We ground our heels then, bouncing on the mounds,

Hoping to make one mad enough to exist,
But nothing came out. Should we believe in nothing?
Maybe the cat just dreamed it was eating something

And turned against the nearest raw material
Till its own bones were curled up in its head
Which then fell smiling down a hole and died.

Or maybe the man meant the holes were the beavers:
The deeper they go, the less there is to see.
We felt the earth dip under us now and then

Through no fault of its own, shifting our ground.
But seeing isn't believing: it's disappearing.
All animals are missing—or will be.

Something was eating us. We thumped their houses,
Then walked downhill together, swinging our flashlights
Up and around our heads like holes in the night.

MAKING UP FOR A SOUL

It's been like fixing a clock, jamming the wheels,
The pinions, and bent springs into a box
And shaking it. Or like patching a vase,
Gluing the mismatched edges of events
Together despite the quirks in the design.
Or trying to make one out of scraps of paper,
The yellowing, dog-eared pages going slapdash

Over each other, flat as a collage.
I can't keep time with it. It won't hold water.
Dipping and rearranging make no pattern.

Imagine me with a soul: I'm sitting here
In the room with you, smiling from corner to corner,
My chest going up and down with inspiration.
I sit serene, insufferably at my ease,
Not scratching or drumming but merely suffering
Your questions, like the man from the back of the book
With all the answers. You couldn't stand me, could you?

My love, if *you* have a soul, don't tell me yet.
Why can't we simply stay uneasy together?
There are snap-on souls like luminous neckties
That light up in the dark, spelling our names.
Let's put them on for solemn visitors,
Switch off the lights, then grope from room to room,
Making our hollow, diabolical noises
Like Dracula and his spouse, avoiding mirrors,
Clutching each other fiendishly for life
To stop the gaps in ourselves, like better halves.

JOHN ASHBERY (1927–   )

Ashbery, who was perhaps the most prominent of the group called the "New York poets" in the fifties, lived in France for several years, where he worked as an editor and art critic. He has written of his own poetry in terms of both painting and music, though most readers may feel that its literary connections with the imagist and surrealist traditions are more important. Like his associates, Ashbery has been particularly active in writing for the poetic stage.

Turandot and Other Poems. New York: Tibor de Nagy Editions, 1953.
Some Trees. Yale University Press, 1956.
Artists' Theatre: Four Plays. Grove, 1960.
The Tennis Court Oath. Wesleyan University Press, 1962.
Rivers and Mountains. Holt, Rinehart & Winston, 1966.
Selected Poems. London: Cape, 1967.
Three Madrigals. New York: Poets Press, 1968.

THOUGHTS OF A YOUNG GIRL

"It is such a beautiful day I had to write you a letter
From the tower, and to show I'm not mad:
I only slipped on the cake of soap of the air
And drowned in the bathtub of the world.
You were too good to cry much over me.
And now I let you go. Signed, The Dwarf."

I passed by late in the afternoon
And the smile still played about her lips
As it has for centuries. She always knows
How to be utterly delightful. Oh my daughter,
My sweetheart, daughter of my late employer, princess,
May you not be long on the way!

TWO SONNETS

1. *Dido*

The body's products become
Fatal to it. Our spit
Would kill us, but we
Die of our heat.
Though I say the things I wish to say
They are needless, their own flame conceives it.
So I am cheated of perfection.

The iodine bottle sat in the hall
And out over the park where crawled roadsters
The apricot and purple clouds were
And our blood flowed down the grating
Of the cream-colored embassy.
Inside it they had a record of "The St. Louis Blues."

2. *The Idiot*

O how this sullen, careless world
Ignorant of me is! Those rocks, those homes
Know not the touch of my flesh, nor is there one tree
Whose shade has known me for a friend.
I've wandered the wide world over.
No man I've known, no friendly beast
Has come and put its nose into my hands.
No maid has welcomed my face with a kiss.

Yet once, as I took passage
From Gibraltar to Cape Horn
I met some friendly mariners on the boat
And as we struggled to keep the ship from sinking
The very waves seemed friendly, and the sound
The spray made as it hit the front of the boat.

OUR YOUTH

Of bricks . . . Who built it? Like some crazy balloon
When love leans on us
Its nights . . . The velvety pavement sticks to our feet.
The dead puppies turn us back on love.

Where we are. Sometimes
The brick arches led to a room like a bubble, that broke
    when you entered it
And sometimes to a fallen leaf.
We got crazy with emotion, showing how much we knew.

The Arabs took us. We knew
The dead horses. We were discovering coffee,
How it is to be drunk hot, with bare feet
In Canada. And the immortal music of Chopin

Which we had been discovering for several months
Since we were fourteen years old. And coffee grounds,
And the wonder of hands, and the wonder of the day
When the child discovers her first dead hand.

Do you know it? Hasn't she
Observed you too? Haven't you been observed to her?
My, haven't the flowers been? Is the evil
In't? What window? What did you say there?

Heh? Eh? Our youth is dead.
From the minute we discover it with eyes closed
Advancing into mountain light.
Ouch . . . You will never have that young boy,

That boy with the monocle
Could have been your father
He is passing by. No, that other one,
Upstairs. He is the one who wanted to see you.

He is dead. Green and yellow handkerchiefs cover him.
Perhaps he will never rot, I see
That my clothes are dry. I will go.
The naked girl crosses the street.

Blue hampers . . . Explosions,
Ice . . .   The ridiculous
Vases of porphyry. All that our youth
Can't use, that it was created for.

It's true we have not avoided our destiny
By weeding out the old people.
Our faces have filled with smoke. We escape
Down the cloud ladder, but the problem has not been
   solved.

LARRY EIGNER (1927–   )

From birth Eigner has been afflicted with severe palsy, which has confined him to a wheelchair and forced him to get his own education. He came to poetry by way of *Origin*, a magazine which published the Black Mountain poets of the early fifties. In his own work he seeks immediacy and force through meticulous typographical arrangements and juxtapositions, and through purposeful ellipsis. He lives in Swampscott, Mass.

From the Sustaining Air. Palma, Mallorca: Divers Press, 1953.

On My Eyes. Highlands, N.C.: Jargon Books, 1960.

The-/Towards Autumn. San Francisco: Black Sparrow Press, 1967.

Another Time in Fragments. London: Fulcrum Press, 1967.

Fleche..

  cruel arrows gone, the
night closes down,
element, noises
from beyond-the-weather cars
     a mental weight   death like space
       with a little communication?
     the clouds level as the earth
     as they travel the world

                all walls becoming one

     the stars induce days of rain
      and you can forget ice,
     the secrets made by men
     are dropped off like shadows

  outside the trees waver again
            the cold around your bodies
it's curious when to die

ELYSEE

He stopped on the irreproachable sidewalk
  the woman croaked

    Ah Paris, he is a good cook

And after soupaire
it lights
yhar schtumach

its just as soon
in the afternoon
    une lune

    the dark insides
    of—

nuage sur le champ

the eyrie tower
cyclops at the zenith
    du bord

    sink away

      the pitch on the meadow

    there are distant blackouts
    within a minute

race de vivre

the corners been far flung

All   Intents

once a man is born he has to die
              and that is time, the
      position of the moon

the earth is never still in one spot
          or perhaps it is, it is
     (part way

                    it is round

  and we are always here
though every second perhaps not

          but here we are, we are

GALWAY KINNELL (1927–   )

A New Englander by birth, Kinnell has lived in Europe, in Iran, and in many parts of the U.S., including the South, where for some time he was a civil-rights activist. He has published one novel, *Black Light* (1966), and a good many translations, especially of volumes by Villon (1965) and Yves Bonnefoy (1968). He has taught at Juniata College, and Colorado, Oregon, and other universities; he lives in Sheffield, Vt.

> *What a Kingdom It Was.* Houghton Mifflin, 1960.
> *Flower Herding on Mount Monadnock.* Houghton Mifflin, 1964.
> *Body Rags.* Houghton Mifflin, 1968.

DUCK-CHASING

I spied a very small brown duck
Riding the swells of the sea
Like a rocking-chair. "Little duck!"
I cried. It paddled away,
I paddled after it. When it dived,
Down I dived: too smoky was the sea,
We were lost. It surfaced
In the west, I torpedoed west
And when it dived I dived,
And we were lost and lost and lost
In the slant smoke of the sea.
When I came floating up on it
From the side, like a deadman,
And yelled suddenly, it took off,
It skimmed the swells as it ascended,
Brown wings burning and flashing
In the sun as the sea it rose over
Burned and flashed underneath it.
I did not see the little duck again.
Duck-chasing is a game like any game.
When it is over it is all over.

599

FOR ROBERT FROST

1

Why do you talk so much
Robert Frost? One day
I drove up to Ripton to ask,

I stayed the whole day
And never got the chance
To put the question.

I drove off at dusk
Worn out and aching
In both ears. Robert Frost,

Were you shy as a boy?
Do you go on making up
For some long stint of solitude?

Is it simply that talk
Doesn't have to be metered and rhymed?
Or is gab distracting from something worse?

2

I saw you once on the TV,
Unsteady at the lectern,
The flimsy white leaf
Of hair standing straight up
In the wind, among top hats,
Old farmer and son
Of worse winters than this,
Stopped in the first dazzle

Of the District of Columbia,
Suddenly having to pay
For the cheap onionskin,
The worn-out ribbon, the eyes
Wrecked from writing poems
For us—stopped,
Lonely before millions,
The paper jumping in your grip,

And as the Presidents
Also on the platform
Began flashing nervously
Their Presidential smiles
For the harmless old guy,
And poets watching on the TV
Started thinking, Well that's
The end of *that* tradition,

And the managers of the event
Said, Boys this is it,
This sonofabitch poet
Is gonna croak,
Putting the paper aside
You drew forth
From your great faithful heart
The poem.

3

Once, walking in winter in Vermont,
In the snow, I followed a set of footprints
That aimed for the woods. At the verge
I could make out, "far in the pillared dark,"
An old creature in a huge, clumsy overcoat,
Lifting his great boots through the drifts,
Going as if to die among "those dark trees"
Of his own country. I watched him go,

Past a house, quiet, warm and light,
A farm, a countryside, a woodpile in its slow
Smokeless burning, alder swamps ghastly white,
Tumultuous snows, blanker whitenesses,
Into the pathless woods, one eye weeping,
The dark trees, for which no saying is dark enough,
Which mask the gloom and lead on into it,
The bare, the withered, the deserted.

There were no more cottages.
Soft bombs of dust falling from the boughs,
The sun shining no warmer than the moon,
He had outwalked the farthest city light,
And there, clinging to the perfect trees,

A last leaf. What was it?
What was that whiteness?—white, uncertain—
The night too dark to know.

4

He turned. *Love,*
Love of things, duty, he said,
And made his way back to the shelter
No longer sheltering him, the house
Where everything real was turning to words,

Where he would think on the white wave,
Folded back, that rides in place on the obscure
Pouring of this life to the sea—
And invent on the broken lips of darkness
The seal of form and the *mot juste.*

5

Poet of the country of white houses,
Of clearings going out to the dark wall of woods
Frayed along the skyline, you who nearly foreknew
The next lines of poems you suddenly dropped,
Who dwelt in access to that which other men
Have burnt all their lives to get near, who heard
The high wind, in gusts, seething
From far off, headed through the trees exactly
To this place where it must happen, who spent
Your life on the point of giving away your heart
To the dark trees, the dissolving woods,
Into which you go at last, heart in hand, deep in:
When we think of a man who was cursed
Neither with the mystical all-lovingness of Walt Whitman
Nor with Melville's anguish to know and to suffer,
And yet cursed . . . a man, what shall I say,
Vain, not fully convinced he was dying, whose calling
Was to set up in the wilderness of his country,
At whatever cost, a man, who would be his own man,
We think of you. And from the same doorway
At which you lived, between the house and the woods,
We see your old footprints going away across
The great Republic, Frost, up memorized slopes,
Down hills floating by heart on the bulldozed land.

IN FIELDS OF SUMMER

The sun rises,
The goldenrod blooms,
I drift in fields of summer,
My life is adrift in my body,
It shines in my heart and hands, in my teeth,
It shines up at the old crane
Who holds out his drainpipe of a neck
And creaks along in the blue,

And the goldenrod shines with its life, too,
And the grass, look,
The great field wavers and flakes,
The rumble of bumblebees keeps deepening,
A phoebe flutters up,
A lark bursts up all dew.

CELLS BREATHE IN THE EMPTINESS

1

When the flowers turn to husks
And the great trees suddenly die
And rocks and old weasel bones lose
The little life they suddenly had
And the air quells and goes so still
It gives the ears something like the bends,
It is an eerie thing to keep vigil,
The senses racing in the emptiness.

2

From the compost heap
Now arises the sound of the teeth
Of one of those sloppy green cabbageworms
Eating his route through a cabbage,
Now snarling like a petite chainsaw, now droning on . . .

A butterfly blooms on a buttercup,
From the junkpile flames up a junco.

3

How many plants are really very quiet animals?
How many inert molecules are ready to break into life?

VAPOR TRAIL REFLECTED
IN THE FROG POND

1

The old watch: their
thick eyes
puff and foreclose by the moon. The young, heads
trailed by the beginnings of necks,
shiver,
in the guarantee they shall be bodies.

In the frog pond
the vapor trail of a SAC bomber creeps,

I hear its drone, drifting, high up
in immaculate ozone.

2

And I hear,
coming over the hills, America singing,
her varied carols I hear:
crack of deputies' rifles practicing their aim on stray dogs
    at night,
sput of cattleprod,
TV groaning at the smells of the human body,
curses of the soldier as he poisons, burns, grinds, and stabs
the rice of the world,
with open mouth, crying strong, hysterical curses.

3

And by rice paddies in Asia
bones
wearing a few shadows
walk down a dirt road, smashed
bloodsuckers on their heel, knowing
the flesh a man throws down in the sunshine

604

dogs shall eat
and the flesh that is upthrown in the air
shall be seized by birds,
shoulder blades smooth, unmarked by old feather-holes,
hands rivered
by blue, erratic wanderings of the blood,
eyes crinkled up
as they gaze up at the drifting sun that gives us our lives,
seed dazzled over the footbattered blaze of the earth.

THE BEAR

1

In late winter
I sometimes glimpse bits of steam
coming up from
some fault in the old snow
and bend close and see it is lung-colored
and put down my nose
and know
the chilly, enduring odor of bear.

2

I take a wolf's rib and whittle
it sharp at both ends
and coil it up
and freeze it in blubber and place it out
on the fairway of the bears.

And when it has vanished
I move out on the bear tracks,
roaming in circles
until I come to the first, tentative, dark
splash on the earth.

And I set out
running, following the splashes
of blood wandering over the world.
At the cut, gashed resting places
I stop and rest,
at the crawl-marks

where he lay out on his belly
to overpass some stretch of bauchy ice
I lie out
dragging myself forward with bear-knives in my fists.

3

On the third day I begin to starve,
at nightfall I bend down as I knew I would
at a turd sopped in blood,
and hesitate, and pick it up,
and thrust it in my mouth, and gnash it down,
and rise
and go on running.

4

On the seventh day,
living by now on bear blood alone,
I can see his upturned carcass far out ahead, a scraggled,
steamy hulk,
the heavy fur riffling in the wind.

I come up to him
and stare at the narrow-spaced, petty eyes,
the dismayed
face laid back on the shoulder, the nostrils
flared, catching
perhaps the first taint of me as he
died.

I hack
a ravine in his thigh, and eat and drink,
and tear him down his whole length
and open him and climb in
and close him up after me, against the wind,
and sleep.

5

And dream
of lumbering flatfooted
over the tundra,
stabbed twice from within,

splattering a trail behind me,
splattering it out no matter which way I lurch,
no matter which parabola of bear-transcendence,
which dance of solitude I attempt,
which gravity-clutched leap,
which trudge, which groan.

6

Until one day I totter and fall—
fall on this
stomach that has tried so hard to keep up,
to digest the blood as it leaked in,
to break up
and digest the bone itself: and now the breeze
blows over me, blows off
the hideous belches of ill-digested bear blood
and rotted stomach
and the ordinary, wretched odor of bear,

blows across
my sore, lolled tongue a song
or screech, until I think I must rise up
and dance. And I lie still.

7

I awaken I think. Marshlights
reappear, geese
come trailing again up the flyway.
In her ravine under old snow the dam-bear
lies, licking
lumps of smeared fur
and drizzly eyes into shapes
with her tongue. And one
hairy-soled trudge stuck out before me,
the next groaned out,
the next,
the next,
the rest of my days I spend
wandering: wondering
what, anyway,
was that sticky infusion, that rank flavor of blood, that
    poetry, by which I lived?

PHILIP LAMANTIA (1927-   )

Born in San Francisco, Lamantia was one of the earliest authentic American surrealists, working in the conventions of André Breton's French movement. Later he broke with surrealism, experimented with drug-induced visionary poetry, and then, in recent poems, returned to a purer spiritualism, mingling elements of classical and gnostic tradition.

Selected Poems, 1943–1966. San Francisco: City Lights Books, 1967.
Touch of the Marvelous. Berkeley: Oyez Press, 1966.

HERMETIC BIRD

This sky is to be opened
this plundered body to be loved
this lantern to be tied
around the fangs of your heart

Lost on a bridge
going across oceans of tragedy
across islands of inflammable women
I stand
with my feathers entangled in your navel
with my wings opalescent in the night
and shout words heard tomorrow
in a little peasant cart
of the seventeenth century

Breath by breath
the vase in the tomb
breaks to give birth to a roving Sphinx
Tremble, sweet bird, sweet lion
hunger for you
hunger for your mother

The children in the lamps
play with our hair
swinging over the void

608

Here is a landscape on fire
Here are horses wet by the sour fluids of women
On the pillars of nicotine
the word *pleasure* is erased by a dog's tongue
On the pillars the bodies are opened by keys
the keys are nailed to my bed
to be touched at dawn
to be used in a dream

If one more sound is heard
the children will come to murder
at the bottom of the lake
at the bottom of the lake

If the children murder
the owls will bleed
the wanton humans
who parade in basements of the sun

When the columns fall into the sea
with a crash involving prophecies and madmen
together in a little cradle
lifted into the robes of desire
and with our mouths opened for the stars
howling for the castles to melt at our feet
you and I
will ride over the breasts of our mother
who knows no one
who was born from unknown birds
forever in silence
forever in dreams
forever in the sweat of fire

SHE SPEAKS THE MORNING'S FILIGREE

Beneath him, earth's breath
risen from inward wars of blood   :
the youth's vision
is a vibrant string plucked by the gods
over the field of stars

Through the night on fire with my blood
whose incense sputters your sleep and washes you
on the threshold caught from the Tinging Stone
I'm tired of cooking the ultimate specter of future poems
weak from demands of the mooneating children of the
25th Century
it's really so late to proclaim my youth of a hundred years!

But you, Io,
walking on sandals of almond & wrapped by hair of eglan-
tine,
open the seashell that sings us back through storms of
smoke
to the burnt altars of childhood that float
in milk I drew from dragons slain with the help of the
sylph:
Clocks rant their dirges of woe to no avail!

Your sleep is my awakening
All the shadows lie canceled by celestial foam
Moon-poisons are cooked to the perfection of Tea
The sun stirs the cauldron Sothis fixes from your tears
that dance as diamonds on opalescent hands breaking the
Seven Seals!
Over & over the dusk of the Chant from the plain of
Segovia
rings up the veil through which the deities move prisms of
desire:
the cup that swallows the sword, the wands that shake
the stars!

Aurora the cat of the morning
has sent a message of aerial fire
to the twelve-faced Aerolith whose name is not permitted
for reading
whose number is water & abyss of the bone
whose age is always about to become and
has always been no less than time

We can play host to the marvelous
and have it burn us to the salt of memory
where an invisible stone contracts all thought
to draw out the words

that shall crackle your sleep
to wake us up beyond the Pleiades

No longer tired now I've supt from the tombs of kings
and raced past the Giant Chairs of Tartesos
to mark the spectrum's path to where you and I
shall be buried in the seed of the Sun
I'm at the gate of the house built by no one
but the One who pulled it down
before it was founded from the sperm of the walking
    sleeper!
From this place my poems can begin
to take on the shape of candles
    and incense sticks

    as you ride midnight mares
    to undo the astral curse
        turn pages of burning books
                or float
        freely
    on the morning's filigree!

W. S. MERWIN (1927–)

Merwin's poetry has evolved from his early graceful lyrics in a neometaphysical style, through a middle period of flatter and wittier poems, to his present extreme individuality of vision and verbal unexpectedness. He was born in New York, and until his recent return to the U.S. lived for many years in England and France. He has translated widely from Latin, French, Spanish, and Portuguese literature, and has written for the B.B.C.

> *The Dancing Bears.* Yale University Press, 1954.
> *Green with Beasts.* Knopf, 1956.
> *The Drunk in the Furnace.* Macmillan, 1960.
> *The Moving Target.* Atheneum, 1963.
> *The Lice.* Atheneum, 1967.
> *Selected Translations.* Atheneum, 1969.

WHEN I CAME FROM COLCHIS

When I came from Colchis
Where the spring fields lay green,
A land famed for fine linen,
Bounded northerly
By the glistering Caucasus,
By the Euxine westerly,

Most I spoke of fine linen
But did, in truth, tell something
Of Jason who had come sailing
And poised upon that shore
His fabulous excursion.
All turned the incredulous ear.

From Troy, over the water
Returning, I recounted
The tale of wrecked walls, but said
That gray waves lap and surround
That shore as any other.
With a shrewd smile they listened.

Now if, amazed, I come
From the deep bourn of your hand,
A stranger up from the sunned
Sea of your eyes, lady,
What fable should I tell them,
That they should believe me?

SONG OF THREE SMILES

Let me call a ghost,
Love, so it be little:
In December we took
No thought for the weather.

Whom now shall I thank
For this wealth of water?
Your heart loves harbors
Where I am a stranger.

Where was it we lay
Needing no other
Twelve days and twelve nights
In each other's eyes?

Or was it at Babel
And the days too small
We spoke our own tongue
Needing no other?

If a seed grow green
Set a stone upon it
That it learn thereby
Holy charity.

If you must smile
Always on that other,
Cut me from ear to ear
And we all smile together.

THE MOUNTAIN

Only on the rarest occasions, when the blue air,
Though clear, is not too blinding (as, say,
For a particular moment just at dusk in autumn)
Or if the clouds should part suddenly
Between freshets in spring, can one trace the rising
Slopes high enough to call them contours; and even
More rarely see above the treeline. Then
It is with almost a shock that one recognizes
What supposedly one had known always:
That it is, in fact, a mountain; not merely
This restrictive sense of nothing level, of never
Being able to go anywhere
But up or down, until it seems probable
Sometimes that the slope, to be so elusive
And yet so inescapable, must be nothing
But ourselves: that we have grown with one
Foot shorter than the other, and would deform
The levellest habitat to our misshapen
Condition, as is said of certain hill creatures.

Standing between two other peaks, but not
As they: or so we have seen in a picture
Whose naive audacity, founded as far as can be
Determined, on nothing but the needs
Of its own composition, presents all three
As shaped oddly, of different colors, rising
From a plain whose flatness appears incredible
To such as we. Of course to each of us
Privately, its chief difference from its peers
Rests not even in its centrality, but its
Strangeness composed of our own intimacy
With a part of it, our necessary
Ignorance of its limits, and diurnal pretence
That what we see of it is all. Learned opinions differ
As to whether it was ever actively
Volcanic. It is believed that if one could see it
Whole, its shape might make this clearer, but that
Is impossible, for at the distance at which in theory
One could see it all, it would be out of sight.

Of course in all the senses in which any
Place or thing can be said not to exist

Until someone, at least, is known to have been there,
It would help immeasurably if anyone
Should ever manage to climb it. No one,
From whatever distance, has ever so much as seen
The summit, or even anywhere near it; not, that is,
As far as we know. At one time the attempt
Was a kind of holy maelstrom, Mecca
For fanatics and madmen, and a mode of ritual
And profane suicide (since among us there is nowhere
From which one could throw oneself down). But there
   have been
Expeditions even quite recently, and with the benefit
Of the most expensive equipment. Very few
Who set out at all seriously have
Come back. At a relatively slight distance
Above us, apparently the whole aspect and condition
Of the mountain changes completely; there is ceaseless
   wind
With a noise like thunder and the beating of wings.

Indeed, if one considers the proximity
Of the point at which so much violence
Is known to begin, it is not our failure
That strikes one as surprising, but our impunity:
The summer camps on near gradients, ski-lifts in winter,
And even our presence where we are. For of those
Who attained any distance and returned, most
Were deafened, some permanently; some were blind,
And these also often incurably; all
Without exception were dazzled, as by a great light. And
   those
Who perhaps went furthest and came back, seemed
To have completely lost the use of our language,
Or if they spoke, babbled incoherently
Of silence bursting beyond that clamor, of time
Passed there not passing here, which we could not under-
   stand,
Of time no time at all. These characteristic
Effects of the upper slopes—especially the derangement
Of time-sense, and the dazzling—seem from earliest
Antiquity to have excited speculation.

One legend has it that a remote king-priest figure
Once gained the summit, spent some—to him non-sequent

615

But to them significant—time there, and returned
'Shining,' bearing ciphers of the arcane (which,
Translated into the common parlance, proved
To be a list of tribal taboos) like clastic
Specimens, and behaved with a glacial violence
Later construed as wisdom. This, though
Charming, does not, in the light of current endeavor,
Seem possible, even though so long ago. Yet
To corroborate this story, in the torrent
Gold has been found which even at this
Late date appears to have been powdered by hand,
And (further to confuse inquiry) several
Pediments besides, each with four sockets shaped
As though to receive the hoof of a giant statue
Of some two-toed ungulate. Legend being
What it is, there are those who still insist
He will come down again some day from the mountain.

As there are those who say it will fall on us. It
Will fall. And those who say it has already
Fallen. It has already fallen. Have we not
Seen it fall in shadow, evening after evening,
Across everything we can touch; do we not build
Our houses out of the great hard monoliths
That have crashed down from far above us? Shadows
Are not without substance, remind and predict;
And we know we live between greater commotions
Than any we can describe. But, most important:
Since this, though we know so little of it, is
All we know, is it not whatever it makes us
Believe of it—even the old woman
Who laughs, pointing, and says that the clouds across
Its face are wings of seraphim? Even the young
Man who, standing on it, declares it is not
There at all. He stands with one leg habitually
Bent, to keep from falling, as though he had grown
That way, as is said of certain hill creatures.

GRANDMOTHER WATCHING AT HER WINDOW

There was always the river or the train
Right past the door, and someone might be gone

Come morning. When I was a child I mind
Being held up at a gate to wave
Good-bye, good-bye to I didn't know who,
Gone to the War, and how I cried after.
When I married I did what was right
But I knew even that first night
That he would go. And so shut my soul tight
Behind my mouth, so he could not steal it
When he went. I brought the children up clean
With my needle, taught them that stealing
Is the worst sin; knew if I loved them
They would be taken away, and did my best
But must have loved them anyway
For they slipped through my fingers like stitches.
Because God loves us always, whatever
We do. You can sit all your life in churches
And teach your hands to clutch when you pray
And never weaken, but God loves you so dearly
Just as you are, that nothing you are can stay,
But all the time you keep going away, away.

SIRE

Here comes the shadow not looking where it is going,
And the whole night will fall; it is time.
Here comes the little wind which the hour
Drags with it everywhere like an empty wagon through
   leaves.
Here comes my ignorance shuffling after them
Asking them what they are doing.

Standing still, I can hear my footsteps
Come up behind me and go on
Ahead of me and come up behind me and
With different keys clinking in the pockets,
And still I do not move. Here comes
The white-haired thistle seed stumbling past through the
   branches
Like a paper lantern carried by a blind man.
I believe it is the lost wisdom of my grandfather
Whose ways were his own and who died before I could
   ask.

Forerunner, I would like to say, silent pilot,
Little dry death, future,
Your indirections are as strange to me
As my own. I know so little that anything
You might tell me would be a revelation.

Sir, I would like to say,
It is hard to think of the good woman
Presenting you with children, like cakes,
Granting you the eye of her needle,
Standing in doorways, flinging after you
Little endearments, like rocks, or her silence
Like a whole Sunday of bells. Instead, tell me:
Which of my many incomprehensions
Did you bequeath me, and where did they take you?
    Standing
In the shoes of indecision, I hear them
Come up behind me and go on ahead of me
Wearing boots, on crutches, barefoot, they could never
Get together on any door-sill or destination—
The one with the assortment of smiles, the one
Jailed in himself like a forest, the one who comes
Back at evening drunk with despair and turns
Into the wrong night as though he owned it—oh small
Deaf disappearance in the dusk, in which of their shoes
Will I find myself tomorrow?

THE LAST ONE

Well they'd made up their minds to be everywhere be-
    cause why not.
Everywhere was theirs because they thought so.
They with two leaves they whom the birds despise.
In the middle of stones they made up their minds.
They started to cut.

Well they cut everything because why not.
Everything was theirs because they thought so.
It fell into its shadows and they took both away.
Some to have some for burning.

618

Well cutting everything they came to the water.
They came to the end of the day there was one left stand-
ing.
They would cut it tomorrow they went away.
The night gathered in the last branches.
The shadow of the night gathered in the shadow on the
water.
The night and the shadow put on the same head.
And it said Now.

Well in the morning they cut the last one.
Like the others the last one fell into its shadow.
It fell into its shadow on the water.
They took it away its shadow stayed on the water.

Well they shrugged they started trying to get the shadow
away.
They cut right to the ground the shadow stayed whole.
They laid boards on it the shadow came out on top.
They shone lights on it the shadow got blacker and clearer.
They exploded the water the shadow rocked.
They built a huge fire on the roots.
They sent up black smoke between the shadow and the
sun.
The new shadow flowed without changing the old one.
They shrugged they went away to get stones.

They came back the shadow was growing.
They started setting up stones it was growing.
They looked the other way it went on growing.
They decided they would make a stone out of it.
They took stones to the water they poured them into
the shadow.
They poured them in they poured them in the stones
vanished.
The shadow was not filled it went on growing.
That was one day.

The next day was just the same it went on growing.
They did all the same things it was just the same.
They decided to take its water from under it.
They took away water they took it away the water went
down.

The shadow stayed where it was before.
It went on growing it grew onto the land.
They started to scrape the shadow with machines.
When it touched the machines it stayed on them.
They started to beat the shadow with sticks.
Where it touched the sticks it stayed on them.
They started to beat the shadow with hands.
Where it touched the hands it stayed on them.
That was another day.

Well the next day started about the same it went on
growing.
They pushed lights into the shadow.
Where the shadow got onto them they went out.
They began to stomp on the edge it got their feet.
And when it got their feet they fell down.
It got into eyes the eyes went blind.
The ones that fell down it grew over and they vanished.
The ones that went blind and walked into it vanished.
The ones that could see and stood still
It swallowed their shadows.
Then it swallowed them too and they vanished.
Well the others ran.

The ones that were left went away to live if it would let
them.
They went as far as they could.
The lucky ones with their shadows.

THE WIDOW

How easily the ripe grain
Leaves the husk
At the simple turning of the planet

There is no season
That requires us

Masters of forgetting
Threading the eyeless rocks with
A narrow light

In which ciphers wake and evil
Gets itself the face of the norm
And contrives cities

The Widow rises under our fingernails
In this sky we were born we are born

And you weep wishing you were numbers
You multiply you cannot be found
You grieve
Not that heaven does not exist but
That it exists without you

You confide
In images in things that can be
Represented which is their dimension you
Require them you say This
Is real and you do not fall down and moan

Not seeing the irony in the air
Everything that does not need you is real

The Widow does not
Hear you and your cry is numberless

This is the waking landscape
Dream after dream after dream walking away through it
Invisible invisible invisible

EARLY JANUARY

A year has come to us as though out of hiding
It has arrived from an unknown distance
From beyond the visions of the old
Everyone waited for it by the wrong roads
And it is hard for us now to be sure it is here
A stranger to nothing
In our hiding places

JAMES WRIGHT (1927–   )

A graduate of Kenyon College, Wright took his advanced studies at the University of Vienna and the University of Washington; he teaches today at Hunter College. In collaboration with Robert Bly, he has translated the work of Neruda and Vallejo.

> *The Green Wall.* Yale University Press, 1957.
> *Saint Judas.* Wesleyan University Press, 1959.
> *The Branch Will Not Break.* Wesleyan University Press, 1963.
> *Shall We Gather at the River.* Wesleyan University Press, 1968.

COMPLAINT

She's gone. She was my love, my moon or more.
She chased the chickens out and swept the floor,
Emptied the bones and nut-shells after feasts,
And smacked the kids for leaping up like beasts.
Now morbid boys have grown past awkwardness;
The girls let stitches out, dress after dress,
To free some swinging body's riding space
And form the new child's unimagined face.
Yet, while vague nephews, spitting on their curls,
Amble to pester winds and blowsy girls,
What arm will sweep the room, what hand will hold
New snow against the milk to keep it cold?
And who will dump the garbage, feed the hogs,
And pitch the chickens' heads to hungry dogs?
Not my lost hag who dumbly bore such pain:
Childbirth and midnight sassafras and rain.
New snow against her face and hands she bore,
And now lies down, who was my moon or more.

AT THE SLACKENING OF THE TIDE

Today I saw a woman wrapped in rags
Leaping along the beach to curse the sea.
Her child lay floating in the oil, away
From oarlock, gunwale, and the blades of oars.
The skinny lifeguard, raging at the sky,
Vomited sea, and fainted on the sand.

The cold simplicity of evening falls
Dead on my mind,
And underneath the piles the water
Leaps up, leaps up, and sags down slowly, farther
Than seagulls disembodied in the drag
Of oil and foam.

Plucking among the oyster shells a man
Stares at the sea, that stretches on its side.
Now far along the beach, a hungry dog
Announces everything I knew before:
Obliterate naiads weeping underground,
Where Homer's tongue thickens with human howls.

I would do anything to drag myself
Out of this place:
Root up a seaweed from the water,
To stuff it in my mouth, or deafen me,
Free me from all the force of human speech;
Go drown, almost.

Warm in the pleasure of the dawn I came
To sing my song
And look for mollusks in the shallows,
The whorl and coil that pretty up the earth,
While far below us, flaring in the dark,
The stars go out.

What did I do to kill my time today,
After the woman ranted in the cold,
The mellow sea, the sound blown dark as wine?
After the lifeguard rose up from the waves
Like a sea-lizard with the scales washed off?
Sit there, admiring sunlight on a shell?

Abstract with terror of the shell, I stared
Over the waters where
God brooded for the living all one day.
Lonely for weeping, starved for a sound of mourning,
I bowed my head, and heard the sea far off
Washing its hands.

BILL ANDERSON (1928–   )

Anderson has published little poetry—no book so far—though he has worked as a journalist, at present with the *Bay Guardian* in San Francisco, where he lives in the Haight district. He writes: "I am interested in expanding my personal definition of 'poetic' activity to include journalistic and revolutionary work."

LETTER FROM A BLACK SOLDIER

Grains of snow ride down here as bits
of light fall on a negative. Pale riders are burned by the
silver ground of this photograph as any agent
would be. It is true that objects would not exist without
instruments to define them, but it does not matter if any
  eye
sees this.

The companies sift through the forest like blind
people living where natural law
won't work. Horses in their sudden arabesques fall
on the eyeballs of the dead, and those great, curved, per-
  fect
lenses register. But they do not really
work. The wind, which nobody handles, probes
at trees and nostrils of the camp. I will tell
you in confidence, it hardly
matters
if any battles have ever occurred or will occur
or even now wheel. The feelings left to us
could as easily enter one opening of the world as
another, and spring with its half-
glory may yet come, clank-clank riding in.
If that happens, it happens.
For now, each contact makes a black spot of sensation
on the skin and that is all the snow
is!

Up the slope, bivouac fires fall apart like
old light. My hands are always cold; the sun gives
out little heat; as soon as it goes down, the winter runs
right back at us. A few days ago, one walker said
the sun helps the enemy no more than it helps us.
As though we were suddenly in
bottomless snow, I am sorry to say we went wild and,
with slow, stopped motions, we hung him upside-
down and split
him. But still, the long red light

is eaten up by somebody. It would remind you
of a deliberate act, a division of the world into two
kinds of apertures: from one lurks he who stands outside
watching; from the other flows whatever
eats up our natural provender.

A man called Brady looks at us this way.
It will be interesting to see if
he can bring the two together in his pictures and make
one splendid animal to which we
could submit. For certainly

some of us are blown down and some of us are raised
up, and none of us can explain this action. Pause.
Recovery. Beat. Beat. Pause. Red meat,
power in the gut. Let the wheeler roll!

It is best if no eye observes this:

I feel like going down into flat darkness and wet
silver. And washing afterward. I hate this action
and would rather sit here and be blown away than ride
any
more. The dry things are cold and the supple
things wet. Sometimes the need of light is
meat in the mouth to

us. We would kill any who do not agree that none of us
should be injured any more. And would be happy if
no more
agents worked on us.

Love.

The snow rides down in its careful way, falling
petal by petal on the muzzles of the transfigured

horses.

OUTBREAK

The masai warrior is not
successful. He made no serious
mistake, he branded
his cattle,

but his heart is a dry stick
anyway. Stones on the ground
tremble and fall

open. If she comes so quickly,
Lord, what must she be
to other men?

PHILIP LEVINE (1928–   )

Levine was born in Detroit. From his Russian-Jewish religious
background, his early work in factories, and his acquaintance
with Spanish poetry during a period of living abroad, he has de-
rived the attitude of constructive bitterness which imbues much
of his poetry. He lives in Fresno, Calif.

On the Edge. Iowa City, Iowa: Stone Wall Press, 1963.
Not This Pig. Wesleyan University Press, 1968.

THE TURNING

Unknown faces in the street
And winter coming on. I
Stand in the last moments of
The city, no more a child,
Only a man,—one who has
Looked upon his own nakedness
Without shame, and in defeat
Has seen nothing to bless.
Touched once, like a plum, I turned
Rotten in the meat, or like
The plum blossom I never
Saw, hard at the edges, burned
At the first entrance of life,
And so endured, unreckoned,
Untaken, with nothing to give.
The first Jew was God; the second
Denied him; I am alive.

GANGRENE

One was kicked in the stomach
until he vomited, then
        made to put back
into his mouth what they had

brought forth; when he tried to drown
    in his own stew
he was recovered. "You are
worse than a nigger or Jew,"

the helmeted one said. "You
are an intellectual.
    I hate your brown
skin; it makes me sick." The tall
intense one, his penis wired,
    was shocked out of
his senses in three seconds.
Weakened, he watched them install

another battery in
the crude electric device.
    The genitals
of a third were beaten with
a short wooden ruler: "Reach
    for your black balls.
I'll show you how to make love."
When two of the beaten passed

in the hall they did not know
each other. "His face had turned
    into a wound:
the nose was gone, the eyes ground
so far back into the face
    they too seemed gone,
the lips, puffed pieces of cracked
blood." None of them was asked

anything. The clerks, the police,
the booted ones, seemed content
    to inflict pain,
to make, they said, each instant
memorable and exquisite,
    reform the brain
through the senses. "Kiss my boot
and learn the taste of French shit."

Reader, does the heart demand
that you bend to the live wound
    as you would bend

to the familiar body
of your beloved, to kiss
    the green flower
which blooms always from the ground,
human and ripe with terror,

to face with love what we have
made of hatred? We must live
    with what we are,
you say, it is enough. I
taste death. I am among you
    and I accuse
you where, secretly thrilled by
the circus of excrement,

you study my strophes or
yawn into the evening air,
    tired, not amused.
Remember what you have said
when from your pacific dream
    you awaken
at last, deafened by the scream
of your own stench. You are dead.

THE DISTANT WINTER

from an officer's diary during the last war

I

The sour daylight cracks through my sleep-caked lids.
"Stephan! Stephan!" The rattling orderly
Comes on a trot, the cold tray in his hands:
Toast whitening with oleo, brown tea,

Yesterday's napkins, and an opened letter.
"Your asthma's bad, old man." He doesn't answer,
And turns to the grey windows and the weather.
"Don't worry, Stephan, the lungs will go to cancer."

II

I speak, "The enemy's exhausted, victory
Is almost ours . . ." These twenty new recruits,

Conscripted for the battles lost already,
Were once the young, exchanging bitter winks,

And shuffling when I rose to eloquence,
Determined not to die and not to show
The fear that held them in their careless stance,
And yet they died, how many wars ago?

Or came back cream puffs, 45, and fat.
I know that I am touched for my eyes brim
With tears I had forgotten. Death is not
For these car salesmen whose only dream

Is of a small percentage of the take.
Oh my eternal smilers, weep for death
Whose harvest withers with your aged aches
And cannot make the grave for lack of breath.

III

Did you wet? Oh no, he had not wet.
How could he say it, it was hard to say
Because he did not understand it yet.
It had to do, maybe, with being away,

With being here where nothing seemed to matter.
It will be better, you will see tomorrow,
I told him, in a while it will be better,
And all the while staring from the mirror

I saw those eyes, my eyes devouring me.
I cannot fire my rifle, I'm afraid
Even to aim at what I cannot see.
This was his voice, or was it mine I heard?

How do I know that in this foul latrine
I calmed a soldier, infantile, manic?
Could he be real with such eyes pinched between
The immense floating shoulders of his tunic?

IV

Around the table where the map is spread
The officers gather. Now the colonel leans
Into the blinkered light from overhead
And with a penknife improvises plans

For our departure. Plans delivered by
An old staff courier on his bicycle.
One looks at him and wonders does he say,
I lean out and I let my shadow fall

Shouldering the picture that we call the world
And there is darkness? Does he say such things?
Or is there merely silence in his head?
Or other voices which the silence rings?

Such a fine skull and forehead, broad and flat,
The eyes opaque and slightly animal.
I can come closer to a starving cat,
I can read hunger in its eyes and feel

In the irregular motions of its tail
A need that I could feel. He slips his knife
Into the terminal where we entrain
And something seems to issue from my life.

V

In the mice-sawed potato field dusk waits.
My dull ones march by fours on the playground,
Kicking up dust. The column hesitates
As though in answer to the rising wind,

To darkness and the coldness it must enter.
Listen, my heroes, my half-frozen men,
The corporal calls us to that distant winter
Where we will merge the nothingness within.

And they salute as one and stand at peace.
Keeping an arm's distance from everything,
I answer them, knowing they see no face
Between my helmet and my helmet thong.

VI

But three more days and we'll be moving out.
The cupboard of the state is bare, no one,
Not God himself, can raise another recruit.
Drinking my hot tea, listening to the rain,

I sit while Stephan packs, grumbling a bit.
He breaks the china that my mother sent,
Her own first china, as a wedding gift.
"Now that your wife is dead, Captain, why can't

The two of us really make love together?"
I cannot answer. When I lift a plate
It seems I almost hear my long-dead mother
Saying, Watch out, the glass is underfoot.

Stephan is touching me. "Captain, why not?
Three days from now and this will all be gone,
It no longer is!" Son, you don't shout,
In the long run it doesn't help the pain.

I gather the brittle bits and cut my finger
On the chipped rim of my wife's favorite glass,
And cannot make the simple bleeding linger.
"Captain, Captain, there's no one watching us."

TO A CHILD TRAPPED IN A BARBER SHOP

You've gotten in through the transom
    and you can't get out
till Monday morning or, worse,
    till the cops come.

That six-year-old red face
    calling for mama
is yours; it won't help you
    because your case

is closed forever, hopeless.
    So don't drink
the Lucky Tiger, don't
    fill up on grease

because that makes it a lot worse,
    that makes it a crime
against property and the state
    and that costs time.

We've all been here before,
    we took our turn
under the electric storm
    of the vibrator

and stiffened our wills to meet
    the close clippers
and heard the true blade mowing
    back and forth

on a strip of dead skin,
    and we stopped crying.
You think your life is over?
    It's just begun.

ANNE SEXTON (1928–)

Miss Sexton's childhood was spent in Weston, Mass., where she still lives. Much of her poetry springs from her experience of emotional illness, from which she has evolved a basically existential attitude of personal hardihood and imaginative ingenuity—an attitude mirrored in her diction and metric.

> *To Bedlam and Part Way Back.* Houghton Mifflin, 1960.
> *All My Pretty Ones.* Houghton Mifflin, 1962.
> *Live or Die.* Houghton Mifflin, 1966.
> *Love Poems.* Houghton Mifflin, 1969.

RINGING THE BELLS

And this is the way they ring
the bells in Bedlam
and this is the bell-lady
who comes each Tuesday morning
to give us a music lesson
and because the attendants make you go
and because we mind by instinct,
like bees caught in the wrong hive,
we are the circle of the crazy ladies
who sit in the lounge of the mental house
and smile at the smiling woman
who passes us each a bell,
who points at my hand
that holds my bell, E flat,
and this is the gray dress next to me
who grumbles as if it were special
to be old, to be old,
and this is the small hunched squirrel girl
on the other side of me
who picks at the hairs over her lip,
who picks at the hairs over her lip all day,
and this is how the bells really sound,
as untroubled and clean
as a workable kitchen,
and this is always my bell responding

to my hand that responds to the lady
who points at me, E flat;
and although we are no better for it,
they tell you to go. And you do.

THE ABORTION

Somebody who should have been born
is gone.

Just as the earth puckered its mouth,
each bud puffing out from its knot,
I changed my shoes, and then drove south.

Up past the Blue Mountains, where
Pennsylvania humps on endlessly,
wearing, like a crayoned cat, its green hair,

its roads sunken in like a gray washboard;
where, in truth, the ground cracks evilly,
a dark socket from which the coal has poured,

Somebody who should have been born
is gone.

the grass as bristly and stout as chives,
and me wondering when the ground would break,
and me wondering how anything fragile survives;

up in Pennsylvania, I met a little man,
not Rumpelstiltskin, at all, at all . . .
he took the fullness that love began.

Returning north, even the sky grew thin
like a high window looking nowhere.
The road was as flat as a sheet of tin.

Somebody who should have been born
is gone.

Yes, woman, such logic will lead
to loss without death. Or say what you meant,
you coward . . . this baby that I bleed.

EDWARD DORN (1929–   )

Dorn is a graduate of Black Mountain College, where he studied under Charles Olson and Robert Creeley. In addition to his poetry, he has published some of the best criticism to have come so far from the Black Mountain poets, and he has edited the magazine *Wild Dog*.

The Newly Fallen. New York: Totem Press, 1961.
From Gloucester Out. London: Matrix Press, 1964.
Hands Up! New York: Corinth Press, 1964.
Idaho Out. New York: Matter Books, 1965.
Geography. London: Fulcrum Press, 1965.
The North Atlantic Turbine. London: Fulcrum Press, 1967.
Gunslinger (Books I and II). Los Angeles: Black Sparrow Press, 1968, 1969.

THE SONG

So light no one noticed
so lightly she could not care
or her deep dark eyes would have turned
saw I surmised in my fear
her walk was troubled for she tried
men's eyes with her grace,
her secret wave
with her fingers
had luck willed,
been real, been an ending to a life
of small tears.

          Thus days go by
and I stand knowing her hair
in my mind as a dark cloud, its presence
straying over the rim of a volcano
of desire, and I take something
so closed as a book
into the world where she is.

Our love.
Like a difficult memory lives and revisits
in certain dreams at night
or during days when I am tired
of the blight of the poorly tuned sounds
    of where I am, times
which make me beholden to please
the motions of those I talk with
eat with sleep with plead with
need. Concerning love
the first trace that slips to the ground
leaving all space above, into which one can enter
was mother? Lespuge is a figure
of dreamed wholeness, the form
is born of that desire
the whole swelling difficulty.

THE BIGGEST KILLING

1

Not by lost killers stranded
on the empty road
the various armies moving
    on to find each other the lost
    killers hail their jeeps
    of victory, colonels sitting
    friendly behind the wheel
but by stranded defeated
killers whose mouths water
for exotic factories
    their new Alabamas
    where they immediately begin
    to assemble old rockets, but better.

2

"And the dreamer turns away

from his visionary herds
and his splendid yesterday"
but we
    live in an earth of well-dressed gangs

638

my friend
waiting on the new Trinity.
And why don't the unctuous catholics
do something but start new wars
and why don't the unctuous protestants.

3

The yellow leaves will be here supposedly
riding the wind on dark branches
beyond a window
beyond summer's yellowing hills oh dead
filthy a dump truck shines in the black mud
November November.

     He remembers Yesterday
as one single day,
the sky was grey, but dark oh day
somewhere in the hills
the wind
everywhere the bleating of this
blissful era comes down against
our land in stark particles of rain.

For no single energetic man requires
anything of us
no single act of cognition
no matter how they rant the time
runs into years and they lead their gangs
through the streets the streets
of our souls and on an actual island
it was you said—they told you
stop ranting about your filthy soul?

     My god man, you should have wept.
What would they do, clean up the streets?
No leader can be exempt from drunk blood,
remember we passed Trinity site,
where 15 years ago we were led by the top gang
of all marching with their eye protectors imagine
they covered their eyes thus those idiot eyes
were not burned out by what they saw of their own
creation. Only a man

will play God and refuse to look at his own creation.
Will Fidel feed his people before his own stomach
is filled? Can Jack
hold up his grimy hands and shade us
from that vileness falling in particles
of fine sifting daily poison sand whose
stirring up he is the anxious inheritor of
he who falls in direct popular birthright to
is there any greater nonsense than
"our leaders would save us"?

My friend, don't breathe too deeply.

Remember we passed Trinity site
returning from Juarez—going north
you could see through ventanas
in the mountains some sixty miles away

still they whisper in the wind
we need you
still they whisper of green elegant glass
there and of emerald plains and say who
will they let in first.
Still the lethal metric bubbles of science
burst there every day and those sophisticated
workers go home to talk politely of pure science,
they breathe, go about in their cars and pay rent
until they advance by degrees to ownership
it is
like a gigantic Parker game of careers.

No complaint.

Still we see the marvelous vapor trails
across the face of the moon.
Still we awaken in the morning
and Yesterday which should be one-half
our whole possibility is lost
in a common nostril so decayed, so cynical
it cannot smell the blood it lifts
and drinks, to all of us.

And spills gaily, like a nutty booze machine
while we are the yellowing leaves, my friends and I
heaped upon the slopes of the New World Trinity
where grieves forth obsolescent landwrack
to infinity.

ADRIENNE RICH (1929-   )

In externals Miss Rich's poetry has developed from early formalism to more recent work in free forms, but in structure and diction it has remained consistently exact and exacting. Much of it mingles intensely personal experience with political and social themes, moving from existential denial to committed radicalism. She has traveled extensively, has lived in England and the Netherlands, and has translated from modern Dutch, as well as other, poetry. She was born in Baltimore, educated at Radcliffe and Oxford, and today lives in New York, where she teaches in the SEEK program at City College.

A Change of World. Yale University Press, 1951.
The Diamond Cutters. Harper, 1955.
Snapshots of a Daughter-in-Law. Harper & Row, 1963.
Necessities of Life. Norton, 1966.
Leaflets. Norton, 1969.

PROSPECTIVE IMMIGRANTS PLEASE NOTE

Either you will
go through this door
or you will not go through.

If you go through
there is always the risk
of remembering your name.

Things look at you doubly
and you must look back
and let them happen.

If you do not go through
it is possible
to live worthily

to maintain your attitudes
to hold your position
to die bravely

but much will blind you,
much will evade you,
at what cost who knows?

The door itself
makes no promises.
It is only a door.

LIKE THIS TOGETHER

for A.H.C.

1

Wind rocks the car.
We sit parked by the river,
silence between our teeth.
Birds scatter across islands
of broken ice. Another time
I'd have said "Canada geese,"
knowing you love them.
A year, ten years from now
I'll remember this—
this sitting like drugged birds
in a glass case—
not why, only that we
were here like this together.

2

They're tearing down, tearing up
this city, block by block.
Rooms cut in half
hang like flayed carcasses,
their old roses in rags,
famous streets have forgotten
where they were going. Only
a fact could be so dreamlike.
They're tearing down the houses
we met and lived in,
soon our two bodies will be all
left standing from that era.

643

3

We have, as they say,
certain things in common.
I mean: a view
from a bathroom window
over slate to stiff pigeons
huddled every morning; the way
water tastes from our tap,
which you marvel at, letting
it splash into the glass.
Because of you I notice
the taste of water,
a luxury I might
otherwise have missed.

4

Our words misunderstand us.
Sometimes at night
you are my mother:
old detailed griefs
twitch at my dreams, and I
crawl against you, fighting
for shelter, making you
my cave. Sometimes
you're the wave of birth
that drowns me in my first
nightmare. I suck the air.
Miscarried knowledge twists us
like hot sheets thrown askew.

5

Dead winter doesn't die,
it wears away, a piece of carrion
picked clean at last,
rained away or burnt dry.
Our desiring does this,
make no mistake, I'm speaking
of fact: through mere indifference
we could prevent it.
Only our fierce attention
gets hyacinths out of those

644

hard cerebral lumps,
unwraps the wet buds down
the whole length of a stem.

AFTER DARK

I

You are falling asleep and I sit looking at you
old tree of life
old man whose death I wanted
I can't stir you up now.

Faintly a phonograph needle
whirs round in the last groove
eating my heart to dust.
That terrible record! how it played

down years, wherever I was
in foreign languages even
over and over, *I know you better
than you know yourself   I know*

*you better than you know
yourself   I know
you*   until, self-maimed,
I limped off, torn at the roots,

stopped singing a whole year,
got a new body, new breath,
got children, croaked for words,
forgot to listen

or read your *mene tekel* fading on the wall,
woke up one morning
and knew myself your daughter.
Blood is a sacred poison.

Now, unasked, you give ground.
We only want to stifle
what's stifling us already.
Alive now, root to crown, I'd give

—oh,—something—not to know
our struggles now are ended.
I seem to hold you, cupped
in my hands, and disappearing.

When your memory fails—
no more to scourge my inconsistencies—
the sashcords of the world fly loose.
A window crashes

suddenly down. I go to the woodbox
and take a stick of kindling
to prop the sash again.
I grow protective toward the world.

II

Now let's away from prison—
Underground seizures!
I used to huddle in the grave
I'd dug for you and bite

my tongue for fear it would babble
—Darling—
I thought they'd find me there
someday, sitting upright, shrunken,

my hair like roots and in my lap
a mess of broken pottery—
wasted libation—
and you embalmed beside me.

No, let's away. Even now
there's a walk between doomed elms
(whose like we shall not see much longer)
and something—grass and water—

an old dream-photograph.
I'll sit with you there and tease you
for wisdom, if you like,
waiting till the blunt barge

bumps along the shore.
Poppies burn in the twilight

like smudge pots.
I think you hardly see me

but—this is the dream now—
your fears blow out,
off, over the water.
At the last, your hand feels steady.

AUTUMN SEQUENCE

1

An old shoe, an old pot, an old skin,
and dreams of the subtly tyrannical.
Thirst in the morning; waking into the blue

drought of another October
to read the familiar message nailed
to some burning bush or maple.

Breakfast under the pines, late yellow-
jackets fumbling for manna on the rim
of the stone crock of marmalade,

and shed pine-needles drifting
in the half-empty cup.
Generosity is drying out,

it's an act of will to remember
May's sticky-mouthed buds
on the provoked magnolias.

2

Still, a sweetness hardly earned
by virtue or craft, belonging
by no desperate right to me

(as the marmalade to the wasp
who risked all in a last euphoria
of hunger)

washes the horizon. A quiet
after weeping, salt still on the tongue
is like this, when the autumn planet

looks me straight in the eye
and straight into the mind
plunges its impersonal spear:

Fill and flow over, think
till you weep, then sleep
to drink again.

3

Your flag is dried-blood, turkey-comb
flayed stiff in the wind,
half-mast on the day of victory,

anarchist prince of evening marshes!
Your eye blurs in a wet smoke,
the stubble freezes under your heel,

the cornsilk *Mädchen* all hags now,
their gold teeth drawn,
the milkweeds gutted and rifled,

but not by you, foundering hero!
The future reconnoiters in dirty boots
along the cranberry-dark horizon.

Stars swim like grease-flecks
in that sky, night pulls a long knife.
Your empire drops to its knees in the dark.

4

Skin of wet leaves on asphalt.
Charcoal slabs pitted with gold.
The reason for cities comes clear.

There must be a place, there has come a time—
where so many nerves are fusing—
for a purely moral loneliness.

Behind bloodsoaked lights of the avenues,
in the crystal grit of flying snow,
in this water-drop bulging at the taphead,

forced by dynamos three hundred miles
from the wild duck's landing and the otter's dive,
for three seconds of quivering identity.

There must be a place. But the eyeball stiffens
as night tightens and my hero passes out
with a film of stale gossip coating his tongue.

GABRIEL

There are no angels   yet
here comes an angel   one
with a man's face   young
shut-off   the dark
side of the moon   turning to me
and saying: I am the plumed
                    serpent   the beast
                    with fangs of fire   and a gentle
                    heart

But he doesn't say that   His message
drenches his body
he'd want to kill me
for using words to name him

I sit in the bare apartment
reading
words stream past me   poetry
twentieth-century rivers
disturbed surfaces   reflecting clouds
reflecting wrinkled neon
but clogged   and mostly
nothing alive left
in their depths

The angel is barely
speaking   to me
Once in a horn of light

he stood   or someone like him
salutations in gold-leaf
ribboning from his lips
Today again   the hair streams
to his shoulders
the eyes reflect something
like a lost country   or so I think
but the ribbon has reeled itself
up
       he isn't giving
or taking any shit
We glance miserably
across the room   at each other

It's true   there are moments
closer and closer together
when words stick   in my throat
                              'the art of love'
                              'the art of words'
I get your message Gabriel
just   will you stay looking
straight at me
awhile longer

JONATHAN WILLIAMS (1929–   )

One of the most active small publishers in the U.S., Williams founded his Jargon Press in Highlands, N.C., in 1951, to bring out works by then neglected poets, especially those associated with Black Mountain College, where he was a student. His own poetry derives from music and painting—including a series of poems written as spontaneous reactions to Mahler's symphonies —from a concern for ecological sanity, and from a sense of social outrage. He is a serious hiker, and has written often about his walks on the Appalachian Trail and in Britain. He has taught at several universities, and has twice been poet in residence at the Aspen Institute for Humanistic Studies.

> *An Ear in Bartram's Tree.* (Selected poems.) University of North Carolina Press, 1968.
> *Mahler.* London: Cape Goliard Press, 1968.
> *Blues & Roots/Rue & Bluets.* San Francisco: Sierra Club, 1968.
> *A Bestiary.* Dial, 1968.

FROM *MAHLER*

Symphony No. 3, in D Minor

> *"Thousands lavishing, thousands starving;*
> *intrigues, wars, flatteries, envyings,*
> *hypocrisies, lying vanities, hollow amusements,*
> *exhaustion, dissipation, death—and giddiness*
> *and laughter, from the first scene to the last."*
> *Samuel Palmer, 1858*

I. *Pan Awakes: Summer Marches In*

Pan's
spring rain
"drives his victims
out to the animals
with whom they become
as one"—

pain and paeans,
hung in the mouth,

to be sung

II. *What the Flowers in the Meadow Tell Me*

June 6, 1857, Thoreau in his *Journal:*

*A year is made up of a certain series
and number of sensations and thoughts
which have their language in nature . . .*

*Now I am ice, now
I am sorrel.*

Or, Clare, 1840, Epping Forest:

*I found the poems in the fields
And only wrote them down*

and

*The book I love is everywhere
And not in idle words*

John, *claritas* tells us the words are not idle,
the syllables are able
to turn plantains into quatrains,
tune *raceme* to *cyme, panicle* and *umbel* to
form corollas in light clusters of tones . . .

Sam Palmer hit it:
"Milton, by one epithet
draws an oak of the largest girth I ever saw,
'Pine and *monumental* oak':
I have just been trying to draw a large one in
Lullingstone; but the poet's tree is huger than
any in the park."

Muse in a meadow, compose in
a mind!

III. *What the Animals in the Forest Tell Me*

Harris's Sparrow—

103 species seen
by the Georgia Ornithological Society
in Rabun Gap,

including Harris's Sparrow, with its
black crown, face, and bib encircling
a pink bill

It was, I think, the third sighting
in Georgia, and I should have been there
instead of reading Clare, listening to
catbirds and worrying about
turdus migratorius that flew
directly into the Volkswagen and
bounced into a ditch

Friend Robin, I cannot figure it, if I'd
been going 40 you might be
whistling in some grass.

10 tepid people got 10 stale letters
one day earlier,
I cannot be happy
about that.

IV. *What the Night Tells Me*

the dark drones on
in the southern wheat fields
and the hop flowers
open before the sun's
beckoning

the end
is ripeness, the wind
rises,
and the dawn says
yes

YES! it says
"yes"

V. *What the Morning Bells Tell Me*

Sounds, and sweet aires
that giue delight
and hurt not—

that, let
Shakespeare's
delectation
bear us

VI *What Love Tells Me*

Anton Bruckner counts the 877th leaf
on a linden tree in the countryside near Vienna
& prays:

Dear God, Sweet Jesus,
Save Us, Save Us . . .

the Light in the Grass,
the Wind on the Hill,

are in my head,
the world cannot be heard

Leaves obliterate
my heart,

we touch each other
far apart

Let us count
into
the Darkness

GREGORY CORSO (1930–)

Born in New York City, Corso grew up chiefly in foster homes, and at age seventeen was sentenced to three years in jail, where he read poetry—Marlowe and Chatterton—and began to write. Later he became associated with Allen Ginsberg and Jack Kerouac in the Beat movement. He has traveled in Europe, South America, and Africa, has lived in Mexico and India, and today lives in New York. In addition to his poetry he has written a novel, *The American Express*, published in Paris in 1961.

> *Vestal Lady on Brattle*. Cambridge, Mass.: Brukenfeld, 1955.
> *Gasoline*. San Francisco: City Lights Books, 1958.
> *The Happy Birthday of Death*. New Directions, 1959.
> *Long Live Man*. New Directions, 1962.
> *The Mutation of the Spirit, a Shuffle Poem*. New York: Death Press, 1964.
> *Selected Poems*. London: Eyre & Spottiswoode, 1962.

BIRTHPLACE REVISITED

I stand in the dark light in the dark street
and look up at my window, I was born there.
The lights are on; other people are moving about.
I am with raincoat; cigarette in mouth,
hat over eye, hand on gat.
I cross the street and enter the building.
The garbage cans haven't stopped smelling.
I walk up the first flight; Dirty Ears
aims a knife at me . . .
I pump him full of lost watches.

ZIZI'S LAMENT

I am in love with the laughing sickness
it would do me a lot of good if I had it—
I have worn the splendid gowns of Sudan,
carried the magnificent halivas of Boudodin Bros.,
kissed the singing Fatimas of the pimp of Aden,
wrote glorious psalms in Hakhaliba's café,
but I've never had the laughing sickness,
so what good am I?

The fat merchant offers me opium, kief, hashish, even
   camel juice,
all is unsatisfactory—
O bitter damned night! you again! must I yet
pluck out my unreal teeth
undress my unlaughable self
put to sleep this melancholy head?
I am nothing without the laughing sickness.

My father's got it, my grandfather had it;
surely my Uncle Fez will get it, but me, me
who it would do the most good,
will I ever get it?

PARIS

Childcity, Aprilcity,
Spirits of angels crouched in doorways,
Poets, worms in hair, beautiful Baudelaire,
Artaud, Rimbaud, Apollinaire,
Look to the nightcity—
Informers and concierges,
Montparnassian woe, deathical Notre Dame,.
To the nightcircle look, dome heirloomed,
Hugo and Zola together entombed,
Harlequin deathtrap,
Seine generates ominous mud,
Eiffel looks down—sees the Apocalyptical ant crawl,
New Yorkless city,
City of Germans dead and gone,
Dollhouse of Mama War.

I HELD A SHELLEY MANUSCRIPT

(in Houghton Library, Harvard)

My hands did numb to beauty
as they reached into Death and tightened!

O sovereign was my touch
upon the tan-ink's fragile page!

Quickly, my eyes moved quickly,
sought for smell for dust for lace
        for dry hair!

I would have taken the page
breathing in the crime!
For no evidence have I wrung from dreams—
yet what triumph is there in private credence?

Often, in some steep ancestral book,
when I find myself entangled with leopard-apples
        and torched-mushrooms,
my cypressean skein outreaches the recorded age
and I, as though tipping a pitcher of milk,
pour secrecy upon the dying page.

WATERCHEW!

He climbs the stair
The steps are old and carpeted   he climbs
He climbs the stair each step is another step
I sit on my bed   he climbs
I get up   bolt the door   put out the lights
I go to the window   I can't scream
I sit back on my bed with a smile   it's all a dream
A knock!
Hail Waterchew! big gubbling goopy mouth
Ho hairy clodbound oaf of beauty   hail!

I renounce the present like a king blessing an epic
I must beat the noon with a gold bassoon
In Waterchew I sleep Norse-proud
On ship deck furs I   O how deep into fear must I wedge
The strangeness I follow fools!

657

DREAM OF A BASEBALL STAR

I dreamed of Ted Williams
leaning at night
against the Eiffel Tower, weeping.

He was in uniform
and his bat lay at his feet
—knotted and twiggy.

'Randall Jarrell says you're a poet!' I cried.
'So do I! I say you're a poet!'

He picked up his bat with blown hands;
stood there astraddle as he would in the batter's box,
and laughed! flinging his schoolboy wrath
toward some invisible pitcher's mound
—waiting the pitch all the way from heaven.

It came; hundreds came! all afire!
He swung and swung and swung and connected not one
sinker curve hook or right-down-the-middle.
A hundred strikes!
The umpire dressed in strange attire
thundered his judgment: YOU'RE OUT!
And the phantom crowd's horrific boo
dispersed the gargoyles from Notre Dame.

And I screamed in my dream:
God! throw thy merciful pitch!
Herald the crack of bats!
Hooray the sharp liner to left!
Yea the double, the triple!
Hosannah the home run!

A DREAMED REALIZATION

The carrion-eater's nobility calls back from God;
Never was a carrion-eater *first* a carrion-eater—
Back there in God creatures sat like stone
—no light in their various eyes.

Life.. It was Life jabbed a spoon in their mouths.
Crow jackal hyena vulture worm woke to necessity
—dipping into Death like a soup.

REFLECTION IN A GREEN ARENA

Where marble stood and fell
into an eternal landscape
I stand ephemeral

Anchored to a long season in a quick life
I am not wearied
nor feel the absence of former things
my relation to my country
the weak dreams   their weaker success
the reactions to death
and lovelessness

And oh and now I know
having had enough of her
how women suffer
And that hate which men bash against men
suffers less and is with end
but a woman's loss   endless
How I wish she were yet again
with all her solemnities

Ah good consoling Greece
She was not the love I know
Having crossed over into her world
I became the sad unlove
which separates us so

Poor America Poor Russia
Thank God the moon has happened them
And France Algeria what sad geo-woe
Burnt peace as obstinate as nature
seems to be the ardor of history

I wipe the dead spider
off the statue's lips
Something there is is forgotten

and what's remembered slips
Butterfly and fly and other insectai
wait themselves to die

And so it's Spring again   so what
The leaves are leaves again   no tree forgot

SEED JOURNEY

There they go
and where they stop
trees will grow

The nuts of amnesiac squirrels
more nuts will be
Bur takes freight on animal fur
And pollen the wind does carry

For some seeds
meal is the end of the journey

A DIFFERENCE OF ZOOS

I went to the Hotel Broog;
and it was there I imagined myself singing *Ave Maria*
    to a bunch of hoary ligneous Brownies.
I believe in gnomes, in midges;
I believe to convert the bogeyman,
take Medusa to Kenneth's;
beg Zeus Polyphemus a new eye;
and I thanked all the men who ever lived,
thanked life the world
    for the chimera, the gargoyle,
    the sphinx, the griffin,
    Rumpelstiltskin—
I sang *Ave Maria*
    for the Heap, for Groot,
    for the mugwump, for Thoth,
    the centaur, Pan;
I summoned them all to my room in the Broog,

the werewolf, the vampire, Frankenstein,
every monster imaginable
and sang and sang *Ave Maria*—
The room got to be unbearable!
I went to the zoo
and oh thank God for the simple elephant.

JOEL OPPENHEIMER (1930–   )

Oppenheimer was born in Yonkers, N.Y., attended Black Mountain College, then entered the printing business. Today he works as a typographer in New York City, where he is also director of the poetry project at St. Mark's Church in the Bowery.

The Dancer. Highlands, N.C.: Jargon Books, 1952.
The Dutiful Son. Highlands, N.C.: Jargon Books, 1957.
The Love Bit and Other Poems. New York: Totem Press, 1962.
The Great American Desert. (Plays.) Grove, 1966.
Sirventes on a Sad Occurrence. Madison, Wis.: The Perishable Press, 1967.

AN UNDEFINED TENDERNESS

an undefined tenderness came
into the relationship. We were
afraid of such things, still, it
became necessary, and we learned
not to put it down—or put it
this way, time and a senseless
friction wore a smooth edge.
finally, i think, we could face to it:
there is no love possible beyond
those first moments of fire and
trembling passion. this makes more
sense than a roomful of roses,
your ass, and my heart. and, desire
burns fiercely in me yet, i
ought to be satisfied.

LEAVE IT TO ME BLUES

from the heart of a flower
a stalk emerges; in each fruit
there are seeds. we turn our
backs on each other so often,
we destroy any community of
interest. yet our hearts are
seeded with love and care sticks
out of our ears. but there is no
bridge unless it is the wind which
whistles our bare house, tearing
the slipcovers apart and constantly
removing the tablecloth covering
it (the table) like a shroud (the
shroud of what the table could mean,
if only we were hungry enough to
care), and we cut ourselves off
because we discovered each man is
an island, detached. man, the
mainland is flipped over the moon.
all i have to depend on is effort,
and the moon goes round and round
in the evening sky. my sons will
make it if they ever reach age,
but how to take care i dont know.
it doesnt get better. on the other
hand, even with answers, where
would we be, out in the cold, with
an old torn blanket, and no one
around us to cry

GARY SNYDER (1930–)

Born in San Francisco, Snyder attended Reed College and studied oriental literature at the University of California. He has worked as a logger and ranger in the forests of the Northwest, and has lived for extended periods in the Far East as a student of Buddhist life and thought. Both experiences are deeply involved in his writing.

Riprap. Kyoto, Japan: Origin Press, 1959.
Myths & Texts. New York: Totem Press, 1960.
Six Sections from Mountains and Rivers Without End.
   San Francisco: Four Seasons Foundation, 1965.
The Back Country. New Directions, 1967.

A SPRING NIGHT IN SHOKOKU-JI

Eight years ago this May
We walked under cherry blossoms
At night in an orchard in Oregon.
All that I wanted then
Is forgotten now, but you.
Here in the night
In a garden of the old capital
I feel the trembling ghost of Yugao
I remember your cool body
Naked under a summer cotton dress.

WORK TO DO TOWARD TOWN

Venus glows in the east,
      mars hangs in the twins.
Frost on the logs and bare ground
      free of house or tree.
Kites come down from the mountains
And glide quavering over the rooftops;
      frost melts in the sun.

A low haze hangs on the houses
    —firewood smoke and mist—
Slanting far to the Kamo river
    and the distant Uji hills.
Farmwomen lead down carts
    loaded with long white radish;
I pack my bike with books—
    all roads descend toward town.

THE MANICHAEANS

Our portion of fire
    at this end of the milky way
(the Tun-huang fragments say, Eternal Light)
Two million years from M 31
    the galaxy in Andromeda—
My eyes sting with these relics.
Fingers mark time.
    semen is everywhere
Two million seeds in a spurt.

Bringing hand close to your belly
    a shade off touching,
Until it feels the radiating warmth.

Your far off laughter
Is an earthquake in your thigh.
Coild like Ourabouros
    we are the Naga King
This bed is Eternal Chaos
        —and wake in a stream of light.

Cable-car cables
Whip over their greast rollers
Two feet underground.
    hemmed in by mysteries
    all moving in order.
A moment at this wide intersection,
Stoplights change, they are
    catastrophes among stars,

A red whorl of minotaurs
                    gone out.
The trumpet of doom
    from a steamship at Pier 41.

Your room is cold,
    in the shade-drawn dusk inside
Light the oven, leave it open
Semi transparent jet flames rise
                    fire,
Together we make eight pounds of
Pure white mineral ash.

Your body is fossil
As you rest with your chin back
    —your arms are still flippers
                    your lidded eyes lift from a swamp
Let us touch—for if two lie together
Then they have warmth.

We shall sink in this heat
                    of our arms
Blankets like rock-strata fold
                    dreaming as
                    Shiva and Shakti
And keep back the cold.

GEORGE STARBUCK (1931–)

Known for his serious "light" verse and his far-out experiments with poetic formalism, Starbuck is director of the writer's workshop at the University of Iowa.

> *Bone Thoughts.* Yale University Press, 1960.
> *White Paper.* Atlantic–Little, Brown, 1966.

OF LATE

"Stephen Smith, University of Iowa sophomore, burned
    what he said was his draft card"
and Norman Morrison, Quaker, of Baltimore Maryland,
    burned what he said was himself.
You, Robert McNamara, burned what you said was a
    concentration of the Enemy Aggressor.
No news medium troubled to put it in quotes.

And Norman Morrison, Quaker, of Baltimore Maryland,
    burned what he said was himself.
He said it with simple materials such as would be found
    in your kitchen.
In your office you were informed.
Reporters got cracking frantically on the mental dis-
    turbance angle.
So far nothing turns up.

Norman Morrison, Quaker, of Baltimore Maryland, burned,
    and while burning, screamed.
No tip-off. No release.
Nothing to quote, to manage to put in quotes.
Pity the unaccustomed hesitance of the newspaper edito-
    rialists.
Pity the press photographers, not called.

Norman Morrison, Quaker, of Baltimore Maryland, burned
    and was burned and said

all that there is to say in that language.
Twice what is said in yours.
It is a strange sect, Mr. McNamara, under advice to try
the whole of a thought in silence, and to oneself.

TRANSLATIONS FROM THE ENGLISH

1. *Pigfoot* (*with Aces Under*) *Passes*

The heat's on the hooker.
Drop's on the lam.
Cops got Booker.
Who give a damn?

The Kid's been had
But not me yet.
Dad's in his pad.
No sweat.

2. *Margaret Are You Drug*

Cool it Mag.
Sure it's a drag
With all that green flaked out.
Next thing you know they'll be changing the color of
    bread.

But look, Chick,
Why panic?
Sevennyeighty years, we'll *all* be dead.

Roll with it, Kid.
I did.
Give it the old benefit of the doubt.

I mean leaves
Schmeaves.
You sure you aint just feeling sorry for yourself?

3. *Lamb*

Lamb, what makes you tick?
You got a wind-up, a Battery-Powered,

A flywheel, a plug-in, or what?
You made out of real Reelfur?
You fall out the window you bust?
You shrink? Turn into a No-No?
Zip open and have pups?

I bet you better than that.
I bet you put out by some other outfit.
I bet you don't do nothin.
I bet you somethin to eat.

PATRICIA LOW (1932-   )

Mrs. Low lives in Lafayette, Ind., where she is, she writes, "a housewife, with the hope of becoming a novelist." Her poems have been published so far only in magazines.

THE FIRST DAY OF THE HUNTING MOON

Father, on the first day of the Hunting Moon,
after we stood the shocks up in the field,
after we tore the walnuts from their skins,
you sent me with a basket up Thunder Hill.
There were no berries in the Hunting Moon;
the hill dripped sunset and red leaves,
and far below me, squatting by a wigwam shock,
the Old One cleaned the plow for spring.

On the first day of the Long Night Moon,
while sunset shivered on the hill, we wrapped
the Old One with his people in the second snow.
Father, the Hunger Moon is here.
Where are the sacks of corn we shucked,
the tubs of walnuts, the meat we hung?
Already our people from their burying ground
whine down on the wind off Thunder Hill.
Father, there were no berries in the Hunting Moon;
there are no sunsets now, and I am cold.

WET WEATHER

Do you look for a rainbow, Love, in this wet weather,
while water reels in the wagon tracks out by the bar
Last week the floodgate splintered in the stampede
of the creek; and this morning, Love, over on the we
rain still whimpers in the ditch along the fence,
the creek still growls in its banks.

Remember, Love, last Indian summer when the sun,
sifting through hickories, latticed the ground?
We sat on the bank and watched slow raindrops
dimple the creek. Climbing the floodgate,
we ran over damp leaves to chase a rainbow home.

In this milkglass weather, Love, rain hammers
sockets in the furrows out in the field;
down on the south *forty*, brown corn silks
lay like squirrel tails dropped at skinning.
O, there'll be no rainbows, Love, in *this* wet weather.
A sun, in this wash, would run and fade on the sky.

SYLVIA PLATH (1932–1963)

Born in Boston, Sylvia Plath spent the latter years of her life in England, where she was married to the British poet Ted Hughes. Her work includes short stories and a novel, as well as her poetry. Her early poems were deliberate in tone, allusive in substance, and she is known today chiefly for the group of dark, intense, often bitter poems written toward the end of her life, poems of racy diction and staccato rhythms. Her death was by suicide.

The Colossus and Other Poems. Knopf, 1962.
Ariel. Harper & Row, 1966.

LADY LAZARUS

I have done it again.
One year in every ten
I manage it——

A sort of walking miracle, my skin
Bright as a Nazi lampshade,
My right foot

A paperweight,
My face a featureless, fine
Jew linen.

Peel off the napkin
O my enemy.
Do I terrify?——

The nose, the eye pits, the full set of teeth?
The sour breath
Will vanish in a day.

Soon, soon the flesh
The grave cave ate will be
At home on me

And I a smiling woman.
I am only thirty.
And like the cat I have nine times to die.

This is Number Three.
What a trash
To annihilate each decade.

What a million filaments.
The peanut-crunching crowd
Shoves in to see

Them unwrap me hand and foot——
The big strip tease.
Gentlemen, ladies

These are my hands
My knees.
I may be skin and bone,

Nevertheless, I am the same, identical woman.
The first time it happened I was ten.
It was an accident.

The second time I meant
To last it out and not come back at all.
I rocked shut

As a seashell.
They had to call and call
And pick the worms off me like sticky pearls.

Dying
Is an art, like everything else.
I do it exceptionally well.

I do it so it feels like hell.
I do it so it feels real.
I guess you could say I've a call.

It's easy enough to do it in a cell.
It's easy enough to do it and stay put.
It's the theatrical

Comeback in broad day
To the same place, the same face, the same brute
Amused shout:

'A miracle!'
That knocks me out.
There is a charge

For the eyeing of my scars, there is a charge
For the hearing of my heart—
It really goes.

And there is a charge, a very large charge
For a word or a touch
Or a bit of blood

Or a piece of my hair or my clothes.
So, so, Herr Doktor.
So, Herr Enemy.

I am your opus,
I am your valuable,
The pure gold baby

That melts to a shriek.
I turn and burn.
Do not think I underestimate your great concern.

Ash, ash—
You poke and stir.
Flesh, bone, there is nothing there—

A cake of soap,
A wedding ring,
A gold filling.

Herr God, Herr Lucifer
Beware
Beware.

Out of the ash
I rise with my red hair
And I eat men like air.

THE MOON AND THE YEW TREE

This is the light of the mind, cold and planetary.
The trees of the mind are black. The light is blue.
The grasses unload their griefs on my feet as if I were God,
Prickling my ankles and murmuring their humility.
Fumey, spiritous mists inhabit this place
Separated from my house by a row of headstones.
I simply cannot see where there is to get to.

The moon is no door. It is a face in its own right,
White as a knuckle and terribly upset.
It drags the sea after it like a dark crime; it is quiet
With the O-gape of complete despair. I live here.
Twice on Sunday, the bells startle the sky—
Eight great tongues affirming the Resurrection.
At the end, they soberly bong out their names.

The yew tree points up. It has a Gothic shape.
The eyes lift after it and find the moon.
The moon is my mother. She is not sweet like Mary.
Her blue garments unloose small bats and owls.
How I would like to believe in tenderness—
The face of the effigy, gentled by candles,
Bending, on me in particular, its mild eyes.

I have fallen a long way. Clouds are flowering
Blue and mystical over the face of the stars.
Inside the church, the saints will be all blue,
Floating on their delicate feet over the cold pews,
Their hands and faces stiff with holiness.
The moon sees nothing of this. She is bald and wild.
And the message of the yew tree is blackness—blackness
     and silence.

FEVER 103°

Pure? What does it mean?
The tongues of hell
Are dull, dull as the triple

Tongues of dull, fat Cerberus
Who wheezes at the gate. Incapable
Of licking clean

The aguey tendon, the sin, the sin.
The tinder cries.
The indelible smell

Of a snuffed candle!
Love, love, the low smokes roll
From me like Isadora's scarves, I'm in a fright

One scarf will catch and anchor in the wheel.
Such yellow sullen smokes
Make their own element. They will not rise,

But trundle round the globe
Choking the aged and the meek,
The weak

Hothouse baby in its crib,
The ghastly orchid
Hanging its hanging garden in the air,

Devilish leopard!
Radiation turned it white
And killed it in an hour.

Greasing the bodies of adulterers
Like Hiroshima ash and eating in.
The sin. The sin.

Darling, all night
I have been flickering, off, on, off, on.
The sheets grow heavy as a lecher's kiss.

Three days. Three nights.
Lemon water, chicken
Water, water make me retch.

I am too pure for you or anyone.
Your body
Hurts me as the world hurts God. I am a lantern—

My head a moon
Of Japanese paper, my gold beaten skin
Infinitely delicate and infinitely expensive.

Does not my heat astound you. And my light.
All by myself I am a huge camellia
Glowing and coming and going, flush on flush.

I think I am going up,
I think I may rise——
The beads of hot metal fly, and I, love, I

Am a pure acetylene
Virgin
Attended by roses,

By kisses, by cherubim,
By whatever these pink things mean.
Not you, nor him

Not him, nor him
(My selves dissolving, old whore petticoats)——
To Paradise.

DAVID RAY (1932–   )

Ray was born in Oklahoma during the days of the Dust Bowl, and spent his childhood in foster homes and orphan asylums. He has taught at Cornell and Reed, and he lives today on a farm in Yorkshire, England.

X-Rays. Cornell University Press, 1965.
Dragging the Main. Cornell University Press, 1968.

GREENS

A boy stoops, picking greens with his mother—
This is the scene in the great elm-shadows.
A pail stands by her feet, her dress conceals
Her chill knees, made bitter by the tall man
Who now lifts a glass, she thinks, with his friends,
Or worse, seeks a younger love in the town
While she with her fading muslin aprons
And her dented tin pail seeks greens, always
Greens, and wins, with her intermittent sighs,
Sympathy, love forever from the boy.
He does not know, this sharp-boned boy who bends
To his mother, that he has been seduced
Already, that he has known anguish, bliss
Of sex—as much as he will ever know.
He does not know, here in the bees' shadow,
He has become the tall and angry man,
The husband wounding the woman who bends,
Sighs and is ecstatic in her clutching
Of sons—bending, dark of brow, by her pail,
Stooped, brushing back the long, complaining strands
Of her hair. She is now too proud to weep,
But not to read the law, to reap greens, greens
Forever in her small pathetic pail.

THE CARD-PLAYERS

How we envy their not caring,
　　　　their sculptural crossing of legs,
their idle tossing of cards!
When they get up they are satisfied
as if from work. They rub
　　　　　　　　　　their hands,
　　　　　　adjust belts
jingle change in their pockets, and
see that their wives have been loyal
　　　　　　　　in their absence.

URSULA

Outside, affectionate eyes
Grateful for steak
And Roquefort dressing;
Smiles and anecdotes
Of prewar childhood Europe.
We had held hands
In the subway.

Inside, huddled in an air
Raid shelter, reduced
To ask immorally,
"Do you mind . . .?"
A spot of air above,
After love, burning
Children running in streets,
Rivers of flaming tar,
Beside an orchard, trees
Blazing with blackened apples.

ROBERT SWARD (1933–   )

Sward worked for seven years in a canning factory on the South Side of Chicago, then in the early fifties joined the navy; he began writing during his time at sea. Since then he has taught at Cornell and has lived in Mexico.

Kissing the Dancer. Cornell University Press, 1964.
Thousand-Year-Old Fiancée. Cornell University Press, 1965.

UNCLE DOG: THE POET AT 9

I did not want to be old Mr.
Garbage man, but uncle dog
Who rode sitting beside him.

Uncle dog had always looked
To me to be truck-strong
Wise-eyed, a cur-like Ford

Of a dog. I did not want
To be Mr. Garbage man because
All he had was cans to do.

Uncle dog sat there me-beside-him
Emptying nothing. Barely even
Looking from garbage side to side:

Like rich people in the backseats
Of chauffeur-cars, only shaggy
In an unwagging tall-scrawny way.

Uncle dog belonged any just where
He sat, but old Mr. Garbage man
Had to stop at everysingle can.

I thought. I did not want to be Mr.
Everybody calls them that first.
A dog is said, Dog! Or by name.

I would rather be called Rover
Than Mr. And sit like a tough
Smart mongrel beside a garbage man.

Uncle dog always went to places
Unconcerned, without no hurry.
Independent like some leashless

Toot. Honorable among Scavenger
Can-picking dogs. And with a bitch
At every other can. And meat:

His for the barking. Oh, I wanted
To be uncle dog—sharp, high fox-
Eared, cur-Ford truck-faced

With his pick of the bones.
A doing, truckman's dog
And not a simple child-dog

Nor friend to man, but an uncle
Traveling, and to himself—
And a bitch at every second can.

CONCERT

Stars walk downhill
To the Plaza
Of a Mexican village.

There, while the band plays,
I read
To all who will listen,
Poems to the stars
Poems to the lovers
The world, the Night.

Each thing awakens,
Raises flute trumpet horn
And plays, or
Like the stones

Write lyrics
Songs in celebration
Of stones, of waking.

The world
Altered, itself
Writing poems
Songs in celebration
Of the sun.

Mexican Band Concert—
Arriving
In the chartreuse (police) jeep
4-wheel drive
Stick transmission,
The boys' Marching Band.

The world ending
As we would have it,
Stones
At their typewriter,
Each at its instrument.

The stars falling,
Lovers
    flying
The band playing,
Drunks at their shorthand,
The moon at its easel,
Dogs listening,
The world again
Without objection,
The world
Walking off
    into space.

WENDELL BERRY (1934–   )

Berry's first book was a long poem in eulogy of John F. Kennedy. Most of his other poetry concerns the history and ecology of his native Kentucky.

> *November Twenty-six, Nineteen Hundred Sixty-three.*
>   Braziller, 1964.
> *The Broken Ground.* Harcourt, Brace & World, 1964.
> *Openings.* Harcourt, Brace & World, 1968.

A MUSIC

I employ the blind mandolin player
in the tunnel of the Métro. I pay him
a coin as hard as his notes,
and maybe he has employed me, and pays me
with his playing to hear him play.

Maybe we're necessary to each other,
and this vacant place has need of us both
—it's vacant, I mean, of dwellers,
is populated by passages and absences.

By some fate or knack he has chosen
to place his music in this cavity
where there's nothing to look at
and blindness costs him nothing.
Nothing was here before he came.

His music goes out among the sounds
of footsteps passing. The tunnel is the resonance
and meaning of what he plays.
It's his music, not the place, I go by.

In this light which is just a fact, like darkness
or the edge or end of what you may be
going toward, he turns his cap up on his knees

and leaves it there to ask and wait, and holds up
his mandolin, the lantern of his world;

his fingers make their pattern on the wires.
This is not the pursuing rhythm
of a blind cane pecking in the sun,
but is a singing in a dark place.

THE WILD

In the empty lot—a place
not natural, but wild—among
the trash of human absence,

the slough and shamble
of the city's seasons, a few
old locusts bloom.

A few woods birds
fly and sing
in the new foliage

—warblers and tanagers, birds
wild as leaves; in a million
each one would be rare,

new to the eyes. A man
couldn't make a habit
of such color,

such flight and singing.
But they're the habit of this
wasted place. In them

the ground is wise. They are
its remembrance of what it is.

THE PEACE OF WILD THINGS

When despair for the world grows in me
and I wake in the night at the least sound
in fear of what my life and my children's lives may be,
I go and lie down where the wood drake
rests in his beauty on the water, and the great heron feeds.
I come into the peace of wild things
who do not tax their lives with forethought
of grief. I come into the presence of still water.
And I feel above me the day-blind stars
waiting with their light. For a time
I rest in the grace of the world, and am free.

LEROI JONES (1934–)

Born in Newark, N.J., Jones is a poet, playwright, and novelist; also the founder and editor of two important publishing ventures, the magazine *Yūgen* and the Totem Press in New York. In recent years he has been an active leader of the militant black nationalist movement, associated with the underground revolutionary press. In 1967 his brutal beating by the police of Newark and subsequent conviction, on charges that seemed trumped up to many observers, in an Essex County court, became a celebrated public issue.

> *Preface to a Twenty Volume Suicide Note*. Totem Press, 1961.
> *The Dead Lecturer*. Grove, 1964.
> *Dutchman and The Slave*. (Plays.) Morrow, 1964.
> *The System of Dante's Hell*. (Novel.) Grove, 1965.

THE POLITICS OF RICH PAINTERS

is something like the rest
of our doubt, whatever slow thought
comes to rest, beneath the silence
of starving talk.
       Just their fingers' prints
staining the cold glass, is sufficient
for commerce, and a proper ruling on
humanity. You know the pity
of democracy, that we must sit here
and listen to how he made his money.
Tho the catalogue of his possible ignorance
roars and extends through the room
like fire. "Love," becomes the pass,
the word taken intimately to combat
all the uses of language. So that learning
itself falls into disrepute.

2

What they have gathered into themselves
in that short mean trip from mother's iron tit

686

to those faggot handmaidens of the french whore
who wades slowly in the narrows, waving her burnt out
torch. There are movies, and we have opinions. There are
regions of compromise so attractive, we daily long
to filthy our minds with their fame. And all the songs
of our handsome generation fall clanging like stones
in the empty darkness of their heads.

                                    Couples, so beautiful
in the newspapers, marauders of cheap sentiment. So
  much *taste*
so little understanding, except some up and coming queer
  explain
cinema and politics while drowning a cigarette.

3

They are more ignorant than the poor
tho they pride themselves with their accent. And
move easily in fake robes of egalitarianism. Meaning,
I will fuck you even if you don't like art. And are wounded
that you call their italian memories petit bourgeois.

                                    Whose death
will be Malraux's? Or the names Senghor, Price, Baldwin
whispered across the same dramatic pancakes, to let each
  eyelash flutter
at the news of their horrible deaths. It is a cheap game
to patronize the dead, unless their deaths be accountable
to your own understanding. Which be nothing nothing
if not bank statements and serene trips to our ominous
  countryside.
Nothing, if not whining talk about handsome white men.
  Nothing
if not false glamorous and static. Except, I admit, your
  lives
are hideously real.

4

The source of their art crumbles into legitimate history.
The whimpering pigment of a decadent economy, slashed
  into life
as Yeats' mad girl plummeting over the nut house wall,
  her broken
knee caps rattling in the weather, reminding us of lands
our antennae do not reach.

And there are people in these savage geographies
use your name in other contexts
think, perhaps, the title of your latest painting
another name for liar.

SNAKE EYES

That force is lost
which shaped me, spent
in its image, battered, an old brown thing
swept off the streets
where it sucked its
gentle living.
          And what is meat
to do, that is driven to its end
by words? The frailest gestures
grown like skirts around breathing.
                        We take
unholy risks to prove
we are what we cannot be. For instance,

I am not even crazy.

JEAN VALENTINE (1934–   )

Miss Valentine, who won the Yale younger poets' competition in 1965, lives in New York City.

> *Dream Barker and Other Poems*. Yale University Press, 1965.
> *Pilgrims*. Farrar, Straus & Giroux, 1969.

SASHA AND THE POET

Sasha: I dreamed you and he
Sat under a tree being interviewed
By some invisible personage. You were saying
'They sound strange because they were lonely,
The seventeenth century,
That's why the poets sound strange today:
In the hope of some strange answer.'
Then you sang *'hey nonny, nonny, no'* and cried,
And asked him to finish. *'Quoth the potato-bug,'*
He said, and stood up slowly.
'By Shakespeare.' And walked away.

DREAM BARKER

We met for supper in your flat-bottomed boat.
I got there first: in a white dress: I remember
Wondering if you'd come. Then you shot over the bank,
A Virgilian Nigger Jim, and poled us off
To a little sea-food barker's cave you knew.

What'll you have? you said. Eels hung down,
Bamboozled claws hung up from the crackling weeds.
The light was all behind us. To one side
In a dish of ice was a shell shaped like a sand-dollar
But worked by Byzantine blue and gold. *What's that?*

Well, I've never seen it before, you said,
And I don't know how it tastes.
Oh well, said I, *if it's bad,*
I'm not too hungry, are you? We'd have the shell . . .
I know just how you feel, you said

And asked for it; we held out our hands.
Six Dollars! barked the barker, *For This Beauty!*
We fell down laughing in your flat-bottomed boat,

And then I woke up: in a white dress:
Dry as a bone on dry land, Jim,
Bone dry, old, in a dry land, Jim, my Jim.

JOHN WIENERS (1934-   )

Wieners, who was a student at Black Mountain College under Charles Olson and Robert Duncan, was born and now lives in Boston. He was cofounder of the important magazine *Measure* in 1957.

The Hotel Wentley Poems. San Francisco: Auerhahn Press, 1958.
Ace of Pentacles. New York: Phoenix Bookshop, 1964.
Pressed Wafer. Buffalo: Gallery Upstairs Press, 1967.

MOON POEMS

The night has come on like a woman sleeping
Like a house full of women, taking sleeping pills
  Their cheeks are puffy and blown up like
    the face of the full moon.

In their ears ring the hymns of the holy night
  And music the sound of the lotus
    unwrapping.
We have come through the desert to this cool place
  where the lotus grow

And we eat their leaves in our opium pipes
  The organs of our body unroll in the church
Sounds so holy and laden with music

    That our cheeks are swollen and blown
      up by the sound

Of the poppy crashing against clouds in the sky.
  And our eyes are pinned with the dilemma
    of dying
And our voices low in the kitchen of the moon
  cooking fires.

LE CHARIOT

A flame burns in the morning.
It is the empty bag of horse

That carries the sun across the sky
And lights the love that blinds your eye.

It turns the night to infinite noon.
Changes the course of the unearthly moon

To ride in your heart instead of heaven.
This is the card that reads as seven.

PAUL ZIMMER (1934–   )

Zimmer, who was born in Ohio, was for a time manager of the UCLA bookstore in Los Angeles, and now works for the University of Pittsburgh Press.

The Ribs of Death. New York: October House, 1968.

PHINEAS WITHIN AND WITHOUT

Phineas dwelled midst lives of many pieces,
In bird flocks and fish schools.

Phineas fell when the grey birds rose,
He drank when the fish were breathing;
He lived so long midst the many pieces
He began to learn their whole.

He puzzled at the small lives,
The twist of a beak or fin;
And marveled at the large lives,
The flick of a school or flock.

Phineas fell when the grey birds rose,
He drank when the fish were breathing;
He lived so long within their without,
He died amidst their whole.

LORD FLUTING DREAMS OF AMERICA
ON THE EVE OF HIS DEPARTURE
FROM LIVERPOOL

Purple Indians pas de bourrée
Around a Chippendale totem pole.
The Ute dips to the Crow,
And curtsies to the Navajo,

While the forest in its wig and stole
Claps its leaves politely.

Cotton and tobacco plants cluster
On the backland hills like
Plaster on a Spanish cloister.
The rivers and the lakes
Are filled with plumèd bass
Who browse urbanely on the watercress.

The sylvan trail to Oregon
Is thronged with gentle post chaise
Gliding toward great fortune;
For this is where the buffalo turn
Broadside to the hunting horns,
And gold is strained like sunshine
Through the heath.

APPLE BLIGHT

Blighted apples will not shine.
Though they are buffed by winds
As diligent as Caesar's valets,
The fog has settled in their skins.

Branches bow down low to death,
Dragged by blighted apples.
Cold leaves curl about the wind,
Strangled by dull apples.

Though apples host the cruelest worms,
The hardest beetles, still they shine,
But when the sickness sweeps the tree
They will not shine, they will not shine.

CLAYTON ESHLEMAN (1935–)

Founder and editor of the magazine *Caterpillar* in New York, Eshleman has lived in Mexico, Japan, and Peru, and has translated many works by Latin American poets, especially Neruda and Vallejo. Among the fourteen books he has published are:

Poemas Humanos/Human Poems, (translations of Cesar Vallejo). New York: Grove Press, 1968.
Indiana. Los Angeles: Black Sparrow Press, 1969.
The House of Ibuki. Freemont, Michigan: The Sumac Press, 1969.

THE BLACK HAT

Yorunomado sat in
black goat's wool tent

a black hat,
a top hat

sat on a radiator
exhaling steam.
When

will it explode?
The man in *the*
or *or*, a fist

craven thru.
I walked

into Yuk Soo
Chinese Laundry

o 396
o 57
o 111
o 384

little pink slips
olive slips   yellow ones
wrapped with string
the wind used to

break our kites,

what I've escaped is
greatly what's let go of me,
to see the sweat
shop the earth is

dew off the field at dawn or
or or
Chinee back over steam mat,
shit, I'm so
fucking lucky,

the perceptions break down
the poem seems to stall
and does
before the greater energy of the world,

I've been given this black
hat of internal anger

still on the hot radiator
To sit here you look at me
I'm riding on my anger
as men did

horses, drove in the spurs,
straddling the trunk of
energy the mind is

heir to, it
bobbles
& Yuk Soo

cuts the prow of iron
    boat
over linen,
rigid

victim of migration,
wife, two daughters
scared little foxes
scared to speak

the ore of or
wife in the same
dress weekly
when does she
leave the shop?

After 40 years she
might as Zukofsky
speak of marriage

There is an area of .
sweetness born of
slavery, for years

the black top hat has
gasped on the radiator
everyone has sat on

watched it shrink
in band carcinomatous
like a chemical

in pure food
drives our stomachs
Yuk Soo

over our belts
—no one

has touched it
Yuk Soo is there
because we're

out of Eden
in Eden,
I'm here
because I left the place
established for me,

(gesture of reaching for
the hat
Xrist it's a snake!
The silliest fear is
the deepest fear—)
as you reached
thru Matthew's
crib slats to touch
on your knees
shaking sobbing
the son, the idea of
son leaving you
Matthew—
marriage
a welt,

hardest
to break up
a welt,
rice

chews, a welt
wants its
anger, inflamed
by a core
        of misery
it surges to
surface again & again
core

is don't touch it,
or
in all its might & fury,
this

is the Selfhood Blake
adored & cleft
again & again
fruit lopped from stem
the earth

is to grow
diurnally
a clerk

come home
to brood
man

split into family
is man
surrounded
treasures
a hill

the earth
is looking at us
a skeleton

whose windows
are teeth
black holes

Matthew
pokes a pencil
into,
primal

to enter
Yuk Soo
get my laundry
leave

peregrination
under the face of
boo

boo boo
poop poo
pup

gh

RONALD JOHNSON (1935–)

Until recently Johnson was known chiefly for *The Book of the Green Man* (1967), a remarkably well-sustained book-length poem about a year's visit to Great Britain. He lives now in San Francisco, where he is a clerk in a gift shop.

A Line of Poetry, a Row of Trees. Highlands, N.C.: Jargon Books, 1964.
The Book of the Green Man. Norton, 1967.
Valley of the Many-colored Grasses. Norton, 1969.

FROM *LETTERS TO WALT WHITMAN*

I

I hear you whispering there O stars of heaven,
O suns—O grass of graves . . .
If you do not say anything how can I say anything?

Let us tunnel

the air
(as a mole's green galleries)
toward the ultimate

,cornfield
—the square of gold, & green, & of tassel

that rustles back at us—

let us burrow in
to a susurration, the dense starlings,

of the real—
the huge
sunflowers waving back at us,

as we move

—the great grassy world

that surrounds us,
singing.

II

Unseen buds, infinite, hidden well,
Under the snow and ice, under the darkness,
in every square or cubic inch,
Germinal, exquisite, in delicate lace, microscopic . . .

Slant sheen/wrinkled silver.

Foxtail & lace-fly out of the vast organic slough
of the earth,
& the exquisite eye
—as myriad upon myriad of dandelions—

seeding itself on the air.

MIRRORS OF THE DARK WATER.

Poems beginning germinal in the instant
—reeling out, unravelling, tendril & silken, into the air—
ethereal growths,

sudden, & peculiar as mushrooms?
Uncrumpling
as moths from cocoons—

under the darkness,
pale wings,
slight densities out of the breadth of summer nights?

A largesse!

Argus-eyed & insistent.

V

Earth, my likeness
. . .

I, too, have plucked a stalk of grass

from your ample prairie, Walt,
& have savored whole fields of a summer's hay in it—

I have known your Appalachian length, the heights
of your Sierra
—I have unearthed the roots of calamus
you left at the margin

of many, hidden ponds,
& have exchanged it with the few, select,
lovers.

I have lain in the open night,

till my shoulders felt twin roots, & the tree of my sight
swayed,
among the stars.

I, too, have plucked a stalk of grass

from your ample prairie, Walt.

IX

Landscapes projected masculine,
full-sized and golden . . .
With floods of the yellow gold of the gorgeous, indolent,

sinking sun, burning, expanding the air.

But are these landscapes to be imagined,
or an actual
Kansas—the central, earthy, prosaic core of us?

Or is the seen always winged, an *eidolon* only to us—&
never
the uncertain capture
of great, golden, unembroidered

slabs?

All is Oz.
The dusty cottonwoods, by the creek,
rustle an Emerald City.

And the mystic, immemorial city

is rooted in earth.

All is Oz & inextricable,

bound up in the unquenchable flames of double suns.

ROBERT KELLY (1935–)

Kelley began writing in the mid-fifties as a formalist poet, while he was a graduate student in medieval studies at Columbia. Later he made what he calls "a total, religious commitment to poetry," and has since then written in more free and comprehensive language, usually also in forms too long to be anthologized. Today he teaches at Bard College, where he conducts the Matter Press. He formerly was associated with two magazines in New York, *Chelsea Review* and *Trobar*.

> *Armed Descent*. New York: Hawk's Well Press, 1961.
> *Round Dances*. New York: Trobar Books, 1964.
> *Lunes*. New York: Hawk's Well Press, 1965.
> *Lectiones*. Placitas, N.M.: Duende Press, 1965.
> *Axon Dendron Tree*. Annandale-on-Hudson, N.Y.: Matter Press, 1967.
> *A Joining*. San Francisco: Black Sparrow Press, 1967.
> *Twenty Poems*. Annandale-on-Hudson, N.Y.: Matter Press, 1967.
> *Finding the Measure*. San Francisco: Black Sparrow Press, 1968.

POEM FOR EASTER

All women are beautiful as they rise
exultant from the ruins they make of us

& this woman
who lies back informing the sheets

has slain me with all day love & now
keeps vigil at the tomb of my desire

from which also she will make me rise
& come before her into galilee

Rising I fall
& what does her beauty matter

except it is a darkness sabbath
where the church—our bodies

everywhere come together—
kindles one small light

from the unyielding the flint
then resurrection

The radio Messiah
I know

that my redeemer liveth
& he shall stand in the last days

up from this earth
beyond blasphemy

beyond misunderstanding
O love this hour will not let me name

they will say I make
a sexual mystery of your passion

whereas we know
flesh rises

to apprehend one other mystery
as the lover's

astonished eyes come open in his coming
to find that he is not alone

LAST LIGHT

there is a meadow
where the grass is now

& then every time,

that older than Christian
moment
      when Christ hangs on his cross
& the world is still

no one knows
if he grieves or rejoices
hangs conscious or asleep or already
dead,

bugs dance,
sun a while set
but sky over west
almost hurts to see
blue going to apple green going to red,

stratus salmon red
in the last light

if I fix wide open eyes
on the mountains' sharp crest
I can make light
rise again from the west,
but just for me

the bugs of night
unfamiliar shapes, dont bite yet

I have believed in time
& in time
come
to this meadow
where all the
moments of time are one

Lao-tze saw these pines
Adam this river,
an 18th century Adam
decorous & white
saw it flowing
his waters away
out
into ocean,

saw
his garden as no more
than source of the stream

watches
it pass

to America the tide
a girl & boy
come from the woods

pines now black
I can look at the sky

on all the lawn
one dandelion
puffball stands immensely alone

like feather-horned Venus
rising behind me
empty sky still light
but not as light as she

almost all
the light lives in the river

in front
of the agony of any being
we are stupid mute,

what is important to each man
he never says,
never learns it till the light
walks out of the sky
& he is left
alone with his failed utterance
impossibly clear in the dark

write everything
the oracle said,
Christ on rood road
tree over river
lovers behind the sundial by the pool,
everything I see or make or am,
seed spores of dandelion
holding light

let what is natural
say what it can

*what is not here
is nowhere*

men
should live in cities
shun
these ghostly edens of twilight

where all we have never been
mocks what we are

noble & foolish & dull
putting off our time of saying

when it is the uttering
not the knowing
that makes it so,

red is dying
pacific turncoat blue turns black

anyone watching me
would know nothing,
would see a dead man
whose hand moves on the paper,
he or the wind
occasionally turning a page

a moth
rises against cloud,
everything louder
under the trees

star out
straight up

above a dandelion
I can barely see

the splendid company of men who move in darkness
along a green continuity has nothing to do with time

for all we see we know nothing,
our utterance alone makes

something of this death,

Adam after hundreds of years
laying him wantonly down to rest.

JIM HARRISON (1937–)

After two years of teaching at Stony Brook, N.Y., Harrison has returned to his native Michigan, where he is coeditor of *Sumac*. Formerly he was poetry editor of the *Nation*.

> *Plain Song*. Norton, 1965.
> *Locations*. Norton, 1968.

POEM

Form is the woods: the beast,
a bobcat padding through red sumac,
the pheasant in brake or goldenrod
that he stalks—both rise to the flush,
the brief low flutter and catch in air:
and trees, rich green, the moving of boughs
and the separate leaf, yield
to conclusions they do not care about
or watch—the dead, frayed bird,
the beautiful plumage,
the spoor of feathers
and slight, pink bones.

RETURNING AT NIGHT

Returning at night

there's a catalpa moth
in the barbary

on the table the flowers
left alone turned black

in the root cellar
the potato sprouts
creeping through the door
glisten white and tubular

in the third phase
of the moon.

SOUND

At dawn I squat on the garage
with snuff under a lip
to sweeten the roofing nails—
my shoes and pant cuffs
are wet with dew.
In the orchard the peach trees
sway with the loud
weight of birds, green fruit, yellow haze.
And my hammer—the cold head taps,
then swings its first full arc;
the sound echoes against the barn,
muffled in the loft,
and out the other side, then lost
in the noise of the birds
as they burst from the trees.

AFTER THE ANONYMOUS SWEDISH

(17th century)

Deep in the forest there is a pond,
small, shaded by a pine so tall
its shadow crosses her surface.
The water is cold and dark and clear,
let it preserve those who lie at the bottom
invisible to us in perpetual dark.
It is our heaven, this bottomless
water that will keep us forever still;
though hands might barely touch they'll never
wander up an arm in caress or lift a drink;
we'll lie with the swords and bones
of our fathers on a bed of silt and pine needles.
In our night we'll wait
for those who walk the green and turning earth,
our brothers, even the birds and deer,
who always float down to us
with alarmed and startled eyes.

DIANE WAKOSKI (1937–   )

A Californian by birth, Miss Wakoski has lived in New York for a number of years, and is associated with the poets called "deep imagists," whose early work was published in *Trobar* magazine. Among her nine published books are the following:

> *Coins and Coffins.* New York: Hawk's Well Press, 1961.
> *The George Washington Poems.* New York: Riverrun Press, 1967.
> *Inside the Blood Factory.* Doubleday, 1968.

PATRIOTIC POEM

George Washington, your name is on my lips.
You had a lot of slaves.
I don't like the idea of slaves. I know I am
a slave to
too many masters, already
a red cardinal flies out of the pine tree in my eye swooping
down to crack a nut and the bird feeds on a tray draped
    with
a thirteen-starred flag. Underneath my heart where the
    fat clings
like bits of wool
I want to feel a man slipping his hand inside my body
massaging the heart, bathing
it in stripes, streams of new blood with stars floating in it
must pass through my arteries, each star pricking
the walls of veins with the prickly sensation of life.
The blood is old,
perhaps was shipped from Mt. Vernon
which was once a blood factory.
Mr. Washington, the pseudo aristocrat with two large
    fish instead of
feet, slapping around the plantation,
managing the country with surveyor's tools,
writing documents with sweet potatoes, yams, ham hocks,
    and black-eyed
peas,

oh I hate southern gentlemen, too bad he was one;
somehow I've always hated the men who ran my country
but I was a loyal citizen. "Take me to your leader,"
and I'll give him a transfusion of my AB negative blood
    with stars
floating in it. I often said this
in a spirit of devotion, chauvinistic passion,
pining secretly for the beautiful Alexander Hamilton but
    making do with
George who, after all, was the first president
and I need those firsts. On my wall, yes the wall of my
    stomach;
on my money, yes play money and real money, money I
    spend and money
I save, in and out of pocket; on documents, and deeds,
    statuary, monu-
ments, books, pictures, trains, old houses, whiskey bottles,
    and even
sewing machine shuttles there is his name
and my commitment, after all, is to names, how else, to
    what else
do we commit ourselves but names
and George I have committed myself to you. No Western
    sheriffs for me;
they only really like men and horses and sometimes gun
    play.
I guess I'm stuck with you, George, despite your absolute
    inability
to feel anything personal, or communicate it,
or at least share it with me.
Thank you at least for being first in your white linen
    and black coat.
My body, the old story, is my country, the only territory
    I control
and it certainly has been torn by wars. I'd like to think the
Revolution is over and that at last I am going to have my
    first pres-
ident, at last I can have an inaugural ball;
the white house of my corpuscles
asks for new blood; I have given so many transfusions to
    others.
When will you make me your first lady, George?
When will I finally become the first president's wife?

THE NIGHT A SAILOR CAME TO ME IN A DREAM

At the point of shining feathers,
that moment when dawn
ran her finger along the knife-edge sky;
at the point when chickens come out of the living room
    rug
to peck for corn and the grains like
old yellow eyes
roll as marbles across the floor;
at that sweet sprouting point when the seed of day
rests on your tongue,
and you haven't swallowed reality yet. Then,
then, yes, at that instant of shimmering new pine needles
came a dream, a blister from a new burn,
and you walked in,
old times,
no player piano or beer,
reality held my toes,
the silver ball of sleep was on my stomach,
the structure of dream
like a harness
lowered over my head, around me,
and I cannot remember what you said, though the harbor
    was foggy,
and your pea coat seemed to drip with moisture.

Thirty years of traveling this ocean.

Perhaps you told me
you were not
dead.

SUMMER

he slid out of the skin, leaving it
like a dried lima bean hull,
white and papery on the road.
his body inched along
the highway,
rippling its new red colors

bits of brown
like stones
seemed strewn along each arm and thigh.
it was a strange transformation
which had been coming.
the moon had warned him flipping like a fish in the sky,
a bowl of sweet cream left overnight emptied itself to the
    snake
living under the hearth.
when the time had come the old skin had shucked off
crackling. no pain
no pulling. he slid his wet body into the sun,
he was dry now
and brown.
the ocean rushed through his head; he heard the crabs
moving sideways on the bottom
and the fish
shouting
with their fins.

LOU LIPSITZ (1938–)

Lipsitz is a professor of political science at the University of North Carolina; his poetry, without being programmatic, combines political and surrealistic aims, showing the influence of Neruda.

Cold Water. Wesleyan University Press, 1967.

PROSPECT BEACH

Here I slept with my face turned
    toward the sun,
my eyes closed and my arms lying
    beside me
like two different animals that
    enjoyed my smell.

What roar, ocean! What an alien
    you are.
You are clear and indecipherable
    and full of fish:
strange and fast ones; and full
    of wild plants.

I watched the striped killies
    swim near shore
and the children splashing about
    holding glass jars;
trying to catch a fish
    in a bare hand.

And I was old, with the taste of sleep
    in my mouth.
Old and solitary, shivering
    in the breeze.
There are none like me here, only
    companions and marvels.

BEDTIME STORY

Nighttime. The faithful prison guard,
Poverty, locks the Negroes in their neighborhoods.
And many white men seal themselves
in the condemned buildings of the soul.

America sleeps, the raw wounds still open.
Mississippi sheriffs enter and stalk
in the forests of dreams; Southern judges,
pounding their gavels, crush small eyes in the brain.

On a highway, a good man is overtaken
by a carload of hoodlums.
Turn away quick!
or you'll see him get it.

Goodnight.

DAVID LAWSON (1940–   )

Lawson was born in Columbus, Ind., and teaches today at East Carolina University, Greenville, N.C. In between, he was a bartender, steel-mill worker, truck driver, etc. He has not yet published a book of his poems.

NO GREAT MATTER

An ugly old man
with camel brown fingers
(lungs as black
as a coal town alley)
stepped from a doorway
onto the curb
beneath a sightless urine-yellow moon
and coughed just twice
before the sidewalk smashed his eyes out.

Forty minutes later,
after every banker's daughter
kissed the son of every lawyer
beneath every lemonade-mellow kiwanis club moon
in Grand Island Nebraska,
the police slithered up
and called for the wagon.

A frowsy old nag
with a mole on her eye
who fancied herself a senior whore,
hung both her chins
on the window ledge
and belched the national anthem,
and told the cops she never saw him sober.

JOEL SLOMAN (1943–)

Sloman was born in Brooklyn, and graduated from CCNY. Recently he lived for awhile in England, and before that was assistant director of the poetry project at St. Mark's Church in the Bowery.

Virgil's Machines. Norton, 1966.

THE TREE

Not yet, not yet,
no green coat for me yet.
Let me stay frozen, my roots sleeping,
still blind to the quick-moving clouds
that draw the dead leaves to them in their whirlpools.
One last fling in this nether kingdom, bound,
oh bound only to forget,
forget life's dreary scum.
I condemn to these depths whoever was responsible for
     this,
even though I bore my son here,
with his green lips, with his amorous teeth that I die from.

It hurts so much,
worse than the pomegranates or the floating berries,
worse than the boar in the thicket exhaling insects,
or the pineapples or the rock mosses.
It cost me more than I dare say
to you, silent white bird that haunts my dreams, my
     dreams of your wings;
to you, ape that accosts me and lives in the hole in my
     spine;
to you, horse whose hoofbeats are the most definite things
     I know;
to you, nameless monster, crawling between rocks, blue
     and black, savage and formless.

The out-of-tune piano is marching on the cold wind to
   the trees,
garbage pails are rolling on their sides,
the womb-shattering bliss of ice just lies on the yellow
   grass
waiting for the shudder to build in the pipes below the
   streets,
waiting for the sea wall to give in, the wind mill to
   collapse,
when you'll only need the atom in your hip pocket to start
   the unheard frenzy.

Meanwhile, lie low. You haven't heard the worst.
Now, the dead leaves quicken beside the voiceless ocean,
pruned limbs grow fervently, the gardens irresponsibly
   verdurous.
Not yet, not yet,
I don't want any more than this green coat.
I feel the caterpillars chewing me up, I'm all in patches
   already.
"Get up!" I tell myself.

Where is that voice coming from?

IN A REMOTE CLOISTER BORDERING THE
EMPYREAN

I'm melted down into a black ooze
created by the silent flood, the center of which is occupied
by those three shots that just rang out.

What was it? When will the flood come?

The shots were blocks apart, rose from sperm or the
   bubbly vacuum
in the sweaty hands the assassin holds out, his feet astride
   boulevards,
being photographed with a shoulder holster, disappearing
   and appearing.
Tense statesmen, worried men of the secret police,
blocking the path on 5th Avenue, ripped apart north-
   bound,

who I watch from the bus, vanish in the fountain's spray,
into the cloisters of the Plaza.

      It was Erhard, rubbing his lamp
in the black Cadillac's shelter, the Allies' black rose
 blooming;
tense men, all of them tense.

       The bullet is picking its teeth.

How do they know how I hate them? What do they think
 I love?
I love the infant orangoutang in the zoo, delicately
 graceful,
climbing and caged, who I hold dearly my relation, the
 family success;
I love the high-branching elm that protects me as well as
 the birds;
the sea that runs by me with its haunting, taunting inhabi-
 tants,
(is the sea wall less brutish than the Berlin Wall?);
and I love Naëtt's limbs most, forgive me for doing so,
loving Naëtt's limbs, loving her name—Naëtt;
I'm human after all, and I contain all, and she contains
 me so well.

In the light of what I love, who can help me?
        Skin rots.
It's an old story. Why must I bring that up?
        Brains rot,
and the foul, grizzled bird unravels the convolutions.
        What is joy?

And the spitting in the lake.
What's this?

Serving a chilled drink.
What's this?

What's this song?
What heart could raise it?
What fool, the moss approaching his lips, wouldn't shout
 it?
Why no such chorus of brothers shunning the lifeless;
Why the ancientest the most praised, the slit-eyed the
 most vehement,

the corrupt the most injured, the slain the most reviled;
who has an idea of right, the confidence of providence,
or the simple prurience of an original imagination?

Like Samson, I'm in the dark,
and continue to ride the bus.